GREAT PASSENGER SHIPS THAT NEVER WERE

GREAT PASSENGER SHIPS THAT NEVER WERE

DAMNED BY DESTINY REVISITED

DAVID L. WILLIAMS AND
RICHARD P. DE KERBRECH

The
History
Press

To Alex A. Hurst, former windjammer mariner and merchant seaman,

ex-Prisoner-of-War, maritime historian, author, publisher, and philosopher.

Godfather of the original *Damned by Destiny*.

First published 1982 by Teredo Books

This edition published in 2019

The History Press
The Mill, Brimscombe Port
Stroud, Gloucestershire, GL5 2QG
www.thehistorypress.co.uk

British Library Cataloguing in Publication Data.
A catalogue record for this book is available from the British Library.

ISBN 978 0 7509 8357 0

Typesetting and origination by The History Press
Printed and bound in India by Thomson Press India Ltd

CONTENTS

FOREWORD TO *DAMNED BY DESTINY*

A great deal has already been written on the history of passenger liners and, in particular, recent decades have seen a veritable flood of publications dealing with this subject. Undoubtedly, the steady decline of the vanishing lines and liners of the classical passenger trades provided the reason for this massive production, which included many outstanding books which have become standard works of reference. However, all these publications deal with ships which really sailed on the routes for which they were built.

Nevertheless, for as long as liners have been constructed, there have always been interesting projects which, for one reason or another, were not completed and the ships concerned were never commissioned on the services for which they were designed. Some of them would have made history for their notable exterior and interior designs alone.

David L. Williams and Richard de Kerbrech undertook the praiseworthy attempt to write the history of these 'liners which were never to be', and the result is a fascinating story. This is the more so as the authors not only trace the individual career of each ship and the stages of the projects, but they also tell us of the men of vision who proposed them and the marine architects who designed and, sometimes, created them. Thus a really unique book has come into being: a book which deserves all the success that I can possibly imagine for it.

Arnold Kludas
Bremerhaven, July 1981

The second *Stockholm* undergoing her sea trials in 1941. Even at this time it was still anticipated that she could be delivered to the Swedish America Line and, accordingly, her interior furnishings and finery were installed in readiness for her entry into service. *Swedish America Line*

FOREWORD TO *GREAT PASSENGER SHIPS THAT NEVER WERE*

When Richard de Kerbrech and David Williams co-author a book together you know you want that book on your shelf at home and in your collection.

So, to have been asked by them to write the Foreword to this book, the sequel to *Damned by Destiny* which was published in 1982, is an honour for which I am very grateful. Richard and David make a great team and have worked together on many books over the years, but *Damned by Destiny* has always stood out as one of their greatest and most important works.

Until now.

And the publication of *Great Passenger Ships that Never Were* – the long awaited and much anticipated sequel to *Damned by Destiny*.

The duo has done it again!

The history of ocean liners has been written, and the stories of individual ships well documented. But it is human nature to speculate 'what if?' and it is natural to want to know more about the ships and projects that never left the drawings boards or slid down the ways thanks to timing, financial crises, war or changing technology. Or those ships that progressed beyond keel laying but never left the shipyard.

These ships deserve their place in ocean liner history because they could have changed history. Some could have been the greatest liners ever built and some could have advanced technology. Would the first *Queen Elizabeth* have been built if White Star had contributed its *Oceanic* to the newly formed Cunard-White Star Line in 1934? Would that company have been formed at all if White Star was able to afford its new flagship? Many *Oceanic* enthusiasts believe she would have made a more interesting running mate for *Queen Mary* than *Queen Elizabeth* was. Would White Star have had the upper hand over Cunard in the new company? How magnificent would *Normandie*'s successor, *Bretagne*, have been? If Q3 had been built would she have seen her 10th, 15th or 20th year in service? If not, the era of ocean liners would have been consigned to the last century.

These 'what might have been' questions can be answered to varying degrees and individual conclusions drawn, thanks to this splendid, well-written and well-illustrated companion to *Damned by Destiny*.

Michael Gallagher (former PR Manager of Cunard Line)
Grays, Essex, February 2018

ACKNOWLEDGEMENTS

Books like this are not written by the authors alone but depend on the support and assistance received from many individuals, institutions and companies alike. We should like here to extend our gratitude and acknowledgements to all those who have kindly contributed information or illustrations, or provided other help throughout the periods covering both the first and present editions of this book, which have made its publication possible.

Sadly, a number of correspondents and friends who assisted us with the first edition have passed away in the interim, to whom we would like now to repeat our thanks and offer our warmest respects: Ed Bearman, Frank O. Braynard, Col. Frank Bustard, Major Aldo Fraccaroli, Shizuo Fukui, Frederic H. Gibbs of Gibbs and Cox Inc, John H. Isherwood, Roy Miller, Tom Rayner, William H. Tantum IV, L.L. von Münching and Peter Wrigglesworth, all in their day nautical historians, authors, artists or photographers of repute.

Much new material and illustrative matter on the various projected ships, otherwise not available, was provided by the kind assistance of the following engineers, designers and maritime specialists, whose support and encouragement was greatly appreciated, namely: Ing. Maurizio Cergol, Maurizio Eliseo, Joseph Farcus, Markku Kanerva, Professor Dr. Kai Levander and Tapani Mylly.

Our gratitude is extended to the following authors, maritime historians and researchers: Harvey Ardman, Andrew Bell, Bruce Beveridge, Jean-Yves Brouard, Nereo Castelli, Mark Chirnside, Luis Miguel Correia, Richard Edwards, Dr. Nico Guns, Frank Heine, Ellen Köster, Marcel Kroon, Tom McCluskie MBE, Bill Miller, Dr. Bruce Peter, Ian Rae and Machteld De Ryck.

Equally we are indebted to a number of professional artists and technical illustrators, in addition to those we have named above: David Briedis, Ricardo Graca Matias, Chris Franks, Bob Hoare, Karsten Kunibert Krüger-Kopiske, Mervyn Pearson, Peter Sparre, Peter Thorne and Tony Westmore; also to David F. Hutchings, a friend of long standing, who was responsible for many of the pen and ink line illustrations, except those credited otherwise, and to Finn Tornquist, for his many digital interpretations of the ships we have described, both of whose kind assistance is warmly acknowledged.

Our thanks go to the archivists and public relations personnel of a number of major companies for their unstinting support and assistance: American President Lines, Chantiers de l'Atlantique, René Bouvard of Compagnie Generale Maritime, Deltamain, Deschimag A.G. Weser, Theodore Ferris and Sons, Fincantieri SpA, Hapag-Lloyd, Harland & Wolff, Klosters Rederi A/S, Meyer Turku Oy, Mitsubishi Heavy Industries, Nippon Kokan, Nippon Yusen Kaisha, Pathé Cinema, Star Cruises, STX France and Wärtsilä. Also, to those with similar responsibilities at the following international institutions and museums: Deutsches Schiffahrtsmuseum, French Lines Archives, Guildhall Library, Hamburgische Versuchenstalt, Mariners Museum at Newport News, Maritime Museum of the Atlantic at

Halifax, Nova Scotia, National Archives at Kew, National Museums of Northern Ireland, Sjöfartsmuseet in Goteborg, Rotterdam Maritime Museum and the United States National Archives and Record Service.

We are also grateful to the Titanic Historical Society and to Simon Mills for their permissions to quote from the respective observations of the *Britannic*'s wreck.

We would also like to express our appreciation to Zorina Hussein, now Zorina Walsh, for diligently typing and re-typing our original manuscript.

We should like to single out for particular thanks Arnold Kludas, who unearthed so many original records of the German schemes and who so kindly agreed to write the Foreword to the first edition, and Michael Gallagher, for his assistance with the many Cunard schemes and for kindly agreeing to write the Foreword to this new, revised edition.

INTRODUCTION TO THE REVISED EDITION

As the result of the immense, extraordinary and continuing interest in the might-have-been passenger liners of the ocean highways, first described in detail in *Damned by Destiny* published in 1982, it was considered to be appropriate to bring out an updated version of that book which includes the story of those vessels which have also fallen the victims of misfortune in the modern cruise ship era.

Considerable new information has come to light since the original volume was published, thanks to the emergence in the years since then of the personal computer with links to the Internet, providing convenient access to a wealth of previously inaccessible records. Thus, this new volume, *Great Passenger Ships that Never Were – Damned by Destiny Revisited*, acts as both an addendum and corrigendum to the accounts related in the original work, the overwhelming majority of which have been retained, while it also brings the story up to date in the new millennium.

The intervening years have witnessed a veritable explosion in the cruise holiday business on a scale hardly conceivable back in the 1980s and, arising from the competitive ambitions of both established and would-be new ship operators, yet more projected ships have been conceived only to fall by the wayside, either undermined by economic issues or the adjustment of marketing strategies to reflect emerging passenger trends, all of which, like the ocean liners described previously, deserve to be recognised and chronicled for posterity.

Of all the tales of the 'might-have-been', there are few more intriguing than those of the great passenger liners and cruise ships which never, for one reason or another, completed a single fare-paying voyage or cruise. This chronological review of these unfortunate and unfulfilled passenger ship schemes of more than a century and a half deals with those projects which only reached the concept stage, those which progressed to the design stage but were never actually built, those which were abandoned and dismantled while still incomplete, and those which were completed but were never operated commercially on their intended routes or in their intended form.

The story behind the conception and design of these projected liners and cruise ships is a fascinating one, for it provides a revealing look behind the scenes at all passenger ship development, whether lucky or unlucky.

The foundation of the story of the ill-fated passenger ships can be said to have been laid as far back as 1859 when Isambard Kingdom Brunel built the *Great Eastern*, a veritable monster in her day, but still small when compared with many of the vessels in this book. Her appearance encouraged immediate competition and rivalry, with plans to build a vessel of similar size, the *Spirit of the Age*. The latter ship's construction was never fulfilled but, from that time onwards, efforts to create successful ocean leviathans became the coveted dream of many ship designers and, inevitably, apart from their many successful creations that actually plied the oceans' highways, there were also, for a variety of reasons, numerous failures.

In the light of some of the proposals included in this work, the reader will find it interesting to know that Brunel, having built by far the biggest ship the world had then known, went on to prophesy with confidence that 100,000 gross ton vessels would eventually be built. At the same time, even if he had not brought all his ideas to the refinement achieved by naval architects over a century later, many of the principles he evolved relating to hull form and movement were not only revolutionary but were also adopted to form the basis of much of the most modern forms of naval architecture, so that today his prophesy has been realised.

Throughout the hey-day of the passenger liner, the completion of really mammoth vessels was regarded as an achievement of great national prestige. Those giants stole the scene in consequence of their prestige value and because they were almost always intended for service on the most illustrious and competitive sea-lane, the North Atlantic. Breaking new ground is invariably at the extreme end of things so that equally, today, there are massive cruise ships which vie with each other for acclaim and to secure the lion's share of the business, much as the ocean liners did in the past. In the modern, highly competitive cruise industry, the pursuit of the biggest, most extravagant and most feature-filled cruise ships mirrors the ambitions of the past to introduce the fastest and most luxuriously appointed liners before their trade was killed off by the aeroplane's monopoly of international travel. In light of this, there are examples of both types here – passenger liners and cruise ships – which, for similar reasons, have fallen by the wayside.

Despite the apparent futility of some of these passenger ship projects (if only when viewed with the benefit of hindsight), which have become the 'might-have-beens' in the history of the ocean passenger ship, all are worthy of favourable recognition in their own right because, through their important relationship with ships completed subsequently, they are an integral part of the whole subject and a vital part of the jig-saw of this chapter of maritime history. For that reason *Damned by Destiny* was appropriately described as being 'the missing link in the chain of maritime history' because, more than anything else, these luckless projects have reflected both the signs of the times and the hazards and difficulties of passenger ship operation, be it to do with line services or cruise vacations.

It should be noted that the contents of this book, within the scope of the subject matter, should not be regarded as definitive since, no doubt, there have been other plans for new passenger ships which did not reach a successful outcome and have not been described herein. As comprehensive a range of ill-fated projects as possible has been included, covering all significant and major ships and schemes of over 20,000grt. In that context, the term 'significant' requires some explanation, given that this term may be construed to have various meanings. Besides those schemes for vessels which would have been significant for their great size by contemporary standards, the focus is also on those projects which would have been significant as the first to either introduce a new method of propulsion, a radical or revolutionary design element, a novel feature which was later more commonly adopted, or a unique and unprecedented mode of operation. Owing to their state of advancement and the circumstances of their failure to enter into commercial service, those vessels, which in various ways fell the victims of war impact, as total losses, or through incompletion or cancellation, have also been treated as significant.

For any project to be successful, it has to be profitably viable, socially acceptable and technologically attainable, measures which, along with others, provide clues as to the reasons why certain of these otherwise well-conceived schemes came to nothing. Disregarding those vessels whose realisation or commercial careers were unfortunately thwarted by war circumstances, there are a number of logical explanations, as will be seen, which account for the lack of fulfillment of the grand projects described in these pages: financial issues, both as far as international trading is concerned as well as with regard to raising investment capital; falling the victim of changed or evolving requirements; being too far ahead of the times or too extreme for contemporary tastes, and so on.

Although, on the face of it, *Great Passenger Ships that Never Were – Damned by Destiny Revisited* might again seem, therefore, to be little more than a catalogue of much fruitless effort, this would be a very superficial viewpoint, since such effort was far from being in vain, and therein lies the essence of this story. As is the case in all new building schemes, there were invariably plans for these ill-destined ships to improve shipboard standards or to further marine technology in some way, and many innovations, which later became commonplace in the passenger liners or cruise ships which followed after them, had their origins in some incomplete project. Often they were, as already stated, simply ahead of their times.

For example: turbo-electric propulsion in the International Mercantile Marine's *Boston* and *Baltimore* proposed some thirteen years before the first large, though somewhat smaller, turbo-electric passenger ship, the *California*, had such engines installed. Likewise, the *Oceanic* was also very advanced where diesel-electric machinery was concerned, a system of power generation installed much later in the *Queen Elizabeth 2*.

The suggestion of dual-purpose passenger ships, suitable for conversion to full aircraft carriers in time of war, was another projected liner's 'first' as proposed in the scheme for the *Flying Cloud*, a concept that was well appreciated later in the many liners converted to escort carriers in the Second World War.

The Swedish America Line's *Stockholm* did not introduce the idea of a purpose-built dual-role cruise ship, since this distinction belongs to the *Empress of Britain* of 1931, but, ten years before the advent of the Cunard Line's *Caronia*, the *Stockholm*'s designers proposed the first permanent accommodation layout suited to this type of ship, whereby practically all cruising passengers would have outside cabins. Yet another example of the influence of a 'might-have-been' is the one-class tourist liner of the 1960s, originally envisaged in the 'Yankee Clipper', designed for Paul Wadsworth Chapman in the late 1930s. It was in this same vessel, re-modeled in 1951, that the first proposal was made for a form of gantry loading, which is now a standard feature of container ship handling.

Other ill-fated passenger ship design features, which have been adopted subsequently, or which have influenced modern cruise ship design, are the inner gardened-verandahs and standardised modular cabins which are now commonplace aboard these ships; also the splitting of the exhaust trunkings to run up the sides of the hull in order to leave uninterrupted open accommodation space along the centre of the ship. Numerous features first proposed for the 'Phoenix' and 'Ultimate Dream' projects, as well as for Carnival Corporation's incredible 'Pinnacle' ship are now to be found aboard the latest generation of cruise ships. For all these reasons, the intrinsic value of these aborted passenger ship projects is surely beyond question.

It is pertinent, too, to note that, thanks to advances in maritime technology as well as progress in social attitudes, some of the objectives which appeared to be unattainable, even unrealistic, in the schemes described in *Damned by Destiny* have not only been achieved since then but in some cases have been surpassed.

Projects such as the 'Yankee Clippers' and 'Liberty Liners', and the giant Cantor and Detwiler tourist ship schemes, which called for vessels of over 100,000 gross tons and 1,250ft in overall length were dismissed by some contemporary pundits as being beyond the limits of practicality and economic viability. Yet today, the Royal Caribbean Cruise Lines' 'Oasis of the Seas' class of cruise ships are more than 250 per cent bigger, at 250,000 gross tons, than that seemingly unattainable tonnage figure, while their length, at 1,186ft overall, is only short of those projected ships of the 1930s and 1950s by a mere 65ft.

Likewise, the apparently unacceptable concept of the 'cafeteria' ship, in which passengers paid up front for their passage fare and cabin accommodation, but were then left to purchase their meals from a selection of restaurants and other food outlets to suit themselves and their personal budgets, has now been adopted aboard certain modern cruise ships, while others offer alternative dining options as an extra carrying a surcharge.

The 'one-class ship' was another projected liners' first, as proposed in the giant transatlantic schemes of the 1930s. Social stratification was already being gradually diluted in that era, from four to three classes, a process that accelerated in the post-war era with two-class accommodation adopted for many of the liners that entered service in the 1950s and 1960s. But it was really in the modern cruise ship that this trend reached its logical conclusion with universal application. Today, all cruise ships are essentially single class although some dining distinctions remain for those paying premium fares.

Perhaps the greatest bequest of all these unfortunate schemes, whether for passenger liners or cruise ships, is less tangible. As lessons in business economics and management, and in research and development, as forms of trial-and-error examples, they have aided the progress of healthy passenger ship operations and advanced the pace of marine engineering. Many of the proponents of these grandiose liners and cruise ships, like their ill-starred projects, have been laid to rest. Others continue to contribute to the advancement of passenger ship design and technology. Among them are naval architects, marine engineers and shipping entrepreneurs whose names will appear throughout this book. They are the leading players in the accounts that unfold in the pages that follow and, although most of them frequently achieved major successes in other undertakings, their fame should not lie more lightly on those conceptions that form the burden of this work and which were 'Damned by Destiny'.

In this new, revised edition we have placed greater emphasis on the technical, commercial, social and political factors that resulted in the loss or abandonment of schemes for new ships, on the basis that fate or destiny are, it is held, beyond the control of man, whereas the designers and entrepreneurs behind these grandiose projects were, for the most part, enlightened, competent and knowledgeable persons in their reasoning. In short, they knew what they were doing and failure had more to do with market forces and world events than matters of a supernatural character. They approached their plans with technical skill or proven business acumen, and few exhibited 'airy-fairy' romantic notions that lacked realism. If there is one criticism that can be leveled at these men, it is that, being able to perceive future trends beyond the ability of others, often their aims were too far ahead of contemporary tastes.

There is another dimension to this subject that is worthwhile reflecting. It seems that nothing stirs the popular imagination more than such things as conspiracy theories, the great disasters and their incongruous coincidences, or the 'what-ifs' of world affairs. Hence, for example, the enduring appeal of the story of the loss of White Star's *Titanic*. In this book we are dealing very much with the potential outcomes that could have arisen had these ships made it into service as planned.

How, for instance, would White Star have fared had the *Britannic* survived the First World War to run a balanced joint service with her sister-ship *Olympic*? Would the *Queen Mary* have even been built if the giant 60,000-ton *Oceanic* had been completed some years earlier? How would the fortunes of the European lines have been affected if either the *Baltimore* and *Boston* pair or Chapman's new *Leviathans* had entered service, offering American travellers, who were by far the majority on the transatlantic run, the means of crossing on their own national flag carriers? And what would have been the effect on Royal Caribbean's 'Oasis of the Seas' class of cruise ships if Carnival Corporation had persisted with its 'Pinnacle Project'?

Conversely, we may also speculate on the potential outcomes had certain world events not occurred. If, for instance, there had not been a Second World War then the magnificent *Normandie* would have continued with her transatlantic service, but accompanied by a consort named *Bretagne*. They would, of course, have been rivaled by a new German giant and, perhaps, even new Italian liners of comparable size. The *Nieuw Amsterdam* would have had a companion ship in the early 1940s. The three *Vaterland*-class ships of Hamburg America would have entered service, while Swedish America Line's elegant *Stockholm* of 1940 would have obviated the need for the smaller ship of that name which was completed in 1948. And then, we could also conjure with the possibility that there would never have been a collision in 1956 to cause the sinking of the *Andrea Doria*. These and other possibilities may be posed for speculation and discussion where the ill-fated passenger ship story is concerned.

This is not the acknowledgements section of our book, but we have elected to express our gratitude here in general terms to all those persons who have kindly given us their assistance over the years, some of whom subsequently became good friends. Sadly, since *Damned by Destiny* was published, a number of them have hoisted anchor and crossed the bar but, nonetheless, our indebtedness for and recognition of their kind help applies just as much as if they were still here with us.

It is hoped that this book will provide an interesting source of reference and enjoyment for shipping and maritime professionals, researchers, historians, marine engineers and naval architects, and general readers alike.

David L. Williams and Richard P. de Kerbrech
Isle of Wight

Note: For the costs and fares to which reference is made in the text, the approximate currency conversion rates (Pound Sterling to U.S. Dollar) can be assumed to be as follows:

Prior to 1940	£1 equals approx $5.00	1970–80	£1 equals approx $2.00
1940–52	£1 equals approx $4.00	1980–95	£1 equals approx $1.50
1953–60	£1 equals approx $3.00	1995–2015	£1 equals approx $1.40
1960–70	£1 equals approx $2.50		

It should be stressed that these figures are only rough, and were subject to fluctuation throughout these periods.

1

THE *SPIRIT OF THE AGE*

This first chapter presents, as a form of scene-setter to the rest of the book, three seemingly far-fetched schemes for ocean passenger vessels covering a period of eighty or so years, all of which could reasonably be considered, when looking back, as little more than wishful thinking. The fact is, though, that whether or not they were realistic or attainable, they reflect the very essence of the story of the ill-fated passenger ship projects – the enduring endeavour to advance and improve the design of ocean passenger ships. Equally, they reveal the extraordinary aspirations and efforts of the inspired men who were behind them. Much time, money and determination were invested in pursuit of the realisation of their ambitions, and while success or even the physical manifestation of the vessels concerned was dubious at best, they symbolise both the spirit and the essence of progress in which ideas first germinate, are then subjected to trial-and-error experimentation until, ultimately, workable solutions emerge.

There is a saying which is pertinent to the ambitious characteristics of the cases described here, indeed to all the projects covered by this book: 'A man's reach should always exceed his grasp'.

The objectives where all three of these designs are concerned may have been beyond the technical capabilities of their time or were an erroneous application of an established and recognised scientific principle, or were so futuristic that they were too far in advance of contemporary tastes and the acceptance of the travelling public. While this may suggest a certain naivety, it should not be concluded that they were just unattainable fantasies. Progress is about rising to challenges, evolving new ideas that break the mould and presenting those ideas in such a way that they engage the public imagination. How else would we have got from the Model T Ford to the Tesla, from the Wright Flyer to Concorde or from Stephenson's *Rocket* to the Bullet Train?

Considered in that light, although they may not have been practicable in themselves, these efforts were still a valid part of that continuing imaginative quest for new possibilities and, in that sense, they were, perhaps, indicators of what the future held in store. Certainly, those who were behind them were genuinely in earnest in pursuing the realisation of their schemes. Thus, no less than the more technically enlightened concepts that followed which also failed to materialise, some perhaps influenced by these more radical notions, they deserve their place herein.

As stated in the Introduction, the projected passenger ships story can be said to have originated in 1859 when Isambard Kingdom Brunel completed the enormous *Great Eastern*. In speaking of an 'enormous' or 'mammoth' ship, we must consider her within the context of her times, since it is clear that what seems to be a gigantic vessel to one generation may not seem to be so to a later one, and the fact of the matter was that the *Great Eastern* was by far the largest vessel afloat when launched, at 18,915 gross tons, and, indeed, that she retained that distinction for almost half a century – forty-eight years to be precise – until she was finally exceeded in size by the *Oceanic* of 1899.

This simple statistic serves to put the nineteenth century into perspective, since it was not until the end of it that 20,000-tonners were becoming a reality although, as will be seen, at least one ambitious idea, which was far ahead of current construction targets, was bruited at that time.

Although regarded as a failure in her day, the *Great Eastern* was the legitimate predecessor of the ocean passenger vessels of

When it is considered that it was not until 1878 that a steamer crossed the Atlantic without square yards, the *Spirit of the Age*, as depicted here, was ultra-optimistic, while the conception of folding masts with no stays could hardly have proved to be of much use in an emergency. At that time, not only did steamship sails provide valuable 'push' in days of high fuel consumption but a better means of 'heaving to' in the event of engine failure. Dated 11 November 1861, this lithograph is by T.G. Dutton. *National Maritime Museum*

the twentieth century. Significantly, she was also the first liner to precipitate a competitive – albeit unsuccessful – reaction, amounting to a challenge not only to improve on her trading performance and potential, but to outdo the ship herself as well as her appointments.

This was the aptly named *Spirit of the Age*, planned in 1861 to challenge the *Great Eastern* for honours in size. In addition, patented features, which sounded as though they had come straight out of a Jules Verne novel, showed the intentions of her designers to surpass her in technical innovations for the comfort and convenience of passengers. The proposed dimensions and tonnage of the *Spirit of the Age* are not known, though the lithograph of her by T.G. Dutton suggests that she would have been of rather similar proportions to Brunel's ship. She was described as 'having great length in comparison with her breadth, and with a very small freeboard'. This vessel would have been operated by the Trans-Atlantic Express Steam Packet Company, on the route alternatively chosen for the *Great Eastern*, which had been intended originally for the Cape route to India – hence her name.

A picture of her designers' thinking with regard to this proposed vessel can be obtained from the patents registered on 19 September 1861 for the *Spirit of the Age*, under the title: 'Silver and Moore's Improvements in Steam Ships Etc.' Silver and Moore, both with the christian name Thomas, were the designers of the liner and their invention, as it was described, consisted of eleven parts.

The first deals with hull subdivision and bulkhead strengthening from the keelson to a hurricane deck. The second part concerns special loading equipment which is imaginatively described as 'facilitating the loading or discharging of coals or cargo, by beam travellers or wheels, flanged or otherwise, running in suspended grooves or working to and fro on rails'.

Sections three to six refer to the proposed engines and machinery layout, although no specific details of the type of engine are given. The machinery and boilers were to be fitted to the sides of the hull, thereby leaving the centre part free and uncluttered. The engine arrangement was intended to drive two paddle-wheels, two screw propellers – one under each stern quarter – and a hydraulic steering apparatus.

Parts seven to nine of the patent deal with passenger comforts and safety provisions ranging from a fire-fighting arrangement based on the ship's hot water pipe heating system, to a ventilation scheme and a between decks lighting contrivance. The description of these latter inventions is typical in style of the whole specification and it makes both interesting and humorous reading. For instance, of the air-conditioning proposal it says:

> The eighth part of our invention consists in ventilating the betweendecks and cabins in a manner more suited to insure health, by carrying off impure air. This we propose to do by inserting trap valves in the decks, communicating with pipes carrying the foul air below, where it will be forced upwards from the bottom of the ship, and taken up through pipes through the floors, and extending above the upper deck. The carbonic gases, which contaminate the atmosphere through the impossibility of their escaping, will be allowed to descend, as it is their nature to do, and be carried up by the upward draught of the ventilating pipes in the bottom of the ship. The trap openings will be covered by gratings. The traps will be made self-acting floats, to close up in the event of water rising underneath. The tops of the ventilating pipes above the upper deck to be in the form of a cap cone fashioned to increase the draft.

Regarding the lighting arrangement, the patent states:

> The ninth part of our invention consists in lighting the between decks. We accomplish this by inserting honeycombed or iron-framed glass in all the corridors or passages throughout the vessel, these diffusers of light to have the appearance of a honeycomb, with conical cells and glass bull's-eyes, so shaped as to fit such cells, the upper part of the cells to have an iron projecting rim, so made as to form cavities for the reception of elastic or other suitable cushions to keep the bull's-eyes from being forced upwards.

Finally, parts ten and eleven describe the rigging and the deck and auxiliary steering equipment. Part ten goes some way towards explaining the novel appearance of the *Spirit of the Age* as depicted in Dutton's lithographed conception. It was proposed that all standing rigging be abolished, suggesting that Messrs Silver and Moore had great faith in the contemporary development of the marine engine in spite of the *Great Eastern*'s debacle during a terrible Atlantic storm in September 1861 when she had her steering shaft ripped off together with both paddle wheels, leaving her almost totally helpless. However, for emergency purposes, the *Spirit of the Age* would have carried hinged spars, flat along her hurricane deck, to take fore-and-aft sails, although it may be difficult to reconcile this rather strange arrangement with the lack of standing rigging.

The impression gained from the patented design for the ship was that the ideas were as obvious in their objectives as they were absurd in their approach. Typical of most patent descriptions of the period, the specification offers little, if anything, in the way of sound, mechanical explanation as to how the desired improvements would – or could – be achieved. The *Spirit of the Age* was never built, the misfortunes of the *Great Eastern* probably having as much to do with this as the improbability of her design.

As the nineteenth century progressed, so marine technology advanced with it, and the conception of large passenger liners moved out of the realms of fantasy, although some quite bizarre craft were being propounded. Among the odd and peculiar suggestions put forward during the latter half of the nineteenth century for large ocean-going vessels was one for a so-called 'roller-boat', whose designer was within a hair's breadth of discovering the principles of the caterpillar track propulsion system or the Squirrel Cage rotor without – it seems – realising it.

The 'roller-boat' was invented in the 1890s by Frederick Augustus Knapp, a Canadian lawyer from Prescott, Ontario, . His idea was that a revolving outer cylinder around a stationary inner cylinder would create less water resistance and minimise sea-sickness.

As the least ship-like concept among those described in this chapter, some of the content of the Canadian patent for the 'roller-boat' design, registered on 13 April 1897 under number 55620, is worthy of inclusion here in order to get some idea of what Knapp was trying to achieve with his incongruous craft which, frankly, would have looked less out of place if it had rolled on land rather than in a marine environment.

The overall description, from the first paragraph of the patent document, reads:

> The object of this invention is to drive a vessel capable of attaining a high rate of speed with absolute safety and great economy and it consists, essentially, of a rotatable double outer hull within which are suspended stationary hulls or compartments containing the freight or passengers and the motive power [and] suitable steering apparatus.

Apart from this broad claim, as in Silver and Moore's patent, there is no explanation within the long and wordy document concerning the mechanical principles by which this strange contraption would make any headway, let alone achieve the incredible speed of around 75 knots required to cross the Atlantic in the 35 hours which was claimed for it! Similarly, the details of the means of propulsion and steering are sketchy at best and require much stretching of the imagination. After explaining that the single cylinder and piston connected to a crank shaft, as shown in the drawing appended to the patent, were intended only to be indicative, Mr Knapp continues:

> In practice, suitable triple expansion engines would preferably be employed and the power might be differently applied to the hull.

Simple matters, such as how boiler fumes would be exhausted and how coal fuel for the steam boilers would be bunkered, are not mentioned. As for the method of steering:

> A windlass contained within the pilot house [is] arranged to wind up chains so as to cause the drag paddles [at either end] to enter the water to a greater or lesser extent, as might be desired.

A 60ft long by 15ft diameter model of the roller-boat, a scaled-down version of a planned 750ft long, 150ft diameter, 35-hour transatlantic roller ship, was built at the Poulson Iron Works, Toronto, and tested in Toronto harbour on 27 October 1897. In practice, it was a complete failure. As the propulsive power of the craft was increased, it was driven deeper into the water rather than forwards, and it became quite

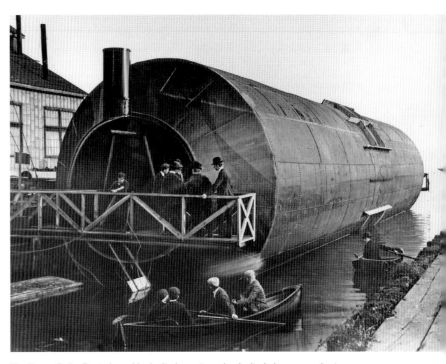

The Knapp Roller Boat viewed by invited guests and uninvited observers prior to commencing her calamitous trials in Lake Ontario on 27 October 1897. *Sunday Sun, Ontario*

The wreck of the Knapp Roller Boat in the ice at Toronto on 10 April 1923. *Toronto Star*

unmanageable. The best speed achieved before it virtually submerged itself was 8 knots. The wreck of the model craft was buried during land-filling along the Toronto waterfront in the 1930s. As the *Toronto Star* cynically commented some years later, the only rolling achieved by Knapp's boat was 'to roll flat the bank accounts of a few suckers'. A sum of $30,000 (£6,000) had been sunk – quite literally! – in the test craft which had a scrap value of just $450 (£90)!

Returning to the more conventional, the new passenger vessels entering service from the late 1880s benefited from the discoveries and inventions of the emerging scientific age, and the construction of even larger liners not only became more feasible but more economically practicable as well. This pioneering period of steam-powered ocean travel is distinguished by the very low number of liner schemes which were not fulfilled. With limited technical knowledge and experience on which to draw, most new ship proposals were eventually realised and lessons were learnt from their performances while actually in service – a potentially costly, though effective, procedure.

Around 1889, serious consideration was given to the design of another large liner and, as in the case of the *Great Eastern*, this vessel was also to be truly a monster when compared to her contemporaries. It was at this time that Sir Edward Harland, of Harland & Wolff in Belfast, produced a design of a 1,000ft liner suitable for the White Star Line. It was a design which, although not pursued any further at that time, was retained for the next thirty or forty years, being perpetuated by Lord Pirrie, a later Harland & Wolff chairman, and setting a sort of symbolic size target for which to aim in all future giant passenger liner thinking. The design was revised from time to time to accommodate the latest improvements to marine engines, and it was said to have been used eventually as the basis for the design of the giant White Star liner *Oceanic*, laid down in the 1920s.

Whether there was any intention to build such a liner in the late 1890s is unknown, but it is unlikely, as shipbuilding practice had not developed sufficiently at that time. Nevertheless, the feasibility of such large passenger ships had been endorsed by a respected authority in the shipbuilding world, and this was surely the main result – if not the object – of the exercise. The eventual construction of a 1,000ft floating palace had now been prophesied but, as fulfillment had

come a little nearer by the turn of the century, aspirations tended to moderate somewhat, and plans for new vessels were for ships of a more immediately practical size which tended to be natural progressions from the largest liners already afloat and in commission.

Politically, Great Britain and Germany faced one another across the North Sea as mighty contestants and the possession of the Atlantic Blue Riband record represented one of the highest national achievements. This invariably attracted the greatest volume of passengers, besides reflecting increased business on the other ships of the company concerned and even, to some degree, on the nation as a whole. So the major companies of both countries led the field with plans for record-breaking, modern sea-queens.

Meanwhile France, Italy and the United States were all emerging as important maritime nations in this field, and the first 20,000-ton liners were soon taking shape on the slipways from 1900 onwards.

The years around the turn of the century also witnessed a revolution in marine engineering which was to have a far-reaching impact on the realisation of many of the ambitions for future passenger liners. To cite but two instances, there was the public display of the *Turbinia*, introducing Parsons' marine turbine, at the Jubilee naval review in 1897, and the commencement of the Allan sisters *Victorian* and *Virginian* in 1903, these being the first passenger liners to be propelled by steam turbines.

A contributor to the Scientific American on 10 November 1900 offered his suggestions for a possible liner of the future – a six-funneled extrapolation of the Hapag *Deutschland*. He reckoned that a 30-knot, 4-day vessel could be produced by increasing the (steam reciprocating) engine size to produce 110,000 horsepower on three screws, with proportionate enlargement to all other dimensions and capacities. On his own admission, however, the author concluded that the development he suggested would not be practicable in reality. Instead, he reasoned that the larger and faster ships of the type to which he referred would only come about with the development and adoption of the Parsons turbine. How right this prediction proved to be! Nonetheless, there also remained a focus on improving hull form as a route to achieving better operational efficiency and improved speed.

Around thirty-five years after Knapp's abortive attempt to demonstrate his craft in Toronto harbour, a noted industrial designer presented his concept for the 'Liner of the Future', a similarly radical approach to transoceanic conveyance.

In that relatively short interlude since 1897, the Victorian and Edwardian periods – typified by their stiff and fussy ornamentation – had passed away and the world was immersed under the influence of the simplism of the Art Deco movement. It was the age of Modernism in every respect: fashion, architecture, interior decoration and furniture and, of course, industrial and transport design. Streamlining, functionality and geometric simplicity were the vogue and these principles were applied to everything from household appliances to road vehicles, from railway locomotives to telephone handsets and ornaments. Although the genesis of Art Deco had been in France, it was in America that Modernism found its greatest expression and its most avid exponents, among them Norman Bel Geddes, something of a design visionary who came to be known as 'the man who designed the future'.

Promulgating the philosophy of Modernism, that the design of an object should be based purely on its purpose – that 'form follows function' – Bel Geddes' view was that everything could benefit from simplification and that every mode of transport could be made to perform better by reducing resistance (air, water or ground) to

the minimum by focusing on how their form affected movement through an environment, no less so with ocean passenger ships. Thus, in pursuit of his crusade to create a sweeping change to the look of everything American, he registered patent D0091759 on 25 October 1933 followed, on 1 November 1933, by Letters of Patent D0049617 and D0049618, all entitled 'Design for a Boat'. In fact, these patents were for the design of his extraordinarily streamlined 'Liner of the Future'.

Dubbed the 'whaleboat', the vessel he conceived was fish-like in general form, almost cylindrical, tapering particularly to its stern end, and fully enclosed with all external projections faired in. It was as streamlined a shape as could be imagined and totally radical when compared with anything then afloat, even the recently commissioned and strikingly modern *Bremen* and *Europa*. It hinted of the cylinder ships mooted in the mid 1800s but also presaged the hull refinements of many years later such as the X-bow, featured in certain cruise ship designs introduced in the twenty-first century, and it may have influenced the *Mauretania/Swift* design envisaged in the 1990s (see page 229). Bel Geddes' patent explained that, while the under-form of the hull was more conventional, 'it will be understood that that portion of the boat which is normally visible, i.e. that part which is normally above the water line thereof, is the dominant feature of my design'.

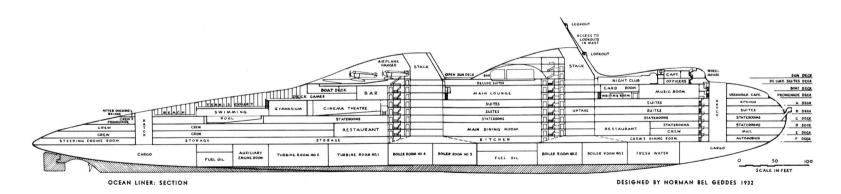

The futuristic whale ship would have accommodated 2,000 First-class passengers and 900 crew according to its designer's calculations. This profile cutaway reveals how the accommodation and public spaces, including a tennis court and swimming pool with beach, would have been laid out. *Norman Bel Geddes*

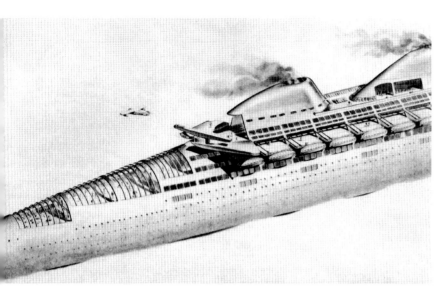

Detail of Norman Bel Geddes 'Liner of the Future', illustrating aircraft handling and stowage abaft the stern-most funnel, an operational dimension that featured in the majority of the transatlantic liner projects from between the wars. *Norman Bel Geddes*

The intended gross tonnage of the 'Boat' was not stated but its long lines of portholes suggested a substantial ship of considerable size and, as noted in Norman Bel Geddes' book *Horizons*, its length would have been 1,088ft. Close-up projections of details, including an impression of a mail plane being handled on a launch ramp abaft the aft funnel, also convey the scale of a ship of great proportions. Of certainty, the 'Liner of the Future' was conceived and designed with transatlantic voyages in mind.

The 'Design for a Boat' patents provide little information on the technical and engineering aspects of the proposed vessel's structure, the novelty claimed being the highly streamlined form of its hull and upperworks.

The *Spirit of the Age* existed only as an illustration and as a crude description in a patent document. Knapp's patented roller-boat did reach the stage of a scaled-down test vehicle which, for an experimental craft, was of impressive size. In a sense, Norman Bel Geddes' 'Liner of the Future' also made it onto the water. When the Paramount film company launched production of the movie 'Big Broadcast of 1938', an extravaganza about a transatlantic race between two ultra-modern liners, it had two large models made to operate on a vast 'pond', one to look exactly like CGT's *Normandie*, bearing the name *Colossal*, and the other based directly on Norman Bel Geddes' 'whaleboat', named *Gigantic*. Of course, the *Gigantic* won the race but what became of these models is not known, although there is another superb model of the 'whaleboat' on display at the Museum of the City of New York.

The important point to make in conclusion is that whereas the *Spirit of the Age* and Knapp's roller-boat may be regarded as having had little, if any, influence on future developments in passenger ship design, the external configuration of Bel Geddes' concept ship, which still stirs the imagination, has, many years later, manifested itself as a direct influence on some of the most modern of today's cruise ship concepts. It is interesting to note that in press releases concerning certain of these new vessels, they are described as being 'unlike anything experienced before, a complete departure from the ordinary' – surely a reference back to the 'whaleboat'.

Having set the scene, we must now return to the beginning of the twentieth century where the great race for passenger ship size and speed honours and an era of immense technological rivalry had begun!

2

EDWARDIAN-ERA ATLANTIC PROJECTS

NORDDEUTSCHER LLOYD'S FIVE-FUNNELLED LINER

Around the beginning of the twentieth century, the Germans were well established as the most superior country operating on the North Atlantic, and this was a most auspicious time for their Bremen-based company. Apart from the Hamburg Amerika Line or Hapag (Hamburg Amerikanische Packetfahrt Aktien-Gesellschaft) *Deutschland* of 1899, the Norddeutscher Lloyd (NDL) had held the Atlantic Blue Riband for five uninterrupted years with their two famous Stettin (now Sceczin)-built liners, the *Kaiser Wilhelm der Grosse* of 1897 and the *Kronprinz Wilhelm* of 1901. Having nailed their flag to the top of the mast with these record-breakers, the NDL intended to see it kept there by the commissioning of even speedier vessels.

So far as the Germans were concerned, their aim was a five-day vessel which would cover the distance between Bremerhaven and New York so as to arrive at the latter port no later than 19.00 hours on the fifth day of the crossing. Such an arrival would permit the Customs and Immigration authorities to carry out formalities on the day of arrival. A ship that could travel at no less than 24.8 knots over the 3,558 miles of distance was therefore required.

Following the *Kaiser Wilhelm der Grosse* and the *Kronprinz Wilhelm*, a third, slightly larger liner, the *Kaiser Wilhelm II*, was begun in 1901 and, with her up-rated engines producing 44,500 indicated horsepower (ihp), was certain to be a 24-knot flyer, but she would still be unable to cross the Atlantic in the five days required. It was well appreciated by the NDL designers that there was very little scope for obtaining further increases in output from the steam reciprocating machinery installed in her.

The company, therefore, sought other means than just increasing engine capacity for the development of a faster vessel, and the projected ship which followed was conceived by their Chief Designer, Professor Dr Johann Schütte. Professor Schütte, known for his contribution to the design of the Schütte-Lanz airship, saw other, more economical means of achieving the desired performance by improving the ship's hull form. In June 1902 he announced his plans for a new liner – a five-funnelled, five-day ship with a cruiser stern! Two important features had been incorporated into his new design, and both had their origins in contemporary warship construction.

The first was a much smaller length to breadth ratio, resulting in a far beamier ship. The second was the replacement of the usual counter stern with a cruiser stern, a feature soon to be adopted universally. The 16,810 gross ton Canadian Pacific liner *Empress of Russia*, running

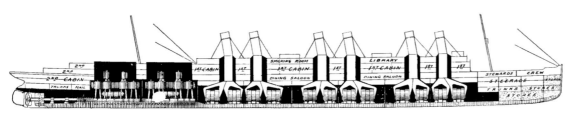

"FOUR-DAY BOAT." *Length, 930 ft. Beam, 87 ft. Displacement, 40,000 tons. Horsepower, 110,000. Speed, 30 knots.*

Cross-section of the 'Four-Day Boat' as it was described in the *Scientific American* of 10 November 1900 showing the boiler rooms and engine rooms by which her proposed 30-knots speed was to be achieved. The drawing demonstrates how, for a given hull size, passenger space has to be increasingly sacrificed in order to accommodate the larger propulsion systems required for greater speeds to be achieved. *Scientific American*

Shipbuilder's model of an express liner intended for the Guion Line, designed by German engineer Robert Zimmermann while engaged at the Fairfield shipyard, Glasgow. Subsequently, Zimmermann transferred to the AG 'Vulcan' shipbuilders at Stettin where his unique paired four-funnel design resulted in five fast German liners, four of which secured Atlantic Blue Riband honours. *Fairfield SB Co*

across the North Pacific, which entered service in 1913, was the first large passenger ship to have a cruiser stern in the event, thereby launching the widespread change of fashion away from counter sterns and thus preceding the *Alsatian* and *Calgarian*, which were the first such liners on the North Atlantic run, by nearly a year. The German five-funnel liner would have preceded them all by eight or nine years.

It had already been demonstrated that cruiser sterns on fast warships were extremely successful. Among the benefits of a cruiser stern was that it obtained a longer waterline length, improving hull flow through the water and aiding propulsive efficiency. It also gave better protection to the screws in harbour as well as greater buoyancy aft in a seaway. This innovative type of stern later became almost a hallmark of Harland & Wolff at Belfast.

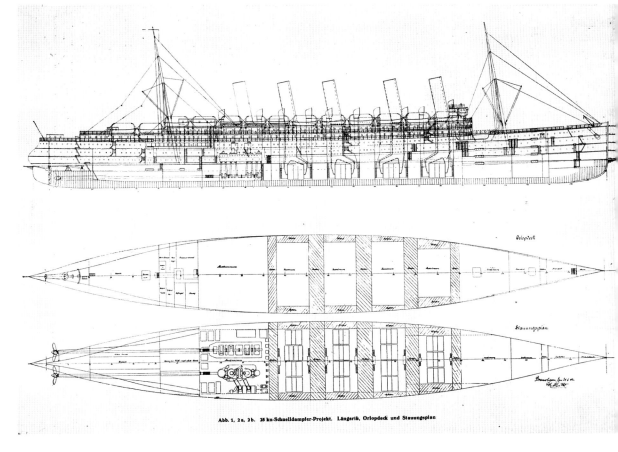

Drawings of the Schütte-designed five-funnelled Norddeutscher Lloyd express liner by Fritz G.E. Moll, dated 24 June 1902. She would have been only the second five-funnelled passenger ship after Brunel's *Great Eastern*. *Schiffbau/Seekiste*

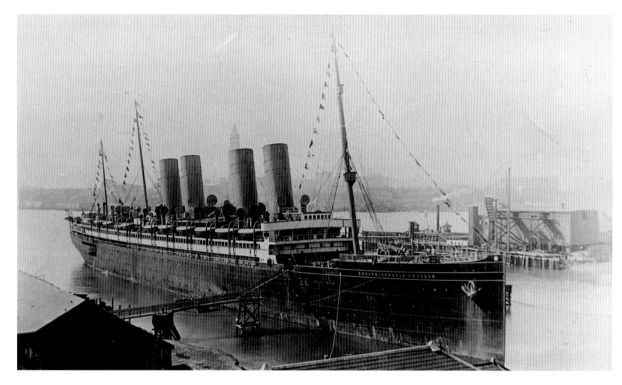

The *Kronprinzessin Cecilie*, which followed the cancellation of the five-funnelled liner. She was seized by the United States while in New York on 6 April 1917, along with fleetmate *Kaiser Wilhelm II*. They were employed as the U.S. Army transports *Mount Vernon* and *Agamemnon*, later *Monticello. Arnold Kludas*

A model of the five-funnelled liner was constructed and tested at Bremerhaven in the great German Experimental Towing Basin, which had also been projected and built under the supervision of Professor Schütte. These tests proved beyond question that the combination of a cruiser stern and more beam in relation to a smaller block coefficient (displacement volume over the product of length × breadth × draught) produced a greatly improved hull form. With smaller engines, the five-funnelled liner would be able to more than match the speed of the *Kaiser Wilhelm II*.

In comparison with the *Kronprinz Wilhelm* and *Kaiser Wilhelm II* one can see how great an improvement had been made in the plans for the new five-funnelled vessel. She would have displaced only 21,069 tons with a gross tonnage of 20,689 and, in spite of her greater dimensions, would have drawn 3ft less water than the much smaller *Kronprinz Wilhelm,* whose draught was 24ft 3in. This was due partly to the influence of the greater beam on the ship's weight, but also to the

intended use of a new type of steel in her construction. Her dimensions were planned to be 690ft 6in overall length and 89ft beam, which compared with 706ft and 72ft for the *Kaiser Wilhelm II*. Thus her length/breadth ratio was 7.76 against 9.81 of the latter vessel. Her engines would have provided a horsepower of 39,000 against the 44,500 of the *Kaiser Wilhelm II*, but she would have been well over a knot faster with a continuous service speed in excess of 25.5 knots.

The contemplated five-funneller not only had an improved hull form compared to that of the *Kaiser Wilhelm II*, but she also had a greater capacity with a complement of 750 First-class passengers, 340 Second-class and 900 Third-class in contrast to the earlier liner's 775, 340 and 770, respectively.

Of her five funnels, the aftermost was a dummy, but the number alone would have been a comfort to the superstitious emigrant passengers, for it was said that these simple folk were reassured of a liner's potential safety by the number of its funnels, and booked their passages accordingly! The only other passenger vessel to be designed with five funnels was Brunel's *Great Eastern* – 43 years previously.

Construction of this superior liner was probably due to start early in 1903 but, before any work could begin, the Norddeutscher Lloyd became aware of the Cunard Line's intention to build two revolutionary turbine liners to wrest the Blue Riband from the Germans. In view of this, the company re-appraised its building plans and, in the face of this new threat, considered it more expedient to stick with established experience and build a second and improved vessel of the *Kaiser Wilhelm II* type. An up-rated version of the five-funnelled liner with bigger reciprocating engines or turbine propulsion might have been able to meet the challenge but, with time against them and with no operating experience of a ship of this type to guide them, the Norddeutscher Lloyd decided on the former course of action.

The five-funnelled liner could have been in service by 1905. Instead, there was a four-year gap between the *Kaiser Wilhelm II* and her near sister, the *Kronprinzessin Cecilie*, and although the former vessel took and held the Blue Riband until 1907, the latter proved to be no match for the *Lusitania* and *Mauretania* which eclipsed the German dominance in achieving the fastest transatlantic passages.

THE *EUROPA* AND THE *NEDERLAND*

Following the cancellation of the five-funnelled liner, the Norddeutscher Lloyd had no ships bigger than the *Kaiser Wilhelm II* or the *Kronprinzessin Cecilie* under consideration during the late 1900s, with the exception of the slower 25,570 gross ton *George Washington*, which was completed in June 1909.

As for the White Star Line, they had answered the German challenge with their celebrated 'Big Four' which entered service between 1901 and 1907. Named *Celtic*, *Cedric*, *Baltic* and *Adriatic*, each of them was in turn the largest passenger liner in the world on completion, although the value of this distinction must be somewhat tempered when it is realised that, even with a gross tonnage averaging 22,500, they were still – after forty-five years had elapsed – little bigger than the *Great Eastern*.

In the meantime, Cunard's reply took the form of exhaustive model tests on designs for two new liners of between 725 and 800ft overall length, tests which resulted in the famous *Lusitania* and *Mauretania*. During this period, the position of the Hamburg Amerika Line (Hapag) was rather ambiguous.

This sketch of the cancelled Hamburg Amerika liner *Europa* (Harland & Wolff Yard No. 391) does not convey particularly well a realistic impression of the ship's planned size even at her original pre-enlargement dimensions. *Arnold Kludas*

Laid down as the *Europa*, the *Kaiserin Auguste Viktoria* was launched under her new name on 29 August 1905. After the First World War, she became the Canadian Pacific's *Empress of Scotland*. The proposed, follow-on *Europa* was to have been a further extension of this design. *Authors' collection*

Despite the limited success of its one record-breaker, the *Deutschland*, which was soon to be withdrawn from her scheduled service to ply eventually as one of the earliest full-time cruising ships, they appeared to have adopted the same policy as the White Star Line. Instead of building more 'racers', they began work on a trio of slower, but steadier and extremely luxurious vessels. As with their later triad of giants – the *Imperator*, *Vaterland* and *Bismarck* – each of these ships was to be a development of the previous one and, consequently, each was slightly larger than the one she succeeded and had corresponding improvements to her appointments. The first of the three, the *Amerika*, was ordered from Harland & Wolff at Belfast in 1903, and she was followed soon afterwards by the *Europa*, which was ordered from the Vulkanwerke shipyard in Stettin, northern Germany (now Sceczin in Poland). While under construction, the *Europa* was renamed *Kaiserin Auguste Viktoria* to honour the Kaiser's consort, and her original name was passed on to the third vessel which had been ordered from the *Amerika*'s builders in September 1906, as Yard No. 391, with a delivery date set for 1909.

Essentially, the three ships were very much alike, though extra length and increased enclosed space made each of them about 4,000 gross tons bigger than her predecessor. The new *Europa*'s gross tonnage was to be 29,700, with an overall length of 718ft. However, in late June 1907, in the early stages of her conception, the design was profoundly modified. The noted maritime historian Arnold Kludas, who conducted detailed research into the origins of the *Europa*, advised as follows:

> The following information, Dr Herbert Bischoff and I have found in the Hapag-Lloyd archives in Hamburg from the records of the meetings of the Board of Directors.
>
> The ship is always referred to as 'enlarged type *Kaiserin Auguste Viktoria*'. Thus, this third steamer of that type was intended as a twin-screw ship with two funnels and four masts. In late June 1907, plans were changed, now a triple-screw liner of 44,500 gross tons was to be built.

Drastic alterations were incorporated into the *Europa*'s design to raise her gross tonnage to 44,500 and increase her length to 780ft, with commensurate enlargement of the passenger accommodation to 4,250, comprising 550 First-class, 350 Second-class, 1,000 Third-class and 2,350 Fourth-class. At this time, immigration to the United States was still increasing and presumably the additional capacity was to be utilised primarily for this purpose.

The revised plans included enlargement of the *Europa*'s propelling machinery from twin to triple screw, driven by the Harland & Wolff combination of reciprocating engines exhausting through a low-pressure turbine. It is not known for certain whether this dramatic change in size would have also altered her general external appearance. This remains a matter for conjecture, for, other than the sketch showing her as first conceived, there is an absence of pictorial impressions of the *Europa*. However, on this, Arnold Kludas made the following observation:

> One can dispute whether the 44,500 gross tons plan was an early *Olympic* version. In any case, the triple-screw arrangement indicates triple expansion engines combined with a low-pressure turbine. Such a big ship would at that time [have had] three funnels as a minimum.

The matter of the vessel's likely external appearance in its larger form is, however, purely academic, since Mr Rupert Cameron, a former Harland & Wolff director, considered it unlikely that the new design for the *Europa* progressed very far, basing his conclusion on the very brief interval which elapsed between the announcement of the ship's increased dimensions and her sudden cancellation in December 1907.

The reason for her cancellation was said to be a need for economic restraint, the causes of which were two-fold. There had been a temporary decline in the passenger-carrying trade in the early years of the twentieth century following the end of the Boer War, when additional tonnage, released from trooping activities, created a surplus of available berths, thereby depressing both passenger volumes and earnings per ship. Hapag's results, like those of everyone else's, reflected this trend. In addition, Albert Ballin, the Managing Director of the Hamburg

Amerika Line, had experienced difficulties with the International Mercantile Marine Company (IMM) which had been masterminded in an attempt to gain control of all the major transatlantic lines.

From April 1902, when the IMM was formed out of the International Navigation Company by the millionaire steel magnate, John Pierpont Morgan from Hartford, Connecticut, many of the major North Atlantic companies were absorbed into this massive all-American finance corporation, holding company or trust. These included the American Line, Dominion Line, Atlantic Transport Line, Leyland Line, Red Star Line and, most significant of all, the White Star Line.

Morgan aspired to cast his IMM net even wider and also to acquire ('M-organize' was the term the press preferred to use) the other major continental lines as well as the Cunard Line – the most important British company to remain independent. Morgan had established something of a cartel with the concerns of which he had already gained control and used his vast reserves to finance almost irresistible boardroom take-overs of his target companies. In the event, the French and British Governments intervened and provided sufficient monetary assistance to enable the Compagnie Générale Transatlantique (CGT) and Cunard to remain autonomous.

As for the two great German lines, which wished to avoid any form of direct take-over, they agreed at an early stage to a ten-year affiliation arrangement which involved mutual cooperation with the IMM on certain joint policies and included a measure of profit-sharing. Notwithstanding this, the IMM eventually acquired a substantial – though by no means a majority – holding in both the Hamburg Amerika and Norddeutscher Lloyd companies. Although this arrangement had relieved the pressure on Hapag to some degree, the fight to remain wholly independent of the IMM had drained valuable funds, and the imposition of financial constraints in order to preserve liquidity may have been a factor where the *Europa* was concerned. In consequence of such a situation, the shelving of the *Europa* project could well have been the outcome.

However, given that within two years of her cancellation, Hapag's plans for the three larger, more impressive and more expensive *Imperator* ships were well advanced, it is possible that financial difficulties may not have been the sole reason for the cancellation decision. Rather, it is perhaps likely that the planned *Europa* had been overtaken by events. With the three *Olympic*-class ships heralded for White Star, Hapag may well have elected to up the stakes with its three 'super-liners' (an expression first used in connection with the *Imperator*) and this essentially made the requirement for the *Europa* redundant. As a matter of related interest, the name *Europa*, which had been dropped on a previous occasion, was also originally mooted for the *Imperator* and then for her near sister *Vaterland*, neither of which, as it turned out, received that name.

J.P. Morgan's ambition had been to dominate the North Atlantic shipping lines totally, but his failure to achieve this objective was pertinently illustrated in an example of what might pass for poetic justice at the time of his death in 1913, at the age of 75. Since he had died during a trip to Rome, arrangements had to be made to return his body to the United States for burial but, ironically, the vessel in which he made this last voyage was the *France*, the flagship of the CGT– one of the few lines which had successfully resisted his challenge!

As it turned out, the cancellation of the *Europa* was not the end of the story, at least not for Harland & Wolff's Yard No. 391. Unlike other shipyards, Harland & Wolff did not, it would seem, enter 'cancelled' on its yard list and then proceed to the next number in the sequence. Instead, the number was treated as vacant, open for allocation for another order.

Turning to another company under the IMM banner, namely the Red Star Line of Antwerp, a proposed passenger ship for them, built under Harland & Wolff's vacant Yard No. 391, reached a more advanced stage. The success of its 1909-built *Lapland* and the impending construction of Holland America's *Statendam*, led Red Star in 1912 to order a large ship from Harland & Wolff for its New York service from Antwerp, laid down as the *Belgenland* on 16 March 1913 for entry into service in 1914. Being somewhat smaller, at 27,000 gross tons, than the scaled-up *Europa* it should be stressed that, despite having the same Yard Number, there was absolutely no correlation between the cancelled *Europa* and Red Star's *Belgenland*. They were completely different ships.

Left: Stern view of the *Belgenland* on the slipway at Harland & Wolff prior to her launch on 31 December 1914. *Harland & Wolff (Robert Welch)*

Right: The *Belgenland* of 27,132 gross tons, near sister to the cancelled *Nederland*. Seen passing down Gravesend Reach, she was the largest ship to use the Port of London at that time. *Tom Rayner collection*

It is claimed that prior to the vacant Yard No. 391 being re-allocated for the *Belgenland*, the IMM had intended that it should be transferred to a large new ship to be named *Ceric*, of up to 80,000 gross tons and 1,000ft in length, to be built for White Star to replace the lost *Titanic*. While the World Ship Society's version of the Harland & Wolff yard list supports this hypothesis to some extent. There is, however, a lack of hard evidence to validate the assertion in its entirety. Nowhere in White Star papers and, specifically, in the company's board reports, is there any mention of such a ship. However, Tom McCluskie MBE, former Harland & Wolff engineer and company historian, and an authority on this period at Harland & Wolff, has indicated that Yard No. 391 was indeed transferred to the IMM initially for a White Star ship with the name *Ceric*. However, the conjecture that the *Ceric* was intended as a replacement for the *Titanic* may be open to challenge given that the interval between the loss of the latter ship and the laying down of the *Belgenland* – just eleven months – seems inadequate for the determination of this replacement action let alone the development of a completely new design for a considerably larger ship. Both the lack of available time and the chronology of events tend

to dictate against such an intention since the *Ceric* was cancelled soon after being announced with virtually no work started on her.

Some months prior to the launch of the *Belgenland* on 31 December 1914, an order for another passenger vessel of comparable size was placed by IMM for the Red Star Line's transatlantic service under a running, cost-plus contract between Harland & Wolff and J.P. Morgan and Company, New York. To be named the *Nederland*, the ship was laid down on 5 March 1914 on Harland & Wolff's No. 2 slipway as Yard No. 469. Although Red Star was not one of the major players on the Atlantic crossing, it enjoyed noted success in the years immediately prior to the First World War, mainly derived from the vast flow of emigrants from central Europe. Presumably, it was the volume of this passenger traffic that was the justification for the construction of not one, but two relatively large liners.

Original design and construction drawings indicate that the *Nederland* would have been a triple-screw ship, similar to the *Belgenland*. Her dimensions would, however, have been slightly greater at 720ft 10in overall length, 670ft length between perpendiculars, 83ft across her beam with a 49ft draught. Her four-cylinder, triple-expansion engines

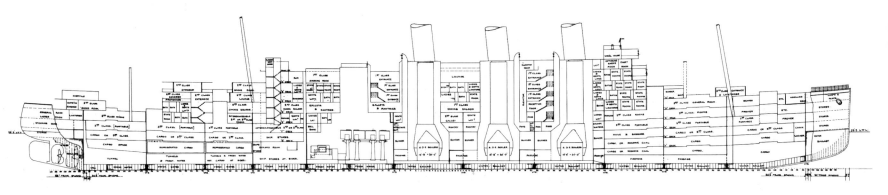

Cross-section elevation drawing of the Red Star liner *Nederland*, dated 25 January 1915. The design of both the *Belgenland* and *Nederland* was by Edward H. Wilding who earlier had been responsible for the *Titanic. Collection Harland & Wolff, Ulster Folk & Transport Museum (HOFM.2010.73)*

with cylinder bores of 35.5in, 56in, 64in and 64in with steam at 215psi supplied by eleven double-ended Scotch boilers suggest that she would have been of combination propulsion machinery with two main reciprocating units driving two outboard propellers exhausting into a low-pressure steam turbine on a central shaft.

According to Tom McCluskie:

The original order for the Red Star line vessel *Nederland* was allocated yard number 469 and was intended to be a 26,500 gross ton passenger vessel. However, work proceeded at a very slow rate due to various factors, the foremost being contractual and financial issues. These difficulties were further compounded by the outbreak of the First World War which saw the contract being negated in its entirety. Work had progressed very slowly and only a partial section of the keel had been laid with little corresponding work on the double bottom/tank top being completed. However, work on manufacturing the necessary frames for the vessel had been proceeded with but only to provide work for the foundry which was facing difficulty in maintaining operation of its furnaces.

With the outbreak of war the Admiralty approached Harland & Wolff with a prospective order for coastal monitor vessels for which the preliminary design work was completed in early November 1914. Matters proceeded rapidly and by the end of that month orders had been placed for an initial three vessels, one to be built in the Govan yard with the other two being constructed in Belfast. The most suitable

building slip was number 2 in the Queens shipyard which was currently occupied by the sections of the *Nederland*. As priority was to be given to Admiralty work the contract for *Nederland* was swiftly cancelled and the completed sections dismantled and removed from the slipway. Subsequently on the 1st December the keel was laid for the first of the Belfast monitors [HMS *Abercrombie* and *Havelock*]. Records indicate that the steel and frames [of the *Nederland*] were later re-used where possible on subsequent vessels.

In fact, the two monitors were laid down on 12 December 1914, just days after the *Nederland*'s partial keel structure had been removed. The *Nederland*'s construction and fate was intertwined with Yard No. 470, intended to be White Star's *Germanic* (discussed in more detail in page 49) which was laid down on 9 July 1914 on adjacent slipway No. 3. The two ships were being built under a 'custom and practice' agreement with Harland & Wolff, including a commission on the whole, as the builder's profit, which was to be reckoned at 5 per cent on the ships and their machinery.

Research by the authors and maritime historian Mark Chirnside, with particular reference to the compensation claim relating to both ships, subsequently presented to the War Compensation Court, would suggest that considerable progress had been made with the *Nederland*'s construction. The claim document states that, by the end of November 1914:

The tank top and double bottom of the *Nederland* seen from the bow on Harland & Wolff's slipway No. 2 on 20 May 1914. *Harland & Wolff (Robert Welch)*

the keel and tank centre plating had been erected and riveted; the vessel had been framed to the height of the double bottom; its tank sides had been plated and almost entirely riveted; the tank top had been half plated; and the stern posts and boss arms castings had been erected.

For Red Star, the outbreak of war would have heralded a retrograde impact upon its then buoyant transatlantic operations and, naturally enough, there would have been concern in the company at the prospect of taking delivery of not one, but two large new ships only for them to be laid up idle pending the cessation of hostilities. Thus the Admiralty's intervention, in giving priority over other work to the construction by Harland & Wolff of vessels for the war effort,

reflected in the cancellation of the *Nederland* and, subsequently, the commandeering of the incomplete *Belgenland,* would no doubt have been welcomed by Red Star. As a consequence, the *Nederland*'s keel sections on the slipway were dismantled and removed in late November 1914 while the *Belgenland* was hastily launched on 31 December 1914 for completion as the utility cargo ship *Belgic,* managed from 21 June 1917 by White Star.

It was anticipated by the Admiralty that, but for a follow-on order for standard ships, construction of the *Nederland* would have resumed after the completion of the naval monitors. The fact was, though, that this would not have been possible since the government retained strict control over the supply and use of all shipbuilding steel under its emergency powers.

After the war, no attempt was made by the IMM or Red Star Line to revive the order for the *Nederland*. For one thing, there was a severe lack of shipyard capacity and first priority was given to the replacement of tonnage lost during the conflict. The *Belgic* was herself laid up for years awaiting her turn to enter the shipyard for conversion back to her originally intended configuration such that she did not make her maiden voyage as the renamed *Belgenland* until 14 April 1923. By then, noises emanating from the United States indicated that a curb on immigration, the very lifeblood of Red Star, was imminent; in fact a quota system was introduced from 1924 which severely reduced the number of migrants.

It is worth considering another factor that dictated against the restoration of the order for the *Nederland* was the transfer or charter of vessels from within the IMM holding group in preference to investment in new tonnage. From 20 January 1925 the former Dominion Line pair *Pittsburgh* and *Regina* became Red Star's *Pennland* and *Westernland* respectively, augmenting the *Lapland* and *Belgenland* on the Antwerp run. Both had a large Third-class capacity thereby giving Red Star an excess of berths at the bottom end of the passenger spectrum. As if to bear this out and reinforce the likely redundancy that would have arisen by having two large ships running on its North Atlantic schedules, the *Belgenland* completed relatively few Antwerp to New York crossings and spent much of her time cruising until she was laid up at London in September 1933. Sold to become the Panama Pacific Line's *Columbia*, running between the US east and west coasts via Panama, she sustained this activity for only a matter of months before being laid up again as unprofitable. In 1936 she was sold for scrapping, just thirteen years to the month from when she had commenced her full passenger-carrying career.

THE *BOSTON* AND *BALTIMORE*

Once international trade began to revive, the major companies began renewing their fleets and replacing their worn-out units. The interval of decline had enabled naval architects to review and improve their ideas for new ships and, with the advent of the White Star's *Olympic*-class, the Cunard's *Aquitania* and the *Imperator* trio of the Hamburg Amerika Line, each in turn being the world's largest ship on entering service, another step was taken nearer to achieving the goal of constructing a 1,000ft-long giant. It was, however, a period when the American presence on the North Atlantic was noticeably absent. This disturbing lack of enterprise concerned American people from many quarters, since they felt that there was a great need for the United States to establish itself as a powerful and progressive maritime nation, with a worthy fleet and an estimable naval presence to match her growing strength and prosperity.

It was with the intention of remedying this lamentable situation that the next two 'unfortunates' were conceived for, had they been completed, they would have been highly enviable vessels. With their proportions, they would not only have been the largest vessels in the world, but also the first to have exceeded the coveted 1,000ft mark. These two liners, which would each have had a gross tonnage of 55,000, had been designed between 1909 and 1914 by William Francis Gibbs and his brother, Frederic H. Gibbs, who were deflected from their intended careers as lawyers by a shared experience on 12 November 1894, when they were eight and seven years old respectively. This was the occasion of the launch of the *St. Louis*, coincidentally, as it turned out, herself a ship of the American Line which, with her sister vessel, the *St. Paul*, was destined to be the largest liner – at 11,629 gross tons – to cross the Atlantic wearing the United States ensign for the next twenty-three years. Inspired as they were by this momentous event, the pair went on to dedicate their lives to naval architecture and, although basically self-taught for the task, their accomplishments have been considerable and their contribution towards the rebirth of the U.S. Navy and U.S. Merchant Marine has made them renowned internationally.

William Francis Gibbs, the senior partner, was born in Philadelphia on 24 August 1886 and was the designer responsible for the reconstruction of the *Leviathan*, ex-*Vaterland*, between February 1922 and June 1923, but there is no question that his greatest success was the record-breaking liner *United States*, completed in 1952. Other less fortuitous plans conceived by him feature within this book. After an eventful and successful career as a naval architect, he died in September 1967.

The Gibbs brothers original design for the *Boston* and *Baltimore* in 1914. The planned location of her home terminal at Montauk Point, Long Island, was a clever stratagem, later advocated by others for the time savings it would permit on the overall transatlantic passage duration. However, the establishment of a new port there, with all its associated infrastructure, would have been punitively expensive. *Gibbs & Cox*

This brief resumé anticipates the events which concern us immediately, and it is necessary to go back to the year 1908, when the Gibbs brothers were embarking on their university careers and when they first conceived the idea of these two giant liners. Remarkably, they not only appear to have mastered the technicalities and intricacies of ship design concurrently with their law studies, but worked on the liner project at their own expense. Then, in June 1913, W.F. Gibbs was awarded two degrees as a Bachelor of Law and Master of Arts at Columbia University and, from then onwards, he financed his ship-design project from the legal fees which he obtained.

The proposed vessels were to have been four-funnellers with graceful counter sterns. The funnels, similar to the Stettin-built German liners, were to have been in two widely spaced pairs, but they bore a general resemblance to the *Olympic*. Their overall length was planned to be 1,001ft, with a beam of 106ft, a depth of 74ft and a load draught of 35ft when they displaced 57,000 tons. Accommodation for 3,000 passengers was to be provided, divided into 1,000 Saloon-class, 800 Second-class and 1,200 Steerage-class,

with a crew of 1,000 but perhaps with an eye to a federal subsidy, their use as armed merchant cruisers or for other military activity also formed part of their design specification.

The Gibbs brothers' liners were to be 30-knot vessels, this speed being produced by quadruple screws driven by 185,000 horsepower 'electric-drive' engines – the first consideration of this method of propulsion for an ocean liner of any size! Outlines for the machinery were prepared at the brothers' request by Mr W.L.R. Emmet of Schenectady, New York State, the Chief Engineer of the General Electric Company. Mr Emmet considered that electric propulsion was the only method by which the extra power to propel the ships at 30 knots could be attained.

These two projected 'speed-queens' were to be oil-fuelled with a cruising radius of 7,000 miles, so that they would only need to bunker in the United States where oil was much cheaper. The presumption is that the architects had calculated that this saving more than offset the additional cost of energy to propel the heavily laden ships, in view of the deeper draught which this entailed, apart from its obvious advantages if and when the ships might be diverted for wartime purposes. It was further intended to operate them from Fort Pond Bay, Montauk Point, on the eastern end of Long Island, with rail links to Manhattan on the Long Island Railroad. The promoters also aimed to involve both this concern and its parent company, The Pennsylvania Railroad, as business partners and as investors in the venture, whereupon booking offices for both railroad companies could become sales points for tickets for transatlantic crossings in the two ships. By dint of using the quick turn-around capabilities of spacious Fort Pond Bay, and thus avoiding the slow trip up the Narrows to Manhattan, it was hoped to save four hours on the crossing time, particularly in thick or foggy weather, enabling the two liners to make four-day passages – an attractive element which appealed to other, later proponents of transatlantic vessels. Indeed, at that time the saving was very significant although the changes in the intervening years, and particularly since the 1950s, may occasion the reader to pause to reflect on the relative merit of this saving of four hours to which the Gibbs brothers attached so much importance as a fundamental element of the *Boston* and *Baltimore* scheme. Today its value pales into insignificance when it is compared with the time of less than six hours that is now taken to cross the Atlantic by modern jet airliners: in other words, a crossing time barely 50 per cent more than the four hours which the Gibbs were hoping to save! The achievement of such a reduction in journey time of approximately 95 per cent in barely half a century can only be described as a revolution and, as it took place, there was little that any passenger liner designer could do realistically to reverse the decline in seaborne passenger traffic which was precipitated thereby.

When they had developed the various elements of their scheme to the stage when it represented a technically viable form of package, the Gibbs brothers approached Mr Philip Albright Small (P.A.S.) Franklin, President of the International Mercantile Marine Company, in July 1916, and he, in turn, introduced them to Mr J. Pierpont Morgan, Jr., the son of the famous shipping magnate. He, for his part, was so impressed by the plans he was shown, which appeared to fit the requirements of the American Line, that he offered immediate financial backing and had both Gibbs placed on the IMM payroll.

At this point it should be remarked that the predicament of the United States Government was that it had lacked a cohesive maritime policy for many years, and in consequence American businessmen had never really been encouraged to invest in shipping of any nationality with any degree of confidence. However, the formation of the International Mercantile Marine Company in 1902 indicated a significant change in attitude, although the emphasis was still on investment in foreign flag fleets as subsidiaries. Nevertheless, one important unit of this great shipping organisation was the American Line, which was entirely American owned and was then in need of new ships. It was undoubtedly for this company that J. Pierpont Morgan Jr intended these two giant vessels.

Indeed, it is safe to assume that this had also been the expectation of the Gibbs brothers from the outset. This conclusion is given the greater weight by contemporary artists' impressions which depicted the two ships in American Line colours – black hull, white superstructure and black funnels with a single, broad white band – and it was now proposed to name them the *Boston* and *Baltimore*, which was broadly consistent with the American Line's system of nomenclature.

In the meantime, the two architects established offices at 11 Broadway, New York, and then had their design tested thoroughly with models at the United States Experimental Model Basin, situated in the Washington Navy Yard, which had been constructed under the supervision of David W. Taylor (later Rear-Admiral D.W. Taylor) – at time of the Gibbs' model tests, in November 1916, Taylor was the Basin's Director. En passant, when a new and larger model basin was commissioned at Camp Carderock, Maryland, in 1937, it was named in honour of Admiral Taylor in recognition of his pioneering work in the fields of naval engineering and experimental mechanics.

The results of the tests on the Gibbs' design for a 1,000ft liner were passed to the United States Government, complete with an exhaustive statement on the economic justifications for the project. By this time, however, the attention of Congress was focused closely on the situation in Europe, and all government funds were being directed into defence channels or being held in reserve for the anticipated national emergency which arose the following year, in 1917.

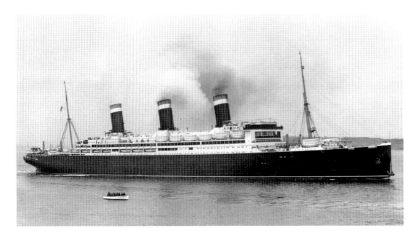

The *Leviathan* ex-*Vaterland* was Capt. Herbert Hartley's last command and the pride of the United States' mercantile marine. As the *Vaterland*, she was in New York when war broke out and was taken over by the United States when they entered the hostilities in April 1917. It was this vessel, re-named *Leviathan* and subsequently reconstructed according to the directives of William Francis Gibbs, that the Germans thought they had sunk when they torpedoed the *Justicia*. In the light of the German error in identification, it is interesting to compare this picture with the two photographs of the *Justicia*, on page 58. *R. Hildebrand*

The revised, post-First World War design for a giant liner of approximately 40,000 gross tons for the International Mercantile Marine Company. *Gibbs & Cox*

In view of the revolutionary idea of 'electric-drive' engines included in the two vessels, the *Boston* and *Baltimore* as they were so briefly named, it is both interesting and significant that it was not until 1928 that the first turbo-electric liner of any size was completed, and that she was built for the Panama Pacific Line, which was a subsidiary of the American Line Steamship Corporation, demonstrating that the idea had taken root within the power-house of the IMM. The vessel concerned was the *California*, the lead ship of almost identical triplets. Of approximately 20,500 gross tons and with 600ft overall length, the three vessels, of which the other two were the *Virginia* and the *Pennsylvania*, served on the New York to San Francisco route via the Panama Canal until 1937. Later, re-named *Uruguay*, *Brazil* and *Argentina*, they operated on Moore McCormack Line's South American schedule, linking New York and the La Plata ports, becoming known popularly as the 'Good Neighbour trio'. All three were broken up in 1964. Their engines consisted of two oil-fired steam turbines generating power for two direct-drive electric motors, one for each screw shaft. Their top speed was 18.5 knots at 17,000shp. Perhaps reflecting their pioneer work in this field of marine engineering for the *Boston* and *Baltimore*, the three sets of turbo-electric machinery were supplied by the General Electric Company.

Meanwhile, another giant liner design was created by the Gibbs brothers for the IMM, incorporating the latest trends in appearance and including other novel features. In comparison with the *Boston* and *Baltimore*, this new ship's tonnage would have been about 40,000, although the long rows of lifeboats indicated a vessel of considerable length. It had three wide, capped funnels and a cruiser stern had been substituted for the conventional counter stern, while a slightly curved and raked bow complemented the liner's graceful sheer. Although this new design had many attractive and advanced features, no ships materialised from it.

When the war had ended and the next opportunity to present the original project occurred, the ships' design had been substantially re-modelled, putting an emphasis on military versatility. The space above the counter stern had been cleared and enlarged to carry and launch seaplanes for reconnaissance purposes. This was one of the ancillary features of the new design, but the most outstanding modification in this new concept was the complete reappraisal of the liner's fuel storage system and facilities. William Francis Gibbs had come to appreciate the potential of using large liners as commerce raiders during wartime from the German example but, realising that fuel limitations had been their 'Achilles Heel', he now gave his ships even more enormous volumes of fuel space. This made it necessary, in view of the additional tanks resulting from this exercise, to devise

a new and carefully controlled ballasting procedure in order to maintain their stability in all conditions as the contents of the tanks were consumed.

Simultaneously, it was also suggested that up to a total of four of these 1,000ft liners should be built. This proposal did indeed become part of the Shipping Board's Merchant Marine Plan of 1919 but, despite this support and the additional naval benefits in this modified design for the *Boston* and *Baltimore*, it was all too late. The post-war Depression in the United States and the vast surplus of war-built emergency tonnage, by then laid up in the United States Reserve Fleet, now put any such scheme beyond realistic contemplation, and so these 1,000ft super-liners were abandoned. Although his high hopes had been blighted, the basic principles of the giant liner concept remained in William Francis Gibbs' mind for the next thirty years, when he was finally given the opportunity to fulfil his dreams in the magnificent *United States*.

THE *BRITANNIC*

While the Gibbs brothers had been persevering with their 1,000ft passenger liner scheme, the outbreak of the First World War had come earlier to Great Britain, and with it had come the postponement of certain new liner projects. A number of these were, however, amended to be used in auxiliary capacities during the conflict. Some of the resulting vessels were to pass through it safely, earning fame and glory for their daring feats and gallant services. Others, less fortunate, were doomed to be 'sent to the bottom', either tragically or heroically as the case might be, and in consequence were prevented from ever operating in the peaceful role which they had originally been meant to fulfil. The *Britannic* was the first of twelve such vessels lost on active service in the two world wars, and she was by far the largest British merchantman to be lost in the first of them.

A magnificent model of the *Britannic*, showing her gantry davit arrangement very clearly. Alongside her is a model of the 5,004 gross tons White Star liner *Britannic* of 1874 which was a famous ship in her day, breaking the Atlantic record with an average speed of 15.25 knots. *Harland & Wolff*

The *Britannic* on the stocks just prior to her launch. At this time, the Harland and Wolff Yard was plagued by myriads of starlings which roosted on the gantries at night. The mess from their droppings was not only extremely unsightly, but so slimy as to be actually dangerous to the squads of men working, so a gang was brought in early, at about 5.30 a.m. each morning to wash it away with high-pressure hoses before the main labour force arrived. When work was suspended on the ship, she was soon in an indescribable state of filth. It might be supposed that the immense weight of bird droppings would have acted as an anti-corrosive sealant to the bare plates but, if such was the case, it was certainly not appreciated! *Harland & Wolff (Robert Welch)*

Originally ordered for the White Star Line as the third ship to follow the *Titanic* and *Olympic*, the *Britannic* was laid down as Yard No. 433 at Harland & Wolff's at Belfast in November 1911. There is a popular belief that the third of the *Olympic*-class was to be named *Gigantic* although no such name appears in Harland & Wolff's Order Book. In the light of the *Titanic* disaster, it is claimed, the name was abandoned. That this was the case has been disputed for years by some maritime historians. Notwithstanding this, Harland & Wolff's former Director and Chief Technical Engineer, Cuthbert Coulson Pounder, wrote in a 1960 technical paper '*Human Problems in Marine Engineering*':

Olympic and *Titanic* had a sister, originally to be called *Gigantic* but, after the loss of the *Titanic*, named *Britannic*.

Some years later he reiterated this statement in a letter written in 1964, which was published in the winter 1977 issue of the *Titanic Commutator*, in which he stated:

The original conception was for three mammoth ships bearing names suitable for such vessels, namely: *Olympic*, *Titanic* and *Gigantic*. After the catastrophe which overtook *Titanic* on her maiden voyage in April 1912, it was decided to drop the name of the third vessel as it was felt that the public might be alarmed at the thought of travelling in a vessel the name of which was *Gigantic*, considering what had overtaken a vessel so large as to be called *Titanic*. The more conventional name *Britannic* was then substituted.

The *Titanic* calamity was, however, to have an even more profound effect on the *Britannic*, for construction of this third ship of the series had hardly begun when the *Titanic* collided with the iceberg on her maiden passage and staggered the world with the terrible news of her death toll. Construction was halted immediately, and many additional safety measures were incorporated into her design following the public enquiry into the disaster. The *Britannic*, as she had become, was given much increased watertight compartmentation, while she was also fitted with a double skin to her hull that extended up beyond her bilges up to a height between the middle (E) and upper (F) decks. The skin ran the length of six boiler rooms and two engine room compartments, in a sort of semi-'wrap around' configuration.

The other alteration was in the provision for extra lifeboats. The *Britannic* was to be fitted with eight sets of a new form of girder crane davits which, it was said, could transfer their boats from one side of the ship to the other, as necessary. These would have enabled her to carry forty-eight boats, but even the five sets eventually fitted (together with other boats under conventional radial davits) looked grotesque and completely spoiled her appearance.

Many of the schemes described in this book never came about in any form, but others did reach fruition, and some even went into commission, if not for their designed purpose, namely the carriage of passengers on a regular schedule. As to the former, no one can state with certainty that they would have matched the claims made for them but, even if some of the entrepreneurs whom we shall encounter had little personal experience of nautical matters, it is undeniable that all of them employed very enlightened marine architects of sheer genius – it would be presumptuous for anyone on a lesser plane to question their findings. However, in certain instances, as in the case of the *Britannic*, when vessels did see sea service, certain of the claims made do give rise to doubts, and the matter

of these girder davits is a clear case in point. Since the whole matter of lifeboats in passenger liners deserves some comment, it may be well to quote first from various contemporary sources. A White Star brochure, for instance, stated:

> The vessel is equipped with the latest and most approved type of electrically-driven boat-lowering gear, by means of which a very large number of boats can, one after the other, be put over the side of the vessel and lowered in much less time than was possible under the old system of davits. ... One of the advantages of the new system is that the passengers take their places in the boats expeditiously and with perfect safety before the boats are lifted from the deck of the vessel, and the gear is so constructed that the fully laden boats are lowered at a very considerable distance from the side of the ship, thus minimising risk in bad weather. Moreover, the whole of the boats on board can be lowered on either side of the vessel which happens to be clear, and the gear has been kept so far inboard as to give a wide passage at either side of the ship for promenading and for marshalling the passengers in the event of an emergency.

The Harland & Wolff rigging plans show eight sets of Topliss gantry davits capable of handling six boats apiece. Provision was made to stow twelve boats forward on the upper deck, twenty-four aft on the upper deck and twelve boats aft on the poop deck, making a total of forty-eight boats, some of which were motorised. The description 'gantry' davit may seem odd, but that is by the way. The *Marine Engineer and Naval Architect* of March 1914 carried quite a feature on the *Britannic*'s boats and gear, much of which repeats the foregoing quotation, but it is worth recording part of it:

> These boats, instead of extending right along the boat deck are arranged in four separate groups with abundant space for marshalling passengers etc. The system of davits used differs from that in any other preceding ship. There are two davits on each side of the deck where the boats are placed. These do not slew, the space apart being sufficient to pass the boats through. They are of lattice girder construction with a swan-necked top turned towards each other in

each pair. They more resemble sheer legs in their action than davits or cranes, being pivoted at their base and moving from a vertical position to a considerable angle inboard or to a considerable angle outboard. Indeed, the angle is so great that the davits command one half of the deck of the ship while, when outboard, they would enable the boats to be lowered vertically into the sea even if the vessel has considerably heeled over. The arrangement is such, too, that the boats may be traversed across the deck so that all of the boats may be lowered on the one side of the ship at the will of the captain. The davits are inclined inboard or outboard by means of powerful screw gear. The height and outreach of the davits enables the boats to be mounted one over the other in tiers and to facilitate the placing of several tiers in the width of the ship. ... limit switches are provided so that in the event of any accident, or any temporary aberration on the part of a man manipulating the gear, the motion of the davits, or both, will be arrested before damage can take place, thus making the gear practically mistake-proof. Another feature is the arrangement by which boats can be lowered on an even keel even in the event of the ship being down by the head or the stern. A further advantage of this davit, which is made by the builders of this vessel, is the fact that the boats can be all open lifeboats of good type, thus dispensing with the troublesome collapsible type.

The *Britannic*'s main reciprocating engines on the left, with those of the *Statendam*, later *Justicia*, at an earlier stage of assembly on the right. *National Museums of Northern Ireland*

Whether or not these gantry davits would have been effective in operation or were able in practice to transfer and lower their boats from either side of the ship as required is a matter for conjecture which falls outside of the scope of this book. It can be asserted with confidence, however, that, in the wake of the *Titanic* disaster, the conspicuous apparatus and the greater number of lifeboats carried by the *Britannic* would have gone a long way in reassuring nervous passengers. It should be kept in mind, too, that the *Britannic* was not the only White Star ship to be so fitted, the *Pittsburgh*, *Regina* and *Doric* all having had two sets of gantry davits when they entered service.

Bigger than both the *Olympic* and *Titanic*, the *Britannic* measured 48,158 gross tons on completion, and her overall length was 903ft. In common with the earlier pair, her engine installation consisted of a combination of steam reciprocating machinery which exhausted through a low-pressure turbine driving a third, central propeller, which gave her a speed of 22 knots.

As a matter of comparison, it may be worth recording the passenger capacity of the *Britannic* and her earlier sisters. The *Britannic*'s figures were 790 First-class, 830 Second-class and 950 Third-class with a crew of 950. Against this, the *Olympic* could carry 1,054 First-class, 510 Second-class, 1,020 Third-class and 860 crew, while the *Titanic* accommodated 905 First-class, 565 Second-class and 1,134 Third-class with a crew of 900.

Above: A splendour which never came into being – an artist's impression of the *Britannic*'s First-class main staircase. *Harland & Wolff*

Left: The *Britannic* at Belfast before being taken up for trade, berthed with the naval monitors that were built in place of the *Germanic* and *Nederland*. The four funnels of the *Olympic* can be seen in the background of this photograph dating from around July 1915. At that time, the *Britannic*'s lifeboats had not been shipped and she appears to be painted in White Star Line's livery. *Bruce Beveridge*

The *Britannic*'s First-class smoking room …

… and the First-class dining saloon. *Both Harland & Wolff*

The *Britannic* would have sported an indoor pool for First-class passengers. *Harland & Wolff*

The *Britannic* was launched on 26 February 1914 but, before she could be completed, the world was plunged into war and, like so many other ships, she was then set aside until the termination of hostilities. However, in November 1915, with the withdrawal of allied troops from the Dardanelles, she was requisitioned for use as a hospital ship. The Dardanelles campaign had been opened up in April 1915 with the invasion of the Gallipoli Peninsula by Great Britain and France, the object being to force a supply route through to Russia via the Bosphorus and the Black Sea. At the same time, the Allies hoped to gain the allegiance of the Balkan States along the way. The operation turned out to be a costly blunder because not only was there a complete failure to achieve the prime objective, but Bulgaria actually joined the enemy. Indeed, it was Bulgaria's aggression against Serbia and Montenegro that precipitated the collapse at the Gallipoli offensive. When these small Balkan countries were overrun in the autumn of 1915, it became necessary to release French and Italian warships to cover landings in order to render assistance in the evacuation of Serbian and Montenegrin troops to Corfu. In consequence of this, there was no alternative to the withdrawal from Gallipoli.

The *Britannic*, under the command of Captain Charles Arthur Bartlett RNR, was ready for her first voyage by 23 December 1915 and then made five round voyages between Naples or Mudros (on the island of Lemnos) and Southampton. Although Mudros was the originally intended port, on her second voyage the *Britannic* only got as far as Naples. On her third voyage the destination was Augusta (Sicily). Voyages four and five followed the scheduled route from Southampton to Mudros via Naples. Her main task was evacuating wounded soldiers from the battle zone and as such she successfully evacuated some 12,000 troops prior to her last voyage. Lemnos, which lies about 50 miles west of the Dardanelles between Greece and Turkey, had been established as the Allied headquarters for the Gallipoli campaign. Leaving Southampton on her final voyage on 12 November 1916, the *Britannic*'s eventual destination was scheduled to be Mudros, where she was to embark more casualties. She called at Naples en route to re-bunker, arriving there on the 17th and remaining for the next two days as she was delayed by a severe storm. When approaching her final destination, all the portholes on both sides were opened to ventilate the cabins, on the order of a member of the medical staff.

On 21 November, at about 08.00 hours, when nearing the end of the voyage outwards, she struck a mine off Port St Nikolo, the principle port of the small island of Kea which is situated south-east of the Gulf of Athens, in the Aegean Sea. The explosion struck her on the starboard side lowest deck forward of the boiler rooms by the third bulkhead. At first there was some dispute about whether it was a mine or whether she had in fact been torpedoed. However, in spite of the unrestricted submarine warfare by then practiced by the Germans, it was considered to be unlikely that she had been torpedoed, as Germany did not want to antagonise United States neutrality. Moreover, the vessel was painted quite clearly in the internationally accepted hospital ship colour scheme – white with a green band interspersed with large red crosses – and the probable cause of her loss was indicated later by Kapitanleutnant Gustav Siess of the submarine *U73*, who stated that his vessel had laid mines in the Kea Channel, through which the *Britannic* had been passing on 28 October, over three weeks before the fateful explosion occurred.

Seen in hospital ship colours, the *Britannic*'s immense gantry davits may be observed in this starboard stern quarter view. *Crown Copyright*

A broadside view of the *Britannic*'s port side. Her hospital ship livery is already showing signs of needing to be spruced-up. *Crown Copyright*

As if to confirm this, the French transport *Burdigala* (12,481grt), struck one of *U73*'s mines in the Kea Channel on 14 November, one week before the *Britannic* went down. The *Britannic*, so it seemed, had almost certainly struck a mine.

In fact, the *Britannic* went down very quickly, sinking within an hour, and there were a number of relevant factors contributing to this. Captain Bartlett made an abortive attempt to beach his ship on Kea Island. Although he had ordered the watertight doors to be closed, this had not happened. Although activated from the bridge, the explosion had caused the electrical control to malfunction. Also the terrific force of the explosion wracked the hull, distorting the doors so they would not close in their tracks. Subsequent dives on the wreck revealed that all the watertight doors remained open. Failing the possibility of being towed in stern first – and even the advantage of this might be open to question – he set the task on attempting to beach his ship but as the *Britannic* gained speed, water was being channelled down through the Firemen's Passage. Perhaps the most salient feature of the events subsequent to the initial explosion was the failure of the forward watertight doors to operate, with the result that water was permitted to flood in unimpeded from between compartments 2 and 3 on the starboard side where the explosion had taken place and, before long, five compartments were flooded and the giant hospital ship was severely down by the head. Then, with a rapidly increasing list, the *Britannic* heeled over to starboard and sank. Like the *Titanic*, her stern disappeared below the surface last. At 9.00 a.m. the Captain and Chief Officer, Assistant Commander Harry Dyke, were still on the bridge and at 9.07 a.m. she sank in 400ft of water.

Of the 1,065 medical staff, Royal Army Medical Corps (RAMC) personnel and crew on board, thirty lost their lives, including nine RAMC staff, and another twenty-eight were injured. Most of the deaths occurred when two lifeboats were smashed by the *Britannic*'s still revolving propellers which had risen clear of the water as the ship's head had sunk deeper and deeper. The survivors were picked up by the cruiser HMS *Heroic* and the destroyers HM *Foxhound* and *Scourge* along with Greek fishing boats. Amongst those saved were two very remarkable individuals, a nurse named Violet Jessop and a 29-year-old fireman, John Priest. Four years earlier, both had survived the *Titanic* disaster, Violet Jessop in the capacity of stewardess, and with this second terrifying experience, they were to be the sole witnesses of the tragic demise of two of the White Star Line's giant ships. Mr Priest later came to be known as 'the man who couldn't be drowned', due to his numerous escapes from sinking and damaged ships. He had been aboard the *Olympic*, the *Britannic*'s younger sister, when she had collided with the cruiser HMS *Hawke* in The Solent on 20 September 1911 and, in February 1916, he experienced his second sinking when he was among the survivors of the former Royal Mail liner *Alcantara*, which was lost in her duel with the German surface raider *Greif* at the entrance to the Skagerrak on 29 February 1916. In spite of shrapnel injuries, he was able to join the *Britannic* for her last three voyages and, after surviving her loss, he was back at sea again in 1917, only to be rescued in April of that year from the British-Irish Sea ferry turned hospital ship *Donegal* after she had been torpedoed.

The loss of the *Britannic* was a tragic one, more particularly since, as a hospital ship, she struck a mine and was not, by any stretch of imagination, a specific target of the enemy – she was typical of so many fine resources wasted by the exigencies of war. She had been meant to enter the White Star's Southampton to New York service in the spring of 1915 but, as things transpired, she lasted less than a year as a hospital ship. Her furnishings and decorations which had never been installed were auctioned off on 4 July 1919. Although she has a number of claims to fame, not least of them being the initial mystery surrounding the precise cause of her loss, if in fact it was a mystery. The *Britannic* will also be remembered as the largest four-funnelled liner ever built, while her triple expansion steam reciprocating engines were the largest of their kind ever to be fitted in a ship built in the UK.

During 1976, Jacques Cousteau and his team located the *Britannic*'s wreck in an attempt to establish once and for all the true cause of the liner's loss. The resultant film investigation was released for television viewing under the title 'CALYPSO's *search for the BRITANNIC*'. Although it shed very little light on the actual cause of the sinking, it is nevertheless an exciting and informative documentary, highlighted by the eerie underwater views of the great ship's hull, vague and indistinct due to the depth and the poor light. Amazingly, much upholstery and furnishing remained to be seen at that time, albeit decomposed by the effects of salt water and ready to disintegrate at the slightest touch.

William H. Tantum IV, an American who was well known in the United States for the interest he engendered in passenger liners and for his involvement in schemes for the recovery of data from some quite important wrecks went down with Cousteau to the *Britannic*'s wreck in the *Calypso*'s small, highly manoeuvrable saucer-like submarine. His subsequent account of the expedition is rather long and repetitive on the whole, but the fact of the matter is that a wreck which has lain on the bottom of the sea for some sixty years has neither the glamour of the original vessel, nor the interest of some ancient craft which may yield unsuspected secrets to archaeologists. Essentially, he reported steel, totally encrusted with barnacles and crustaceans, wherever the team looked. The following are a few extracts from his account:

… we landed the submarine right on the side of the ship … this small saucer submarine … in diameter maybe 16 or 18 feet … this little thing … it's like taking an aspirin tablet and putting it against an Entext model on the side of the hull. There I was on the side of the BRITANNIC, right near a porthole. Incidentally, all the glass in those portholes was completely gone … the hull in that area was completely encrusted with barnacles and sealife and all kinds of growth … say two or three inches … of growth. We … proceeded around the stern. You can see her two propellers – her port side and centre propeller very well. Her starboard propeller is really down into the mud, into the sand, very deeply … we proceeded right along the main deck railing right past the first set of lifeboat davits – the large special lifeboat davits which she has – you could see them turned out. Some of them still have the cable and gear hanging from them, others don't … some of the deck area looks like it was put on yesterday, it's so smooth. Others are rotting or breaking away, full of barnacles … all of the doors are actually rotted away or they have fallen into the hull or have gone down to the seabed. There are no funnels up on this ship … the wooden sections of the bridge – the outer sections are all rotted away.

From the No. 2 to the No. 3 bulkhead, right straight up to the deck, she is opened up (as if with) a can opener. All her ribs (frames) and

sections of her keel are blown completely away, they are not even there! The ribs [sic] that are there are bent and blown out. She's blown completely through, right from starboard to port, port to starboard! The only thing holding the bow to the rest of the ship is the deck and some deck plates. Incidentally the bow is bent – it is not like the rest of the hull, straight and laying on its side. It is bent at an 85° angle the other way. In other words, when she first touched bottom with her bow, it twisted and … as the survivors and witnesses stated, that she first went [listed] to port, then … to starboard and then … to port again and rolled over. The water rushed into the funnels and the funnels broke off simultaneously and she went down on that angle on her starboard side. So actually her bow was already twisting in the sea bed at this point and just holding from the amount of metal of the deck area left … (proceeding) along the sea bed you see a lot of stern wreckage such as metal cots, rusting away. Again, no wood can be seen … some pieces of machinery can be seen … laying there … about 180 metres behind the BRITANNIC we found the third funnel flat, just completely laid out like the fourth funnel …

On 19 September 2008, some thirty-two years after Jacques Cousteau and William Tantum's exploration of the wreck, the *Britannic*'s owner, Englishman Simon Mills, dived on the wreck. By contrast his observations were as follows:

As *Thetis* descends to the wreck of the *Britannic* the light slowly decreases with depth. Just as noticeable is the gradual change in the external colour temperature, as the colours with the longer wavelength in the visible colour spectrum decrease. The first to go is red, quickly followed by orange, yellow and green, as each colour is filtered from the increasingly deep water. At 108 metres we can clearly see the desert-like bottom of the Kea Channel; a flat, muddy and featureless landscape, with only the occasional rock interrupting the monotony of sand.

As we move forward something begins to emerge from Cousteau's 'Stygian gloom'; what at first appears as a huge shadow gradually reveals itself to be the *Britannic*, sister-ship of the *Titanic*. Sister-ships perhaps, but there is a world of difference between the two wrecks.

The *Titanic* rests 12,460ft down in the cold, pitch-black waters of the North Atlantic, twisted and broken into two main sections some 2,000ft apart; the *Britannic*, on the other hand, lies barely 400ft down at the bottom of the spectacularly clear and warm waters of the Kea Channel, and even after more than ninety years on the seabed she is spectacularly intact.

Moments later the submarine lights are switched on, as the *Britannic* suddenly becomes an oasis of unbelievable colour and life. To all intents and purposes the wreck has become an artificial reef, comprising a complex and unique ecosystem. Unlike the *Titanic*, on the *Britannic* there is hardly a rusticle in sight – at least, not on the exterior. The coralligenous substrate on the wreck has instead become home to all of the main Aegean benthic organisms, including filter feeders such as sponges, bivalves, bryozoans and tunicates; the higher parts of the hull support white colonies of Filograna tube worms, with the upper sides of the wreck dominated by a huge variety of sponges, particularly around the deck railings and the level of the Promenade Deck. Further down the sponges are not so big, as the coralline hard and soft red algae, and an incalculable number of saddle oysters, cover the wreck from top to bottom. Large lobsters can be seen sitting in the open portholes on the higher port side of the wreck, also an occasional moray eel holed up in one of the ventilators, while numerous schools of fish (predominately anthias) are everywhere.

The *Britannic* lies on her starboard side, seemingly sleeping, at an approximate angle of 80°. Much of the hull is supported by the seabed, except for where it drops away closer to the upper works of the ship, in some places creating a substantial overhang beneath the superstructure.

We start our tour from the bow, where the metal plates of the ship's prow are corrugated as the foc's'le was pushed into the seabed. As we move back over the wreck, across the buckled base of the still-attached foremast (the lookout's cage is still attached but the wooden floor is gone), about 140ft from the bow a huge chasm suddenly opens up beneath the forward well deck, where the hull broke as a direct consequence of the weight concentrated in this area while the stern of the ship was still above the surface. For so long mistaken for an internal explosion, the reality is that a huge chasm, maybe 60ft across, opened up as the almost detached bow dropped down to the seabed – a bit like cracking open an egg! Even so, in spite of the apparent devastation both of the two-and-a-half-ton Stothert and Pitt cargo cranes still remain fixed resolutely in position.

The forward starboard gantry davits are twisted but still remain attached, while higher up the engine telegraphs and ship's wheel pedestal on the bridge have fallen from their mountings, remaining attached to the hull only by their chains; the wheelhouse telemotor remains fixed, with a few red floor tiles still attached around the base. The port running light is undamaged and as we move further aft it is clear that although the boat deck bulwarks have rotted away, practically every davit remains firmly attached, obscured only by thick layers of saddle oysters. All of the pine decking is long gone, even though from a distance, the ridges of caulking give the appearance of it still being there, while nearly all of the teak woodwork and handrails display a reasonable degree of preservation. All four funnels lie just to the north of the wreck, largely intact although in the process of gradual collapse under their own weight, while the massive open funnel casings show no evidence whatsoever of any internal structural collapse. Remembering that the 100-ton boilers in Boiler Room No. 6 were still seated firmly in their cradles only five years ago, this comes as no surprise; if anything it confirms that Harland & Wolff really knew how to build a ship!

Two huge and very old fishing nets hang lifelessly from the two aft girder davits, so thickly encrusted that in places it is difficult to see their latticework structure, and as we drop down below the *Britannic's* perfectly preserved stern the massive 23ft-diameter port propeller, the cause of all the casualties of the sinking, is unmissable. In fact all three propellers still remain attached, the lower starboard propeller, with one blade partially buried in the seabed, partially obscured by another old fishing net hanging from the 102-ton rudder, still turned slightly to port.

After two hours our time was up. Kostas turned the switch and the *Thetis* gently began the short journey to the surface; in spite of the slightly rough conditions the recovery goes without a hitch and ten minutes later we are once again safely secured on the fantail of the RV *Aegaeo*.

Although owned by Simon Mills, the *Britannic's* wreck is designated as a war grave and is protected by the Greek authorities.

THE STRANGE CASE OF WHITE STAR'S *GERMANIC*

Concurrent with the construction and brief career of the *Britannic*, another large liner was forecast for the White Star Line, listed as a forthcoming new build in the company's 1913 list of new tonnage and already bearing the name *Germanic*. Indeed, the Eleventh Annual Report of the International Mercantile Marine Company (IMM), of 51 Newark Street, Hoboken, New Jersey (a rare document held in the New York Public Library), for the fiscal year ended 31 December 1913, states:

> Your directors have authorised the construction of a steamer of about 33,600 tons and 19 knots speed for the New York–Liverpool service of the White Star Line, to be named *Germanic*, and to be of the *Adriatic* type, with such alterations and improvements as experience has suggested and as are made possible by her greater size. It is expected that the *Germanic* will be completed in time to enter the service in 1916, and that she will be an exceedingly attractive steamer.

To back this up, in June 1914, White Star's then Chairman and Managing Director, Harold Sanderson, stated that the new ship would be about 746ft in overall length: a '*larger ship than Adriatic but smaller than the Olympic*'. Her intended gross tonnage made her marginally larger than rival Cunard's *Mauretania* and *Lusitania*. Further technical details indicate that she would have a 720ft length bp and 88ft beam and be propelled by combination machinery of twin triple expansion steam reciprocating units exhausting into a low-pressure steam turbine on the central propeller. She was assigned Yard No. 470 by Harland & Wolff.

The *Germanic's* keel was laid on 9 July 1914 on slipway No. 3 but owing to the outbreak of the First World War with Germany less than a month later, the ship's name was amended in September 1914 to *Homeric*. This new name appeared among a number of steamers listed 'under construction' for December 1915 with payments against her account of £103,041 14s 5d at that date.

The keel structure of the *Homeric* ex-*Germanic* (Yard No. 470) on slipway No. 3, quite probably showing the greatest extent of its construction. The process of removal for the second time began on 19 September 1917. *Harland & Wolff (Robert Welch)*

Another view of Harland & Wolff's slipway No. 3 and the keel structure of the *Homeric* ex-*Germanic*, seen either while under construction or during demolition. *Harland & Wolff (Robert Welch)*

Subsequently dismantled by government order from December 1914 to make way for two naval monitors, the keel was re-laid starting on 27 May 1916 only for work to be stopped for the second time on 3 April 1917. Eventually, all the structure completed up until that time was likewise dismantled, commencing on 30 August 1917.

According to the research of White Star historian, Mark Chirnside:

Although completion was far off, the ship's keel and centre plate had been riveted and was framed to the height of the double bottom. The costs accrued to November 1914 were around £40,000 of which £35,000 was for the cost of materials, and two payments had been made, £25,000 in October and £25,000 in November, a total of £50,000. However in May 1916 Slipway No. 3 was released, the structure dismantled and then re-laid. Then nearly twelve months later the structure was then broken up in September 1917 by the Deputy Controller of Auxiliary Shipping in order to make room for government work. The second construction on slipway No. 3 had cost £35,000 and £8,000 to dismantle.

Plates marked with each ship's Yard No. [469 and 470] were delivered from the rolling mills. All materials were procured and purchased and paid for by Messrs Harland & Wolff from outside, except the rivets which were supplied out of their own stores and immediately charged to White Star Line's account. The understanding with Harland & Wolff ensured that the builder had no motive to resort to cheap or inferior materials or work. They were given carte blanche, within the limits of reason and of bona fides, to procure the best materials and workmanship; and the purchasers, who were closely allied in business with the builders, seem to have been justified in regarding themselves as safe in dispensing with supervision or tests.

After the War the IMM Co., White Star and Harland & Wolff appealed to the War Compensation Court with a claim relating to two passenger ships, Yard Orders No. 469 (the *Nederland*) and 470 (the *Germanic/Homeric*) which had both been ordered for the IMM. The claimants declared that when the two ships had reached a certain stage of construction the Admiralty obliged the builders to dismantle them to vacate the slips for government work; as has been seen No. 470 was dismantled twice. The claim for the scrapping of both ships was for £104,197, this being the cost of the work and materials ditched and the cost of dismantling after deducting the amounts realised by the sale of recovered materials.

Further research conducted by the authors reveals that the settlement of compensation in respect of the *Nederland* and *Germanic/Homeric* was by no means straightforward – the British Government, in the form of the Admiralty and the Shipping Liquidation Department, completely resisting the claim. The proceedings that followed descended into acrimony, especially when it was suggested that the owners and builders of the two vessels (described as 'hulks') had forfeited the part-built ships as an act of patriotic generosity. Both Lord Pirrie, for Harland & Wolff, and Harold Sanderson, for the IMM, openly expressed their displeasure. An appeal against the initial rejection of the claim was lodged and this finally succeeded, although the outcome was far from satisfactory. On 1 April 1924, the War Compensation Court awarded settlement for both vessels at £55,315, barely half of the cost that had been incurred. The Holland America Line experienced similar resistance when it sought compensation for the lost *Justicia* ex *Statendam* (see The *Justicia ex Statendam* on page 55).

The *Columbus* during construction at the Schichau shipyard, Danzig, prior to being handed over to White Star for completion as the *Homeric*. Arnold Kludas

The *Homeric*, which was begun as the Norddeutscher Lloyd *Columbus*. *Tom Rayner collection*

In 1919, the proposed intermediate vessel was abandoned altogether in favour of captured or seized German tonnage. At that time the *Columbus* was nearing completion for Norddeutscher Lloyd at the Danzig (now Gdansk) shipyard of F. Schichau, but under the War Reparations Scheme agreed under the Treaty of Versailles she was handed over to Great Britain's HM Shipping Controller on 28 June 1919. During June 1920 White Star Line bought the new ship at her builders, giving her the name of the cancelled vessel, *Homeric*.

Construction continued in Danzig to White Star's specifications under the supervision of Harland & Wolff, much to the disdain of the German shipyard. At 34,351 gross tons, the *Homeric* was quite a prize, being the largest twin-screw, reciprocating-engine ship in the world when she entered service on 15 February 1922, sailing on her maiden voyage from Southampton to New York. Meanwhile, the *Columbus'* former sister, the *Hindenburg*, one of the few half-built German ships not commandeered by the Allies, was completed for Norddeutscher Lloyd, eventually sailing on her maiden voyage in December 1923 under the name *Columbus*, the two former sister-ships to some extent rivalling one another.

With the aforementioned tonnage and a length overall of 774ft (751ft bp) and a beam of 83ft 4in, the size of the *Homeric* was not greatly at variance to the specification of the originally conceived *Germanic/Homeric* but her service speed of 18 knots would leave a lot to be desired where White Star's 'express' service was concerned.

To sum up this rather convoluted saga: the proposed *Germanic* ultimately became the *Homeric* but another *Homeric* (the ex-*Columbus*), a sequestrated Germanic vessel, was commissioned in her place. As to what became of the Yard No. 470, there was a more positive outcome following the end of the war. Apparently, subsequent to the cancellation of the *Germanic/Homeric*, it was allocated to the proposed giant White Star vessel *Oceanic* as first mooted in 1923. However, as White star were unable to raise the finance necessary for such a major project, work on the giant vessel's design was suspended and the contract transferred instead to a new *Laurentic*, the second of the name and a considerably smaller vessel. Although originally ordered by the IMM, the company apparently did not really want the *Laurentic*, as they had acquired a surfeit of German tonnage following the Armistice. With the costs of shipbuilding rocketing, the contract with Harland & Wolff was, for the first time, placed on a 'fixed price' basis and not 'cost plus' as had been the previous arrangement.

IMM's Mr P.A.S. Franklin had originally intended the *Laurentic* to be the finest 'cabin' ship on the Canadian service but later dictated that there was to be no unnecessary expenditure on her. As a consequence of the extreme shortage of steel for new buildings at Harland & Wolff, coupled with the General Strike of 1926 which caused a halt on all work throughout the shipyard, the construction of the *Laurentic* was delayed by nine months. She was eventually launched without ceremony on 16 June 1927 and completed just under five months later. Propelled by the somewhat outdated combination machinery of twin reciprocating engines exhausting into an LP turbine, she was reputed to be the last ever coal-burning transatlantic liner.

Despite its rather labyrinthine genesis, the physical manifestation of Harland & Wolff's Yard No. 470, originally intended as the *Germanic*, later renamed *Homeric*, and which subsequently, though briefly, transmogrified into the projected giant *Oceanic*, was finally realised in the form of the *Laurentic*.

The *Laurentic*, the final manifestation of Yard No. 470 was the last coal-burning transatlantic liner. *Tom Rayner collection*

THE *ANDREA DORIA* AND *CAMILLO DI CAVOUR*

In the early 1900s, the Italian merchant marine was emerging as one of considerable size and importance on the world's sea-lanes following the unification of the country as a single sovereign state. It was a period still dominated by the nationalistic spirit of 'risorgimento' and 'irridentism' and this continued to influence much of Italian affairs including shipping.

But the Italian ocean liner companies, of which there were many, were not well organised. They operated on the same routes, competing with each other, and none particularly predominated in such a way that it could commission larger ships to vie with those of the dominant shipping lines operating out of north-west Europe. That situation was set to change.

By 1914, the Navigazione Generale Italiana's (NGI) largest North Atlantic ships were the three 8,900grt *Ancona*, *Taormina* and *Verona* but it was soon to order the *Giulio Cesare* which, after her delayed

Left: The *Dante Alighieri* was the largest Transatlantica Italiana liner prior to the planned large sisters *Andrea Doria* and *Camillo di Cavour*. *Nereo Castelli*

Below: Drawings of the deck layouts of the *Andrea Doria* and *Camillo di Cavour*. The name of the latter honoured one of the champions of the 'risorgimento' movement. *Maurizio Eliseo*

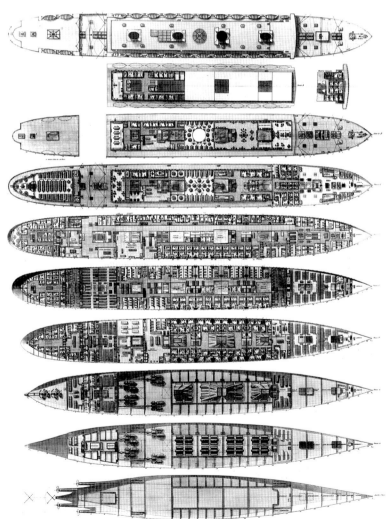

completion at Swan Hunter and Wigham Richardson on Tyneside, would become Italy's first ocean liner to exceed 20,000grt. Around the same time, the Lloyd Sabaudo had the 15,000grt *Conte Rosso* under construction at Beardmore's yard at Dalmuir although she was forfeited when the British Admiralty commandeered the partially built hull and had her completed as the aircraft carrier HMS *Argus*. A slightly larger replacement, *Conte Rosso,* would enter service in March 1922.

Another Italian company, the Transatlantica Italiana, had even more ambitious plans for two considerably larger 32,000grt ships for the Atlantic service to New York. At the time, the biggest ships owned by the company were the 9,750grt *Dante Alighieri* and *Giuseppe Verdi*, the planned new liners representing an astonishing 300 per cent increase in size. Equally surprising, they were to be built in a domestic shipyard when foreign builders were still providing the majority of Italy's new tonnage. Named *Andrea Doria* and *Camillo di Cavour*, the designs for these major ships, comparable in size to the new liners then building for Holland America and Red Star, were drawn up in detail by Ansaldo SpA for construction at its Sestri Ponente facility.

Bearing a close resemblance to the new Compagnie Générale Transatlantique (CGT) flagship *France*, they were flush-decked for most of their length with an aft structure separated from the main superstructure to provide access space to cargo hatches served by four winches situated near the base of the main mast. They had a straight stem, a counter stern and four upright funnels. Of these, the aft-most would have been a dummy. Hull dimensions were 782ft overall length, 738ft length between perpendiculars and 95ft 6in beam. Height from the keel to the top-most deck would have been 54ft 4in and at full load displacement the ships would have had a draught of 29ft.

The design provided for nine decks, a raised boat deck plus decks A to H, with decks C to H extending the full length of the hull. Perhaps mindful of the recent disaster to White Star Line's *Titanic*, the ships' plans showed a total of fifty-two double-banked lifeboats, eight stowed at main deck level (deck B) on the separate aft structure, the others along either side of the boat deck (deck A) on the main structure.

Propulsion was to be by steam turbines with thirty-two double-ended boilers providing steam for the four turbine units driving quadruple screws. As expressed on the Ansaldo specification, the engines would have generated 48,000shp to give a speed of 25 knots. Though not the swiftest liners of their time, nonetheless the *Andrea Doria* and *Camillo di Cavour* would have been fast ships.

As an aside, it is worth noting that, during that period, Italian designers were among the most enthusiastic proponents of the internal combustion engine and it is a matter for speculation as to whether any consideration was given to making this pair motor-ships, although as such they may have found it difficult to achieve the designed service speed. Professor Ingenieur Giorgio Supino, the Italian engineer, was among the first to propose diesel engines for passenger liners of this size and it should be borne in mind that, as a reaffirmation of those ambitions, during the 1920s Italian companies placed several large motor-ships in transatlantic service. Indeed, by 1927 Italy owned the world's largest motor liner, the *Augustus*. About 1915, Professor Supino proposed two alternative designs for a diesel-driven transatlantic passenger liner. It was envisaged that the ship should be of 36,000 tons, with a length of 750ft and a speed of

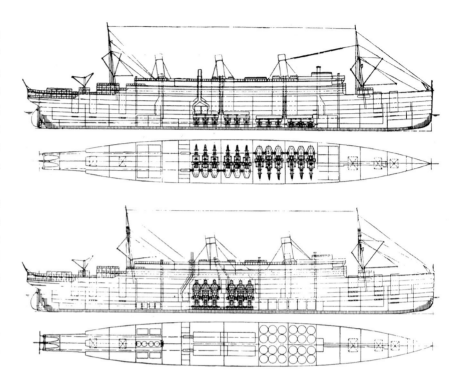

Two alternative proposals for a diesel-driven transatlantic passenger liner designed by Professor Ing. Giorgio Supino, the Italian engineer, about 1915. *Authors' collection*

21 knots, driven by two Junkers engines, in the first design with the engines arranged vertically, in the other arranged horizontally, each to have six double cylinders (cylinder diameter 820mm = 32.2in; stroke 2 × 820mm. = 64.4 inches), generating a total of 30,000bhp at 110rpm.

The *Andrea Doria* and *Camillo di Cavour* would each have carried a total of 2,322 passengers in four classes, split 420 first, 338 second, 176 third and, exploiting the vast volume of emigrants then leaving Italy for the United States, 1,388 in steerage accommodation. Crew numbers would have been 448, making a total maximum complement of 2,770. This represented a relatively low crew-to-passenger ratio even disregarding the immigrant passengers who would mostly have provided for themselves.

The First-class accommodation was spread over decks A to C. A gymnasium for First-class passengers was located aft on A deck with the main First-class public spaces situated on B deck – a Music Room at the forward end, then two Libraries on the port and starboard sides, and a Grand Hall. The upper section of the two-deck main restaurant was on B deck, the lower section on C deck. Above the restaurant was a large, circular skylight located between the second and third funnels. A smaller First-class dining room was located aft on B deck. There were two private dining salons on C deck and, towards the stern end, the First-class smoking room. Right aft on the same deck was the Second-class smoking room.

The Second- and Third-class cabin accommodation was distributed over decks D to F, mainly aft, with the emigrant sleeping quarters, in dormitories, on E, F and G decks. The bakery, the Second- and Third-class kitchen and the emigrant kitchen were on D deck where there was also a bank, a printing office and, right aft, a Second-class lounge.

For some unexplained reason, the First-class kitchens were located down on E deck, two decks below the First-class dining areas. The engine room extended up from H deck through into G deck. There were additional galleys on decks G and H as well as much of the crew's quarters.

Simultaneous with the Transatlantica Italiana's plans for the *Andrea Doria* and *Camillo di Cavour*, another Italian company, the 'Italia' Società di Navigazione, announced that it too was intending to build a pair of new large liners for transatlantic operation. In the event, none of these ships was built. The outbreak of the First World War severely undermined the Italian passenger shipping business even though the ships of neutral countries were able – at some risk – to continue with scheduled commercial services as best they could in the circumstances. However, it was Italy's entry into the war in 1915, joining the alliance of Great Britain, France and Russia, that effectively killed off these schemes. The fact that the Hamburg Amerika Line, a German company, held a majority stake in the Transatlantica Italiana may also have adversely affected the prospects for turning the plans for the *Andrea Doria* and *Camillo di Cavour* into reality. Equally, Hamburg Amerika had assisted financially in the establishment of the 'Italia' company. On the outbreak of hostilities with Italy, there would have been an understandable reluctance on the part of Hamburg Amerika to invest further in the construction of new ships for the companies of what had become an adversary.

By the time the war had ended, the shape of Italian passenger shipping business – for those companies that remained in existence – was about to enter another period of flux. The Transatlantica Italiana struggled on through the 1920s but as traffic declined to an alarming extent and heavy losses were incurred it led to the suspension of all New York sailings in 1927 as the company concentrated on its South American services. Subsequently, with its operations reduced to Mediterranean routes alone, the Transatlantica Italiana was finally wound up altogether in 1931.

THE *JUSTICIA* EX-*STATENDAM*

Yet another vessel which suffered a similar fate to White Star's *Britannic* was building at Harland & Wolff at the outbreak of the 1914 War. Given Yard No. 436, this was to become the British troopship *Justicia*. Originally ordered as the *Statendam* for the Holland America Line, she was laid down on 11 July 1912 and launched on 9 July 1914 but, after the war had started, work on her proceeded at a much slower pace. Then, following negotiations with her Dutch owners, she was requisitioned when almost complete for conversion into a troopship.

On 7 April 1917 she was handed over to the White Star Line who managed her for the British Government under the name *Justicia*. The intention had been to award her to the Cunard Line to replace the lost *Lusitania*, and it was for this reason that she was given a name ending in 'ia' instead of in 'ic'. Cunard's initial choice of name had been *Neuretania* before they settled for the more topical – and possibly more comprehensible – *Justicia* (the word was to carry the connotation of 'Justice'), but all this proved to be of little consequence because, in the event, Cunard did not have the officers and men with which to man her anyway. The *Justicia* was therefore re-allocated to the White Star Line, who had spare men from the lost *Britannic*, for them to manage for the duration of the war. It is uncertain whether the ship would have been returned to the Cunard Line after the war or transferred back to the Holland America Line who had ordered her in the first place.

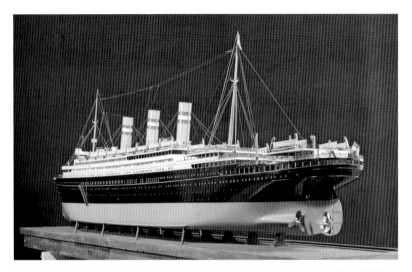

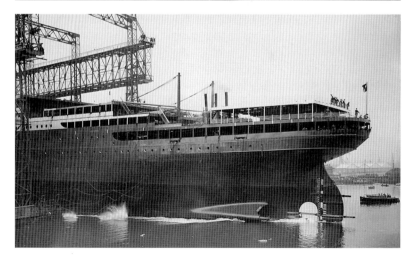

Clockwise from above: Two liners which shared a similar fate seen under construction at Belfast – both became war losses, preventing them from entering commercial service. The *Britannic* is on slipway No. 2, the *Statendam*, to the left, is on slipway No. 3. *Collection Harland & Wolff, Ulster Folk & Transport Museum (HOFM.HW.H1963)*; A beautiful builder's model of the original *Statendam*, completed as the *Justicia*. *Rotterdam Museum Maritiem*; The *Statendam* on slipway No. 3 prior to her launch looking down from above her bow. *Collection Harland & Wolff, Ulster Folk & Transport Museum (HOFM.HW.H2093)*; Launch of the *Statendam* on 9 July 1914. *Harland & Wolff*

Another, ground level, view of the *Statendam* on the building way. *Collection Harland & Wolff, Ulster Folk & Transport Museum (HOFM.HW.H2094)*

Her gross tonnage was 32,235 and her overall length 776ft. In passenger service the *Justicia* would have carried 3,430 passengers in three classes: 800 First-class, 600 Second-class and 2,030 Third-class, whilst the crew would have numbered 600. Although the Holland America Line's projected flagship was of modest proportions compared with the ships then being built or contemplated for the Hamburg Amerika, White Star and Cunard Lines, this was certainly not the case with regard to her public rooms and standards of internal décor. Indeed, it is widely held that, had the *Statendam* been completed for the express mail service as scheduled, the quality and spaciousness of her interiors would have far exceeded that of any of her contemporaries. For instance, she would have boasted a First-class social hall over 20ft high, which would have been amongst the tallest of the day. Both her First-class dining saloon, which would have been capable of seating 563 at one sitting, and the huge palm court, were designed with the kind of creative freedom more akin to the unfettered artistic expression of the 1920s.

Like all Harland & Wolff liners of the period, she was a triple-screw vessel fitted with combination machinery. In the *Justicia*'s installation the outer shafts were driven by four-cylinder triple-expansion engines and these exhausted into a large direct-acting low-pressure turbine which drove the centre screw, the maximum indicated horsepower being 22,000. Steam was supplied by twelve boilers, and her designed speed was 18 knots. The aftermost funnel was a dummy. It was claimed that the physical diameter of her funnels was reduced from the designed dimension in order to save on the cost of sheet metal.

After leaving Belfast for Liverpool, the *Justicia* commenced her first trooping voyage on 15 April 1917 and, initially, she was painted all grey but later, in November 1917, she was given a dazzle-painted scheme. This camouflage idea had been contrived during that October by an Admiralty working group under the leadership of Norman Wilkinson, the marine artist, and its application was soon widespread. Unlike later camouflage paint schemes, particularly those used during the Second World War, the principle of dazzle painting was not to conceal the ship against her background. Instead, the aim was to break up the ship's silhouette by contrasting areas of light and dark paints, making identification difficult and, more particularly, judgement

Seen from the *Arlanza*, the *Justicia* as completed, painted in wartime grey.
L.L. von Münching

Justicia in dazzle-painted camouflage, seen during a call at Halifax after crossing the Atlantic in December 1917. *Courtesy of the Maritime Museum of the Atlantic, Halifax, Nova Scotia*

of size and bearing, especially in poor visibility and, in general terms, to falsify perspective. The *Justicia*'s dazzle paint consisted of patches of black, blue and light grey and was intended, in part, to disguise her as a single-funnelled freighter.

In her short career, the *Justicia* completed nine round voyages between Liverpool and New York, with calls at Halifax in both directions. She loaded thousands of tons of cargo at New York and at Halifax she embarked 4,445 troops in May 1917 and another 4,160 that June. Between October 1917 and January 1918 she transported around 12,000 Chinese coolies to Liverpool, to serve as labourers behind the Allied front line in France. Her first brush with the enemy, was on 23 January 1918 when she was attacked unsuccessfully by U-boats in the position 54° 40'N, 05° 05'W, while en route from Halifax to Liverpool. Her luck ran out later that year, though, shortly after leaving Liverpool bound for New York on her nineteenth Atlantic crossing. The beginning of her end came on Friday morning, 19 July 1918, when she was 20 miles off the Skerryvore Rock in the Inner Hebrides, she was attacked by the submarine *UB64* commanded by Kapitänleutnant Otto von Schrader and torpedoed in the engine room. Other torpedo attacks failed to sink her and,

later in the same day, she was taken in tow for Lough Swilly on the north-west coast of Ireland. Early the following day the attack was resumed, again unsuccessfully, by *U54*. However, a further strike by this submarine at about 09.00 hours proved to be decisive. With two fatal hits in her port side, she sank by the stern and finally disappeared below the surface at 12.40 hours.

The *Justicia* had no passengers or troops aboard at the time of the attack, but she was carrying a crew of between six and seven hundred men. Of these, nine engine room ratings (firemen, trimmers and greasers) and a 3rd Engineer Officer were killed when the first torpedo exploded in her engine room. The survivors were transferred to the escorting ships and, of these, the destroyers HM Ships *Marne*, *Millbrook* and *Pigeon* succeeded in sinking a third submarine – the *UB124* under command of Lt Wutsdorf – which had not actually taken part in the attack. She had developed so many leaks from the depth charges exploded around her that she made a fruitless attempt to escape by diving right under the stricken liner.

The *Justicia* had taken a good deal of punishment and was quite a long time sinking. There is evidence to show that she was amongst the first vessels to be provided with protective net-defence, which was first introduced in that year. Moreover, it is of interest to note that a contemporary newspaper (The *Daily Mirror* of 25 July 1918) reported that the *Justicia*'s gunners exploded four out of the ten torpedoes fired at their vessel by gunfire, which was no mean feat.

For their part, the Germans were said to be particularly jubilant over the sinking of the *Justicia*, having mistaken her for the ex-*Vaterland*, their wonder ship 'stolen' from them by the Americans. This vessel, which had been interned in New York for over two years, had been seized along with many other German ships on 4 April 1917. The Germans felt that their actions, although preventing them from ever regaining possession of the monster vessel, would also effectively deny the Americans the use of her but, in the event, the *Vaterland* was to continue operating long after the war as the *Leviathan* and, indeed, carried American troops to fight the armies of Imperial Germany during the last months of the conflict.

The *Justicia* sinking, finally vanquished by her attackers. Her wreck lies some 12 nautical miles north-west of Malin Head. *Authors' collection*

The *Statendam* of 1929. She may have had some of the furnishings intended originally for the previous *Statendam*. *Authors' collection*

As for the sunk ex-*Statendam*, hers was a great loss, for she was a fine looking ship and would undoubtedly have been a profitable and popular liner had she been able to fulfil her destiny. As with the *Nederland* and *Germanic/Homeric*, the British Government resisted her owner's claim for compensation, disputing whether there had ever been a contract between the two parties. Recognising, however, that the cost of a replacement for the *Justicia* could cost them £2 million should the claim go to trial, the British authorities opted to make an offer. A letter from the Ministry of Shipping, dated 26 April 1920, contained the following statements:

> It seems probable that if the Petition of Right comes to trial, the court may be disposed to find that the Suppliants are entitled to compensation on some basis or other.
>
> In the circumstances, the Lords Commissioners of His Majesty's Treasury authorise settlement on the basis proposed, viz. by a cash payment of £500,000 to the Company [Holland America] in addition to the value of steel already supplied to the Company, or to be supplied under the agreement referred to, costing, at the then export prices current at the date of the agreement, about £1,145,000. The Company will also retain the fittings etc. ordered for the *Justicia* but not aboard at the time of her loss.

The steel was used for the construction of a fleet of modern freighters, while it is for consideration whether the fittings were installed aboard the new and more fortunate *Statendam* which was ordered from the same builders in 1921 to replace the original liner. She was launched in 1924 at about the time that the United States promulgated laws restricting immigration into their country, and this had the effect of work on the new liner being suspended temporarily. When it resumed, Harland & Wolff was so plagued with strikes in its yard that the ship was towed over to the Wilton-Fijenoord shipyard at Schiedam, and she was completed there in March 1929, being the largest vessel that yard had ever handled.

The remains of the *Justicia* ex *Statendam*, situated between Skerryvore and the Irish coast in the position 55° 39'N, 07° 42'W, are now regarded as a world-class dive site by technical divers who have taken some stunning photographs of the wreck. Lying at a depth of 230ft on its port side, the wreck is split apart and the decks have partially collapsed. Her three huge propellers can be seen and her boilers, scattered in pairs, are also discernible. For all its appeal as an underwater sporting challenge, it makes a desolate monument to a once fine ship.

3

'SHIPS-OF-STATE' PROJECTS
IN THE INTER-WAR PERIOD

THE *FLYING CLOUD*-CLASS

As the clouds of war receded there was an upsurge in interest in new giant liners during the 1920s from Germany and, later, Italy. The response to these initiatives came from English, American and French sources in five separate projects, each of which had outstanding and interesting features of its own. Of these, two were successful, culminating in the three largest passengers liners ever built, the *Normandie* and the two *Queens*, which elevated luxury ocean travel to its highest peak. The other three proposals were not so fortunate, since each was blighted for a quite individual reason, although financial problems played a significant part in the downfall of all of them. One of the three was, however, to become the catalyst for a far more ambitious plan to introduce a uniquely novel, alternative form of ocean liner, the attainment of which would occupy the next thirty-five years.

The first of this latter group was American in origin, being an idea for a comprehensive express transatlantic service which called for the construction of six (initially ten) liners to operate a high-speed shuttle schedule specifically to meet the requirements of American businessmen and travellers. Based on the principles of high productivity and intense equipment usage, the scheme was germinated in 1924 as a result of a meeting between Dr Walter Boveri, of Brown Boveri and Co. Ltd of Baden, Switzerland, and Mr Lawrence R. Wilder, who was the Chairman of the New York Shipbuilding Corporation at Camden, New Jersey – the shipbuilding division of Brown Boveri's American subsidiary, the American Brown Boveri Electric Corporation. By 1926 the detailed design work on the proposed ships was well under way and, in this context, it is interesting to note that technicians at

the New York Shipbuilding Corporation had been model-testing and studying the feasibility of designs for 1,000ft Atlantic liners ever since 1914.

At this juncture, with the project destined for realisation as a viable business proposition, Lawrence Wilder sought the financial participation of interested parties, and herein lay the apparent strength of the scheme, since it was one that had gained the confidence of certain established shipping men who were prepared to invest their own money in its success.

Amongst those who joined Lawrence Wilder in promoting the project were Joseph E. Sheedy, former European Vice-President of the U.S. Merchant Marine's Emergency Fleet Corporation, and Mr H.B. Walker, President of the American Steamship Owners Association. Besides this, the venture owed much of its credibility and impetus to the convictions of its founder, Lawrence Wilder himself.

In the summer of 1927 the Transoceanic Corporation of the United States was formed with a capital of $50 million to manage the project and to administer the construction of the six ships. Concurrently, the Blue Ribbon Line, registered as The New York–London–Paris Steamship Company, was established as the North Atlantic operating company. It was proposed to run the ships, one of which would sail every other day from either side of the Atlantic between Montauk Point, Long Island, and Southampton or Plymouth, and Le Havre, the aim being to provide an electric railway connection between New York and Montauk Point for the passengers, and that this would also be built by the American Brown Boveri Electric Corporation. The choice of Montauk Point as the home terminal was the same as that chosen by W.F. Gibbs for his twin American Line super-liners and for much the same reasons. Montauk Point would permit quicker turn-arounds and it would be possible to deliver westbound passengers to their destinations hours sooner.

The American public came to hear of the Blue Ribbon Line project for the first time on 14 September 1927, when the *New York Herald Tribune* carried an exclusive story on the scheme by their shipping correspondent, John Kelly. From his 'scoop', details of the ships began to emerge, but a subsequent announcement revealed that much of the dimensional and statistical information had to be viewed with some caution, since the specifications for the ships continued to change for some time and were obviously still under development. One thing that was evident, however, was that the liners were of a very novel design. They were to be four day 'clipper' vessels capable of a continuous sea speed of 31 to 33 knots and a maximum speed of 35 knots. According to Kelly's article, there were to be ten 20,000-ton liners, 800ft in length with a beam of 80ft and a 24ft draught, but this was soon to be revised to six ships of 35,000 tons, each with an overall length of 900ft and a beam of 90ft, maintaining the high length/ beam ratio of 10:1 which was apparently fundamental to their design. 'Departure' displacement would have been around 50,000 tons, which included bunker capacity for the round trip.

Accommodation numbers also tended to fluctuate, varying from 400 to 800 per ship in First-class only. There was to be space for 1,000 tons of express cargo and mail. The cabins were to be a little larger than Pullman drawing rooms, which measured some 15 × 10ft, and there would be a total absence of extravagant public rooms, swimming pools and similar passenger amenities of like nature. If this description sounds to be somewhat Spartan, the explanation given seemed to be justified, for it appeared that the need to devote a disproportionate amount of space to engines of massive size, which were essential to the high speeds required for the service, overrode all other considerations. As if to allay any doubts passengers may have had about crossing in these ships, Wilder himself pointed out that there would nevertheless be a fair degree of comfort aboard. The dining rooms would be positioned in the after part of the vessels, as would the promenade space. This latter situation was necessitated by what was the most striking and revolutionary feature of the ships, since they had been designed as aeroplane-carrying auxiliaries and, as a result, the funnels and masts were to be set to one side of a long, uncluttered upper deck in order to leave a large, clear area on which the aircraft could land and take off. Twenty-four aircraft were to be carried by each vessel in commercial service to expedite rapid delivery of mail and passengers in a hurry, but

An artist's impression of one of the Blue Ribbon liners – the first to be named *Flying Cloud*. Although she was intended for exclusive First-class occupancy, it was said there would be few frills, ostentation or grandeur to her planned décor. *Marine Engineering*

The scene at New York on 31 July 1927 as Clarence Chamberlin prepares to make the very first flight from a passenger liner, the *Leviathan* of United States Lines, to demonstrate how expedited mail deliveries could be made from ships at sea. *Authors' collection*

the number would be increased to a hundred machines in wartime. These aeroplanes were to be housed in a hangar under the runway deck, and a number of aircraft mechanics were to be included as part of the regular crew.

The concept of ships carrying aircraft was very much in vogue in the late 1920s as a result of Clarence Chamberlin's successful flight off the *Leviathan* in August 1927 and the experiments with the *Île de France*, but the Wilder suggestions had little in common with these catapult-launched single aeroplane trials. His ideas, instead, reflected a strong naval influence. The New York Shipbuilding Corporation had, after all, just completed the U.S. Navy's giant aircraft-carrier *Saratoga*. It was proposed to give the first ship in the fleet the very appropriate name of *Flying Cloud*, since it was taken from one of the most celebrated of the American-built clipper ships and, more tenuously, it was held to have a certain connotation with her possible function as an aircraft carrier.

At this time, it was estimated that each of the six units would cost around $21 million (almost £4 million) to build. Tests on 20ft models of the liners were conducted on 17 October 1927 at the

Experimental Model Basin at the Washington Navy Yard and, from the findings which stemmed from them, it was estimated that the high-pressure, super-heat turbine engines intended for the *Flying Cloud* ships would need to generate 130,000shp for a service speed of 33 knots and 160,000shp for a maximum speed of 35 knots.

When considered individually, the liners under contemplation for the Blue Ribbon Line were not particularly large, especially when compared with others being forecast at that time or already under construction for other lines, but the project as a whole was both colossal and expensive.

The Blue Ribbon Line's backers were putting up $50 million (£10 million) of private capital but, naturally enough, a request for a loan from the United States Government, under the provisions of the 1920 Merchant Marine Act, was a key point of the proposals, and an outline submission for a Shipping Board Construction Fund loan was made on 21 November 1927. Further hearings were scheduled for early 1928.

Wilder and his associates were well aware of the great need for such a subsidy in order to get their project off the ground and, realising that Congress had to be more than convinced of the economic viability of the scheme before committing so large a sum as the $94.2 million that was required, they had the entire concept examined by a series of committees of so-called 'disinterested experts'. These covered such aspects of the enterprise as design, marine engineering and propulsion, operation and economics, and they were assisted very ably by some extremely influential consultants. Included amongst them were Theodore E. Ferris, the noted American naval architect, Elmer A. Sperry, of the Sperry Gyroscope Company, and Sir Charles Parsons of the Parsons Marine Steam Turbine Company. A great deal of publicity was given to this exercise in the American press and, in the light of subsequent events, it became misconstrued as an attempt to acquire business endorsement and technical approval for the scheme as an influencing factor in applying for federal aid.

Detailed statements on the Blue Ribbon Line proposal were presented to the U.S. Shipping Board during hearings on 10 and 24 January 1928. In his submissions, Wilder aimed to sell the idea of six auxiliary aircraft carriers for use in a national emergency –

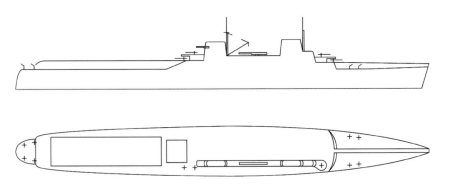

Pre-empting Japanese plans for the conversion of its ocean liners into aircraft carriers, the U.S. Navy's Bureau of Construction & Repair drew up plans for partial carrier conversion of the *Flying Cloud* ships in the event of a national emergency. Instead of a full-length flight deck, the narrow, forward launch ramp was retained. *Chris Franks from a U.S. Navy drawing*

six potential warships which were not affected by the restrictions and limitations of the 1921 Washington Naval Conference – and also the freedom from dependence on vessels under foreign flags for the carriage of transatlantic passengers and freight as an added inducement. To add weight to his arguments, he pointed out that over 60 per cent of the traffic then being carried was of US nationality or manufacture. In exchange, Wilder sought, in the first place, a 75 per cent construction costs loan and, in the second, a revision of the Mail-Carrying Act to the advantage of fast ships. Finally, because insurance was limited on any one ship, he requested protection in the event of total loss in the form of cancellation of the loans against the ships to the extent not covered by amortisation and insurance.

In spite of the strong representations made by the scheme's originator, the Shipping Board was apparently not impressed by the carefully compiled proposals and expressed an unwillingness to assist the project financially. In a complete rejection of the construction loan application, Chairman T.V. O'Connor, speaking on behalf of the Board on 27 April 1928, described the plan as 'technically open to criticism, economically unsound and financially nebulous'. As a result of this pronouncement, many of Lawrence Wilder's supporters, including Dr Walter Boveri, then decided to dissociate themselves from the

Blue Ribbon Line, and certain of them, in marked contrast to their earlier standpoint, became critical of the whole venture and of its prospects. Such overt scepticism from persons previously so closely connected with the scheme did little to enhance the now slender chances of success for the *Flying Cloud* and her sisters.

Much to his credit, Lawrence Wilder remained undeterred in spite of this setback. He severed his connections with his Swiss employers and, in so doing, purchased from them the shipbuilding division of the American Brown Boveri Electric Corporation – the now defunct New York Shipbuilding Corporation. His intentions were to proceed alone with the Blue Ribbon Line project if necessary.

As events turned out, this necessity did not arise because, although voices of uncertainty were being raised from certain quarters, other people were impressed, both by the potential of the scheme and by the sincerity of the Blue Ribbon Line's promoter. Outstanding among those whose careers became involved with the efforts of this company and the Transoceanic Corporation was Captain Herbert Hartley, master of the *Leviathan* and Commodore of the United States Lines. Disillusioned with the prospects for the revitalisation of the United States Lines' fleet, Captain Hartley resigned his position to become Director of Operations for the new enterprise in which his aspirations for a strong U.S. Merchant Marine appeared to have a rewarding outlet. One aspect which may have had a particular appeal to Hartley was Wilder's interest in purchasing the United States Lines' ships, including the *Leviathan*, as part of the Blue Ribbon operation. As a result of the failure to gain a Shipping Board loan, Wilder did not expect to have any of the new ships in service before 1931, so he wished to acquire the United States Lines' fleet as an interim measure, in order to gain experience and goodwill in readiness for the express ship service.

Within a month, Herbert Hartley was accompanying Lawrence Wilder on visits to the White House to lobby President Coolidge for support for both the Blue Ribbon Line and the purchase of the United States Lines. They were busy months, and the former Commodore was involved in many other activities, including giving radio talks on the express ship proposition and making visits to Montauk Point to clarify the berthing and passenger handling requirements.

This huge cigar-shaped craft, named *Leviathan*, was the brain-child of a New Yorker named Darius Davison. Dating from 1852, this was the 'Vernes-ish' prediction of the future of ocean travel by a mid–nineteenth-century-engineer. Of 700ft in length and 50ft maximum beam, she was intended to carry 3,000 passengers across the North Atlantic in relative luxury at an average speed of 25 knots. Other cigar-shaped vessels were in fact built, although the *Leviathan*, as she was named, was not amongst them. However, those which were completed proved to be impractical. *Authors' collection*

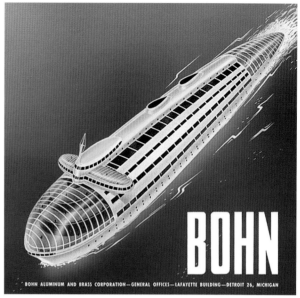

A model of the whale ship designed by Norman Bel Geddes. Its form was more elegant than the descriptive name it was given. In the foreground can be seen the funnels of a model of either of the United States Lines' ships *Manhattan* or *Washington*. The Italian dictator Benito Mussolini offered $200,000 for the whale ship design and patents but the offer was declined by Bel Geddes who preferred to have an American shipbuilder construct his revolutionary vessel. *Authors' collection*

Symbolising the modern era with its ultra-streamlined form, Norman Bel Geddes' whale ship was featured in one of a series of futuristic adverts created for the Bohn Aluminum & Brass Corporation company between 1945 and 1948. *Authors' collection*

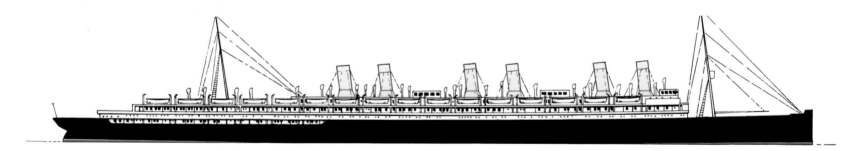

A six-funnelled transatlantic liner with a displacement of 40,000 tons and measuring 930ft in length, as suggested in *The Scientific American* of 10 November 1900. *David Hutchings*

Shown in American Line colours, the Gibbs' design of 1914 for the *Boston and Baltimore* for the IMM reveals an elegant vessel in the style that was the vogue in the Edwardian era. *David Briedis*

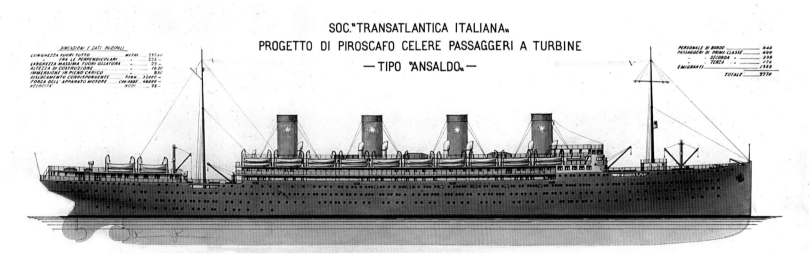

SOC."TRANSATLANTICA ITALIANA"
PROGETTO DI PIROSCAFO CELERE PASSAGGERI A TURBINE
— TIPO "ANSALDO" —

Ansaldo SpA elevation drawing of the *Andrea Doria* and *Camillo di Cavour* from 1914. *Maurizio Eliseo*

Profile drawing of the *Britannic* in White Star Line colours. *Peter Sparre*

The Holland–America's *Statendam* in a magnificent artist's impression. As finally completed as the *Justicia* she was much the same size as Norddeutscher Lloyd's *Columbus*, but very different in appearance. *Captain Stephen Card*

Two more views of the beautiful display model of the *Statendam*. As the *Justicia*, she logged over 55,000 sea miles in her short wartime career. *Both Rotterdam Museum Maritiem*

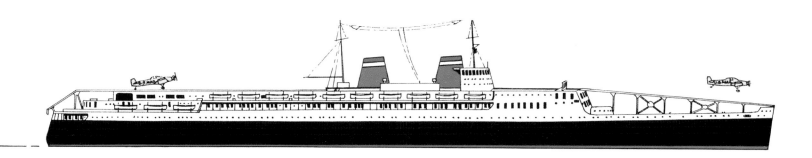

A profile view of the *Flying Cloud* passenger liner/aircraft carrier design. *David Hutchings*

An artist's impression of the *Justicia* in the grey livery in which she commenced her service as a wartime auxiliary. *Ed Bearman*

Another view of the model of White Star's giant *Oceanic*. *Richard Edwards*

Opposite: The White Star Line's *Oceanic* making an imaginary departure from New York. *Peter Wrigglesworth*

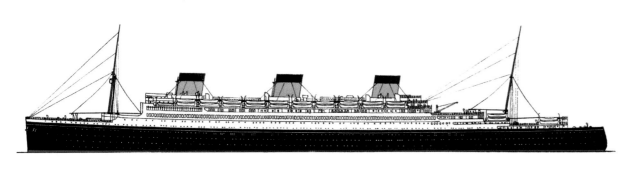

Since 1982, when *Damned by Destiny* was published, the only creditable image that has been used of the *Oceanic* is John H. Isherwood's three-funnelled profile, seen here. This has been the accepted definitive image that has been circulated in the world-wide media ever since the 1960s and it formed the basis of the painting of the ill-fated *Oceanic* created by the late Peter Wrigglesworth (see previous page). Mr Isherwood felt it was largely a product of guesswork on his behalf.

I hope you realise that this drawing is not authentic! It is from an outline only, published in a shipping journal, filled in by my imagination and [based on] a study of White Star and Harland & Wolff general practice at the time. The arrangement, as it happens, filled in the 'outline' fairly well and gave a reasonable 'general arrangement' – but basically it is, I suppose, largely my own imagination.

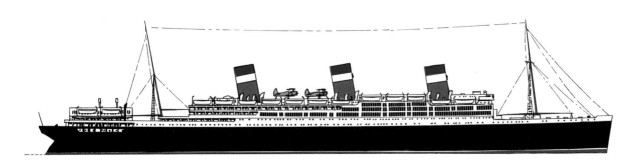

In fact, Mr Isherwood's interpretation was more accurate than he realised – see the authorised Harland & Wolff plan on page 73.

John H. Isherwood

Middle Illustration: Theodore Ferris' initial design for new liners for the United States Lines showing a marked similarity to the *Leviathan* ex-*Vaterland*. The evolved design that followed revealed a closer resemblance to the modern lines of Norddeutscher Lloyd's flyers *Bremen* and *Europa*. *David Hutchings*

Left: The graceful lines of the second, modernised Ferris design for the *Leviathan II* and *Leviathan III* can be appreciated in this oblique-angled depiction. *Finn Tornquist*

During May and June of 1928 he assisted with the preparation of a revised submission to the United States Navy for approval of the planned ships under the loan provisions of the recently implemented Jones-White (Merchant Marine) Act of that year, so named after the sponsoring Senators Wesley Jones and Wallace White. Its principal provisions were the creation of a federal loan fund from which shipbuilders could borrow up to 75 per cent of new construction costs and US shipping companies could be paid operating subsidies.

That the Blue Ribbon Line scheme made no further progress, in spite of all these efforts, was mainly due to doubts about the strength of Wilder's financial backing at this point. Doomed to failure, the decline of the enterprise was rapid and, by late November 1928, after less than a year with the company, a disenchanted and disappointed Captain Herbert Hartley was suing the Transoceanic Corporation for $75,000 – the unpaid amount due to him under the terms of his contract. Ironically, it could be said that Hartley's association with the Blue Ribbon Line project was in itself partly instrumental in bringing about its downfall. After he had decided to resign as Commodore of the United States Lines on 24 January 1928, he had called in at the offices of the U.S. Shipping Board to discuss his decision with friends on the Board who were sympathetic to his sense of frustration. As it turned out, the Board was engaged in discussions on the Transoceanic Corporation's loan application at the time of his arrival, and he was invited to sit in on their deliberations, which he duly did. Later, it was claimed that less than a quarter of an hour elapsed from the time that the news of Hartley's resignation from the U.S. Lines was received to the Board giving tentative approval to the express ship application. However, within three days, and largely as a result of unfavourable statements in the press, the United States Senate ordered the Shipping Board to investigate the financial status of the Transoceanic Corporation and the way it was proposing to use government funds in the construction of new ships. Without any question, this investigation had a significant bearing on the subsequent judgement relating to the company's loan request.

Still worse was to follow because, before the year was out, the activities of Lawrence Wilder and Herbert Hartley in pursuance of their Blue Ribbon project had quite unwittingly provoked yet another investigation by the Senate into Marine lobbying practices, and it was this which led to Hartley terminating his employment with the Transoceanic Corporation in October 1928. He had, in fact, been under considerable attack in the press, particularly from the Hearst Newspaper Group, in which it was alleged that he had influenced the Shipping Board over the *Flying Cloud* issue when he had visited them on 24 January 1928. Much stress was placed on the fact that the scheme was one that was in line with the sentiments he had expressed previously in his desire for a better U.S. Merchant Marine and that, within twenty-four hours of his resignation from the U.S. Lines, his new position with the Blue Ribbon Line was announced.

There is little doubt that his visit to the U.S. Shipping Board at the very crucial moment when it was in session on that fateful day was pure coincidence – but it proved to be a very unfortunate and costly one. Moreover, Hartley undoubtedly had his enemies in the press and was not entirely popular in all quarters, although this had stemmed from his time as captain of the *Leviathan*, since he was a shipmaster who tended to maintain a certain dignity and aloofness aboard, and not to associate with the passengers to the degree that had become expected of masters of the big passenger ships. In another age and in other circumstances this was common enough practice, but, where the *Leviathan* was concerned, it was not an attitude which everyone understood and of those who took offence at it, one may be sure that some journalists were numbered amongst them.

At all events, whatever their motives, the American press made a great deal of all this and, as a result of their columns on the subject, the title 'fast ship project' was given an unfortunate new meaning by playing on the colloquial connotation of the word 'fast', which carried the implication that the Blue Ribbon Line project was a fraudulent attempt to swindle money out of the United States Government, while unfortunate individuals, such as Captain Herbert Hartley, were regarded as the victims of the proponents' deceit. In short, the press wanted it all ways, but the latter suggestions were no more true or fair than the first ones had been.

Lawrence Wilder's plans were undoubtedly rather ambitious, even though they were based on the successful American concept of mass-marketing, but there is no question that he himself had real faith in the principle of the scheme. This was clearly evident when he addressed the Propeller Club of New York on the subject of his projected ships on 18 October 1928. Considering the moribund state of the project at that time, nobody in his audience could have doubted his enthusiasm or sincerity and, indeed, he campaigned alone for nine more long years to win support for the 'clipper' liners and, at the time of his death in 1937, he was in the process of putting the plan before the U.S. Shipping Board for the second time.

While Lawrence Wilder may have lacked an appreciation of some of the costs and problems involved in managing and operating six such ships, so far as his own personal experience was concerned, he had availed himself of the best expertise available and, despite the judgement of T.V. O'Connor and his Board, it would be difficult to fault him on that score. Granted that there was already stiff competition on the North Atlantic seaway, but this was known. It is easy to say that he failed to take account of the imminence of the leaner years which lay ahead, but less easy to justify that contention, since his scheme was not grandiose in the sense that he was advocating outsized vessels, though its grandeur lay rather in the number of them. The fact was that other owners were building ships for the route in the period in which Wilder was involved, and these proved to be successful.

One aspect of his scheme that cannot be questioned was his far-sighted faith in the integral relationship between ships and aircraft. It is for this reason that the aeroplane auxiliary element in the *Flying Cloud*'s design was, perhaps, the greatest legacy to posterity of the Blue Ribbon project, for it triggered the concept of building passenger liners with a basic structure expressly suited for conversion to full aircraft carriers in wartime. It undoubtedly influenced both the Japanese Government with its aircraft carrier/liner programme, in which many vessels were completed, and the U.S. Maritime Commission's own P-4-P design, both described in detail in later chapters. In fact, many well-known passenger liners were considered for adaptation to aircraft-carrying roles in the Second World War, including the Norddeutscher Lloyd's famous record-breaker *Europa*.

Thus the *Flying Cloud* and her stillborn sisters faded into history, to become yet another sad chapter in the review of unrealised ventures in the realm of the passenger liner. Meanwhile, there were other developments on the other side of the Atlantic.

THE LLOYD LITTORIO'S *REX* AND *DUX*

The period immediately following the end of the First World War had been a difficult one for shipping in general and passenger shipping in particular. For Italy, beset with the continuing after-effects of the war, coupled with the financial recession of the early 1920s, the situation was further exacerbated by the restriction on immigration into the United States on which Italian passenger shipping lines largely depended for their profitability.

Moreover, the three main surviving Italian transatlantic carriers – Navigazione Generale Italiana (NGI), Lloyd Sabaudo and the Cosulich Line – were all in need of urgent fleet enhancement, but in those straightened times finance was not readily available.

The government of Italy had been in the hands of the Partito Nazionale Fascista since 1922 which, intent on elevating Italy's international standing, set about formulating a plan which would generate the funding required for new construction from both public and private institutions as the means to regenerate the Italian merchant fleet as a whole and its transatlantic passenger fleet in particular. In parallel with these initiatives, discussions proceeded between the principal operators and the Italian Government with a view to achieving this goal.

The Lloyd Sabaudo, the only company of the three that was actually turning a profit, took over the Cosulich Line in the late 1920s as a subsidiary. As for the NGI, at that time it was under the financial control of the Banca Commerciale Italiana, a government institution, meaning that for all practical purposes it was publicly owned. This prompted proposals that the NGI should be fully nationalised and reconstituted in the form of a completely new company, the Lloyd Littorio, as the first move of a strategy to ultimately merge together all the main Italian passenger shipping companies. The proposals included plans to supplement the newly constituted Lloyd Littorio fleet with two large new express liners, to be constructed using public money. At that time, NGI's largest existing ships were the near sisters *Roma* of 32,600grt and *Augustus* of 30,400grt, the former turbine driven, the latter a motor-ship, the pair having entered service, respectively, in September 1926 and November 1927.

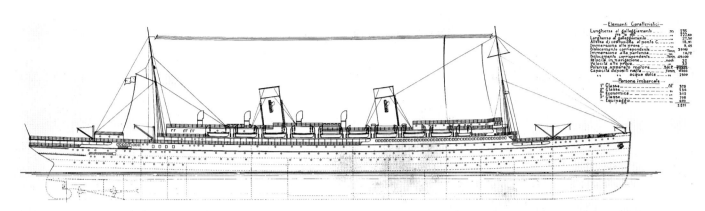

Ansaldo SPA general arrangement drawings for the Lloyd Littorio's *Rex* and *Dux*, Type G variant, dated 10 January 1927. *Maurizio Eliseo*

The planned new liners would be significantly larger at around 40,000grt; not as large as the Norddeutscher Lloyd's *Bremen* and *Europa* but in the same league as the French Line's recent new addition, the 43,150grt *Île-de-France*. However, it was claimed that their intended speed would be closer to, if not faster than, the former pair which then were the holders of the Atlantic Blue Riband. Their overall external appearance, like that of the *Île-de-France*, would have been conventional in contrast to that of the German flyers. By that it is meant that they would have had an external layout and profile in keeping with the established styles of the early 1920s and would not have exhibited a modern, rakish design.

The names *Rex* and *Dux* were announced as being intended for the planned sister-ships. Their design was the subject of detailed official studies performed by the Directorate of Ship Construction (Direttore della Construzioni Navali) at the Ansaldo S.A. Cantiere Navale shipyard at Sestri Ponente, Genoa, under the umbrella of project designation Pm.594. There would appear to have been more than one variant under consideration. Details of a Type G transatlantic express ship were released on 10 January 1927, complete with side elevation drawing, and these form the basis of the description of these projected ships as outlined in this chapter.

The available details reveal that the *Rex* and *Dux* would have measured 773ft length overall, 749ft length between perpendiculars, and 90ft 6in in the beam. Depth from the keel to the top deck would have been 62ft 2in, while the draught at full load displacement

was given as 31ft 1in. With such dimensions, there is more than a suspicion that the design for the Lloyd Littorio pair could have been an extrapolation and revival of the plans for the *Andrea Doria* and *Camillo di Cavour*, envisaged some twelve years earlier for Transatlantica Italiana, dusted-off and given a new lease of life. However, the estimated gross tonnage of the *Rex* and *Dux*, at 39,140, was at some variance to the 32,000grt of the earlier design, possibly accounted for by an extra deck.

Steam turbine machinery with a maximum rating of 213,000shp would have permitted a service speed of 32 knots at 200,000shp. Even with these larger engines, the reduction of funnel numbers from four to two was clear evidence of the improvements to boiler efficiency achieved in the intervening years.

Passenger numbers for the express ships reflected the near eradication of emigrant berths since 1924 and the corresponding rise of Tourist-class travellers. As four-class ships, the total passenger complement of 1,631 was divided 375 First-class, 236 Second-class, 312 Third-class 'Economica' (Tourist) and 708 Third-class. Crew numbers would have been 600.

While the Lloyd Littorio plan was a solution of sorts, it did nothing to deal with the underlying fact that all three competing Italian lines needed investment in new fleet units – an expensive and inefficient arrangement if funding had to be found for them all. It became apparent to Italy's Ministry of the Merchant Marine that the approach to regeneration of the Italian passenger fleet could not proceed in this way but had to take into account all the main operating companies.

Another, larger *Rex*, ordered by Navigazione Generale Italiana but which entered service as an Italia Line ship. She is seen dressed overall, probably during her maiden voyage. *Authors' collection*

Both the *Rex* and the *Conte di Savoia*, seen here, were sunk by Allied aircraft in Italian coastal waters during the Second World War. *L.L. von Münching*

The Italian Government openly favoured the nationalisation of the entire passenger fleet in parallel with a complete rationalisation of services to optimise Italian presence on the world's main passenger routes. The process to achieve this, pursued against some resistance from the private companies concerned, began with a synchronisation agreement concluded in 1928 which coordinated the sailing schedules of NGI and Lloyd Sabaudo from Genoa, and to a lesser extent of Cosulich, based in Trieste. Effectively, this marked the abandonment of the Lloyd Littorio plan and, with it, the cancellation of the projected *Rex* and *Dux*. It also signified the imminent end of the three companies as independent concerns. Just over three years later, from 2 January 1932, the Italia Flotte Riunite or Italia Line was formed, absorbing NGI, Lloyd Sabaudo and Cosulich, all of whose ships from that time adopted a common livery – their funnel colours incorporating the red, white and green of the Italian national ensign.

While these developments resulted in the *Rex* and *Dux* being stricken, two other even larger liners that had been ordered in the interim by NGI and Lloyd Sabaudo filled the vacuum, entering service, respectively, in September and November 1932. They were the *Rex* and *Conte di Savoia*, the name *Dux* having been apparently considered for the latter ship. She and her consort certainly achieved the desired elevation of the 'Sunny Southern Route' to New York and in so doing reinforced Italy's status as a major transatlantic player, culminating in the *Rex* taking the Atlantic Blue Riband in August 1933 at an average speed of 28.92 knots.

The Italian Government's aim to bring all passenger shipping under its financial control was finally attained from the beginning of 1937 with the creation of the Società Finanziara Marittima (Finmare) as the parent company of Italia Flotte Riunite as well as of the Lloyd Triestino, Adriatica Line and Tirrenia Line. Simultaneously, Italia Flotte Riunite was renamed Società Italia di Navigazione, although to the world at large it remained the Italia Line.

Worthy of mention here, in this discussion of the unfolding efforts to enhance recognition of the Italian Merchant Marine and its passenger fleet, is a short-lived and most unusual scheme for a large passenger ship which involved NGI a few years previously. No doubt, it was viewed at the time (the early 1920s) as an opportunity

The launch of the *Francesco Caracciolo* on 12 May 1920. At that time she was destined for completion as a battle-cruiser. Later revisions to the plans for her envisaged service as a battlecruiser, then as an aircraft carrier before she was sold for completion as a large passenger-cargo liner. *Aldo Fraccaroli*

to introduce additional passenger tonnage of any sort against the backdrop of economic recession and lack of shipyard capacity. Among all the projects described in this book, the concept was, though, totally unique in its character and the only one that was not conceived from the outset as a passenger vessel.

This was the *Francesco Caracciolo*, originally ordered and designed as one of four 'super-Dreadnought' battleships for the Italian Navy. She was laid down at the Castellamare di Stabia Dockyard in October 1914 but when naval construction plans were reviewed in early 1916 all work was suspended. The three sister-ships were cancelled completely, their materials diverted for use on other naval craft, but the *Francesco Caracciolo*, whose construction had been the most advanced, remained on the slipway. Three and a half years of inactivity passed until, in October 1919, work resumed but to a much modified design as a high-speed battle-cruiser. Launched on 12 May 1920, the hull was towed to La Spezia for completion but work was halted for a second time while yet more revised plans were considered, this time for modification into an aircraft carrier.

Five months later, on 25 October 1920, the incomplete ship was sold to the NGI for six million lire for conversion into a 'high-speed' passenger-cargo liner. Taken in tow for a second time, the hull of the *Francesco Caracciolo* was next moved to Baia, near Naples.

There are no details of how a hull built with heavy scantlings, armour plating along its sides and internal compartmentation to naval specifications could or would have been altered for efficient running as a merchant vessel, let alone how passenger accommodation and cargo holds would have been arranged in spaces never intended for such use. As originally intended, the *Francesco Caracciolo* would have had a full load displacement of 34,000 tons. Her length was 691ft. Steam turbines, later up-rated (during the battle-cruiser phase) from 70,000 to 105,000shp would have driven quadruple screws giving her a maximum speed of 28 knots. The passenger-cargo configuration would have resulted in a gross tonnage of 25,300 and a service speed of just 18 knots (hardly fast!) from a powerplant reduced to twin turbines producing 20,000shp through twin shafts.

In the event, the quite bizarre project came to naught, abandoned altogether in 1921 when it became apparent that insufficient consideration had been given to the costs involved in such a conversion only to produce a dubious outcome – a potentially uneconomic lone ship with modest passenger capacity and unable to fit into schedules with other purpose-built liners.

Few ships can have gone through four iterations, each for a quite different role, without ever undertaking any of them, despite considerable expenditure on multiple design work, more than two years of physical construction and two towage operations. Aborted altogether, the *Francesco Caracciolo* spent five years mothballed before being broken up from late 1926, concluding a wasteful loss to the NGI company's scant resources and bringing an end to this brief, strange and frustrating episode.

WHITE STAR'S FALLEN STAR, THE *OCEANIC*

The next project precipitated by the sudden domination of the Atlantic passenger trade by the Germans and Italians had been on the cards in Great Britain for almost fifty years, but it was only considered seriously at this time when prestige and a truly competitive ripost to these foreign liners was demanded. This was, in fact, the 1,000ft long White Star liner basically designed as far back as 1880 by Sir Edward Harland. Now brought to life again, to ultimately become the *Oceanic*, the ship's design was improved radically to match and exceed the best foreign ships afloat.

Claims have been made that the *Oceanic* was perceived in two distinctly different forms, according to general arrangement plans and other drawings sourced from Harland & Wolff – one precluding the other. However, while it cannot be substantiated, the authors are of the opinion that there were probably two distinct phases to the pursuit of a giant new express liner for White Star during the mid to late 1920s, each of which reflected the thinking of different holding concerns, but both of which, in essence, were stages of progression from the original concept of Sir Edward Harland. The first phase occurred while the company was still a subsidiary of the IMM; the second phase, which was to eventually emerge as the *Oceanic* design, followed after the White Star Line was acquired by the Royal Mail Group.

Knowledge of a serious intention to commission a giant new White Star liner first came to the attention of the maritime world in August 1926, when an announcement indicated that a giant 25-knot liner to replace the *Homeric*, whose service speed was inadequate, was under consideration by the White Star Line. *Lloyds List* reported the press statement by Mr P.A.S. Franklin, President of the IMM, made as he stepped ashore from the *Majestic* in New York on 3 August 1926:

Mr P.A.S. Franklin said they were making all the plans for the future development of the White Star Line and with that object in view were proceeding with the preparation of plans and specifications for a new mammoth steamer of the *Majestic* and *Olympic* class which would embody the outstanding features of those vessels.

The press statement also suggested that the new vessel would bear a 'family resemblance' to the old *Olympic*. Some have argued that this was somewhat misleading since the final, more familiar design of the *Oceanic* showed a liner with three squat motor-ship-type funnels. This appearance was far more in common with the Royal Mail liner *Asturias* which entered service in March 1927, the first of a long line of Harland & Wolff-built motor-vessels propelled by double-acting four-stroke diesel machinery, as well as the later *Britannic* of 1930. But it is contended that the vessel Mr Franklin was referring to was not the *Oceanic*. At that time, as far as is known, the planned ship had no name, for there is no mention of the *Oceanic* as such until 1928. Drawings obtained from Harland & Wolff, dating from 1926 show a four-funnelled steamship with a cruiser stern. Its tonnage has been estimated at around 55,000 gross with dimensions comparable to those of the contemporary *Bremen* and *Europa* and a service speed of 25 knots. It is most probable that this was the ship referred to by P.A.S. Franklin in his statement.

Less than a year later, in January 1927, the White Star Line returned to British ownership when the International Mercantile Marine began to shed its foreign flag subsidiaries, the buyer being the Royal Mail Steam Packet Company. Lord Kylsant, the Chairman of the Royal Mail Group, was a champion of the motor-ship and, due to his influence, from that point it was proposed that the new express liner was to be propelled by diesel-electric engines – a revolutionary innovation for the adoption of which there was no proven precedent. For this reason, viewed retrospectively, the installation of these marine engines in what, from 1928, was known as the *Oceanic* would have been a greater gamble than the installation of steam turbines in the *Lusitania* and *Mauretania* had been in 1907, since the liner *Carmania*, built two years earlier, had acted as something of an engine test-bed

A model of the planned giant White Star liner *Oceanic* based on J.H. Isherwood's profile drawing (see first colour section) and Peter Wrigglesworth's painting. *Richard Edwards*

for the two Cunard record-breakers. Quite obviously, the *Oceanic*'s future owners and her builders were fully aware of the immensity of the decision to install such engines, but their subsequent caution and protracted hesitation in deciding firmly whether the generating machinery for the liner's electric drives should be diesel instead of turbine only contributed to her eventual cancellation.

These requirements resulted in a quite different configuration, a vessel exhibiting classic motor-ship lines and of somewhat greater size in order to accommodate the much larger engine installation that was now planned.

In the end, the question of the *Oceanic*'s engines was finally resolved in favour of a diesel-electric power unit. However, before any substantial progress could be made with her construction, the effects of the Great Depression began to be felt. Due to the severity of the economic crisis, abandonment of the project at such an early stage was the only logical course of action open to the White Star Line in their endeavours to try to remain in business. Had the debate over the engines not taken so long, until financial pressures had become even more severe, it is conceivable that the ship would have been so advanced that a decision would have been made to complete her. As it was, only the keel had been laid. Before reflecting on the fate of the *Oceanic*, it is first necessary to take a look at the unfortunate ship to see how much more progress towards the eventual realisation of a 1,000ft liner had been made on this occasion.

A debate has persisted for years as to whether or not construction of the *Oceanic* was actually started. Over the years, reference has been made by some authors to a full or partial keel structure but some have challenged the veracity of these assertions, particularly in the absence of photographic evidence. Thankfully, the Belfast correspondent of *Lloyd's List* compiled reports at the time which leave little doubt on this matter, despite the contrary views of certain persons who actually worked at Harland & Wolff, though not in the 1928–30 period. Written by someone who was there in person, working on behalf of the most prestigious, scrupulous and dependable maritime journal, it is felt that these accounts really leave little grounds for further dispute.

In fact, the stage reached with the *Oceanic* was the furthest of any of the pre-*Normandie* 1,000ft liner projects, for her construction was indeed actually started, as the *Lloyd's List* reports that follow explicitly confirm. The *Normandie*, the first ship to break the coveted 1,000ft barrier, measured 1,029ft length overall and 981ft between perpendiculars.

Work on the new ship's design took almost two more years, reaching its climax when the contract for her construction was placed on 18 June 1928. In their historic announcement, the White Star Line declared that their new liner, to be named *Oceanic* after the company's pioneer ship, was to be built as expected by Harland & Wolff Ltd at Belfast. On 19 June 1928, The Belfast Correspondent of *Lloyd's List* reported:

It has been decided to proceed immediately with the White Star liner of the super *Olympic* type which has been talked of for the past two years. The intimation is contained in the following announcement issued by Messrs Harland & Wolff today:

'Messrs Harland & Wolff Ltd are now laying the keel of the mammoth passenger liner which the White Star Line have ordered from them. The vessel is being laid down in the firm's East Yard at Belfast. The actual dimensions are not yet available for publication but I understand the vessel will be larger than *Majestic*.

'The importance of this announcement to Belfast cannot be over-estimated. It means that once more Queen's Island is to have the honour of building the largest ship in the world. It has been decided that the vessel will be built in the East Yard which launches into the Musgrave Channel. No. 14 berth which has been idle since the completion of the Lago Shipping Company's tankers has been allotted for the purpose. It is one of the largest berths in the port and can easily take a vessel of such dimensions.

'The news has given great satisfaction in Belfast, where the shipbuilding industry at Queen's Island is at present very fully occupied with a large amount of high-class liner tonnage. This order will increase the amount of new work on the stocks to almost 200,000 tons.'

Construction was expected to take about three and a half years, and the final cost to be in the region of £3.5–£6 million. The *Oceanic* was to measure 60,000 gross tons with an overall length of 1,010ft, a beam of 120ft and a draught of 38ft.

The full details of her intended engines were only released many years later, after the Second World War, by Mr Cuthbert Coulson Pounder, Director and Chief Technical Engineer of Harland & Wolff. These showed that the quadruple-screw *Oceanic* would have had forty-seven six-cylinder, exhaust turbo-charged, four-stroke single-acting trunk diesel engines producing a total of 275,000ihp and coupled in pairs to electric generators. In each six-cylinder engine the cylinder bores were 670mm (26.38in) and 930mm (36.31in) stroke delivering 3,400 brake horsepower (bhp) at 260rpm. The total weight of the installation would have been some 17,000 tons, equal to the displacement tonnage of a smaller liner of the day! She was to have been Great Britain's answer to the *Bremen* and, with a shaft horsepower (shp) of 200,000 producing a speed in the region of 30 knots, might well have rivalled the latter for the Atlantic Blue Riband honours.

The first keel plates of the *Oceanic*, Yard No. 844, were laid down nine days after the memorable order for her construction was announced. She was to be built on slipway 14 in the famous Musgrave or East yard on Queen's Island, a massive shipbuilding complex built during the First World War for the construction of wartime-standard

Cuthbert Coulson Pounder's sketches of the engine arrangement of the *Oceanic*, described as: diesel-electric drive, 200,000shp and quadruple screw. *C.C. Pounder*

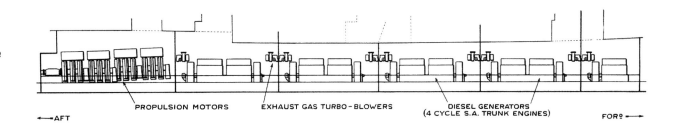

PROPULSION MOTORS   EXHAUST GAS TURBO-BLOWERS   DIESEL GENERATORS
(4 CYCLE S.A. TRUNK ENGINES)

←—AFT   FOR⁰ ←—

Below: Accredited side elevation and plan view of the *Oceanic* as prepared by the Harland & Wolff Design Office. Pounder's elevation that was derived from these lines inspired all subsequent interpretations of the ship's external appearance. *Harland & Wolff*

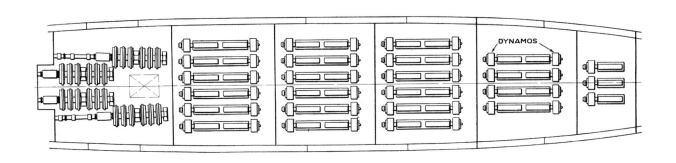

DYNAMOS

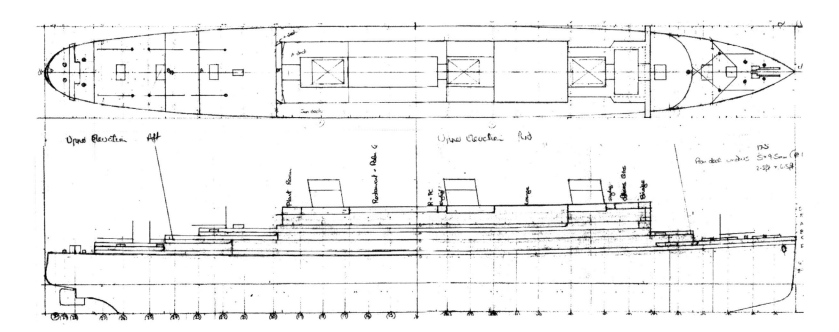

vessels but which also became the future birthplace of many other celebrated ships. The building of yet another revolutionary White Star liner was thus begun, albeit with little pomp or ceremony.

This absence of publicity is reinforced by a lack of photographic records depicting the early stages of construction of the *Oceanic*, although a British Pathé newsreel dated 15 October 1928, entitled '*Ulster's Loyal Welcome*', shows Princess Mary, Viscountess Lascelles, viewing the keel plates of what is purported to be the *Oceanic* during a visit to the shipyard. In the film, the keel structure is described as '*the keel plate of the 1,000 ft long Britannic, to be Ulster's pride and the biggest liner in the world*'. White Star's new *Britannic* was, of course, under construction at that time in the South Yard and it is quite possible that the Pathé team confused the names of the two ships. The slipway in these images had a caisson at the seaward end which would make it too short for a 1,000ft vessel. However, in noting this impediment, the *Lloyd's List* correspondent explained on 27 June 1928 how Harland & Wolff proposed to manage the slipway's limitations:

> The interest created by the announcement regarding the big White Star liner continues unabated. Material is still coming in and the keel plate as it is laid down on the blocks in the East Yard gives a fair indication of the length of the vessel, showing that it is to be at least 1,000ft long. The upper portion of the vessel will extend into ground not served by overhead equipment and it is intended to put down right away further tower cranes to handle material and pile this part of the slip and extend it at the seaward end. All this will take time so that it will certainly be six or nine months before the construction gets properly going but the fact that it has been started is a great matter for Belfast.

Tom McCluskie, who is of the opinion that the *Oceanic* was never laid down, has speculated that the ship's structure shown in the film was possibly the keel plates of another unidentified ship. As has already been stated, it has been mooted from many quarters that, in fact, no plates were ever laid down for the *Oceanic* despite the *Lloyd's List* reports to the contrary. It is for consideration, if this latter assertion

was the case, that the keel plates that Princess Mary inspected, which were likewise seen by the *Lloyd's List* correspondent, may well have been stage-managed and set out cosmetically for appearances only. It is only for speculation but, given that this exercise would have involved a fair amount of cost, it could perhaps have been intended to give the impression that the yard was earnestly progressing the work on the giant ship as a means of influencing Whitehall in respect of the financial aid that White Star was seeking when, in reality, nothing substantive had actually occurred at all.

Whatever the true intentions of White Star and Harland & Wolff, it was not long before it became apparent that all was not well with the new ship. Erring on the side of *Lloyd's List* and assuming that work on the keel plates had indeed begun, the absence of any real progress from that point was a clear indication that something was amiss. The fears were eventually substantiated on 23 July 1929 when all work was stopped on what was, by then, said to be the almost complete keel structure of the *Oceanic*. Three days later, *Lloyd's List* reported:

> The Company states that it has been decided to defer work on the *Oceanic*, the keel of which was laid at Belfast last year, and to give priority to the construction of a new motor vessel of 27,000 tons – a sister ship to the *Britannic* which was launched on 6 August for its Liverpool and New York passenger service; these two vessels will be the largest British motor ships and the largest liners sailing from the port of Liverpool.

A formal announcement the same September confirmed that further work was to be deferred temporarily pending final decisions on her propulsive machinery. Meanwhile, the keel section was to remain undisturbed on the slipway as pointed out by the *Lloyd's List* correspondent:

> The keel plates of the monster vessel, however, will remain undisturbed on its present slip, No. 14, until the important problems that face both owners and builders, primarily with regard to the propelling power to be adopted, have been solved so that the construction can be proceeded with.

In spite of this reassuring statement, the vessel was to be mentioned for what was probably the last time at the White Star Line's Annual General Meeting the following 8 May, when Lord Kylsant, in his Chairman's report, repeated, in so many words, the formal announcement of the previous September, and then … there was silence …

The question remained as to whether the problem with the *Oceanic* was simply one of an engineering nature. Undoubtedly the advent of the turbine-driven record-breaker *Bremen* in 1929 must have given rise to plenty of cause for doubt over the *Oceanic*'s engines, but perhaps the real reason for her abandonment was an economic one. The world financial crisis was worsening rapidly in late 1929, and the Royal Mail Group was known to be having money difficulties. It had become like a monster that had outgrown itself, and was encountering increasing difficulties in maintaining its position as a leading shipping concern. The government was not prepared to stake a loan to help to build the new liner on such a shaky foundation, particularly when it also had the problem of

being expected to provide similar aid to the rival Cunard Line, the other major British company with a predominant North Atlantic interest, which was also about to embark on the construction of a new express ship for its premier service. Such national rivalry was impractical during the unfavourable economic circumstances then prevailing, and could not be encouraged at the expense of the taxpayer.

In this saga of the *Oceanic*, it is also for speculation what the impact was on Harland & Wolff's business to have a slipway occupied but inactive for at least the known twenty-two-month-long period of idleness.

Without doubt, the ailing White Star Line could not finance the project on its own, and so the giant *Oceanic* was discarded and priority given in 1932 to a more economic sister-ship of the *Britannic* – the 27,759 gross ton *Georgic*. Meanwhile, the *Oceanic*'s keel structure was broken up discreetly and the giant liner was gradually forgotten, denying Harland & Wolff the honour of building the first ocean liner of over 1,000ft in length. In 1955, Mr C.C. Pounder wrote:

Seen in a post-war view, the RMMV *Britannic*, completed in 1930, berthed at the Liverpool Landing Stage. *J.McCann*

In the event, the *Oceanic* was replaced to some extent by the building of a sister-ship to the *Britannic* named the *Georgic*. The ships were similar in appearance, except that the latter vessel had a rounded facing to the fore end of her superstructure. These were the only two British motor ships built for the transatlantic run. It will be noted that the *Georgic* had four double-banked sets of boats per side under Welin davits with falls. With their typically stumpy funnels and overall appearance, the *Britannic* and *Georgic* were clearly influenced by the design of the giant liner *Oceanic*. B. & A. Feilden

The White Star Line was later merged with the Cunard Line, the conventional steamers *Queen Mary* and *Queen Elizabeth* were built, and work on the great diesel liner was not resumed. Thus was a history-making engineering achievement lost for the nation.

It cannot be confirmed but it is possible that some of the steel cut for the *Oceanic* may have been used in the *Georgic*'s construction. It seemed slightly ironic that, soon afterwards in the very depths of the Depression, rumours began to circulate to the effect that the White Star Line, as if with the bravado of a condemned man, was contemplating another giant of over 70,000 gross tons. Or was this an example of journalistic clairvoyancy? Perhaps a premonition of a combined Cunard–White Star Line and of the birth of number 534, the *Queen Mary*, of 1,019ft overall length. In 1934, when Cunard was also struggling, amalgamation with White Star was the principal condition laid down by the British Government for a loan to enable work to resume on this vessel.

THE UNITED STATES LINES' SISTER-SHIPS – THE TWO *LEVIATHANS*

An equally ill-fated American project, the fifth major scheme to be announced in the late 1920s, now appeared on the scene. This was a far more viable proposition than that of the *Flying Cloud* liners, as it was requested initially by the United States Department of Commerce in the terms of the sale of the United States Lines to Paul Wadsworth Chapman and his associates in 1929. Plans for a pair of 31-knot super-liners for a weekly service, to compete directly with the *Bremen, Europa, Rex* and *Conte di Savoia*, had to be ready by 13 February 1930 at the latest.

The contract for the United States Lines, of which this stipulation formed an essential part, was won by Paul Wadsworth Chapman after a highly competitive struggle, and this is quite an interesting story on its own. From August 1921, after the financial collapse of the United States Mail Line, the various ships of its fleet had remained under the control of the Shipping Board of the Department of Commerce. The vessels were operated on a bare-boat charter basis for the Shipping Board under the collective name of United States Lines, the management being performed by a consortium composed of the Moore McCormack Company, the Roosevelt Steamship Company and the United American Lines. The Department of Commerce was anxious, however, to shed its responsibility for the United States Lines on to total private ownership and, to be sure that the fleet did not return to them again, they sought a group of businessmen who were financially sound to take control of it.

One person who was very keen to steer the future course of the *Leviathan* and her companions was William Francis Gibbs, who made several bids for the United States Lines fleet in association with Mr J.H. Winchester, the head of a charter firm of long standing. The first offer by Gibbs and Winchester came in 1926, and it was to buy the fleet outright. This was rejected, but they soon followed it with two other modified bids in the same year. The second of these was a proposal to buy the American Merchant Lines freighter service as well as the United States Lines with a down payment of $200,000 (£50,000) – a very low figure which later formed part and parcel of newspaper allegations – and it carried with it an offer to build two companion ships to the *Leviathan* with an investment of $30 million (£7.5 million). This was the first mention of prospective consorts for the *Leviathan*, but this bid was said to have been blocked by political and press activities and no progress was made.

As their next move, the Gibbs–Winchester team proposed to recondition the *Mount Vernon* and *Agamemnon*, two former German liners sequestrated during the First World War, as part of an offer to purchase the United States Lines fleet, but this also failed. In fact, 1928 saw a great deal of interest in this company when the U.S. Shipping Board opened bids for the purchase of the ships on 15 January. There was, for instance, a bid of $6 million by P.A.S. Franklin of the American Line SS Corporation on behalf of the IMM, which had faded as a force in the shipping world since commencing to dispose of its foreign assets. Though regarded as a rather low offer at the time, compared with others that were tabled, the IMM's bid was probably the most financially sound, as later events were to demonstrate. Against this,

the Gibbs and Winchester partnership were now offering $10 million (£2.5 million), but this was exceeded by a bid of $16,300,000 (£4,075.000) from a syndicate headed by Paul Wadsworth Chapman, a wealthy Chicago financier. Lawrence R. Wilder, bidding in the name of the Blue Ribbon Line, entered the field later in the year, but the real fight for ownership of the line was between the Gibbs–Winchester team and the Chapman group.

Although Gibbs and Winchester had the greatest experience of shipping behind them, Chapman's group had strong financial support and its bid finally won the day, with the provision that two ships comparable with the *Leviathan*, costing not less than $25 million (£6.25 million) each, should be built by them within two years of the purchase of the fleet. Other smaller ships were also planned as part of this deal. Little was known in shipping circles of P.W. Chapman, the leading character in the purchase of the ailing United States Lines. He had been born in Jerseyville, Illinois, into a family of lawyers and bankers, and his own business background had been in finance and public utilities (service industries), where he had had considerable success. Now, his emergence as President of the United States Lines was to precipitate an equally keen interest in passenger shipping and its coordination with air travel.

While Chapman may have lacked shipping experience himself, he made up for this deficiency in his board appointments. Among those selected was Joseph E. Sheedy, who had been active with the Blue Ribbon project until its federal rebuff in April 1928, to become Vice-President, and William Perrott, the former Operations Manager of the United States Lines while it was under government control. Perrott was to be responsible for managing the construction programmes of the new company.

In order to comply with the stipulations of the contract with the U.S. Shipping Board, one of America's most distinguished naval architects, Mr Theodore E. Ferris, was commissioned to design the two giant liners of at least 45,000 tons which were required. Simultaneously, Mr Ernest H. Rigg, Chief Naval Architect at the New York Shipbuilding Corporation, was engaged to design two ships for the secondary mail service to Hamburg. Both men had played a prominent part on the Blue Ribbon Line technical committees, and

Theodore Ferris was particularly well known for his design work on the Ward Line coastwise steamers *Morro Castle* and *Oriente*.

The initial proposals for the express liners for the Channel ports service, which were released in mid 1929, were for two more-or-less updated versions of the *Leviathan*, with which they were intended to run. Each was to have a capacity for 3,000 passengers and 1,000 crew, and each was to carry two catapult-launched mail seaplanes. In appearance, they were rather disappointing, having a close resemblance to the earlier, 15-year-old ship, with three tall funnels and a counter stern. Unlike the *Leviathan*, however, they would have had a slightly raked bow and all the lifeboats would have been carried on the boat deck. They were also considerably larger, with a gross tonnage in excess of 60,000 and an overall length of over 1,000ft. A service speed of 26 knots was envisaged. It was anticipated that construction of the two liners would begin early in 1930 with the building costs put at $28 million (£7 million) per ship. However, in February of that year, Theodore Ferris put forward vastly amended designs for the United States Lines' new super-liners.

In size, these modified ships were somewhat smaller than the previous pair, but they would be much faster and they featured a profile design more in keeping with the styles of the time. Although they resembled the contemporary *Bremen* in many respects, they also bore a close similarity with the much later *Queen Elizabeth* and would have pioneered features first introduced in the latter vessel.

Right: The *Bremen* (51,656 gross tons) and the *Europa* (49,746 gross tons) captured the Atlantic Blue Riband from the *Mauretania* and their success was, in some measure, a spur to other grandiose schemes. The *Bremen* is seen underway in The Solent in this photograph. *Kirk*

Below: Theodore Ferris' second design for the super-liners covered by Paul W. Chapman's project for the two *Leviathans*, their design perhaps influenced by the lines of Germany's record-breakers. *Bremen* and *Europa*. *Frank Braynard*

A half-model of Ferris' second design in his New York office in 1930. Theodore Ferris himself is just visible on the left of the picture. *Towline*

In spite of the Depression and the rock bottom value of shipping shares, over $440,000 (£110,000) was spent in testing and proving the design, and in preparing the proposal for submission to the U.S. Shipping Board for approval under the terms of the contract, in order that the vessels would qualify for government construction loans as approved ships under the terms of the Jones–White Act of 1928.

Twenty-two scale models were made for testing in the United States Model Basin at Washington, D.C., with the assistance of sixty naval architects. The designs that were selected for further appraisal as a result of these tests were approved by the American Bureau of Shipping and Lloyds of London. Concurrent with this research, a fifty-seven-page bound booklet was published covering the economic aspects and the mail subsidy possibilities of the proposals, while Theodore Ferris addressed the Society of Naval Architects and Marine Engineers in New York from a thirty-two-page paper on the subject of his super-liners on 20 November 1931.

The design specification finally agreed had two versions: one for geared-turbine propulsion and the other for turbo-electric propulsion. Both versions were basically identical in appearance, but their dimensions varied slightly. The turbo-electric design was slightly bigger with a gross tonnage of 60,000 on an overall length of 985ft, compared with 56,000 gross tons and 963ft for the geared-turbine version, but both vessels were narrow enough to pass through the Panama Canal locks. The two liners were to be quadruple screw, with a maximum speed of 32 knots and a service speed of 29.5 knots. Designed maximum shaft horsepower was 180,000 at 174rpm for the geared turbine version, and 200,000 at 180rpm for the turbo-electric ship. The propelling units in the geared-turbine vessel consisted of four-pinion, single-reduction engine types arranged on the four shafts with the inboard propellers turning outward and the outboard ones turning inward. In the electric-drive ship there would have been a single motor on each shaft, screw rotation being the same as for the other version.

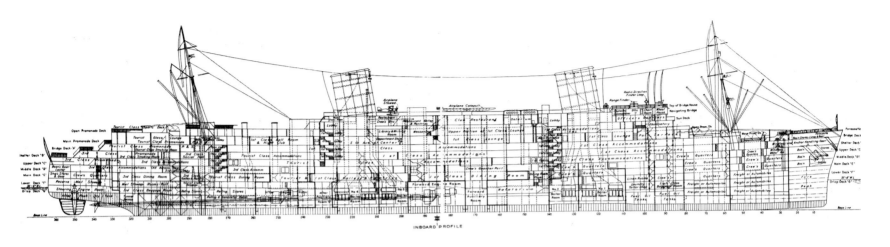

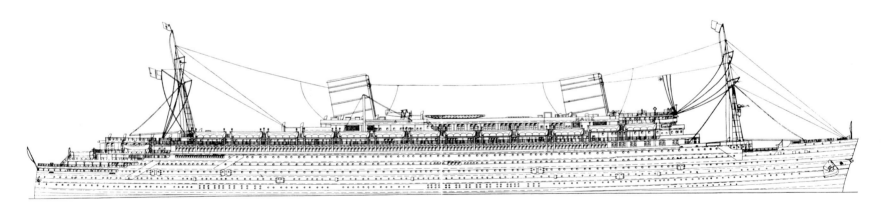

External elevation and inboard profile drawings of the second Ferris design, which were published in December, 1931. *Marine Engineering*

On the design aspect, they had a cruiser stern similar to the later *Queen Elizabeth*, two widely spaced funnels with squashed-hat cowls, a curved and raked stem with a bulbous forefoot, and a rounded fore end to their superstructure. Watertight subdivision was in accordance with United States Navy standards in anticipation of their use as auxiliaries. The Ferris liners were to be built of high-elastic nickel steel which would save weight while increasing structural strength, and aluminium was to be used extensively for the deck houses to reduce weight still further. Among the features incorporated into the two liners were a novel solarium on the upper deck with a living garden, a shopping arcade to be called 'Fifth Avenue', and the inevitable aircraft catapult and seaplane to dispatch the mail one day early. Passenger accommodation was provided for 2,800 passengers in three classes, the largest percentage being in First-class. It was estimated that the cost of these modified liners would be approximately $30 million (£7.5 million) each. With government approval and with federal aid, in the shape of a promised $31 million construction loan, Mr Chapman hoped to have one ship in service by 1936 and the second by 1940.

These two ships were to be named the *Leviathan 2* and the *Leviathan 3*. Whilst the object was obvious, such nomenclature was rather out of keeping with that normally used for Atlantic liners and, perhaps, was rather more reminiscent of modern-day Hollywood sequels. However, due to the repetition involved and to avoid possible confusion with the existing *Leviathan* (ex-*Vaterland*), these two names will not be used within this text. All seemed to be set fair for this latest American enterprise, but time was fast running out for P.W. Chapman. As a result of the economic slump, the returns for the first two years were disappointing, to understate the case. The total number of passengers carried by the company had fallen from 80,161 in 1929 to only 65,408 in 1930. By the end of 1931 the number had dropped to a mere 43,310. By then unable to fulfil their commitments, the Chapman team defaulted in its payments to the Shipping Board and the government was, therefore, compelled to foreclose in October 1931. The business was thereupon offered for sale again, and this time it was bought by what remained of the old International Mercantile Marine.

The new owners inherited the twenty-year-old *Leviathan* and the two Ernest Rigg-designed cabin ships *Manhattan* and *Washington* that Mr Chapman had ordered on 24 May 1930. They were not, however, bound to a contract that insisted on the construction of two new giant express liners, and, in view of the prevailing economic climate, the new owners reappraised completely the proposal for the Ferris sisters from a much more critical standpoint. The viability of the scheme depended to a great extent on the United States mail subsidies, as there was expected to be much competition for passenger traffic from other express luxury liners on the North Atlantic route, and these subsidies seemed, unfortunately, to be calculated to the disadvantage of the express ship. The mail rate over 20 knots did not increase in the same proportion for speeds in excess of this figure as it did below it. Under 20 knots, an extra $1 per mile was paid for each additional knot in speed, yet over 20 knots the rate was increased by only 50 cents for each additional knot. Consequently, a 20-knot vessel, with its smaller engines, could earn more net profit carrying mail than a 30-knot ship whose larger engines made her very much less economical to run and reduced her earnings from passengers due to the loss of cabin accommodation to the increased space required by the machinery.

This seemed to decide the issue for the new owners of the United States Lines, and little more was heard of the two giant sisters. However, they reappeared briefly when, in 1936, the Merchant Marine Act amended the differential on the mail subsidies to operate to the advantage of the faster vessels, and a new proposal to build the two Ferris passenger liners was included in the Act while it was in bill form. With the repeal of the 18th Amendment (Prohibition) also militating in their favour, the outlook seemed to be brighter once more, but this fresh proposal was voted out before the Bill became an Act of Law, and that concluded the matter. As for Paul Wadsworth Chapman, one might suppose that his somewhat retrograde experiences with the United States Lines had dampened his embryonic enthusiasm for passenger shipping, but this was far from being the case! Despite this initial setback, in which he had lost control of the United States Lines, his belief in the monster passenger liner had been confirmed and he was to become one of the greatest campaigners for vessels of such

The *Manhattan*, with her sister the *Washington*, were the biggest ships built in the United States at the time of their launch in1932–33, being 24,289 tons gross. It has been suggested that they were a substitute for the cancelled large express liners but, in fact, they had been ordered simultaneously. In the event, they proved to be most successful, raising questions as to the necessity for giant ships-of-state. *Deutsches Schiffahrtsmuseum*

immense proportions. Over the next twenty years he maintained his association with Theodore Ferris and, together, they produced plans for colossal liners in which they demonstrated great ingenuity and their unswerving belief in such vessels. Although the commercial value of these ships was open to question, one could only marvel at their very size and magnificence.

Meanwhile in Europe, during this inclement period, shipping was also in a steep downward spiral, but new plans, aimed partly to cope with these difficult circumstances, were nevertheless still being devised. Yet, as was so often the case, willing investors were hard to find, and many otherwise good schemes never had an opportunity to prove themselves for this reason. Since the end of the First World War, the Hamburg Amerika Line, having re-established most of its

passenger services, had contented itself with rather small and not particularly attractive liners to carry out its schedules. However, in the early 1930s, it seemed that they might be ready to return to their former splendour in the days of Imperial Germany.

The company announced that it intended to build the first of a number of 30-knot super-liners, whose size and standard of luxury would exceed anything else then afloat or projected. About the same time, the Canadian Pacific Line reported that it proposed to build a sister to the *Empress of Britain*, a successful ship which had been earning a good income for her owners, while the Italia Line were said to be planning a third vessel to complement the *Rex* and *Conte di Savoia*. None of these ships materialised, however, and the blame for this probably lay in the continued effects of the Depression.

THE 'YANKEE CLIPPERS'

Resuming the Chapman/Ferris story, as intimated earlier, after emerging from their experience with the two *Leviathans*, Paul Wadsworth Chapman, in collaboration with his colleague Theodore Ernest Ferris, next evolved their latest, most elaborate and most gigantic proposal for two passenger liners to fly the United States ensign. This effort, developed from the earlier plans for the United States Lines, not only confirmed Chapman's enthusiastic belief in giant passenger liners, but also indicated his genius as a prophet of maritime trends. The outstanding characteristic of the two new liners now planned was that they were to be one-class ships aimed specifically at the Tourist-class traveller. (Such predominantly tourist liners did not become commonplace features of the passenger shipping scene until the 1960s.) Credit for the scheme was entirely due to Chapman, the entrepreneur, but praise for the design of the ships deservedly belongs to Ferris.

Projected at a time when sheer size was so important, these two ships would have been monsters – phenomenal, colossal ocean wonders! At the time, they were the largest passenger liners ever conceived, yet their sleek proportions concealed their immense size, for their displacement would have been about 105,000 tons each, with a gross tonnage slightly less at 100,000. (In comparison, the *Normandie*, quoted in 1938 as 86,495 gross tons, would have constituted the biggest of the giant liners ever completed, but this figure was subsequently considered to be unreliable and she was, in

reality, 83,423 tons – this surprising variation having possibly arisen due to differences in measurement – putting the *Queen Elizabeth*, at 83,673 gross tons, at the top of the league until the advent of the *Queen Mary 2* in 2004, at 149,215 gross tons.) Their other main dimensions were an overall length of 1,250ft and a beam of 144ft.

The crews would have numbered between 1,500 and 1,750. 5,000 cabins were to be provided on each of these super-liners for a total of 10,000 passengers, and each cabin was to have a private bath. Fares across the Atlantic were to be $50 (approximately £10 at contemporary exchange rates) per passenger each way, meals costing extra, and with the 'run of the ship' for all. Private single occupancy of cabins was an optional extra at an increased price, and meals were to be served in three popular and distinct types of restaurants, at appropriate prices, in addition to the passage fare.

The design of the two liners envisaged them as completely enclosed ships with air-conditioning throughout. As for the interior decorations of these mammoth vessels, their commodious spaces would, without doubt, have given rise to great ingenuity and creativity within the limitations of the fare and the class of passenger to be carried. Both Chapman and Ferris had a strong inclination towards adopting new ideas and inventions, and it is certain that, in addition to the luxurious décor and furnishings that were characteristic of all the great liners of the period, there would have been all manner of modern shipboard facilities and new-fangled contrivances in the two liners. It was intended to operate the two 'Yankee Clippers', as they were dubbed, at 34 knots, with a reserve maximum of 38 knots.

A model of the 'Yankee Clipper' design. *Frank Braynard*

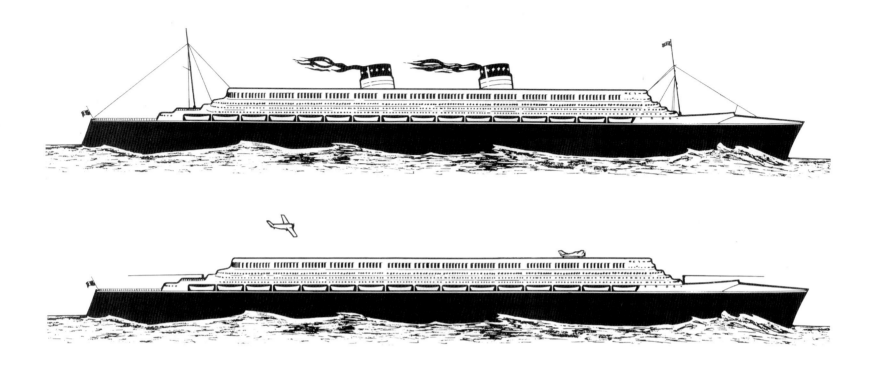

Two sketches of the 'Yankee Clipper' design, the top one showing the vessel in conventional guise, the lower one with her funnels telescoped, her ventilators collapsed and with her masts lowered, providing a flying deck run way measuring 140 × 800ft. *Roy Miller*

This was to be achieved with a geared-turbine installation producing 380,000shp and driving four propellers.

A contingency feature of the design, for auxiliary deployment during national emergencies, was their use as troop transports, with a capacity for 40,000 men each. Additionally, they featured Lawrence Wilder's innovation of an aircraft-carrying capability, for their two masts were to be telescopic and the funnels could be retracted below the level of the upper deck, leaving a clear flight deck 800ft long and the full width of the ship. Aeroplane storage space was provided beneath the flight deck and, in order to keep the upper superstructure levels clear for flying operations, the lifeboats were placed on the main deck.

Meritable as it was to propose such grand liners which, in their very size, capacity and mode of operation, were intended to make ocean travel affordable to the general public – to the masses on average

pay – such giant vessels would at the same time have imposed major infrastructural and logistical issues at ports of departure and arrival. Besides the matter of processing so many people through booking halls, customs and passport controls, there also would have been the challenge of providing and organising adequate onward transportation, let alone the means of replenishment of food and beverages on this scale for each subsequent voyage. With regard to the proposed conveyance of up to 40,000 military personnel as a wartime auxiliary, one has only to look at the photographs of the *Queen Mary*'s crowded decks when she carried a record 16,683 American troops and crew across the Atlantic in July 1943 to get a scale of what this would have entailed, despite the fact that Cunard and the War Ministry had meticulously pre-planned that particular voyage. Added to which, should one of these ships have fallen the victim of a torpedo attack, the magnitude of the potential casualties would surely have raised questions as to the wisdom of exposing such a large and valuable military resource to danger as a single entity. Nonetheless, this did not dissuade others later, as will be seen, from proposing equally mammoth liners with broadly similar specifications as far as their peacetime and wartime complements were concerned.

As it turned out, these fine ships, the very epitome of the giant liner concept, never came to be built. The year was 1937, and the *Normandie* and *Queen Mary* were already in service, gaining for France and Great Britain, respectively, the distinction of being the only countries up to that time to place passenger liners of over 1,000ft in length into service. The Chapman/Ferris project should have been America's answer to them and, in its scale, it would have far surpassed the two European giants and placed the United States at the top of the league amongst the maritime nations operating the North Atlantic route.

Almost coincidentally with the release of the Chapman/Ferris scheme, the United States Maritime Commission was set up, replacing the U.S. Shipping Board, and one of its first major tasks was to establish some sort of order to the heterogeneous merchant fleet then owned by the United States, since it comprised out-dated war-prize vessels of foreign origin and a variety of 'one-off' ships. Their approach to the problem was, basically, the introduction of standard ship types, and these received priority over mammoth express liners in the national expenditure. This policy was not only very unfortunate for Messrs Chapman and Ferris, but its very wisdom might be called into question, especially when one considers, despite the misgivings expressed above, just how heavily America had to depend on her allies for troop-carriers under the Lease–Lend scheme in the ensuing world war.

Even though it was their second major set-back, this was by no means the end of the road for Chapman and Ferris. In 1949, after the war was over, the construction of their two 'class-distinction-less' ships was advocated once again, with a third ship also suggested, for operation in the Pacific. This, however, is jumping ahead of our chronology, and we must first continue in the pre-war days when a new generation of giants were emerging on the drawing board, intended for transatlantic service.

NORDDEUTSCHER LLOYD'S
AMERIKA AND *VIKTORIA*

While the Hamburg Amerika Line was occupied with a project for a new *Vaterland* class (see page 113), the Norddeutscher Lloyd was involved with plans to supersede its record-breaking sisters *Bremen* and *Europa*. This particular project was evolved entirely with a view to the reacquisition of the Atlantic Blue Riband for Germany, to be exploited as a symbol of Nazi achievement. Two ships were contemplated, although only one was planned immediately. The involvement of the German Government in the design process was evident from the start by the collaboration of its naval experts with both the architects from the Deschimag A.G. Weser shipyard at Bremen and technical representatives from Norddeutscher Lloyd itself.

Work commenced in 1937 under the supervision of Dr. Ing. Gustav Bauer, the chief engineer of the project, who was well known for his Bauer-Wach exhaust steam turbine. Some years before, in the mid-1920s, he had also been responsible for the design of the propulsion machinery of the *Bremen*. Designed as a four-day ship

Artist's impression of the projected Norddeutscher Lloyd giant *Viktoria*, also known as the *Amerika* or, more plausible, the second ship of the type. *Ed Bearman*

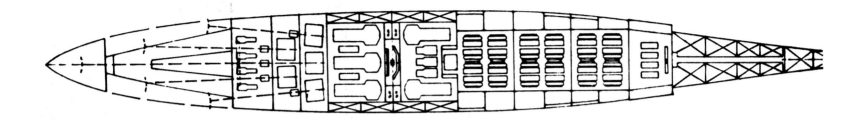

for the North Atlantic, the new liner would have been a prodigious vessel, vying only with the *Queen Mary* and *Normandie* – with an overall length of 1,070ft, her registered tonnage would have been well in excess of 80,000 gross tons. Her length between perpendiculars would have been exactly 1,000ft, the moulded beam 112ft and her draught 35ft with a displacement of 65,000 tons. Christened *Amerika*, the first of the new liners was planned as a replacement for the slow and ageing *Columbus*. In addition to her transatlantic employment, she would have been used for off-peak cruises for the Deutsche Arbeitsfront's 'Kraft durch Freude' (Strength through Joy) movement in conjunction with the cruise ships *Wilhelm Gustloff* and *Robert Ley*.

As the prime task of the new vessel was to wrest the Atlantic Blue Riband from the *Queen Mary*, she would have had turbo-electric engines producing a maximum shaft horsepower of 300,000 to give her the formidable speed of 36 to 38 knots! In order to attain these speeds the fuel oil consumption would have been approximately 100 tons per hour! In comparison, the fuel consumption of the contemporary and similar-sized *Queen Elizabeth* was only 45 tons per hour. Thus the indication is that the *Amerika* would hardly have been an economical proposition and that such a high designed speed could only have been justified to satisfy the rather nebulous matter of national prestige. The normal output of each of the five main turbines would have been 49,700shp which, after power conversion from the turbines to the propulsion motors and after some transmission losses, would have given a total delivered service rating of

An inferior but rare partial deck plan of the Projekt 305/1937 for the *Amerika and Viktoria*, showing the ships' Oberskommandobrücke, Sportdeck, Sonnendeck, Promünadendeck and Hauptdeck. *Deschimag AG*

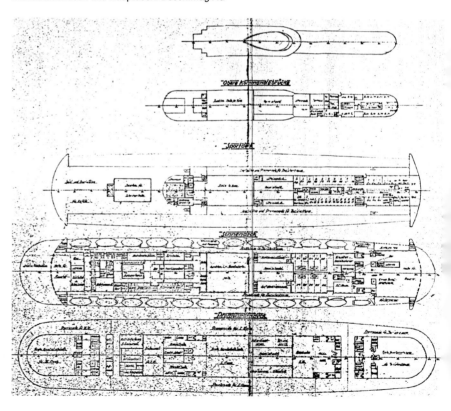

246,000shp. Driving five screws, one to each propulsion motor and turbine set, the resulting service speed would have been of the order of 34 knots. This arrangement of five propeller shafts in the design of the *Amerika* was determined because the maximum shaft horsepower to any one screw was limited to 60,000 and this was consequently the only approach by which the required total power output could be achieved. Steam to her five turbines would have been supplied at a pressure of 867 pounds per square inch (psi) from twenty-four boilers with a total heating surface of 720 square metres.

The *Amerika* would have been built to the highest standards according to the instructions of Germanischer Lloyd, with watertight subdivision to the requirements of international agreements. The usual high standard of interior appointments were to be incorporated, while her approximate complement would have been 2,000 passengers in three classes – 400 cabin, 700 tourist and 900 third. The total crew number was estimated at 1,000.

A vast amount of effort went into developing the design of the *Amerika*, designated Projekt 305/1937, the results no doubt to have been applied to the second ship at the appropriate time. Papers from the Board of Trade's German Division (Documents Unit) released on 9 June 1947, reveal that, during 1938, propellerless models were built by the Deschimag shipyard and put through tank tests in Hamburg by the Hamburgische Schiffbau-Versuchsanstalt (Research Institute for Ship Construction, Hamburg). These were most successful, and the keel-laying ceremony for the new ship was duly prepared for the autumn of 1939, when it would have taken place formally in the presence of Adolf Hitler. However, before this was possible, the outbreak of the Second World War occurred and the project was deferred temporarily due to more important war work, but the Führer did not allow this German wonder ship, supervised under his decree by the Reichverkehrsministeriums (Ministry of Transport), to be neglected.

During the war, in October 1941, it was announced that the Hamburg Amerika Line (Hapag) and the Norddeutscher Lloyd would be merged into one organisation, the Deutsche Amerika Line, and that when the war was victoriously concluded, the first ship to be built for the new company would be the giant express liner. The name *Viktoria*, as seemed appropriate, was now mentioned, but could this have been the identity of the second of the two planned liners, given that the *Bremen* had been lost in a fire outbreak on 16 March 1941, intimating that the entire building programme was to be accelerated? This would seem to be a reasonable assumption, given that two liners were planned and there is no documentary evidence of a deliberate change of name. There was talk of making the vessels even larger, with a gross tonnage in excess of 90,000.

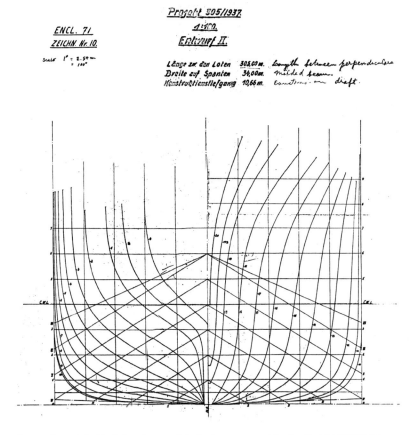

Among the detailed hull drawings and deck plans prepared for the Projekt 305/1937 were a series of body plans (transverse hull cross-sections) such as this one, all based on the projected ship's length between perpendiculars. The model numbers appended to the series of drawings, of which there were several sheets, indicate that a number of different models of the design were tested. *Hamburgische Schiffbau-Versuchenstalt*

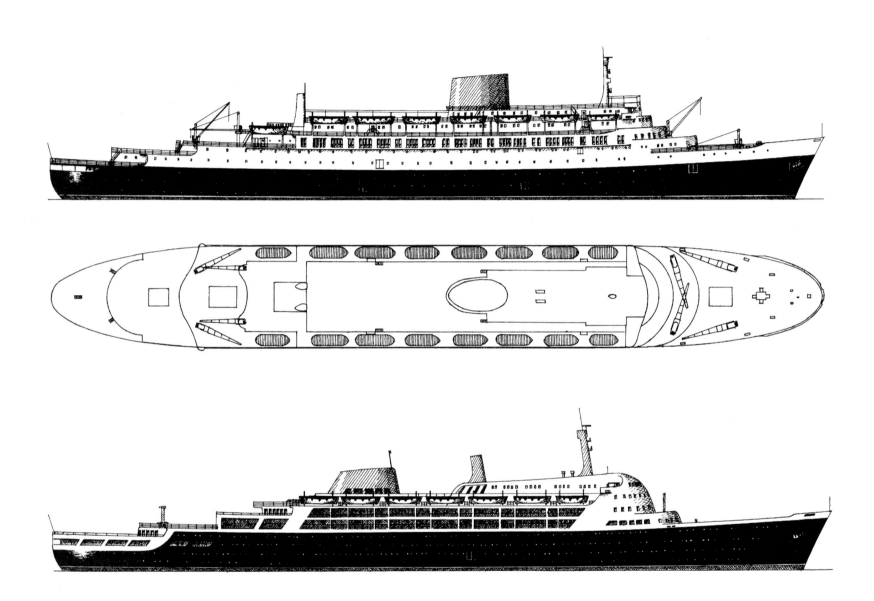

One attempt to introduce new German passenger ships to make good the wartime losses was Bremer Vulkan's Projekt 6/53B developed with Norddeutscher Lloyd in mind. Modest by comparison to the *Amerika* and *Viktoria* giants, it was not pursued and second-hand tonnage was adapted instead. The name *Bremen* was assigned to the 6/53B concept. The lower elevation shows a development of the planned vessel's design. *Karsten Kunibert Krüger-Kopiske*

The Nazi Government held the view that, in the interests of the German nation and to control debts, the transatlantic service would be best operated by a single, state-owned company, an objective that it had been pursuing since 1934 under an agreement named the Hapag–Lloyd Union. The two shipping lines were compelled against their better judgement to enter into this collaboration although, apparently, they were to be permitted to sell passage tickets under their existing names. All this was academic because the war circumstances had curtailed all international commercial voyages from Germany. As it turned out, the planned amalgamation never came about, although in July 1970 the Hapag and NDL concerns did merge voluntarily to become the Hapag–Lloyd AG. As for the giant ships, construction of the *Amerika* was never even started, let alone that of a sister-ship *Viktoria*. In the economically austere wake of the Second World War, following the defeat of Germany, the entire project was abandoned, yet another unfulfilled vision cut short by the war. Yet, as late as 1947, Norddeutscher Lloyd officials were said to have been still actively interested in a liner of the *Amerika/Viktoria* type.

All the same, nothing resulted, and reports over the subsequent twenty-five years that new liners were under construction for either the Hamburg Amerika or Norddeutscher Lloyd lines proved to be erroneous. Certainly, new German liners were subjects for discussion – a proposal to NDL from Bremer Vulkan in 1953 for the much smaller Projekt 6/53B, as one example – but little more transpired beyond this. Indeed, West German Government officials had more to say on the subject than any of the operating companies!

In 1956, the New York *Herald Tribune* correspondent, Walter Hamshar, reported that the West German Transport Minister, Dr Hans-Cristoph Seebohm, had announced the imminence of two new 25,000 to 30,000-ton vessels (possibly a manifestation of the Bremer Vulkan Projekt 6/53B concept), one for each of two companies, for North Atlantic operation. These medium-sized liners would have carried large amounts of cargo, but fewer than 900 passengers and would have featured nuclear power drive. While no companies were named specifically, Hamshar felt sure that the Norddeutscher Lloyd and Hapag were the operators concerned. With hindsight, it is perhaps more probable that the other line involved, apart from the Norddeutscher Lloyd, was the newly established Hamburg Atlantik Line. The Norddeutscher Lloyd had just recommenced its North Atlantic services with the *Berlin*, formerly the Swedish America Line's *Gripsholm* and, while Hapag concentrated on cargo services, the Hamburg Atlantik's aim was specifically the passenger market.

As events proved, neither of these companies proceeded with new tonnage, either then or for some time afterwards. Instead, they opted for drastic 'face-lifts' on older, second-hand vessels. In the NDL's case, this was the *Pasteur*, former flagship of the Compagnie Sud-Atlantique, noted more for her enormous funnel than for anything else, which eventually emerged as the fifth *Bremen* in July 1959. The Hamburg Atlantik Line, for its part, completely rebuilt the laid-up *Empress of Scotland* ex-*Empress of Japan* as the two-funnelled *Hanseatic*. When her new career was brought to an abrupt end by fire in September 1966, she was replaced by another *Hanseatic*, the ex-*Shalom* of Zim Israel Lines. Then, in February 1969, the Hamburg Atlantik Line, by now called the German Atlantik Line, complemented the second *Hanseatic* with the 24,981 gross ton *Hamburg* and, in so doing, became the first German passenger company to complete a new liner after the Second World War. Nine years later, in 1978, a new *Europa*, of 33,819 gross tons, was ordered by Hapag–Lloyd. She entered service in January 1982, only the second major new German passenger vessel in fifty-one years, but she was a dedicated cruise ship, not an ocean liner.

Viewing the economic miracle achieved by West Germany in the years subsequent to her defeat, and by Germany as a whole since reunification in October 1990, this might seem to be odd on the face of it. But it is probably fair to say that the reasons lie in the changed face of the whole North Atlantic liner scenario as a result of the advance of air travel which, to a great extent, killed the whole former concept of the passenger liner running on regular routes to predetermined schedules. Germany is now among the world leaders in cruise ship construction and it has an estimable and growing national flag cruise fleet owned by, besides Hapag–Lloyd, TUI Cruises and AIDA Cruises.

Mention was made earlier in this chapter of the Deutsche Artbeiftsfront cruise movement established in Germany in the 1930s and, in passing, mention should be made of the frustrated plans of that organisation, as they constitute an ill-fated passenger ship project of sorts. Having completed the *Wilhelm Gustloff* and *Robert Ley*, the head of the Deutsche Artbeiftsfront, Dr Robert Ley (the person), indicated in an interview with *The Motor Ship* in March 1938 that far bolder plans were in the pipeline to satisfy the aspirations of its 18 million worker members. The plan was to build one new motor vessel every year for twenty years. Following the *Wilhelm Gustloff* and *Robert Ley*, orders were to be placed with Schichau at Danzig and the Flensburgwerft yard for two more ships of the 25,000 to 28,000 gross ton type, with more to follow, although later ships in the programme would fall in the 12,000 to 15,000 gross ton category to permit access to smaller anchorages on the Baltic coast. None of this transpired, no doubt more to do with the Nazi Government's emphasis on military spending rather than on commercial projects, besides which the two large cruise ships that had been completed were lost during the war that followed.

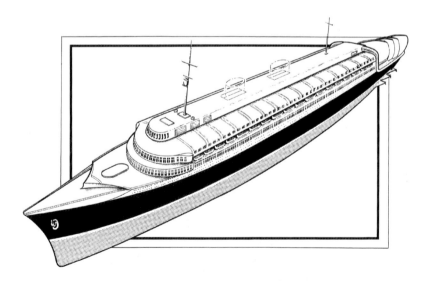

A rendering of the Hardy and de Malglaive 'Liner of the Future' showing her funnels lowered and raised (ghosted). *Bob Hoare*

THE TRANSATLANTIC LINER OF THE FUTURE

As a precursor to another planned new express liner, this being for the Compagnie Générale Transatlantique as a consort to the *Normandie* and subsequently developed as the *Bretagne* (see page 92), Pierre de Malglaive, a close colleague of Vladimir Yourkevitch, the design coordinator of the *Normandie*, was himself studying express super-liners for the North Atlantic trade in collaboration with the noted British naval architect, Alfred Cecil (A.C.) Hardy.

Bearing in mind the anticipated need to compete with the impending challenge of air transportation, they evolved a ship that would be able to cross the Atlantic in 3.5 days, with disembarkation on the 'States-side' at Montauk Bay. Exploiting a primary point of many earlier schemes – principally that by the Gibbs brothers for the *Boston* and *Baltimore* – a fast boat-train service down Long Island to New York would have saved a further ten hours by eliminating 170 miles of the ship's journey as well as the slow process of docking in New York harbour. Similar provisions were proposed for the European side, between Plymouth and London and between St. Malo and Paris.

Described as 'The Transatlantic Liner of the Future', the detailed design study was presented to the Institute of Marine Engineers, London, on 14 December 1937. The liner so conceived was massive and far larger than any ship suggested previously, with a length of 1,350ft between perpendiculars and even greater length overall. The gross tonnage of the subject vessel was never quoted but, based on its linear dimensions, it would probably have exceeded 150,000 tons.

The proposed engine room arrangement, intended to drive six screws, paralleled the vast scale of every other aspect of the ship. This consisted of six electric main propulsion units of 396,000 total horsepower. Electricity to these motors would have been supplied by six Velox turbo-generators, each with a capacity of 51,000 kilowatts and complete with its own 'fuel-valve' type boiler. Such a power plant would have consumed 2,150 tons of fuel oil a day and necessitated the design of immense storage tanks and a unique ballasting system to maintain trim as the oil was consumed. Pierre de Malglaive and A.C. Hardy calculated that such an arrangement could provide a comfortable service speed of 37 knots.

Another sketch of this futuristic design, showing how the funnels would have looked when lowered. The proponents said of their concept in December 1937, 'Our ideas are advanced not in the sense of a detailed specification of the ship of the future, but as an indication based upon rational lines of what shape the transatlantic mammoth will take if developments follow their present trend.' *David Hutchings*

The exterior of the 'Liner of the Future' was equally spectacular, being streamlined to the finest degree. Like the 'Yankee Clippers', it also featured telescopic masts and retractable funnels, albeit for different reasons, and it is difficult to say who was influenced by whom. Without doubt, many prominent naval architects and designers in this period were propounding similar radical design innovations simultaneously. During a voyage, flue gases and smoke would have been exhausted through vents at the stern. The two conventional funnels placed amidships, which normally were to be withdrawn through flaps in the upperdeck, would have been used in harbour or when there was a strong following wind.

As for the superstructure, an alloy inverted hull over the main deck was suggested to provide the least air resistance, with the elimination of as much external gear as possible, and the lifeboats stowed under cover. The top (Sports) deck would have been covered by a glass reinforced roof to specifications prepared by the Pilkington Glass Company, and this would have been capable of resisting the battering of the heaviest Atlantic gales. Another innovation would have been retractable docking wings on the bridge which would have laid flush with the ship's sides at sea and extended for harbour manoeuvring.

Interior features of the 'Liner of the Future' included gyro-stabilisers, even though the only previous experience with these in a large vessel – aboard the Italia liner *Conte di Savoia* – had only been partially successful and, from economic considerations, they had taken up an unconscionable amount of space. As for the passengers, escalators and travellators (powered horizontal conveyors) were planned to facilitate more rapid movement from deck to deck.

The harbour installations and shore requirements, which were an integral part of Pierre de Malglaive and A.C. Hardy's study, were not overlooked either. The boat-train connections mentioned were no mere simple rail-track affairs – on the contrary, the designers envisaged rail-plane type, on overhanging monorails which could travel at speeds up to 200mph. A test line for one of these propeller-driven vehicles was constructed by Mr George Bennie at Milngavie, near Glasgow, over the London and North-Eastern Railway. In so doing, he successfully proved the system's functionality if not its practicability.

Nothing ever came of the 'Liner of the Future'. Messrs Bassett Lowke, a celebrated model-making firm, built a display model, while most of the shipping and engineering journals of the day carried features on the design but, as Pierre de Malglaive and A.C. Hardy explained, it had been no more than a design investigation: a prediction of the most likely future trends as they saw them, and not a specific design contract from a shipowner. However, as CGT were firming up their plans for the future Bretagne, it was said that the 'Liner of the Future' was one of the options first considered by the company.

THE *BRETAGNE* – ONE SHIP, TWO CONCEPTS

The Norddeutscher Lloyd was not the only company interested in new tonnage for the North Atlantic run in the years immediately prior to the Second World War. The Italia Line had two 'very fast' liners of 60,000 gross tons under consideration which were to be built more or less concurrently, but these never got beyond the 'talking' stage. In France, the Compagnie Générale Transatlantique (CGT) was well aware of the German plans for high-speed super-liners, and it knew that good progress was being made with the Queen Elizabeth across the Channel. The fact that the Normandie might, in these circumstances, remain a lone ship on their service (since the Île-de-France was too slow to provide a balanced schedule with her) clearly affected her chances of success, and this had not escaped their notice. Thus, CGT wanted running mates desperately for the famed record-breaker and, of course, an equally important ambition was to regain the prestigious Atlantic Blue Riband.

In October 1938, CGT announced that a definite decision had been made to build a consort to the Normandie. In his book 'Normandie, Her Life and Times', Harvey Ardman reveals that initial thinking was along the lines of the 'Liner of the Future' concept that de Malglaive and Hardy had described in their talk at the Institute of Marine Engineers, London, ten months earlier:

This liner, according to CGT, would closely resemble the vision discussed the previous year by Pierre de Malglaive and A.C. Hardy at the Institute of Marine Engineers. It would cost $60 million and take four years to build.

This was more than a little misleading as it turned out, although, extreme as it was, the design under consideration did in fact incorporate some of the features of the 'Liner of the Future'.

In April 1939, the problem assumed a new urgency when CGT's liner Paris was destroyed by fire at Le Havre, and the French Government then authorised the expediting of plans for a new liner. Consequently, the CGT turned to the existing design drawings of the Normandie in order to save both time and expense. From these, it was proposed to develop a suitable consort: a liner in the classic French style perpetuating the character of its illustrious predecessor. Eventually the new building specification emerged. This indicated that the projected second ship, to be named Bretagne, other than taking the form of the 'Liner of the Future' would instead be modelled directly on the successful lines of the Normandie, as had been widely expected, but would incorporate minor alterations influenced by the operational experience gained from the earlier ship, as well as the benefits of technical progress made since the Normandie's inception. The gross tonnage of the new vessel was expected to be approximately 85,000, while her linear dimensions would have been virtually identical to the previous vessel.

The CGT required a service speed of at least 32 knots for the Bretagne which could have been achieved, at a price, as a result of the engineering advances made since the Normandie's power plant had been constructed in the early 1930s. However, details of the size and type of the propulsion machinery planned, in order to enable the new ship to attempt the Atlantic record were not released, and one can only speculate whether or not the Bretagne would have had a turbo-electric arrangement, such as that installed in the Normandie, or steam turbine engines like Cunard's Queens. The fact that the hull strength and layout had been designed around machinery of the turbo-electric type and weight suggests that this would have been the most probable.

Vladimir Yourkevitch's masterpiece, the *Normandie*, at her builder's yard in April, 1935. On her trials she achieved 31.9 knots over several miles and, on her maiden voyage, crossed from Cowes to the Ambrose Light at an average speed of 29.94 knots, capturing for herself the Atlantic Blue Riband. *Jean-Yves Brouard*

When approached in December 1974, René Bouvard, official historian of CGT, revealed that there was an absence of drawings and sketches in the company's possession, possibly destroyed during the war and, therefore, it was only possible to guess at the new liner's likely appearance, and to what extent engineering improvements would have influenced her externally. Undoubtedly she would have borne a general resemblance to the *Normandie*, particularly with the unmistakeable Yourkevitch hull shape. The CGT technical officials he consulted were quite positive that she would have had only two funnels, compared with three in the former ship. Thus, sketches and drawings of the *Bretagne* that have been created since that time show a vessel broadly similar to the *Normandie* but with two squat funnels instead of three, and a more modern spoon style of stern.

The French Minister of Merchant Marine, Louis de Chappedelaine, announced at the annual banquet of the Federation of French Pilots on 27 May 1939 that the Compagnie Générale Transatlantique was expected to order the *Bretagne* from the Penhöet shipyard of Chantiers et Ateliers de St Nazaire within the next three weeks. The keel laying was planned for early 1940, with the launching by autumn 1942 and completion in the spring of 1944. There was also speculation on a second similar vessel later, for which the name *Provence* was mooted. While it was expected that the *Bretagne* would surpass the imminent *Queen Elizabeth* in size and speed, Louis de Chappedelaine declared that she '*might not be quite so luxuriously fitted out as the Normandie but she would be faster*'.

The essence of that announcement was confirmed by Marcel Olivier, a CGT director, when he arrived in New York as the French Commissioner General to the World's Fair. He added that the new liner was expected to cost 1,000 million francs (c. £5.2 million), approximately 25 per cent more than the *Normandie*. Her engines would develop a nominal 250,000shp to give the ship a top speed of 35 knots and a cruising speed of 33 knots. The choice of the name *Bretagne* was also explained:

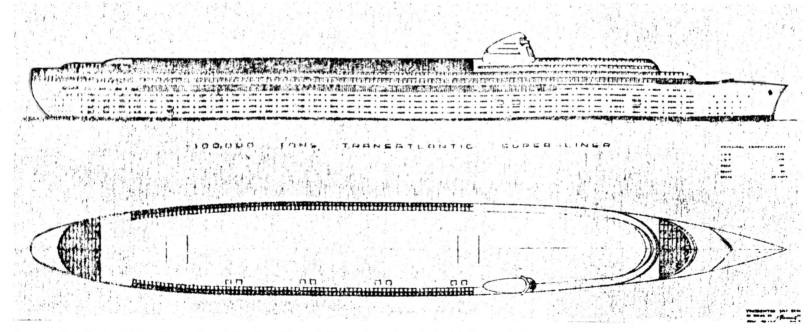

A poor-quality but uniquely interesting profile and plan view of Yourkevitch's grand one-class giant, originally conceived as an option for the *Bretagne* and here seen in a post-war derivative with single offset funnel of modern style. *Vladimir Yourkevitch* (*Harvey Ardman*)

The new liner would be named *Bretagne*, a well-deserved tribute to the province, which, apart from the catering department, supplied 90 per cent of the owners' crews.

Meanwhile, Vladimir Yourkevitch, the famed designer of the *Normandie*, entered the scene himself by submitting his own new ideas for the design of the proposed super-liner *Bretagne*. Formerly a naval architect in Imperial Russia, he had emigrated from France to the United States of America in 1937 sailing, naturally enough, in the *Normandie*. He established offices in New York and commenced to evolve his own design specifications for the next generation of ocean liners, liners that could compete favourably, as was thought, with passenger aircraft, whose impending threat Yourkevitch could see looming on the horizon. It was the plans which resulted from this exercise which he now offered to the CGT.

These revealed another truly prodigious vessel, much larger than the *Normandie*, with a registered tonnage in excess of 100,000 tons. The dimensions of the Yourkevitch design were 1,148ft overall length and 138ft beam, in comparison with the *Normandie*'s figures of 1,029ft and 118ft, respectively.

As in the case of the improved version of the *Normandie*, no revelations were forthcoming as to the intended prime-mover in the machinery of the Yourkevitch concept, although a service speed of 34 knots was confidently forecast for this massive liner. Much of this extra speed would have been achieved as a result of the extreme streamlining of the hull and superstructure. In consequence of these hydrodynamic refinements, the Yourkevitch design had a quite unusual profile. The hull exhibited much less of the flare that typified the *Normandie*, being long and slab-sided, although the Yourkevitch bow form was retained. A cruiser stern contrasted with the elliptical counter of the earlier liner. The superstructure was long, quite uncluttered and with rounded steps between decks forward and aft. There were no visible projections from either the hull or the superstructure – not even bridge or docking wings – and the concealment of deck gear was taken a stage further from the *Normandie* with the lifeboats enclosed under sliding glass panels on the upper deck. Two modernistic funnels were situated athwartships of each side of this upper deck and, with the absence of masts, these would have contained the radio aerials and lookout posts. Between the funnels, a broad platform, inclining slightly to the stern, was suggested for the operation of aeroplanes carrying express mail and, presumably, for any impatient or unpunctual members of the passenger list. It was intended that, when not employed for this purpose, this open deck area would be available for passenger recreation, although in practice it might well have proved to be unsuitable since such an exposed deck, subject to strong sea winds, apart from the apparent wind created by the speed of the ship herself, might have presented a serious hazard to passengers.

Yourkevitch's proposals for the *Bretagne* represented a considerable departure from his earlier thoughts on passenger liners but, if the exterior design was radical, then the suggested interior arrangements were revolutionary, especially where a company like the CGT was concerned.

Even though Yourkevitch proposed a high grade of luxurious appointments for his ship, in keeping with the customary standards aboard existing vessels of the CGT fleet, accommodation was nevertheless provided for only a single class of passengers, totalling an incredible 5,000. The approximate fare level for this one-class complement was tourist, and one thing that Yourkevitch had in mind particularly for this type of ship was the provision of cheap passages for the growing mass of travel-hungry tourists – America's so-called 'two-week vacationists'. Consequently, shipboard facilities were geared to the requirements of such passengers.

Cabin space would have been entirely in two-berth units, each of them with a private bathroom with a shower and toilet, indicating a conversion to the Ferris/Chapman philosophy of mass-handling in transatlantic travel. Applying the principle further, Yourkevitch suggested for his liner what he described as 'Pleasure-Planning' facilities, which consisted primarily of inexpensive restaurants and other forms of low-cost catering service, which would enable passengers to decide their own meal expenses separately from their ticket price. With regard to entertainment, a similar approach was intimated, with a wide variety of different recreational and leisure centres instead of an extravagant concentration of effort on the traditional ocean liner public rooms. Certainly a ship of the type draughted by Vladimir Yourkevitch would have been completely different from anything that the CGT either were, or had been, operating.

With an eye to military adaptation, a more than usually important consideration at that particular time, as well as the influence that this might have had on government funding, Yourkevitch had designed the ship so that it could be converted readily into a troopship, with a capacity for 13,000 fully equipped soldiers.

The Compagnie Générale Transatlantique, although apparently impressed with Yourkevitch's proposals, nevertheless rejected them. It was still quite definitely in the 'luxury liner' business, and there would be no place for such a ship in the fleet of a company whose name was synonymous with unsurpassable standards of shipboard comfort, spaciousness and service.

This may have been a short-sighted decision, although no liner company at that time would have conceded that passenger aircraft would one day be regarded as a serious threat to the livelihood of their ships. A typical view, expressed anonymously some ten years earlier and quoted in *The Sway of the Grand Saloon* by John Malcolm Brinnin, rather dismissed the aircraft as a novelty and, at the same time, hinted that it might perhaps even be inherently unsafe:

> The simple truth is that aerial transport can never be made to pay. Flying has come to stay but I cannot believe that the airway will ever replace the seaway. We can step aboard a Cunarder at either Southampton or Liverpool with a feeling of assurance that we shall be in New York with timetable punctuality, travelling in luxury and safety. The aircraft can never hold such assurance.

Indeed, even twenty years later when the menace of aircraft competition was fully appreciated, no established transatlantic passenger company opted for such a drastically different type of vessel as Yourkevitch's *Bretagne* and, in any case, in the summer of 1939, CGT was still anxious to promote the image of exclusive luxury and old world culture, cuisine and sophistication which was associated with its name.

Quite apart from this, there were time and cost factors to consider. It would have taken some appreciable time to have worked up detailed construction plans for a completely new design, whereas the *Normandie*'s plans already existed. Against this, Yourkevitch claimed that a vessel of the type that he was proposing would cost less to build than the 800 million francs (say £4.2 million or $20 million, at August 1939 rates of exchange) the *Normandie* had cost.

Whilst disputing Yourkevitch's figures, CGT director Marcel Olivier, speaking in June 1939, confirmed that the company's preference was to abide by the super-*Normandie* concept and, by way of comparison, based on this approach, he revealed that the *Bretagne* was expected to cost his firm no more than 1,000 million francs (approximately £5.2 million or $25 million).

Understandably, Vladimir Yourkevitch was disappointed at the outcome, but his frustration was diminished by the knowledge that it would have been impossible to have proceeded immediately with his ship anyway, as no dry-dock or building berth of sufficient capacity was then in existence.

On 23 August 1939, the very day that Yourkevitch's latest creation, the Compagnie Sud-Atlantique's *Pasteur*, satisfactorily completed her sea trials, CGT indicated that it was proceeding with its new liner as forecast, to be based on the *Normandie*'s blueprints. The keel-laying would now take place towards the end of 1940 since adherence to the original building programme as outlined earlier was prevented by an obstacle at the shipyard. The only suitable slipway at the Penhöet yard large enough to accommodate the giant *Bretagne* was already occupied by the 35,000-ton aircraft carrier *Joffre*, one of a pair which were being built for the French Navy. This was regarded as causing little more than a minor delay, and it was intended that the construction of the *Bretagne* would go ahead once the carrier was launched. Within days of the announcement, though, war had broken out in Europe but, in spite of this outbreak of hostilities, there were no intentions to abandon the scheme.

However, in the winter of 1939–40, while the logistical problems at the shipyard were being ironed out, no one even remotely considered the possibility of a threat to the *Bretagne* of far greater significance, namely the French nation being overrun and occupied by the German army. Such a notion seemed to be beyond credibility but, as it turned out, within six months that was precisely what happened. In occupied France, those shipbuilding facilities which had not been prudently sabotaged in time found themselves in the service of their German overlords.

A rendering of a futuristic German ocean liner, 'Das Ozean-Schnellschiff von Morgen' (ocean express ship of tomorrow) by N. von Romer. The painting reveals the impact of some of Norman Bel Geddes' theories upon the artist's interpretation of his subject. *Authors' collection*

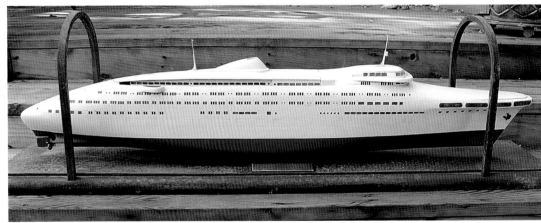

A display model of the developed whale ship as planned for construction for shipbuilding magnate Henry J. Kaiser. The brass plate reveals the ship's intended name – SS *Henry J. Kaiser* – and the details of its dimensions. *Melissa (gypsiegirls)*

This drawing of the *Amerika/Viktoria* design gives force to the maxim that a really well-designed ship seldom looks its size. In fact, she would have been close to 90,000grt, which would have been extremely extravagant in her fuel consumption had she entered commercial service. *David Hutchings from Deschimag AG general arrangement plans*

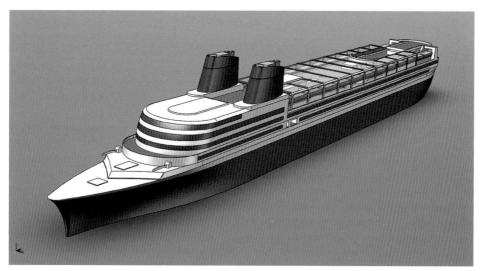

Vladimir Yourkevitch's concept of the *Bretagne*, the projected consort for the *Normandie*, unexpectedly revealed an almost total abandonment of aesthetic values in favour of purely functional characteristics. *Finn Tornquist*

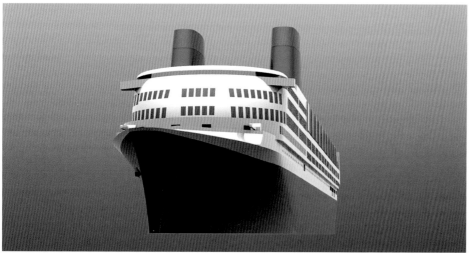

Her twin, athwartships funnels and high, long superstructure gave her an unattractive profile. *Finn Tornquist*

Another representation of Yourkevitch's distinctive concept for the *Bretagne*. *Finn Tornquist*

An interesting take on Yourkevitch's version of the *Bretagne* in the form of a French Line poster heralding the entry into service that never happened. *Finn Tornquist*

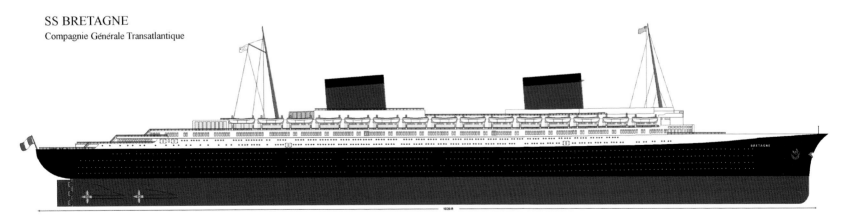

Based on statements made by CGT officials at the time, as well as speculation on the effects of the engineering advances in the late 1930s that had resulted in the evolution of the *Queen Elizabeth* from the earlier *Queen Mary*, artists have generated speculative interpretations of the likely appearance of the *Bretagne*, as similarly evolved from the *Normandie*: with twin funnels and a rounded or spoon stern, as depicted here. It is likely that, in practice, had the actual funnels been as squat as shown in this illustration they would have required heightening. *Stanislav Eigi*

The Atlantic Steam Navigation's *Silver Falcon* in an impression of her underway. Note the company's angular, pale blue on white bird-like emblem at the bow. *Mervyn Pearson*

An artist's impression of the *Stockholm. Swedish America Line*

Oblique views of the simplified models of
the two, alternative *Rotterdam* 1940/1941
designs. *Both Rotterdam Museum Maritiem*

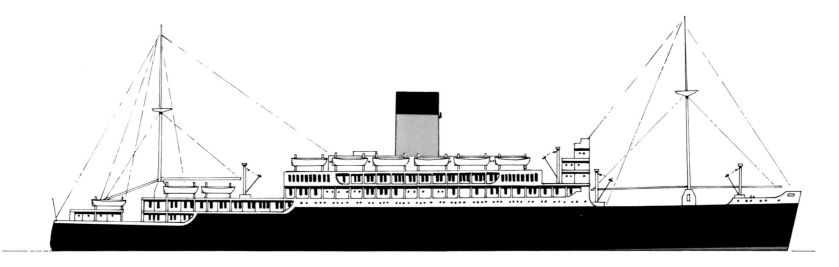

The design of the *Jason*, considered by Blue Funnel Line as a consort to Shaw Savill's *Dominion Monarch. David Hutchings*

KASHIWARA MARU

世界をむすんで一世紀 新世を拓く
三 日本郵船

An artist's rendering of the *Kashiwara Maru* from NYK publicity material. Prior to the cruise ship era, the *Kashiwara Maru* and her sister, *Izumo Maru*, would have been Japan's largest passenger ships. *Nippon Yusen Kaisha*

Of the five large passenger ships that were completed and which put to sea but were denied commercial service through the impact of the World Wars, the aircraft carriers *Hiyo* ex-*Izumo Maru* and *Junyo* ex-*Kashiwara Maru* survived the longest, the latter for over three years. *Takeshi Yuki*

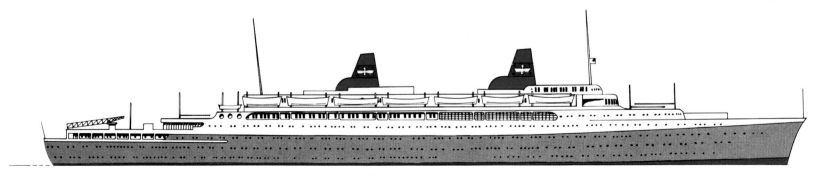

The P-4-P passenger liner/aircraft carrier in the colours of the American President Lines for whom she had probably been intended. *David Hutchings*

The *France* depicted in the early stages of her design evolution, before the smoke-dispersing fins were added to her funnels. In this form, she hinted of CGT's version of the abandoned *Bretagne*. *Compagnie Générale Transatlantique*

Designed by Antoine Barthelmy, the *France* of 1962, at Southampton's original Ocean Terminal. She was conceived to satisfy quite different commercial objectives from the *Bretagne*, but was quite possibly her reincarnation in a post-war version that was the largest that CGT could produce within the limitations of the financial help that the French Government was then prepared to offer. *Chris Howell*

Consequently, the incomplete *Joffre* was broken up on the slipway and, once vacated, this was used for quite different purposes far removed from the halcyon affairs of transatlantic travel.

So it came about that, in May 1945, the Compagnie Générale Transatlantique not only lacked its super-liner *Bretagne*, but had also lost the beautiful *Normandie*, gutted by fire so unfortunately during the war – a loss which was only partly remedied by the advent of the *France* in 1962, despite the acquisition as an interim flagship of the *Liberté* ex-*Europa*, a war reparation.

As for Vladimir Yourkevitch, on the completion of work on his *Bretagne* concept, he became involved once more with the *Normandie*. Sadly, in February 1942, he had witnessed the needless devastation of his great liner in New York, and the stories of his frustrated attempts to save her from capsizing and total loss are well known. While she was being converted into a troopship for the U.S. Government, welders had accidentally ignited a pile of burlap-wrapped kapok life-jackets which started a massive conflagration, a fire that was rapidly out of control. The gutted ship, top heavy from the huge volumes of water hosed into her, sank at her berth.

Throughout 1942 and 1943 Yourkevitch was closely involved in the preparations to raise the great ship from the mud and slime of her Manhattan cradle and, after this had been accomplished, he worked on elaborate and comprehensive plans for her complete reconstruction. When these were rejected, he prepared yet new suggestions and, even as the *Normandie*'s hull was being dismantled at the Lipsett breakers yard across the harbour at Port Newark, New Jersey, he was finalising yet another proposal to rebuild her as a medium-sized liner.

After the war, in parallel with the efforts of Paul Chapman, Theodore Ferris and A.C. Hardy, Yourkevitch continued to promote his ambitious plans for massive 'cafeteria-type' ships, as they were called, such as his *Bretagne* design. In 1946, his *Bretagne* plans were further streamlined, resulting in the elimination of one of the funnels, whilst the one that remained was given an even more modern look and was still situated on the extreme edge of the hull on the starboard side.

Although nothing resulted from Yourkevitch's campaign for revolutionary transatlantic tonnage, it influenced his approach when he was engaged as consultant to Hyman Cantor in 1956 for the Sea Coach Line project. The design for the *Peace* and the *Goodwill*, described in detail later (see page 172), was a direct development from the *Bretagne* concept, with a close similarity in both overall dimensions and general layout. When this scheme failed in the early 1960s, it dashed the last hope of putting Yourkevitch's mass-transportation ideas into practice.

Vladimir Yourkevitch may have been a visionary but, if he be described thus, it must be as a visionary of genius, as evidenced by his achievements with the *Normandie*, and it is certain that his name will remain recorded on the rolls of fame so long as maritime history continues to be read. He died on 16 December 1964, aged 79, and, as events proved, his most grandiose and inspired conceptions died with him. It is some two millennia since Christ said 'A prophet is not without honour, save in his own country …' and that maxim is not only as true today as it was then, but all too often he never receives the full honours that he merits anywhere at all in his lifetime. This is an unpalatable truth of which this book provides a number of examples.

The world was about to be plunged again into hostilities and, when it emerged from the shadow of total conflict for the second time in thirty years, the various shipping companies would once again take stock of their various situations, and ideas such as the 'Liner of the Future' and the earlier 'Yankee Clippers' would continue, for a while at least, to have an influence on plans for new express liners for the transatlantic service.

INTERMEDIATE PROJECTS FOR TRANSATLANTIC SERVICE

THE ATLANTIC STEAM NAVIGATION COMPANY'S DESIGN

An ambitious proposition being fostered in Great Britain in the 1930s involved new intermediate ships, that is liners of around 30–40,000 gross tons, for the North Atlantic crossing. With the dissolution of the White Star Line in 1934, one of the company's executives, Major Frank Bustard, attempted to establish a good, second-grade transatlantic service to supplement the express mail schedules provided by the Cunard White Star Line. Cunard later placed the motor-ships *Britannic* and *Georgic* in a somewhat similar service based at London, which proved to be very successful, but Major Bustard regarded Liverpool, at one time the Mecca of Britain's passenger shipping trade, as being a more suitable terminus port, especially if a good train service to the capital could be arranged.

The first step was the formation of a new company, the Atlantic Steam Navigation Company (the Atlantic Line) in late 1934, with offices in Cockspur Street in London, registered two years later on 8 November 1936. Having formed the company, its directors, Major Bustard and Mr A.G. Wansborough, commenced negotiations with the London, Midland and Scottish Railway Company for a suitable express rail link between Euston and Liverpool. With this accomplished, the next move was to acquire the necessary ships with which to operate the service.

Initially, Major Bustard approached Philip Albright Franklin, the IMM's President, on 27 November 1934 intent upon tendering to purchase the vessels of the Red Star Line which had been put up for sale as part of the IMM's budgetary measures implemented during the Great Depression. The ships included in the sale were the *Belgenland*, *Pennland* and *Westernland*, in addition to the former Atlantic Transport Line cargo-passenger steamers *Minnetonka* and *Minnewaska,* which the Red Star Line had operated since 1930. Initially, the plan was to carry tourist passengers only on the five ships at a one-way fare of £10, with *a la carte* menus as an extra. The British Government, however, would not support the purchase financially because the proposed vessels would have been competing with the Cunard White Star Line which had already received Treasury assistance.

As a result of official prevarication and negativity, this opportunity was lost. Consequently, the Red Star Line was sold instead to Arnold Bernstein, the Hamburg shipowner. The sale only covered the *Pennland* and *Westernland* which, as it transpired, made substantial profits for their new German owners, while the *Belgenland* was transferred within the IMM to the Panama Pacific Line and renamed *Columbia.* The *Minnetonka* and the *Minnewaska* were sold for scrapping only ten years after they had been completed.

In view of the outcome to these initial procurement moves, it was necessary to conisder the construction of two new liners for the embryonic Atlantic Line service. *Lloyd's List* reported on the new company's bold intentions on 9 September 1936:

The new company aims at catering for a far wider class of traffic than that covered by the existing lines serving the North Atlantic and has as its preliminary objective the placing of orders for the construction of two passenger and cargo liners, each of approximately 30,000 tons gross and of an improved *Manhattan*-type [vessel]. It is believed that these orders will be placed in the comparatively near future and we understand that plans embodying the essential details of the vessels have already been approved. It is probable that the liners will be of the two-class type, though this is subject to alteration, and they will have a speed of something over 20 knots, sufficient to enable them to complete the voyage from this country [UK] to America within the week. The service will be between Liverpool and New York with a call in each direction in an Irish port, probably Dublin.

It is understood that the cost of the new liners will be well over £1 million each but no public issue of capital will be made, it being intended to run the new line as a private concern.

Major Bustard approached Vickers-Armstrongs to have designs prepared for the two sister-ships which presumably would eventually have been built by that shipyard. According to the *Lloyd's List* of 25 September 1936, that appeared to be all but certain:

A contract for the construction of two 30,000 gross ton passenger liners for the North Atlantic service is, we understand, shortly to be placed with Vickers-Armstrongs Limited, Barrow-in-Furness, by the Atlantic Line, the new company recently registered under the title Atlantic Steam Navigation Company and formed for the purpose of a new passenger and cargo service between Liverpool and New York via Dublin.

The vessels will have an overall length of 725 feet, a breadth of 90 feet and a speed of about 22 knots. There will be two classes of accommodation – First [Cabin-class*] and Tourist – the numbers to be carried in each class being 500 and 1,000 respectively, and there will be sailings from Liverpool and New York every ten days. The ships will be operated on the same principle as railways. Passengers will be charged a fare for transportation and accommodation and will pay separately for their meals but inclusive fares will be quoted if desired. Tourist accommodation will be from £10 for the single voyage and, while no definite decision has yet been arrived at in regard to First-class fares, it is expected that these will be from £20 single.

The registered offices of the Atlantic Line are in London and the head office will be in Liverpool. The house flag will be a white and blue swallow-tailed flag and the funnels of the vessels will be painted light blue with a white band under a black top. The hull will be dark blue with a white band and the boot-topping will be light blue. The superstructure will be painted white.

It should be noted by reference to the inserted comment [*] that the planned accommodation grades had been reported erroneously. Reflecting the trend which had emerged since the Atlantic Conference agreement of February 1936 they were, in fact, to be Cabin- and Tourist-class.

The liners conceived by Vickers-Armstrongs' Ship Design Department were attractive three-funnelled ships, nearer to 33,000 gross tons. With a length between perpendiculars of 685ft, they had an elegant rake at the bow extending out to the full length of the hull. There was speculation in the American press during late 1936 that the two vessels were to be named *Silverswift* and *Silverfalcon* (alternatively stated to be *Silver Swift* and *Silver Falcon*) though no hard evidence can be discovered to support this assertion.

The ships were pleasing in every respect. They were commercially sound vehicles, and there was more than a hint of the White Star's planned *Oceanic* of seven years earlier in the shipbuilder's profile. Perhaps this is not so surprising, since Major Bustard held an executive position with the White Star Line at the time of the brief *Oceanic* episode.

Steam turbine engines geared to twin shafts would have given them a service speed of 22 knots, permitting a proposed sailing schedule that offered a departure from either side of the Atlantic every ten days, leaving on alternate Saturdays and Wednesdays. As intimated by *Lloyd's List*, it was intended to operate the Atlantic Line service from Liverpool via Dublin (Dún Laoghaire) to New York. The Dublin call was deliberately included to exploit the strong family links between the Irish people there and in the USA. The Vickers-Armstrongs drawing revealed some detail of the intended layout of the propulsion system, showing the main engine room located aft beneath the third, dummy funnel. The two boiler rooms, separated by a diesel generator compartment, were located, respectively, beneath the first and second funnels.

With shipyard prices negotiated at £2.4 million per vessel and tentative delivery dates agreed to permit the commencement of the new service in late 1938, the ingredients for the project were all but complete. This was a viable and sensible scheme which was

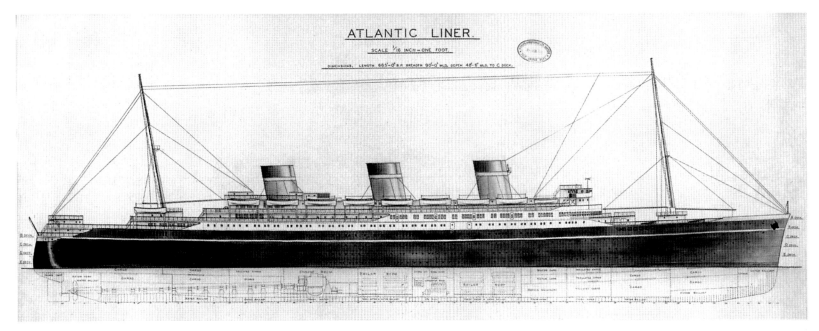

ATLANTIC LINER.

SCALE ⅟₁₆ INCH = ONE FOOT.

DIMENSIONS, LENGTH 665'-0" B.P. BREADTH 90'-0" MLD. DEPTH 48'-6" MLD. TO C. DECK.

The Vickers-Armstrongs design for the Atlantic Steam Navigation Company's liners. *Frank Bustard*

An artist's impression of the *Silver Falcon* in the River Mersey outward bound from Liverpool. *Mervyn Pearson*

not intended to compete with other UK-based liners in any way for passengers travelling by the premier express services. Instead, it was directed at winning for Great Britain a further handsome chunk of that lucrative part of the trade which catered for the passenger who was not so wealthy – the traveller who really did not care so much about the speed of the crossing, especially if it meant paying a higher fare for the pleasure. At the time, this trade was dominated by the Continental and American lines, primarily with the steamships *Champlain*, *Manhattan* and *Washington*.

Having catered for all possible contingencies, on 4 October 1938 Major Bustard approached the Bank of England for financial assistance, presenting his formal case for a loan application entitled *'Statement Prepared by Major Frank Bustard, OBE, M Inst T, in Relation to the North Atlantic Route'*. The problem was that, having effectively elected to go it alone as a private concern rather than raise the required capital in the city through a share issue, the Atlantic Line needed both a mortgage and a loan to finance the construction of the ships. The former, for the amount of £2,475,000 at 4 per cent interest would, no doubt, have been arranged with Vickers-Armstrongs while the size of the proposed loan, at £2 million spread over two years, required an institution of the scale of the Bank of England to act as provider. This, however, could not be granted by the Bank without the approval of the Treasury and due to a negative attitude of the government of the day, which did not appear to appreciate the value of having a comprehensive secondary transatlantic service, the loan for these two well-conceived liners was opposed by successive Chancellors of the Exchequer, Neville Chamberlain and Sir John Simon. In the absence of the loan, a mortgage alone was insufficient to permit matters to proceed.

This was not only a great disappointment to Major Bustard, but a most unfortunate loss for Great Britain, for a valuable section of the North Atlantic traffic was abandoned almost entirely, while two potential hospital ships, which would have been invaluable in the world war which was looming, were also forfeited. One of the features of the design of these ships was their suitability for conversion to this role during wartime – a conversion for which Major Bustard had made clear that they would be made available immediately.

Nevertheless, Bustard pursued his project with undaunted determination, and he next approached other established shipping companies, including the Orient and Anchor Lines, for consideration of his plans, in the hope that they would be prepared to subsidise his enterprise. For various reasons, however, these concerns were unable to involve themselves collaboratively in the project and, with the approach of war – the final and inevitable confrontation with the Third Reich – it became increasingly difficult to pursue the project further.

It was thought that Major Bustard had reluctantly conceded defeat and terminally abandoned his scheme for the *Silver* twins on the outbreak of the Second World War, in which he served in the Army Reserve, but that was not the case. It had only been shelved for the duration and, following the cessation of hostilities and after re-establishing offices in Cockspur Street, London, he attempted to re-kindle the project in a last-ditch bid to revive his plans for a secondary North Atlantic service from Liverpool. Alas, yet again, the timing was not auspicious. Immediately post-war, there was a severe shortage of liner tonnage with nothing suitable or even available in the second-hand market and there was little prospect of having new vessels constructed for some time to come.

Right up to his death, Major Bustard (later Lieutenant Colonel Bustard, and the last surviving ex-White Star Line Director) felt that the lack of positive support for his constructive and practical suggestions was a great pity. The fact that his ships were never realised can only be regarded as an unnecessarily blank page in the history of Great Britain's maritime trade.

Before closing this section, a few brief biographical notes about the man must surely be in order, for the personal vitality which this dynamic individual displayed in his business affairs was equally evident in his private and social activities. Frank Bustard was born in Liverpool in February 1886 and, following a distinguished career in the army, he was equally successful in the passenger shipping business. He was also well known for his extrovert involvement in sports activities, being a member of the so-called 'Champion Eight' of the Liverpool gymnasium and a contestant for the Liverpool and Merseyside Amateur Wrestling Championship.

Having accepted defeat with his aspirations for transatlantic ships, Bustard turned his attention to implementing a unique approach to freight and passenger services on short sea routes around the UK, initially using adapted wartime tank landing ships and then with purpose-built vessels based on the same principles. Having become part of the nationalised British Transport Commission in 1955, his company, Atlantic Steam Navigation, was eventually swallowed up in the European Ferries Group in November 1971 as one of the first 'privatisation' disposals made by the newly elected Conservative government.

Lieutenant Colonel Frank Bustard died barely three years later, in January 1974, aged 87, but his memory lives on in the RoRo ferry operations which he pioneered as a novel mode of commercial vehicle transportation by sea and which continue to this day.

THE TWO *STOCKHOLMS*

During the decade of the 1930s, the liner projects which fell by the wayside were very much the minority of all those begun. Most of the plans bore fruit and many big passenger ships, which subsequently became famous, proceeded without obstacle from the drawing board to the slipway, and from the slipway to the water to begin the ships' first and lifelong association in their own element. In due course, the maiden voyages completed this perfect maritime metamorphosis. Amongst the many success stories of the period were the later P&O *Straths*, the German trio *Gneisenau*, *Potsdam* and *Scharnhorst* for the Far East service, and the Union Castle Line's *Athlone* and *Stirling Castle*. Other new liners were the Orient Line's *Orion* and *Orcades*, the *Pretoria* and *Windhuk* of the Deutsche-Ost Afrika Line, while the Gdynia America Line took delivery of the smaller *Batory* and *Pilsudski*. However, the crowning event of the mid 1930s was the entry into service of the *Normandie* and *Queen Mary* and, viewed with hindsight, what greater proof could there have been that the ocean passenger liner had reached a glorious and most spectacular peak at that time?

This great shipbuilding boom did not end with these ships for, as the barometer of world trade rose ever upwards, so even more ships began to take shape on the drawing boards and in shipyard berths. The list of new buildings was impressive, to say the very least,

and it included a new *Mauretania* and a second *Nieuw Amsterdam*. In addition, there was the *Capetown Castle*, the *Pasteur*, the *America*, the *Dominion Monarch* and finally, of course, the greatest of them all, the *Queen Elizabeth*, due for completion in 1940. In fact, these years were so favourable for passenger ships of all categories that it is hard to believe that any scheme could have fallen the victim of bad luck.

Nevertheless, ill-fortune comes in many forms, and no ship could have had a greater need of good luck than the liner whose story is now related. It began in 1935 when the relatively youthful Swedish America Line, just twenty years old, embarked upon its most ambitious project to that time. Preliminary design work was started on a large liner for the North Atlantic route, a vessel which would place Sweden on a level with the more established maritime nations on the world's prestige sea route. Planned to be of around 28,500 gross tons on completion, the new ship, given the name *Stockholm*, was ordered from the Monfalcone yard of the Cantieri Riuniti dell'Adriatico in 1936 and laid down on 10 March the following year.

The *Stockholm* was an unusual liner and a quite unique experiment. Designed by the Swedish America Line's technical director, Mr E. Th. Christiansson, she was to be a purpose-built, dual-role, regular service vessel and 'off-peak' cruise ship — a trend more commonplace three and a half decades later, but not at that time.

En passant, Mr E. Th. Christiansson died in 1981 at the age of 80. He went to sea as a boy of 14 and sailed in various ships, on deck and in the engine room, until he came ashore and took a job as a ships' plater while he studied for his engineering examinations. After this somewhat unorthodox start, he had a most successful career as a ship designer.

With her smaller consorts, the *Gripsholm* of 1925 and the *Kungsholm* of 1928, the *Stockholm* was intended to make pleasure cruises to the North Cape, the Caribbean and the Baltic when not employed on the North Atlantic service. Her passenger accommodation was, therefore, styled with her twin-purpose career in mind and it differed vastly from the accommodation in other great transatlantic liners of the period. The usual system of two corridors was abandoned in favour of a single broad, central passageway along the whole length of the stateroom decks. As a result, all cabins would have been very large, and practically all cruising passengers would have had outside cabins. This was reflected in her passenger numbers for, while on the North Atlantic, the *Stockholm* would have carried 1,350 in four classes – De-Luxe, Cabin, Tourist and Third – whereas on cruises she would have carried only 620 passengers in one class.

The launch of the first *Stockholm* on 29 May 1938. *Italcantieri*

In addition to her unconventional accommodation layout, the equipment and fittings of the *Stockholm* included many novel features. The most interesting of the installations to be fitted in the vessel was her air-conditioning plant. This treated and controlled the air temperature and humidity to all her saloons and passenger cabins, and it made her the first passenger liner to be so fitted.

Even more thought was given to the passengers' comfort with regard to stability and vibration, and a number of features were incorporated into the design to improve these factors. First, the *Stockholm* had big, streamlined bilge keels; secondly, anti-rolling tanks capable of reducing roll from 15° to 5° were fitted; finally, in the most fundamental approach to the stability of the ship, she had a very carefully thought out length/beam ratio. The proportions which resulted were an overall length of 678ft and a beam measurementof 83ft, giving a ratio of 8:1. Her draught would have been 28ft when fully loaded.

The *Stockholm* was designed as a triple-screw motor-ship, and was the largest vessel of her time with this machinery/propeller combination. Her engines consisted of three ten-cylinder C.R.A.-Sulzer SD72 single-acting main units giving a total of 22,000bhp. It had been suggested originally that she should be fitted with twelve ten-cylinder medium-speed engines geared in fours to the three propeller shafts. These would have been manufactured by the Atlas Diesel Company of Stockholm, but the Swedish America Line preferred the direct drive arrangement of the C.R.A.-Sulzer design. The *Stockholm*'s service speed was to be 18.5 knots with a maximum speed of 20 knots.

With her construction financed on a barter arrangement in exchange for coal, the *Stockholm* was the first and, with the exception of the Clyde-built *Kungsholm* of 1966, the only really large liner ordered by Sweden. Unfortunately, however, as already indicated, she was a very unlucky ship. The building of the vessel proceeded through 1937 and 1938 and was distinguished at that time by the extensive use of electric arc welding in the hull structure.

The new liner was launched by HRH Princess Ingeborg, mother of Queen Astrid of Sweden, on 29 May 1938. She was nearing completion by the end of that year, with her sea trials scheduled for March 1939 but, unfortunately, on 19 December 1938 the vessel was gutted by fire.

The first *Stockholm* during fitting out. *Authors' collection*

The first *Stockholm* ablaze and listing to port at her fitting out berth. *Lloyds, Trieste*

Unlike her predecessor, the second *Stockholm* was launched with masts and funnels in position. *Swedish America Line*

The second *Stockholm* immediately after her launch on 10 March 1940. *Swedish America Line*

The blaze spread through the ship rapidly, being fanned by strong gusts of the seasonal winds, and fire-fighting was made particularly difficult by the toxic fumes which developed from the burning insulation material already fitted on board – acetic acid was created in the presence of the extinguishing water, a hazard not foreseen when the material had been selected. On account of the vast quantities of water pumped into her, the unlucky liner gradually lost stability and finally sank at her fitting-out berth.

After the fire had been extinguished, the charred hulk was examined in an attempt to establish its cause, but the findings were inconclusive. Among the various suppositions as to the origin of the outbreak was an electrical short circuit, burning coal or sparks from a rivet furnace, or even a discarded cigarette. The inspection did, however, reveal quite clearly that the ship and most of her fittings were beyond salvage. Almost immediately it was decided to construct another virtually identical liner, also to bear the name *Stockholm*, using the undamaged parts of the wreck wherever possible, including the original oil engines. Work was consequently resumed on the vacant slipway and the second hull, Yard No. 1203, was launched on 10 March 1940.

This new *Stockholm* was completed in 1941 and in appearance she was already a hint of the post-war Swedish America Line ships *Kungsholm* of 1953 and *Gripsholm* of 1958. The new *Stockholm* measured 29,305 gross tons, a measurement later increased to 30,390. She had ten decks, six of which extended the full length of the ship. All the features and appointments of the original vessel were present in the replacement and she was a very luxurious and beautiful liner in every respect.

The *Stockholm*'s First-class Main Lounge. *Authors' collection*

The *Stockholm*'s First-class Gallery. *Cantieri Riuniti dell'Adriatico*

The *Stockholm*'s First-class Card Room. *Cantieri Riuniti dell'Adriatico*

The Tourist-class Lounge of the *Stockholm*. *Cantieri Riuniti dell'Adriatico*

The *Stockholm*'s Tourist-class 'Show Boat' restaurant designed by Oscar Nilsson. *Cantieri Riuniti dell'Adriatico*

A twin-bed Tourist-class cabin on B-deck. *Cantieri Riuniti dell'Adriatico*

In a spirit of competition, most large liners had generally provided not only luxury in the First-class accommodation but also a magnificence of décor and standards vastly in excess of the experience and expectations of all passengers, invariably causing admiration but, sometimes, criticism. The Orient Line had broken with the older traditions in their *Orion* and *Orcades* in 1935 and 1937, but these were for the Australian run. The *Stockholm* provided luxury with greater simplicity and across the board and, had she gone into service on the North Atlantic, her accommodation would have produced a sensation. Her designers were, in fact, some years ahead of their times, since these trends only appeared on the route after the Second World War.

The *Stockholm* carried out her sea trials in the spring of 1941, but the outbreak of the Second World War in September 1939 had led to the immediate blockade of the Skaggerak and thus, due to the long delay since the first ship had been laid down and Italy's involvement

in the conflict from June 1940 as part of the Axis, it was impossible for the fine new liner to be delivered to her owners. The President of the Swedish America Line was said to have wept when he saw his splendid ship and knew that he could not have her in his fleet.

Later in the same year the vessel was sold back to the Italians, who at once set about converting her into a troopship. This work was finished in 1942, and she reappeared as the *Sabaudia*, to be managed for the Italian Government by the Italia Line. Perhaps surprisingly, in view of her recent conversion, she was immediately laid up at Monfalcone. Contrary to popular belief, neither this vessel, nor the *Rex* nor the *Conte di Savoia*, were used for trooping in the end, because of their large size and obvious vulnerability to air attack in the Mediterranean – a vulnerability demonstrated graphically by the attack on the Taranto naval base by aircraft of the Fleet Air Arm in November 1940. For a while she was used as a German

The second *Stockholm* undergoing her sea trials, a starboard side, stern quarter view. Note that she is flying both the Swedish and Italian flags, the former on the main mast and the latter on the foremast. *Swedish America Line*

The *Sabaudia* ex-*Stockholm*, alongside at the Cantieri Riuniti dell' Adriatico yard at Monfalcone. The change of paint and angle of view belies her size. *Aldo Fraccaroli*

The *Sabaudia* being towed to Vallone di Zaule, near Trieste, in *c.*1944. She had never received her full complement of boats. *Aldo Fraccaroli*

accommodation ship in Trieste following the Italian capitulation, and then she was towed to the supposed safety of Vallone di Zaule in the Gulf of Muggia, just south of Sabba, not far from Trieste.

It seemed that fate was still banked against the luckless liner. On 6 July 1944, the *Sabaudia* was spotted at her anchorage by British aircraft, bombed and set on fire. The conflagration could not be controlled and the blazing ship drifted helplessly until she finally went aground. Later, the half-sunken, burnt-out hulk was bombed for a second time in May 1945 and became a total loss, lying near the wrecks of the *Duilio* and *Giulio Cesare*.

When the war ended, the *Sabaudia* was refloated by Messrs D. and C. Tripcovich, only to be declared unfit for restoration. Thus, the wreck was sold on to the firm of Messrs Goriup for dismantling, ironically at the San Rocco Repair Yard, also in the Gulf of Muggia. The work started in 1947 and was completed by 1950. This was a tragically ignominious end for such a fine ship, which had never been put to any good use at all. Miraculously, the main engines were once again recovered practically intact and these were sold, one to be fitted to the MV *Trieste*, a new cargo liner, Yard No. 1780, building at the Cantieri Riuniti dell'Adriatico's San Marco shipyard.

The *Sabaudia* ablaze after Allied aircraft had attacked her with rockets and bombs. *Authors' collection*

A graveyard of liners. The scene at Vallone di Zaule on 16 October 1947, showing the wreck of the *Sabaudia* (foreground), the *Duilio* (left) and the *Giulio Cesare* (right background).
Aldo Fraccaroli

Looking aft close along the side of the destroyed *Sabaudia* ex-*Stockholm*, she makes a sad spectacle of a once elegant but doubly ill-fated liner. Note the buckled plates and the men on the side of her hull, small in comparison to the immense structure. *Alex Duncan*

The name *Stockholm* can, perhaps, be considered to have been an unlucky one from the point of view of the Swedish America Line for, apart from the two giant liners of that name lost in 1938 and 1944 as described above, the next *Stockholm*, built in 1948, was involved in the tragic collision with the *Andrea Doria* on 26 July 1956, a disaster which resulted in the loss of fifty-three lives and the sinking of the Italian liner.

HAPAG'S SECOND *VATERLAND*, ANOTHER WARTIME LOSS

Just as the loom of impending war in the Pacific changed the destinies of the *Izumo Maru*, *Kashiwara Maru* and the P-4-P ships (all described in the next section), so the actual outbreak of hostilities in Europe interfered with the futures of other newly planned ocean liners intended for the Atlantic. Under the control of Hitler's National Socialists, Germany had once again become a powerful and assertive industrial nation. Once more, efforts were being made to elevate the prestige of her merchant fleet to a position befitting her political and military status. One objective was to regain the premier rank on the North Atlantic

route which had been held briefly by the *Bremen* and *Europa*, but the resurgence of the German passenger fleet had wider goals. Indeed, the aim was to have the best ships with the highest standards on every sea route, to compete directly with every foreign company.

The Hamburg Sud-Amerika Line had announced plans to refit and complement the *Cap Arcona* on the River Plate service while the Deutsche Ost-Afrika Line was proposing the construction of two 25,000 gross ton vessels (or bigger), for a fast South and East Africa service to challenge the new Union-Castle motor-ships. The war, however, interrupted both schemes while they were still in the preliminary planning stages. Yet another project, but one which proceeded much further, involved the Hamburg Amerika Line (Hapag) which had not owned a first-rate giant passenger liner since the pre-First World War *Bismarck* trio.

Hapag's North Atlantic presence since the early 1920s had been in the form of the *New York*, *Hansa* ex-*Albert Ballin*, *Hamburg* and *Deutschland*, a quartet which, in spite of some excellent public rooms, were commonly regarded as being somewhat slow and spartan. Certainly, they had few of the luxurious accoutrements and little of the aura of extravagance and gracious living normally associated with this prestigious route.

In a bid to improve their standards on the Western Ocean, the Hamburg Amerika Line began to consider replacements for their four older and smaller liners around 1935. Two years later the first of a class of three turbo-electric passenger ships was ordered from Blohm and Voss at Hamburg as Yard No. 523. The builder's models revealed a magnificent two-funnelled vessel with a turtle-back forecastle similar to that on the *Normandie*, a feature that indicated that her genesis too had been on the drawing board of Vladimir Yourkevitch. Although never christened officially, the name *Vaterland* was definitely intended for the new liner and she was referred to as such in official Hapag documents. Laid down in 1938, one of the most interesting features of the 41,000 gross ton ship was the proposal that her engines should consist of a turbo-electric machinery installation. Designed to produce 62,000 total shaft horsepower for a maximum speed of 25.5 knots, the propulsive power arrangement consisted of eight Benson forced circulation boilers to drive the steam turbine ends of

These views of a waterline model of the new *Vaterland* showed her to be a vessel of great individuality. *Both Hapag-Lloyd*

A flight of the imagination. On the request of an unknown interested party, a model of the *Vaterland* was made with streamlined funnels. While such a style would have made for an elegant profile, this was never the intention of the Hamburg Amerika Line. *Ellen Koester*

the AC generator sets which, in turn, would drive the motors on the twin-screw shafts. The boilers would generate steam at 950psi and a super-heated temperature of 877° Fahrenheit.

The *Vaterland*'s principal dimensions were 827ft in length overall and 98ft 6in beam with a designed displacement of 36,000 tons, making her comparable in size to the *Oriana* and *Canberra* of the early 1960s. She was intended to carry 1,322 passengers on the North Atlantic run, divided into 354 First-class, 435 Tourist-class and 533 Third-class. In the winter months she would have cruised with a smaller passenger complement.

Welding was used extensively in the construction of the *Vaterland*. The shell butts of her hull were welded but the seams were riveted, while on the upper decks both the seams and butts were welded. The decks themselves were riveted to the hull shell by an angle bar.

Work on the ship proceeded regardless of the outbreak of war, as there was a possibility that her berth would be required for one of the planned diesel-powered super-battleships of the *Gross Deutschland*-class. Conceived under the 'Z' Plan – the blueprint of the renascent Kriegsmarine – there were to be six of these monster battleships, each with a displacement of 65,000 tons, an overall length of 912ft and a main armament of eight 16-inch guns. Their proposed diesel propulsion arrangement, comprising three engines producing 165,000 shaft horsepower, was chosen for the increased range it would give the ships, whose operations would, of necessity, have to be independent of overseas bases. The anticipated need for the *Vaterland*'s slipway arose in 1940, so she was launched without ceremony on 24 August of that year. The super-battleship that was laid down on the vacated slip was herself cancelled soon after work on her had begun and she was broken up on the stocks. As for the *Vaterland*, all work on her construction was halted following her launch owing to the lack of raw materials, and the incomplete liner was chained to the wharf in the Kuhwerder Harbour where she was used as a store-ship for furniture wood.

On 25 July 1943 she was badly damaged during a particularly heavy air raid on Hamburg. Bombs penetrated the steel of her decks, exploding below and blowing out some of her decks, while the wood stored aboard her was set alight and the resulting blaze caused

The *Vaterland* on the slipway at Blohm & Voss in an advanced state of construction prior to her launch. Her Yourkevitch-style bow and turtle-back foredeck are evident. It has been suggested that a second ship of this class was also started but no evidence can be found to support such an assertion. *Arnold Kludas*

The launch of the *Vaterland* on 24 August, 1940 – a bow view and a stern quarter view, with the almost-completed battleship *Bismarck* beyond. *Both Arnold Kludas*

The wreck of the bomb-damaged *Vaterland* in Hamburg in 1945. *L.L. von Münching*

With her fore-deck blasted upwards by exploding bombs, the never-completed *Vaterland* seen prior to being broken up. *Crown Copyright*

further extensive damage to both the steel decks and the hull itself. It is interesting to note that, in spite of the explosions and the intense heat, none of the welded seams of the shell or decks opened up – a testimony to the good workmanship which had gone into the vessel.

The *Vaterland* was abandoned in her damaged and sorry state until the end of the war when, once again, Germany was made to forfeit her merchant fleet as reparations to the Allies, to whom it was left to decide the future of the scarred wreck. Although much of the damage was superficial and could have been restored fairly easily, it was considered to be too expensive to replace all the annealed steelwork. Consequently, the half-completed *Vaterland* was broken up locally in 1948. During this period, much of the Blohm and Voss shipyard was demolished under the supervision of the British Control Commission and the confiscated material, which included machine tools, medical instruments, theodolites and quantities of scrap metal, was shipped back to England from the 'Backloading Depot' at the Togo Quay, Hamburg. Amongst this was the scrap metal from the *Vaterland*, which was destined to reappear in post-war Britain as part of the materials for one reconstruction project or another, perhaps demonstrating that some fortune comes from every adversity.

Had the *Vaterland* and her sisters been completed and survived the war, the inference is that they would have been confiscated and would have passed to some other flag, but they would certainly have made their mark and enhanced the prestige of whatever country had operated them.

HOLLAND AMERICA'S 1940/1941 *ROTTERDAM* CONCEPTS

Despite having lost its *Statendam*, as the *Justicia*, in the First World War (page 55), for which the British Government compensated the company as detailed earlier, and despite the protracted completion of the replacement ship of the same name – laid down in 1921, launched in 1924 and delivered in 1929 – the Holland America Line (Nederlandsche Amerika Stoomvaart Maatschappij or NASM) was generally lucky in its procurement of new ships.

The *Nieuw Amsterdam* (second of the name), completed in 1938 as a companion to the *Statendam* of 1929 (third of the name), was a notably successful ship and one of the most elegant and popular liners ever placed in the North Atlantic passenger service. However, the difficulties the company experienced with regard to raising the necessary funds to pay for that ship provide an indication of the obstacles that Dutch shipping lines in general had to overcome in order to augment their fleets. The Dutch Government was resolutely opposed to the use of public funds to finance private business projects, insisting instead that companies should raise the capital they required through normal commercial channels.

In 1933, arising from the long-term fallout from the Wall Street crash and the ensuing Great Depression, the Holland America Line – whose revenues, like most other transatlantic shipping lines, had suffered badly – was on the brink of total collapse. Against this backdrop, the Dutch Government was approached for an injection of aid to keep the company going. The initial response was to set up a commission to evaluate the health of Dutch merchant shipping as a whole. It recommended that the three largest lines, Rotterdam Lloyd, Nederland Line and Holland America should pool their resources by merging into a single operating concern covering all worldwide shipping routes. Many Rotterdam businessmen opposed this advice and, led by William van der Vorm, they proceeded to invest personally in the Holland America Line to keep it independent. Their confidence in the company's underlying prospects proved to be well-founded and gradually paid dividends, such that by the mid 1930s it was deemed that a running mate for the *Statendam* should be built.

Again, the Dutch Government was requested to support the initiative but once more it declined. At the time, however, there was high unemployment in The Netherlands and the Rotterdam region in particular, costing the government heavily in 'dole' relief payouts. When it was pointed out that a project of the magnitude of a large, new transatlantic passenger ship would give the local economy an urgently needed boost by creating a lot of jobs, the government relented. The only condition imposed was that as many Dutch shipbuilding operations as possible should play a part in the ship's construction. Hence, although the *Nieuw Amsterdam*, as the new ship became, was nominally built by the Rotterdam Drydock Company, both the Wilton-Fijenoord shipyard and R.M. De Schelde of Vlissingen (Flushing) were also involved, the latter yard responsible for her Parsons quadruple-geared turbine engines.

A year after the 36,287grt *Nieuw Amsterdam* entered service, Holland America's directors decided that, given her excellent performance, a second ship of her size was required, not only to permit a more balanced three-ship service with regular sailings from either side of the Atlantic but to help boost further the company's improving fortunes.

For a third time, the Dutch Government was petitioned for financial assistance to permit the company to proceed with an order. It was disclosed by the Director of the National Bank for Reconstruction that

Holland America was seeking a loan of $8.5 million, approximately one-third of the cost of the new ship, plus a 100 per cent guarantee for that loan and a further 20 per cent of credit to be raised from private investment sources. The remaining amount of the ship's cost was to be paid for out of the company's own cash reserves. The government, no longer concerned about high unemployment as a justification, adamantly refused the request, insisting that commercial concerns should not unnecessarily depend on state support for their business expansion.

Undaunted, despite having to find the total amount of a new ship's construction cost itself, a potentially insurmountable obstacle, Holland America proceeded nevertheless with the design phase which had commenced in 1939. The German occupation of The Netherlands

Holland's most-loved, most elegant and most successful passenger liner, the *Nieuw Amsterdam* of 1938. *Kenneth W. Wightman*

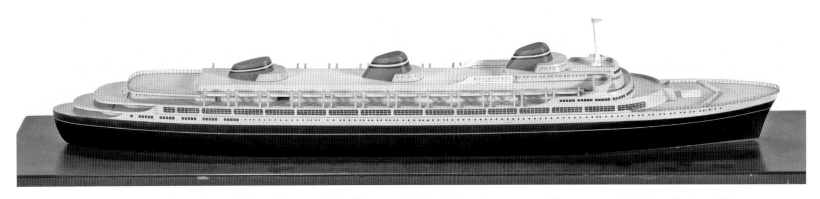

The planned consort to the *Nieuw Amsterdam* would have had a completely different profile. Two design options were considered as revealed in these display models: a three-funnelled vessel with a spoon stern … *Rotterdam Museum Maritiem*

from May 1940 along with the cessation of scheduled services did not help the situation, but the loss of the *Statendam*, destroyed during the fighting around the docks area of Rotterdam, gave greater impetus to the pursuit of a new running mate for the *Nieuw Amsterdam*. As it was impossible to foresee how long the war and the occupation would last, the needs of the post-war future, whenever it came, had to be addressed. So it was that the planning of the *Nieuw Amsterdam*'s consort, referred to as the '1940/1941' design, continued in earnest.

The chief designer of the *Rotterdam* of 1959, Ing. Wim H.W. Stapel, later revealed the intended size and linear dimensions of the projected ship. They were to be comparable to those of the *Nieuw Amsterdam* at 36,595grt, length between perpendiculars 725ft, beam 95ft and depth to the waterline 56ft 6in. Like the earlier ship, she would have had geared steam turbines with the Rotterdam Drydock Company, as before, the prospective builders. Dr Nico Guns, the respected Dutch shipping historian, explained why the selection of the shipyard was pretty much a foregone conclusion:

Both the Rotterdamsche Droogdok Maatschappij (RDM) and Wilton-Fijenoord (WF) were angling in the HAL [Holland America Line] pond for the potential order which, in my view, would almost certainly have gone to the RDM because of the excellent experiences HAL had with RDM in building *Nieuw Amsterdam*, whereas WF was considered to be not so experienced and equipped for such a large project.

There were, in fact, two variants of the '1940/1941' design, one with three funnels, the other with two. Models of the variants are in the collection of the Rotterdam Maritime Museum and, as a matter of interest, they indicate slightly different full-size measurements based on their 1:200 scale. Marcel Kroon, the information manager at the museum, provided the authors with the dimensions of the two models from which the full-scale length and breadth can be calculated. These show that the three-funnelled variant (M3521) would have had a waterline length of 763ft and a beam of 99ft, whereas the two-funnelled variant (M3523) would have measured 789ft 7in at the waterline with a beam of 95ft. In comparison, the *Nieuw Amsterdam* had an overall length of 760ft and a beam of 88ft 2in.

Both models reveal forward-thinking in the exterior design, having a markedly more modern overall appearance than the *Nieuw Amsterdam*. They feature streamlined funnels, rounded and enclosed superstructures, the three-funneller with a spoon stern, the other having a cruiser stern, and an absence of stick masts. Like the supposedly alternative variant of Hapag's *Vaterland* (see illustration at the bottom of page 114) they were ahead of their time, a portent of the future.

As far as the name of the projected ship is concerned, this has been the matter of some speculation. The models in the Rotterdam Maritime Museum have the name '*Rotterdam*' displayed alongside them – a probable choice – but it is not known whether this name was appended when the models were made back in 1940–41 or

… or a two-funnelled ship with a cruiser stern. In both cases, the funnels would have had streamlined contours in contrast to those of the *Nieuw Amsterdam*.
Rotterdam Museum Maritiem

added later by museum staff. Dr Guns had this to say about the name of the *Nieuw Amsterdam*'s consort:

> Most likely, in the period 1938 to 1940, the HAL referred to the third ship as the 'second *Nieuw Amsterdam*' just as they had done [previously] in the case of the 'second *Statendam*'. I say 'most likely' because the HAL were always quite reluctant to give any clues away as to the intended name for a new liner. While planning of the 'second *Statendam*' [in fact third ship of the name] started in 1935, it was not until 1937 that the name *Prinsendam* started to be mentioned. Towards the end of 1937, the HAL management decided to ask the American travelling public for the name they would prefer for the new ship. This resulted in the old name of the colony of Nieuw Amsterdam. There had been a *Nieuw Amsterdam* (I) at the beginning of the 20th century. Management decided it was a much better name than *Prinsendam*, and so it was to be.
>
> When thinking of a name for the 'second *Nieuw Amsterdam*', it is highly likely that the HAL management thought of *Rotterdam* (IV).

> By then, there had already been several ships named like that. They may even have been thinking of *Statendam* (IV). Again, publicly and officially, they will have postponed mentioning the name as long as possible. But it is very well possible that the previewed or intended ship has been referred to as '*Rotterdam*'.

The occupation of The Netherlands lasted for five years, time enough for things to change, and at the war's end, in the general recovery from the immense destruction, Holland America was preoccupied with making good the heavy losses it had sustained from its pre-war fleet – sixteen vessels sunk out of a total of twenty-five, including the *Statendam*, *Zaandam*, *Zuiderdam* and *Pennland*. There was no time then to give thought to a new frontline ship for the North Atlantic service. Thus, the '1940/1941' design was abandoned and forgotten. But fourteen years later a magnificent new *Rotterdam*, to an altogether and, as was thought at the time, more radical design, became Holland America's new flagship, a much-loved ship which presently graces the Rotterdam waterfront, hopefully preserved there in perpetuity.

5

UNREALISED PROJECTS FOR OTHER OCEAN ROUTES

The 'Yankee Clippers' scheme was not the only unsuccessful liner project in the United States in the mid 1930s. The Dollar Line, which operated from the US west coast to Japan, ambitiously planned to build two 'super-liners' for its San Francisco to the Orient service. Heralded to be close in size and speed to the *Bremen* and *Europa* which operated on the North Atlantic route, this was something of an exaggeration, no doubt intended for a public that, by then, was entranced by record-breaking sizes and speeds.

A contemporary account, complete with profile drawing, described them with greater accuracy as being more moderate in size and of 'conventional appearance', lacking any radical features that typified the new giant express ships introduced on the North Atlantic run, although they would still have been the largest and fastest ships serving on the Pacific at that time. They were to have had a slightly raked bow and a counter stern. Their full superstructure would have been topped by two moderately streamlined funnels and they would have had two stick masts. In many respects, from the overall description, they sounded reminiscent of the *President Coolidge* and the *President Hoover*, the two ships they were intended to complement. The two older *Presidents*, handsome turbo-electric liners built in 1931, provided only a relatively small representation on this route compared with the many modern vessels owned by the Nippon Yusen Kaisha and the Canadian Pacific Lines, and so it was intended that these somewhat larger new liners, up to half as big again, should also challenge this foreign domination of the transpacific routes. The project, however, was short-lived.

With the majority of Congressmen being from land-locked and land-orientated states, and with the financial losses of the *Leviathan*

ex-*Vaterland* on the North Atlantic being ever present in their minds, these factors combined to put a federal subsidy out of the question. The *Leviathan* was judged by the members of Congress by her losses to be unsuccessful, thereby influencing their consideration of the proposed ships for the Dollar Line and thus killing them off when they might well have been successful on a quite different route and in quite different circumstances. This is not to say that Congress was right or wrong in the matter, but it does demonstrate that the prospects for these two superlative, modern ships which never came into existence, were damned by the continuing presence of another, ageing one. Had the *Leviathan* never existed, or had she been sunk by a German U-boat during the First World War, the Dollar liners might have reached the water! The word 'successful' is frequently used of ships, though its meaning is not always clear. A vessel which performs well but is run at a loss may still be a success if she engenders the national prestige intended for her. Two similar vessels on the same route, but under different flags, may produce quite different financial results if one is hedged by onerous regulations and restrictive practices, and the other is not; hence the flight to 'flags of convenience' in relatively recent times.

With no other financial support available, the Dollar giants were doomed from the outset and never got beyond the preliminary planning stage. It seemed that, at around this time, many Americans shared the belief that they could not operate a super-liner profitably or successfully and, as it turned out, their doubts, and those of congressmen specifically, appeared to be substantiated when, in 1938, the United States Maritime Commission (USMC) was compelled to intervene in the affairs of the Dollar Line, which had been slipping deeper and deeper into financial trouble, in order to protect the federal loans already made to the company. The result of this action was the reorganisation of the company, resulting in the formation of the American President Lines which was soon to have new ideas of its own.

ALFRED HOLT'S *JASON* – A RELUCTANT CONSORT

In the United Kingdom, the mid 1930s saw the beginning of an upsurge in the construction of new passenger liners, as detailed earlier, a fact which reflected the vast improvement in international commerce following the Depression and the particularly auspicious situation in the shipping world as a whole – a direct result of this upturn in international trade. Not all of these new passenger ship projects were successful, however, and one scheme that failed was

proposed by the Shaw Savill and Blue Funnel Lines, which from 1935 had operated the Blue Funnel and Shaw Savill Joint Service route to South Africa and Australia.

In the late 1920s, Shaw Savill had already lost two tentatively planned 20,000 gross ton, 17-knot passenger liners as a result of being taken over by the Royal Mail organisation. Now, their new plan involved the construction of a series of 900ft-long motor vessels as an extension of their famous Empire Food ships. In the event, the unjustifiably high cost of liners of this calibre for a route which did not warrant them proved to be a fatal ingredient. From this point, further discussions on the question of constructing new ships for the Dominion trade centred around a design for somewhat smaller quadruple-screw motor-ships, and the outcome of them was the placing of an order by the Shaw Savill Line for the 682ft *Dominion Monarch* in 1937. Lord Essendon, the Chairman of Shaw Savill and Albion, who was a committed advocate

Shaw Savill & Albion's quadruple-screw motor-ship *Dominion Monarch*. She almost became a war casualty when she was dry-docked at Singapore just before it was captured by the Japanese in February 1942. *Tom Rayner collection*

of the large passenger-cargo type of vessel, urged his Blue Funnel counterparts to follow suit, and it was generally expected that they, too, would follow with a similar vessel.

In fact, a decision in principle was made to this effect in the summer of 1939. Although Alfred Holt and Company, owners of the Blue Funnel Line, were basically opposed to the large liner concept, the directors agreed, somewhat reluctantly, to the construction of a similar vessel to the *Dominion Monarch* in order to provide this vessel with a suitable consort in the joint service and as a replacement for the ageing *Nestor* and *Ulysses*. However, certain detailed preferences in the design of the Blue Funnel ship would have made her substantially, as well as visually, different from the *Dominion Monarch*.

Given the name *Jason* for discussion purposes, she would have had similar dimensions and tonnage to the *Dominion Monarch* but, instead of the exclusive First-class accommodation of 500 in the Shaw Savill ship, the *Jason* would have had cabin space for 1,000 tourist passengers only, at the expense of some of the refrigerated cargo capacity.

The Blue Funnel also chose a different propulsion arrangement, preferring a simpler twin-propeller drive system. There would have been two Burmeister and Wain engines instead of the *Dominion Monarch*'s four Doxford diesels. One of the reasons behind their preference for this simpler engine arrangement may have been the vast maintenance problems initially associated with the latter ship's quadruple engine installation – a disadvantage which almost resulted in her capture by the Japanese at Singapore in 1942.

Externally, the two liners would have had a very similar appearance except that the *Jason* would have had one funnel and two masts, whereas the *Dominion Monarch* had two funnels and one mast.

The order for the *Jason* was forecast for 1940, but the outbreak of war interfered with this and the plan was then abandoned. It is probably safe to say that the Blue Funnel directors greeted this enforced abandonment of the scheme with some relief, since they had never given their full support to the building of such a ship in the first place. As for Shaw Savill, in the absence of a firm commitment to the *Jason*, they had been compelled to terminate the joint service arrangement with the Blue Funnel Line. In February 1939, when the 27,155 tons, 682ft *Dominion Monarch* went into

The front cover of the Blue Funnel/Shaw Savill Joint Service sailing schedule, dated January 1939. *Bjorn Larsson*

service, she inaugurated the Australia and New Zealand route from Southampton, calling at Tenerife, Cape Town, Durban, Fremantle, Melbourne, Sydney, Wellington and Lyttleton. Thereafter, Shaw Savill reorganised its Australian services completely and, in spite of a tacit agreement to the provision of a consort to the *Dominion Monarch*, Blue Funnel displayed no great urgency in trying to reinstate the close working arrangement they had enjoyed on the Empire run hitherto.

As things turned out, with the services of the two companies no longer closely linked, when Blue Funnel did proceed with new vessels after the war, they opted for a completely different solution to their new ship requirements. This took the form of the much smaller cargo vessels of the *Patroclus* type, and the second of these ships, which entered service in 1950, was given the name *Jason*.

The Blue Funnel and Shaw Savill Joint Service was briefly revived in 1954 with Shaw Savill contributing their *Athenic*, *Ceramic*, *Arawa* and *Dominion Monarch* to the service. Ironically, one of Blue Funnel's contributions was the post-war *Jason*. This second attempt was short-lived, as the entry into service of Shaw Savill's *Southern Cross* in 1955 on the round-the-world service may well have superceded the joint itinerary.

It is interesting to note that, despite the fact that they originated from distinctly different approaches, both the *Dominion Monarch* and the *Helenus*-class ships were highly successful.

THE *IZUMO MARU* AND *KASHIWARA MARU*

At this point we should return to 1936 to witness the commencement of another ship project which became disrupted by the deteriorating international political situation. Early in that year, a statement had been issued that the next Olympiad, to follow the games in Berlin, would be held at Tokyo in 1940. This venue was subsequently transferred to Helsinki before being finally abandoned altogether, but the immediate result of this decision was that Japan swiftly realised that vast numbers of people might be expected to attend so spectacular an event of such international importance. Both the Canadian Pacific and Dollar Lines would benefit from the consequent upsurge in passenger

traffic, but the Japanese had no intention of allowing their foreign competitors to dominate the battle for profits which this increased influx of people to their country would bring. This consideration, therefore, prompted a decision to build Japan's first large passenger liners, and two luxury vessels were consequently evolved for the Nippon Yusen Kaisha's (NYK) express Pacific service from Yokohama to San Francisco. These ships were expected to elevate Japan's status as a passenger-carrying maritime nation but, as things turned out, they were destined instead to be among the first doomed liners ordered for a route other than the North Atlantic.

From the very outset, the design work was influenced very strongly by the requirements of the Japanese Government's naval rearmament policy, and the two liners were immediately earmarked for conversion into aircraft carriers should it become necessary. The reasons for this went back to 1927, when the Japanese Government resolved to implement a naval building programme which would provide their country with a naval force strong enough to challenge the combined strengths of the US and British Pacific Fleets, but would not contravene the strength limitations laid down by the Washington Naval Conference of 1921. With the reinforcement of the naval air arm particularly in mind, this was to be achieved by the construction of a number of passenger ships which would serve commercial purposes during peacetime, but designed so that, in the event of a national emergency, they could be rapidly transformed into aircraft carriers.

The first group of liners to be completed within the concepts of this new strategy were the 17,000 gross ton NYK motor-ships *Asama Maru*, *Tatsuta Maru* and *Chichibu Maru*, built for the San Francisco run, but never actually requisitioned by the Japanese Navy. A second group of three similar ships planned for the NYK's European service was cancelled in 1935 on economic grounds. With the expiry of the first London Naval Treaty on 31 December 1936, Japan moved into a treaty-free era and unwisely aggravated the political scene by both proliferating her rearmament scheme and by blatantly exposing its fundamental intentions, in an appendix to the Imperial Japanese Navy Fleet Register, for all the liners concerned were listed as reserve aircraft carriers.

From 1938 onwards, another five passenger vessels were built which were also intended for conversion to aircraft carriers. These were the NYK 17,000 gross ton motor-ships *Nitta Maru*, *Kasuga Maru* and *Yawata Maru*, which became the carriers *Chuyo*, *Taiyo* and *Unyo* respectively, and the smaller Osaka Shosen Kaisha motor-ships *Argentina Maru* and *Brazil Maru*. Of these, only the former was requisitioned to become the auxiliary carrier *Kaiyo*.

Meanwhile, the negotiations over the design and building costs of the two larger ships planned from 1936 proceeded rather discordantly, with neither the size, speed nor the question of cost-sharing being resolved. Eventually, however, agreement was reached on ships of 27,700 gross tons and 25 knots speed, with 60 per cent of the building costs being met by the Ministry of Trade. This amounted to 8.2 million yen over five years. The design of the two ships was to be

The original conception of the *Kashiwara Maru*, to which her final form bore not the slightest resemblance. *Nippon Yusen Kaisha*

shared between the Ministry of Trade, the Admiralty and the Central Planning Department of the Japanese Imperial Fleet.

The Nippon Yusen Kaisha gave the names *Kashiwara Maru* and *Izumo Maru* to the two liners that emerged from the final design. The former was ordered from Mitsubishi Heavy Industries at Nagasaki, and the latter from Kawasaki Heavy Industries at Kobe. Unlike the other new NYK liners, these two vessels were to be turbine steamers with a passenger capacity of 890 in three classes, divided 220 First, 120 Second and 550 Third. The *Kashiwara Maru* was laid down on 20 March 1939, but there was a delay on her sister-ship and work on her did not begin until 30 November of that year. On 10 February 1941 it was decided to take advantage of their suitability for conversion and they were purchased by the Imperial Japanese Navy while still on the stocks. Conversion to 'flat-tops' began immediately and the *Izumo Maru* soon reached a stage of construction as advanced as that of her sister.

Until after the Battle of Midway in July 1942, all the ex-merchant aircraft carriers were listed under their mercantile names although, certainly in the case of the two large liner conversions, this did not accurately reflect the situation. The *Izumo Maru* was launched under that name on 24 June 1941 and did not receive her naval name, *Hiyo*, until the date when she was commissioned on 31 July 1942. In contrast, the intended *Kashiwara Maru* was christened as the *Junyo* when she was launched two days after her sister. Nonetheless, she did not become a full naval vessel until 3 May 1942, the date of her commissioning.

The *Junyo* displaced 28,300 tons when fully loaded, the *Hiyo* somewhat less at 27,500 tons, and both had an overall length of 722ft with a beam measurement of 87ft 7in. Geared turbines, supplied by destroyer-type boilers producing 56,630shp and driving twin screws, gave them an operational speed of 24 knots. On trials, in May and August 1942, respectively, the *Junyo* achieved a maximum speed of 26 knots while the *Hiyo* managed 25.6 knots. Their aircraft capacity was forty-eight, with a reserve maximum of fifty-three aircraft, comprising a combination of torpedo and dive bombers.

In many respects the *Junyo* and her sister were test beds, for their design incorporated many features which were under trial for the later Japanese fleet aircraft carriers *Taiho* and *Shinano*.

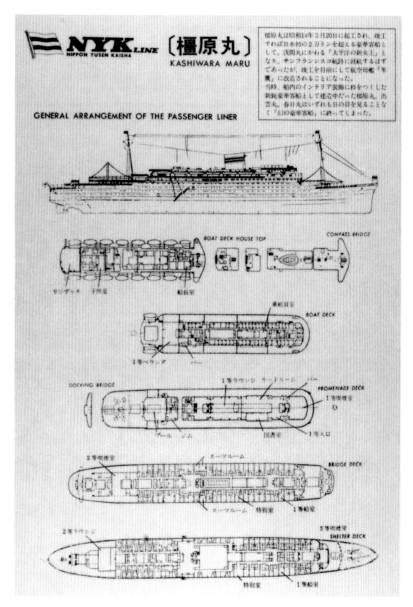

Side elevation drawing and partial deck plan of the *Kashiwara Maru*.
Nippon Yusen Kaisha

Publicity impressions of the interiors planned for the NYK sisters, the First-class Smoking Room … *Mitsubishi Heavy Industries*

… and their First-class Main Foyer and staircase. *Mitsubishi Heavy Industries*

No one seeing the *Kashiwara Maru* on the stocks, and observing her scantlings and the degree of her subdivision, would have supposed her to be a passenger liner. The top picture was taken on 31 January 1940 … *Mitsubishi Heavy Industries*

…and the lower one on 20 May 1940. *Mitsubishi Heavy Industries*

Notable amongst these was an island bridge superstructure situated on the starboard side and surmounted by a funnel which inclined outboard at 26°. The *Junyo* and *Hiyo* were the first Japanese carriers to be completed in this way. In addition, they were given light overall armour of two layers of 25mm (1in) Ducol steel, and the flammable supplies and munition storerooms were similarly protected. The 690 × 89ft flight-deck was constructed entirely of steel plate – a distinct improvement on the earlier wooden decks of Japanese aircraft carriers. Compared with normal passenger ships, the number of their watertight bulkheads was greatly increased, to such an extent that no one seeing their hulls under construction would have gained any impression that they were looking at passenger vessels. In fact, the conversion of the *Kashiwara Maru* and *Izumo Maru* was much more extensive than any of the other former passenger liners and, on its conclusion, they were more correctly rated as light fleet carriers. Only the *Aquila*, rebuilt from the Italia Line passenger liner *Roma* for the Italian Navy, underwent a more extensive conversion.

The *Junyo* and *Hiyo* differed in appearance considerably from other Japanese aircraft carriers, being shorter and higher out of the water than those ships that had been designed for the purpose from the start. They also lacked the characteristic lipped bow of other Japanese warships. Both vessels packed a fair amount into their short naval careers during which they engaged in some of the high-profile naval actions of the Pacific War. Aircraft ferrying, troop transportation and other reinforcement duties occupied them but torpedo and fire damage, as well as shortages to their air groups, rendered them inactive on several occasions.

The *Junyo*'s baptism of fire came, only a month after her completion, in the Aleutian Islands campaign, designated the MI/AL Operation. The Aleutians are a chain of volcanic islands owned by the United States which are strung out from Alaska to about 450 miles east of the Kamchatka Peninsula in Russian Asia. Partly as a diversionary tactic from the main Japanese offensive on Midway Island, the *Junyo* was sent, under the command of Rear-Admiral Kakuta, with the smaller *Ryujo* to attack Dutch Harbour and support the invasion and occupation of the islands of Kiska and Attu.

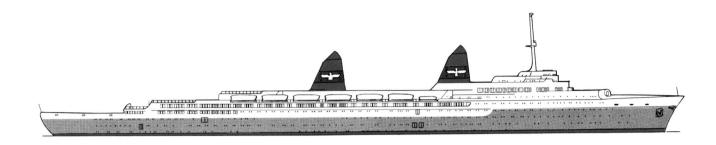

The P5-S2-E1 design, drawn in profile from U.S. Maritime Commission plans dated 21 May 1946. *David Hutchings*

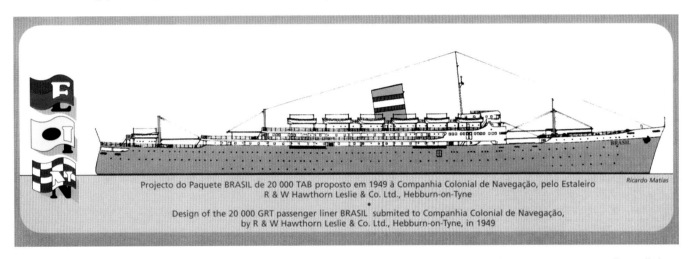

Projecto do Paquete BRASIL de 20 000 TAB proposto em 1949 à Companhia Colonial de Navegação, pelo Estaleiro R & W Hawthorn Leslie & Co. Ltd., Hebburn-on-Tyne

Design of the 20 000 GRT passenger liner BRASIL submitted to Companhia Colonial de Navegação, by R & W Hawthorn Leslie & Co. Ltd., Hebburn-on-Tyne, in 1949

Ricardo Matias

In 1949, R. & W. Hawthorn Leslie submitted its design proposal to Companhia Colonial de Navegacao, Portugal, for a 20,000grt passenger liner called the *Brasil*, seen here. From the actual blueprint its dimensions were: length overall 598ft; length bp 560ft; breadth moulded 72ft; depth to 'O' deck 38ft. In the event, the Company did not take up Hawthorn Leslie's proposal but instead went to Cockerill of Hoboken, Belgium, and the vessel that emerged, completed in 1952, was the 21,765grt *Vera Cruz*, followed by a sister, the *Santa Maria* in 1953. *Ricardo Graca Matias*

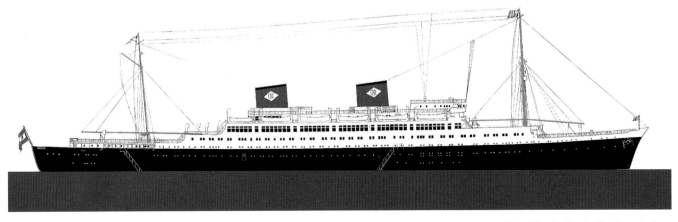

Measuring 21,500grt and 616ft in length the Empresa Nacional Elcano's type 'F' passenger liner concept was considered for the North Atlantic route in around 1945. Accommodation would have been provided for 434 passengers. *Navaera Elcano*

The original design for the twin vessels proposed for Nippon Yusen Kaisha through the 1950s into the 1960s. *David Hutchings*

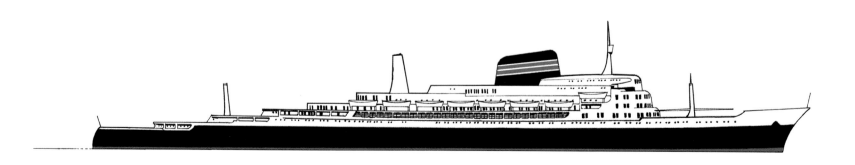

Reflecting significant activity in the Nippon Yusen Kaisha drawing office, the design for the two passenger liners was continually amended to 'keep up with the times'. Here, for comparison, are two of the modified designs, the first showing the substitution of a *Rotterdam*-like flue for a conventional funnel with a dummy structure ahead of it to balance the profile. In the second, the dummy funnel has been removed from an extended top structure and the open sides of the promenade deck have been enclosed. *Both David Hutchings*

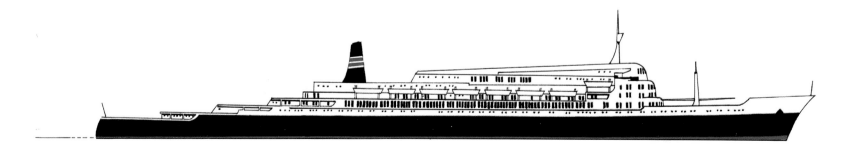

An exaggerated image of Hyman Cantor's Hotel Dixie super-liners *Peace* and *Goodwill* from a postcard promoting the '$50 to Europe' fare. All rooms were to be of the studio type, air-conditioned with twin beds, private shower and toilet, and TV, amenities that were not available on the Atlantic run until the advent of the *France* in 1962. The card implored recipients to lobby their Congressmen and Senators to approve the Bill for the ships' construction. *Authors' collection*

An alternative interpretation of the Detwiler 'United Nations'-class ships, revealing twin athwartships signal masts and the funnel located further forward than on the engines-aft variant (see page 182). As stated already regarding Norddeutscher Lloyd's *Amerika/Viktoria*, the *United Nations* was another example of a ship whose well-conceived design did not convey the full immensity of its scale. This splendid, never-before-seen painting was inspired by an impression of these ships which appeared in a colour magazine from the late 1950s. *Tony Westmore*

Artist's impression of the design for the replacements to Achille Lauro's emigrant carriers *Roma* and *Sydney*. *David Hutchings*

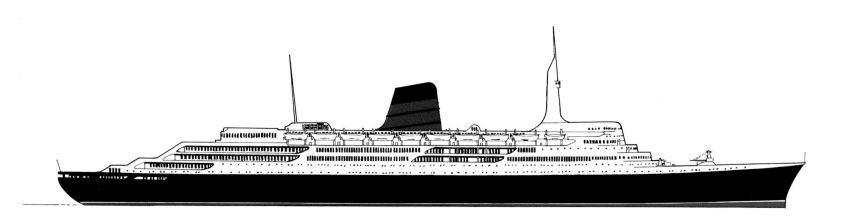

Profile of Cunard's ill-fated Q3, based on drawings dated 30 March 1961 when the funnel design was yet to be finalised. This rendering, visualised by the authors, is thought to show the most likely configuration based on contemporary styling. *David Hutchings*

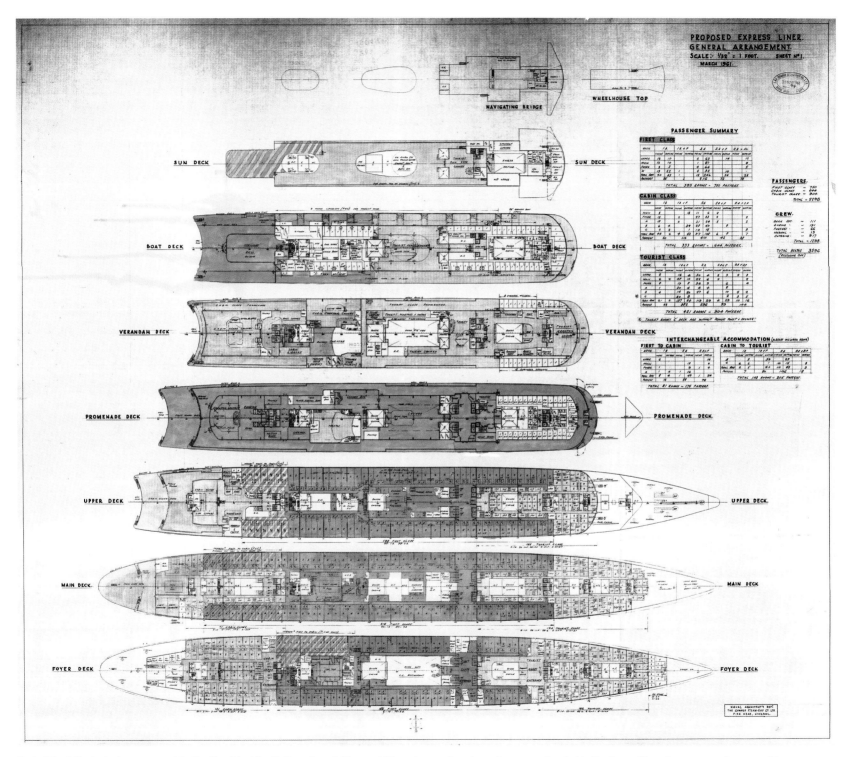

Part of the Q3's deck plans prepared by the Naval Architect's Department, Liverpool. The colour-coding shows the areas allocated to the three different passenger classes: red for First-class, blue for Cabin-class and green for Tourist-class. Some of the cabin spaces were cross-hatched in two colours to indicate they were interchangeable. *Michael Gallagher*

A striking impression of an imaginary departure from New York by the Q3. Had she been built, would the Q3 have received the name *Queen Victoria* as many commentators from the time had expected? *Mervyn Pearson*

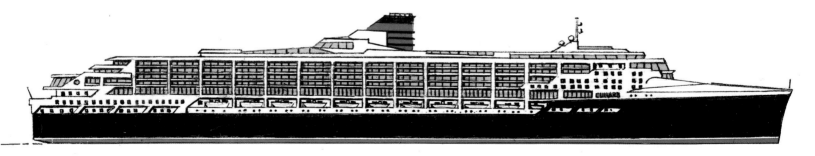

A side view of a variant of Cunard's Q5 with a single funnel. Though, perhaps, less graceful in appearance than the earlier *Queen*s, this configuration generally looked better than the two- and three-funnel options that were also considered. *David Hutchings*

CRUISE SHIP OF THE FUTURE ?

A coloured impression of *Wärtsilä*'s SWATH Cruiser from a trade magazine advert. *Authors' collection*

The cruise ship with everything but an 18 hole golf course.

M eet the cruise ship of the future — MACS, short for Multi Activity Cruise Ship. Developed by NKK and IKO Maritime A/S, is like a full-fledged floating resort, incorporating a host of leisure and entertainment facilities to make getting there more than half the fun — Just what passengers of the future will demand. One of the key features of MACS is a 54-meter beam, which improves sea friendliness and makes it possible for each of the 1,000 cabins to have either an ocean or garden view, with natural lighting. Another feature is the twin skeg aft hull shape, which not only improves propulsion efficiency but also provides an inside harbor complete with stern gate. This inside harbor, together with a floating pier, allows all types of water sports — windsurfing, sailing, water skiing, diving, the works. MACS, the cruise ship of the future, from NKK. Suddenly, the excitement is back in ocean voyaging.

Another magazine advert extolling the virtues of the Nippon Kokan MACS 3000 cruise ship and demonstrating that it was targeted at the millennium and beyond. *Authors' collection*

The *Hiyo* ex-*Izumo Maru* as completed. *Fujifotos*

The task force arrived off Dutch Harbour on the morning of 4 June 1942, but its impact as a decoy group was minimal. If the whole operation was not entirely a tactical blunder, given that the main objective of taking the two Aleutian Islands was achieved, nonetheless it had a disastrously unfortunate result in that it provided the Americans with the means to establish eventual air superiority over the Japanese. Of the few planes to attack shore installations – most turned back because of the extremely adverse weather conditions – was one Zeke (Zero) fighter which was critically damaged and forced to crash land at the eastern end of Unalaska Island. Subsequently discovered relatively intact, and put through exhaustive test flights, it provided the vital information regarding the few design weaknesses of this superb plane which, at that time, outmatched every comparable Allied machine. For the *Junyo*, the initial operation ended on 24 June but she was then assigned to a back-up reinforcement mission from 28 June through to 7 July 1942.

After this sortie, on 31 July 1942, the *Junyo* was effectively joined by the *Hiyo*, and together they formed the Second Aircraft Carrier Division, part of Vice-Admiral Nobutake Kondo's newly created Vanguard Force. They engaged actively in the Battle of the Santa

Cruz Islands from 11 to 27 October of that year and it was during this action, on 21 October 1942, that an outbreak of fire in the *Hiyo*'s starboard generator room caused extensive damage and forced her rather ignominious withdrawal from the engagement. She limped away to Truk for emergency repairs and subsequently underwent full repairs at Kure which lasted from 11 to 29 December. Meanwhile, the *Junyo* distinguished herself by the part she played in the battle. Her planes made a significant contribution by attacking Henderson Field on Guadalcanal and in providing fighter protection to the surface ships. They attacked the American carrier USS *Enterprise*, though without inflicting damage, and dealt the death blow to another *Yorktown*-class vessel, the USS *Hornet* which had to be finished off by American destroyers to ensure she could not be captured by enemy forces.

A variety of missions followed for the *Junyo*, during the period from November 1942 through to April 1943. She was used for reinforcement runs, also to provide air cover for transportation convoys. In May 1943 she was rejoined by the *Hiyo* and they were assigned to Operation Kita-Go later that month, escorting battleships returning to Japan from Singapore, only to be stood down when it was cancelled.

A month later on 10 June 1943, the *Hiyo* fell foul of a torpedo attack from the United States submarine *Trigger* when she was 17 miles from Miyake Island, en route from Yokosuka to Truk. Struck by two torpedoes, one in the bow, the other in way of No.1 boiler room, she was left dead in the water, settling by the bow. Although water began entering her lower hangar deck she was kept afloat by determined damage control. Able to make way at a very slow 6 knots and fortunate that the submarine did not press home the attack, she was able to make her way to Tateyama, escorted by two destroyers and the light cruiser *Isuzu*. Eventually able to reach Yokosuka, the ensuing repairs took from 12 June to 15 September.

Once more operating alone, the *Junyo* continued with aircraft ferrying duties and made a long voyage with the *Ryuho* from Saeki to Singapore from August to September 1943, calling at Manila, Palau and Tarakan. This was followed by a series of troop transport missions – the TEI Operations – between Iwakuni and Truk that lasted to the end of October. On 5 November 1943, it was her turn to be hit by a torpedo fired by the USS *Halibut* while she was on passage through

Testing of the *Hiyo*'s fire-fighting sprays on her flight deck while at Yokosuka on 7 October 1943 following lengthy repairs after she sustained torpedo damage on 10 June that year. *Imperial Japanese Navy*

the Bungo Suido (the channel between Shikoku and Honshu). The torpedo destroyed her steering gear and left her with a jammed rudder. She began to flood, settling by the stern with a slight list, but again the valiant efforts of her crew saved her and she was towed into Kure by the heavy cruiser *Tone*. During the repairs it was decided to give her a full refit which culminated in equipment trials and, as a consequence, she was out of action through to 29 February 1944.

By June 1944 the two vessels were back in action in the Battle of the Philippine Sea, the Operation A-Go, and, together with the *Ryuho*, they formed the Japanese Aircraft Carrier Force B under Rear-Admiral Takaji Joshima, this being a unit of Vice-Admiral Jisaburo Ozawa's First Task Fleet.

Late in the afternoon of 20 June, when north-west of Luzon, Force B was attacked by American dive- and torpedo-bombers from the aircraft carrier USS *Bellau Wood*. The *Hiyo* was hit by bombs on the top of her bridge and on the flight deck. Almost all of the bridge personnel were killed. In the next wave, the attacking aircraft struck her with a torpedo in way of her starboard engine room causing severe damage, notably to her fuel tanks which had sustained critical fractures. Two hours after the attack, already dead in the water and listing to starboard, she was wracked by a massive explosion when the vapour from the leaking tanks was ignited. She was promptly engulfed by uncontrollable fires, rolled over and sank approximately 300 miles west of Saipan.

The same day the *Junyo* also sustained damage when she was hit by two bombs which exploded alongside her funnel. Her funnel was completely shattered and fell into the sea, her signal mast was destroyed and fires broke out in her island structure. Further near misses buckled her flight deck and caused the steering room to flood. Despite this, she was able to continue to operate, although air operations were temporarily suspended. Ordered to retire with other units of the fleet to Nakagusuku Bay, Okinawa, she eventually managed to escape to Japan where she underwent repairs and a refit at Kure which lasted until 14 July 1944.

After completing her repairs, the *Junyo* was restricted to training and transport duties in connection with the continuing operations around the Philippines. On one voyage, while thus employed, she carried 18-inch shells for the super-battleship *Yamato*; on another she returned with 200 survivors after the sinking of the *Musashi*, the *Yamato*'s sister-ship. The *Junyo* was torpedoed for a second time on 9 December 1944 while off Cape Nomo-zaki, south of Nagasaki, by the United States submarines *Redfish*, *Plaice* and *Sea Devil*, although which of them actually hit the carrier is uncertain. One torpedo hit her starboard engine room; another clipped her stem, breaching the bow plates, leading to extensive flooding and causing her to list heavily to starboard. Despite the fact that the ingress of water increased her draught to over 33ft she was still able to make 13 knots on a straight course. Fortunately, the central bulkhead dividing her two engine rooms held and, as her aviation fuel tanks were empty, there were no explosions or fire as had afflicted the *Hiyo*. By manoeuvring her into shoal waters, which the attacking

Poor, but rare, views of the *Hiyo* in action during the Battle of the Philippine Sea from a section of newsreel film. Attacked by US warplanes, she blew up and sank shortly after this footage was taken. *Pathé*

The *Junyo* ex-*Kashiwara Maru* laid up at Sasebo on 26 September 1945, as she was found by the American occupation forces. The squared-off darker area of hull colouring was intentional, as part of a Japanese Navy camouflage scheme. U.S. National Archives

submarines could not safely enter, she was spared further assault, sheltering there until the menace had passed. She then made her way to Sasebo for patching-up, where she arrived under escort of the battle-cruiser *Haruna*, but, due to the protracted nature of the repairs, she saw no further active service.

The *Junyo* sustained further slight damage when hit by bombs on 20 January 1945 while in dry-dock but this had little impact on her restoration because the repairs were abandoned incomplete that March due to a lack of materials. From 24 April she was relegated to reserve status and anchored at Ebisu Wan where she remained until the Japanese surrender. During this same time she was camouflaged, the work continuing into June. On 20 June she was declassified as a guard ship but barely two months later, on 5 August, she was stripped of all armament and other equipment and was left little more than a hulk. She was eventually found in this condition by the Allied occupation forces on 2 September. An inspection conducted by U.S. Navy technical officers on

8 October 1945 revealed that she was unfit for reconstruction and was not even fit for temporary deployment, like other captured carriers, on repatriation duties returning Japanese troops from Indo-China under the supervision of the Americans. Instead she was condemned to breaking up on 28 May 1946, the work being completed by 1 August 1947, a short life indeed for what was such a promising vessel at the outset.

During the war, it was reported that the *Junyo* (meaning 'falcon') and *Hiyo* ('flying hawk') were also known by the names *Hayataka* ('fast or swift bird') and *Hitaka* ('flying or soaring bird'), respectively. In fact, for a while, they were identified as being four different ships. It appears that the words *Hayataka* and *Hitaka* are, in fact, alternatives for the more familiar names *Junyo* and *Hiyo* according to the complexities and potential ambiguities of the Japanese language. It can be said with certainty that four separate aircraft carriers with these names never existed, but there is ample evidence that the U.S. Naval records, together with Lloyds Casualty Reports, and other sources of the same calibre, were still confused up to and after 1959. There were other Japanese carriers besides the *Junyo* and *Hiyo* which were subject to this incorrect identification, among them being the three that were re-built from the small NYK motor-ships *Nitta Maru*, *Kasuga Maru* and *Yawata Maru*. Although officially renamed *Chuyo*, *Taiyo* and *Unyo*, they were also identified as *Okitaka*, *Otaka* and *Kumotaka*, respectively. It was all rather confusing.

An interesting postcript to the story of the *Kashiwara Maru* and *Izumo Maru* concerns the only remaining relic of these vessels, of which few people are aware. This is the *Junyo*'s 18in ship's bell which was presented as a war-prize to Fordham College, New York. The bell was sent to Fordham by Admiral Chester Nimitz in answer to a request for a trophy, which could be retained as a memorial to the Fordham students killed during the war. Flown from Japan to Pearl

A view from water level of the *Junyo*'s starboard side, showing her inclined funnel. Note the submarine alongside her hull. *U.S. National Archives*

Looking aft and down on to the *Junyo*'s flight deck after the Japanese surrender, with American officers surveying the carrier. Note the positions of the (removed) deck-edge guns. *U.S. National Archives*

Conceived as the passenger liner *Kashiwara Maru*, the ship lived a violent life as the aircraft carrier *Junyo*, and was survived only by her bell in an American University – thus did Destiny cast her dice. Here, far removed from the war zones of the Aleutians, New Guinea, the Solomons and the Philippine Sea, Harry S. Truman tolls her bell for the first time in its new site at Fordham University for its charter centenary on 11 May 1946. Admiral E. King, the President's naval aide, stands beside him. *Fordham University Library*

Harbour, the bell was collected there by the light cruiser *Detroit* and transported to Philadelphia. It was finally dedicated at Fordham in December 1945, tolled for the first time by President Harry S. Truman, and it remains there to this day. According to the Rev. Edward S. Dunn of the University Library, speaking back in the early 1980s, the bell is tolled on all festive occasions, but its primary function is to signal the start of Fordham's annual Academic Procession of Graduation!

Had the Second World War not intervened and had these two ships been completed as intended, there is no doubt that these they would have been a great credit to the Japanese Mercantile Marine. As events proved, they joined the ranks of those vessels denied entry into the service for which they had been intended. However, unlike the majority of the big ships which are included in this unhappy roster, they crowded a great deal into their relatively short lives, contributing to the history of sea warfare, seeing a variety of action by no means unmixed with success, and suffering damage, only to come back and fight another day until their respective fates were finally sealed. Taking account of their actual sea time, few passenger liners can have had so concentrated an experience of excitement and action in so short a time – whatever the roles in which they found themselves cast.

THE U.S. MARITIME COMMISSION'S P-4-P DESIGN – ANOTHER FALSE START!

Almost concurrently, and in reply to the design and construction of the *Kashiwara Maru* and *Izumo Maru*, the newly formed American President Lines (APL) planned competitors for these rumoured Japanese vessels. A report in the *New York Times* of 28 April 1939 stated that three sister-ships to the *President Coolidge* were envisaged, but this plan was dropped following a close inspection of this vessel and her turbo-electric machinery by Commander (later Admiral) H.L. Vickery, Director of the Technical Division of the United States Maritime Commission. This government organisation then submitted its own alternative proposal for the American President Lines' Pacific route.

Under the Merchant Marine Act of 1936, the United States Maritime Commission (USMC) was established in June 1936 as a replacement for the U.S. Shipping Board. Its primary function was to launch a massive long-range shipbuilding programme for the revitalisation of the U.S. Merchant Marine. Commenced in 1937, the initial target of this programme was to produce 500 new ships at the rate of 50 vessels annually. To this end, the Maritime Commission had not wasted any time in producing its designs for standard ship types to replace the many ageing units in the American merchant fleet. These designs were

The *President Coolidge* in Dollar Line colours.
A. Palmer

Sister-ship of the *President Coolidge*, the
President Hoover photographed at Shanghai
in August 1931 during her inaugural call after
completing her maiden transpacific voyage.
Collection of Lieut. Oscar W. Levy, USN Retd

A model of the P-4-P design, revealing the similarities to the *Flying Cloud* concept. The illustration first appeared in the *Pacific Marine Review* of October 1940. *Mariners Museum*

classified with a letter and number code which indicated the type of ship, length of hull, engine type, number of propellers, etc. which were referred to by a comprehensive nomenclature.

The letters C and T referred to cargo ships and tankers respectively and, just as predictably, P was used to indicate passenger vessels. Although she was created by William Francis Gibbs before the inception of the Maritime Commission, the United States Line's *America* was given a P4-S2 designation, the number 4 indicating a length between 700 and 800ft – in her case 723ft overall – the S2 revealing that she was a twin-screw steamship.

Early in 1939, a further P4 design, that for the transpacific passenger liners, appeared on the Commission's drawing boards. Known as the P-4-P or P4P (the last P possibly referring to Pacific), this design was in many ways a resurrection of the *Flying Cloud* passenger liner/aircraft carrier intended for transatlantic service, although somewhat smaller. The vessels' dimensions would have been 35,500 gross tons with an overall length of 759ft and a beam of 98ft. Draught would have been 32ft and her displacement approximately 41,000 tons.

This early Maritime Commission design was distinctive – even revolutionary – in its approach to the hull specification, which featured a combination of high strength and low weight. This was to be achieved in a number of ways. It was intended to weld the hulls of the P-4-P ships wherever possible, while they had also been designed in such a way as to obviate the necessity for expansion joints. Further weight reductions would have been achieved through the layout and design of the propulsion machinery. Additionally, the P-4-P ships would have had no fresh water tanks – the proposed installation of a large evaporating plant making this unnecessary. As a result of this and of the increased efficiency of the main propelling plant, it was stated that in this particular design it would be possible to make a complete voyage without utilising ballast tanks.

For protection in the event of collision, the ships were to be given subdivision of an extraordinarily high standard, perhaps reflecting national defence needs. The hull was to contain fourteen main watertight transverse bulkheads with numerous other additional watertight and oil-tight barriers. Apart from the safety features incorporated in the hull structure, the P-4-P design was also noteworthy for the elaborate security arrangements for the prevention of fire. A highly efficient fire detection system was to be installed in each ship and incombustible materials were specified for all bulkheads, deckheads, linings and partitions.

Regarding the propulsion machinery, there were to be two triple-expansion steam turbines, each driving its own propeller through double reduction gears from an entirely independent engine room. The machinery in the forward engine room would have driven the port propeller, while that in the aft engine room would have driven the starboard one. The two turbines would have operated on a re-heat regenerative cycle producing a total normal output of 58,000 shaft horsepower and a maximum total output of 88,000 shaft horsepower. This would have sustained a sea-speed of 25 knots.

Accommodation would have been provided for between 800 and 1,000 passengers in three classes, with a crew of

500. An ultra-modern air-conditioning installation was proposed, supplying every cabin and stateroom with heating in the winter and with cooling and dehumidification in the summer. All lighting aboard the ships would have been of the fluorescent type, which would have saved generator capacity – an additional weight reduction – while it was also regarded as lending itself more readily to artistic innovation in lighting effects. Passenger liners on the Orient routes were noted for their high standards of comfort and roominess, passenger complements invariably being lower than those aboard ships of equivalent size on the Atlantic run. The P-4-P vessels would have been no exception to this rule, with more than adequate provision of all the usual passenger amenities.

The planned decoration for the lounges, dining rooms and other public centres were distinguished by the use of light, relaxing pastel shades. Separate swimming pools were to be provided for each of the Cabin-, Tourist- and Third-class passengers, while the games and promenade deck spaces were to be unusually large and unobstructed in consequence of the auxiliary (wartime) features of the P-4-P design.

The cargo space for each ship was to be 535,000 cu ft, of which some 7 per cent would have been refrigerated. Large holds were to be fitted forward and aft, with ample facilities for handling cargo through conventional hatches, as well as through side ports. Special provision was also made for the carriage of a number of automobiles in an enclosed space at the forward end of the promenade deck.

The P-4-Ps were specifically designed as passenger ships suitable for rapid modification into aircraft carriers in times of national emergency. Like the *Flying Cloud*, their twin funnels would have been situated to one side of the upper deck, but it was not planned to fit a permanent flightdeck aboard these ships, as would have been the case with the earlier design, since there was no aeroplane-carrying application intended for them during their commercial service. In fact, apart from the offset funnels, the auxiliary characteristics of the ships would not have been readily apparent. This approach had the benefit of providing promenade, boat and sun decks in the superstructure for increased passenger space, in addition to the four decks in the hull proper. In comparing the P-4-P conception with the *Flying Cloud*, the emphasis had been switched from adaptability to convertibility, the

former being primarily a passenger liner, while the latter had been first and foremost an auxiliary aircraft carrier.

Nevertheless, since the successful utilisation of the P-4-P's auxiliary capability depended on a fast and economic conversion, this was to be made possible through the incorporation of special features in the design and construction stages. Beneath the light superstructure, which was to be fitted as a pre-fabricated unit, and therefore readily removable, the main deck was to be strengthened in readiness for the construction of a flight deck. All decks were to be flush throughout the ships in order to facilitate the installation of hangars, workshops and stores for armaments and aircraft spares and, in addition, the passenger accommodation was to be laid out in such a way that it would suit adaptation to officers' and crews' quarters during military employment.

The Maritime Commission's comprehensive design plans were disclosed to naval architects and marine engineers in New York in January 1940 for their consideration. They were received with enthusiastic approval and W.F. Gibbs was among the many famous names who endorsed them. At the same time, details were released about the Commission's proposed construction programme for the P-4-P liners and it was announced that, initially, there would only be two such vessels, and not three as originally intended. These two would be built (it was thought) on the east coast for the Commission's own account and chartered by them to the American President Lines for service on the California–Orient route (San Francisco–Los Angeles–Yokohama–Kobe–Shanghai–Manila), with calls at Hawaii both ways. The ships were to be ready for service in 1943. Furthermore, it was stated that additional vessels of the P-4-P type would be built later for the San Francisco–Australasian run.

A slight interruption, which threatened to endanger the P-4-P's prospects, occurred in February 1940 when the House of Representatives substantially reduced the amount of money in the Ship Construction Appropriations Bill. Subsequently, the Senate Appropriations Committee reviewed the pruned bill and favoured the restoration of an amount equal to the original appropriation, which would be specifically earmarked for the liners destined for the Pacific trade. These wishes were endorsed by the rest of Congress, and it was now expected that tenders would be invited for the construction of the two liners.

There was, however, a further delay in May 1940 when the Maritime Commission postponed the opening of tendering until 18 June to permit shipbuilders further opportunity to study the design specifications. The *New York Times* had reported that at least one interested party had expressed anxiety about the strength of the hull, considering that, in view of the horsepower and speed requirements, the hull structure was too light in weight. In spite of the apparent disquiet on this score, no alterations were made to the P-4-P hull details and, perhaps significantly, only one tender for construction was received.

This came from the Seattle-Tacoma Shipbuilding Corporation of Seattle, Washington, on the west coast, there being no interest expressed from the east coast. On 10 September 1940 it offered to build the two vessels for $28,458,000 (approximately £7,115,000) per ship on a fixed price contract, or $23,715,000 (approximately £6,000,000) on an adjusted price basis, the delivery of the first one to be late in 1943 and the second in the summer of 1944. In spite of this, the two liners were never built.

The press blamed the shipyards, alleging that they were not interested in building Maritime Commission designs, completely disregarding the fact that Seattle-Tacoma had made a bid, if a lone one. As for the Commission itself, they made no apparent response to the single tender they did receive, though whether they regarded the price as being too high or had some other reason was never disclosed. Whatever the cause, the projected P-4-Ps were dropped in August 1941, in order that all shipyards could concentrate their efforts totally on designs specifically required to prepare the country to be on a proper war footing. These included P2-type transports, later adapted for civilian work, and the highly successful *Essex*-class of fast attack carriers.

After the war, the American President Lines proceeded to pursue other new building policies and, throughout the subsequent fifteen years, were involved in a number of ambitious and exciting projects.

LAURO'S *ROMA* AND *SYDNEY* REPLACEMENTS

While it is true to say that few of the passenger liner projects chronicled in this book were designed for other routes than the North Atlantic, this was simply because the most luxurious and ambitious ocean transport was synonymous with the world's most illustrious sea route. But as aeroplane traffic between America and Europe increased following the Second World War and the sea traffic reciprocally declined, attention was focused briefly on other sea passages on which some shipping companies still saw a future in the large ocean passenger carrier. That is not to say that the plans for ships designed to serve on other routes than the North Atlantic were any less progressive, resolute or consequential, a consideration that equally applies later to the unfulfilled cruise ship projects that were conceived following the end of the passenger liner era. Like the earlier *Jason*, the ships whose brief proposition is described in this chapter were intended to operate in the Australia trade, albeit primarily as emigrant carriers.

In 1962, the Italian company, Flotte Lauro of Naples, established in 1923, was seeking replacements for the old *Roma* and *Sydney*, two former wartime escort carriers completed from what were originally standardised cargo ship hulls. Following reconstruction, the pair worked various emigrant routes including to Canada and South America but by the mid 1950s they were more or less permanently operating between Genoa and Sydney. Much of their Tourist-class accommodation was relatively basic and, to meet the more discerning expectations of a later generation of emigrant passengers as well as to increase passenger capacity overall, new larger ships were contemplated and subsequently ordered.

Details of the ships are, unfortunately, rather scarce, but two vessels of approximately 30,000 gross tons were contracted from Ansaldo's Leghorn (Livorno) shipyard on 27 February 1962 and given the Yard Nos 1604 and 1605, the former to the account of Egeria Società di Navigazione, the latter to Achille Lauro, both Flotte Lauro companies. Despite having disparate ownership, they would have maintained the same joint service as the earlier pair. Each of the liners was to

The Lloyd Triestino liner *Galileo Galilei*, seen here, was completed in 1963 with her sister-ship *Guglielmo Marconi* by Cantieri Riuniti dell'Adriatico for the Genoa to Sydney service. Though slightly larger, it is thought that the twin *Achille Lauro* ships planned as replacements for the *Roma* and *Sydney* would have had a broadly similar appearance to these ships which exemplified Italian liner styling in that period. *Lloyd Triestino*

Flotte Lauro terminated its pursuit of new ships for the Australian emigrant run by acquiring and converting two former Dutch liners. The *Willem Ruys*, seen here ... *Ray Sprake*

... became the *Achille Lauro. Frank Heine*

be a twin-screw turbine vessel with a service speed of 27 knots and able to carry approximately 1,700 passengers, 1,000 more than the complements of the older ships they were to replace. Flotte Lauro hoped to have these new liners in service by 1965 and 1966 and in all probability, following the then current trend of Italian design, they would have looked somewhat similar to the contemporary *Leonardo da Vinci* or the *Guglielmo Marconi* and *Galileo Galilei* which also operated the Australian emigrant service.

Financing of the two ships was arranged through the Istituto Mobiliare Italiano (IMI), a public financial institution first set up in 1931 with powers to intervene with assistance to companies having sustainable economic positions by granting medium-term loans through its Autonomous Shipping Loans Department, an agency jointly created with a pool of Italian banks. However, during 1963, after construction on yard numbers 1604 and 1605 had begun, the IMI failed to pay the first installment towards their cost as had been agreed in the build contract. Arising from the default, Ansaldo immediately suspended work on the ships and then, in 1964, cancelled the orders altogether. This was an interesting situation that differs completely from other cancelled projects related in these pages in that it was not the intended owner that ended the project by revoking the contract, but the builders. A court action was launched against Ansaldo by Flotte Lauro which was concluded in 1966, though whether or not this favoured the plaintiff is not known, besides which by that time Ansaldo no longer existed as an autonomous company, having been merged with Navalmeccanica SpA and Cantieri Riuniti dell'Adriatico to form Fincantieri.

Very little work had been done on the two ships by the date of the cancellation and, as the litigation process was unfolding, it had become increasingly apparent to Flotte Lauro that the cost of building new ships was considerably greater than that of converting and streamlining two existing ones. So, when a British shipbroker alerted Flotte Lauro that two Dutch liners, *Willem Ruys* and *Oranje*, had come on to the market at a very good price – they were due for disposal due to poor results from their round-the-world service, Lauro elected to buy them, rather than pursuing the commencement of construction on the new vessels. Thus, the *Willem Ruys* and *Oranje*

were rebuilt into the *Achille Lauro* and *Angelina Lauro*, respectively. In the event, it turned out to be a particularly astute economic decision by Lauro because the combined total purchase price of the two second-hand vessels plus their associated reconstruction costs came to less than half of what it would have had to pay for the two new-builds.

This was a relatively minor episode in the continuing saga of thwarted schemes, if only for its brief duration – though not necessarily for its intended route, as pointed out above – for which, in part, the overriding reason for its failure was simply that it was a sign of the times: the decline of the traditional ocean liner trades and the need to contain costs, especially where state financial backing was either unavailable or unreliable.

By the mid 1960s, the times were hard where the passenger liner was concerned, and getting harder. The evolution of transport from one country to another, involving the crossing of seas or oceans, has occasionally been accelerated by some fundamental change as, for instance, when steam superceded sail. Yet the sailing ship was a long time in ebbing away and, for a long time, was able to compete with steam while running in parallel and on equal terms, until it was gradually forced into trades which were uneconomic for the supplanting screw-driven vessel. The ocean passenger liner expired much more quickly before the modern, highly developed aeroplane and, being so specialised in its form, it had virtually nowhere else to turn. A buoyant future era in which large passenger vessels would once again be sustainable in the form of dedicated cruise ships would then have seemed nothing more than an improbable dream, beyond the most imaginative contemplation of all but a very few. Incredibly, James L. Bates, the Director of the USMC Technical Division, had been gifted with extraordinary foresight when, as early as 1944, he said:

During the half dozen years immediately succeeding the present conflict, all facilities for passenger transport, whether air, water or land, will be utilised to capacity. Later, air travel should attract more and more of the available First-class passengers, principally because of its superior speed which is a permanent and compelling advantage over other

Meanwhile the *Oranje* … *Authors' collection*

… was modified to become the *Angelina Lauro*.
Skyfotos

forms of passenger transport. Ultimately, it is believed that the water transport of passengers will be so decreased as to become rather a minor factor outside of the cruise for relaxation and recreation.

The fact is that changes never take place overnight, but the death of the passenger liner in the true sense of the word – as a vessel which plies on a regular schedule – nonetheless occurred in a remarkably short span of maritime chronology, and the Italian decision even to convert two existing vessels, rather than to build from scratch, was to some extent a bold gesture in the very shadow of death. It is true though that, at that time, they held the emigrant contract and, in this sense, enjoyed the patronage of the Australian Government, besides which this had turned out to be a prudent solution to its immediate need.

Apart from those relatively few ultra-prestigious vessels that enjoyed government patronage and subsidy, the so-called 'liners of state', the *raison d'etre* of shipowning was, and still is, to earn profit, even if this so often takes a low priority in shipping company histories. By the 1960s, with the ever-spiralling costs of construction and the increasing cost of money as interest rates increased, quite apart from higher wage bills and so much else, and with flying machines, for all their drawbacks, having caught the public imagination, it is small wonder that Nos 1604 and 1605 never advanced far beyond their keel plates in the Livorno yard.

NIPPON YUSEN KAISHA'S PROJECTED LINERS OF THE 1950S

Sometimes it is difficult to pinpoint precisely when a scheme started, but it can be said that a very ambitious project in Japan realistically originated in November 1953, when the urgent need for two large Pacific passenger liners was stressed in a plan entitled '*The Establishment and Promotion of the Tourist Industry Council and its Execution*', which was presented to the Prime Minister by the Tourist Industry Council for the Cabinet.

More or less concurrently, the Nippon Yusen Kaisha were considering a construction programme within the context of reviving its passenger shipping trade following the losses suffered in the Second World War, which had left it with the small *Hikawa Maru* alone. Although it had not yet invited any tenders for the envisaged liners, the company went to great lengths in planning their interiors and developing their external appearance in keeping with the ever-changing fashions, in readiness for the moment when it would be possible to start building them. However, since the implications of financing large new liners would have been extremely difficult for a single private enterprise in the severely depressed Japan of the 1950s, particularly after the discontinuance of the war indemnity for high-cost reconstruction projects, the company lent its weight to the arguments of the Tourist Industry Council in urging that the realisation of the ships should be regarded as a national undertaking.

Even more pressure for action on these Pacific ocean-going liners came in January 1956, when the Liberal Democratic Party's Special Committee for the Tourist Industry held a conference on '*Basic Elements Concerning the Promotion and Planning of the Tourist Industry*'. The result of this was that, in August of that year, the Japanese Cabinet issued a statement in which it supported the concept of the building of the passenger liners but, as it turned out, these were but empty words and no action eventuated from them.

The Nippon Yusen Kaisha had figured in the centre of this drive for new Japanese passenger tonnage from the very beginning and, sensing that success was, perhaps, now not too far away, it organised internal company changes in preparation for ordering the ships. In February 1959, it set up the Passenger Ship Arrangements Chamber and in that August formed the Passenger Ship Planning Section. These departments immediately set to work on the final design of the proposed liners and, in due course, they released a specification for them as well as an artist's impression which depicted a sleek and handsome single-funnelled vessel. With a gross tonnage of 33,400, the other principal statistics were a length of 689ft (thought to be the between perpendiculars measurement), a beam of 92ft and a draught of 30ft. Geared turbines driving twin screws would have given them a service speed of 24.5 knots. The passenger capacity was for 1,200 persons, divided between 200 First-class and 1,000 Tourist-class.

A spirited artist's impression of one of the twin NYK liners as originally conceived. Had they been built, these vessels would have exceeded the size of the *Izumo Maru* and *Kashiwara Maru* as the largest ocean liners under the Japanese flag. *Nippon Yusen Kaisha*

While 1959 was a very busy year within the Nippon Yusen Kaisha, it was also a significant one in the campaign to persuade the Japanese Government to approve the construction of the ships and to make adequate financial appropriations for them. Six years had already passed with no outcome, and the fact that the Olympic Games were scheduled to be held in Tokyo in October 1964 made it imperative to progress matters with greater urgency. It was obviously important to place the liners in commission in time for this event and, to this end, the completion target date for the first vessel was set at July 1963, and a year later for the second. The implication of the Olympics brings to mind the previous project involving the *Kashiwara Maru* and *Izumo Maru*, which had also been planned with that event in mind.

In the meantime, pressure for action was mounting from all quarters, with deputations from the Japan Shipowners Association in May 1959, the Yokohama Municipal Assembly that June, and even from branches of the Japanese Chamber of Commerce in both Honolulu and Los Angeles.

Finally, influenced by such an overwhelming weight of both public and professional opinion, a close examination of the ships' design and operating potential was carried out by the Ministry of Transportation. As a result, they were able to recommend that the budget for the fiscal year 1959–60 should include provision for a two-ship programme of the type proposed by the Nippon Yusen Kaisha. The budgetary allocation requested amounted to 2,375 million yen, (£2,339,901) which covered direct expenditure, treasury loans and indirect investments.

Artist's impressions were released of some of the interiors of the planned NYK twins. This is one of the passenger lounges. *Nippon Yusen Kaisha*

A twin-bedded cabin suite. *Nippon Yusen Kaisha*

The lido area and swimming pool. *Nippon Yusen Kaisha*

The ship's show lounge or theatre. *Nippon Yusen Kaisha*

During all the debate and procrastination, the new NYK liners ... *Nippon Yusen Kaisha*

Nevertheless, the construction of the new Nippon Yusen Kaisha liners was not achieved, in spite of this government involvement and endorsement. No money for the ships was included in the budget for 1959–60, and it was not until 1962–63 that an appropriation of any sort was made for passenger liner projects of any kind, and then it amounted to a mere 15 million yen (£14,749) for investigating the expense of passenger ship reconstruction.

The officials of the Nippon Yusen Kaisha felt that the patriotic resolve for national reconstruction had been abandoned in this instance but, as the company required such ships for its own purposes in order to restore its long-interrupted passenger services, it considered other ways and means of raising the funds required. These included Public Holding Corporation and Joint-Stock Corporation financing systems, but none achieved the desired results. The Japanese Government, for its part, explained that there was a need for an overall strengthening of maritime traffic in all its forms, and that money could not be concentrated on a single cost-intensive project. This was the official policy which, on the face of it, was based on a certain common sense and, despite every effort, it remained unshaken and no government budget to help to finance the big passenger liners was ever forthcoming. However, much as one may agree with the rationale of the government's point of view, it is difficult to ignore the inescapable

conclusion that a great deal of fruitless effort would have been avoided had it not taken so long to reach its decision, apart from the fact that, aside from economic considerations, the NYK was quite correct in its opinion that the policy of reconstruction on grounds of a patriotic national revival had been allowed to drop.

Quite apart from that, the fact of the matter was that as a result of this decision, those who travelled by sea to Japan for the Tokyo Olympics of 1964 were obliged to rely on other national flag carriers.

Meanwhile, throughout this long, indecisive period, the Nippon Yusen Kaisha had been pursuing various improvements in the design of its planned ships, taking account of the changes in shape which were coming into fashion all over the world. Subsequent renditions showed a gradual transition of the liners' profiles from the original form through to a stage where there were twin exhaust flues aft and a conventionally shaped dummy funnel forward of them, rather like the Moore McCormack sisters *Argentina* and *Brasil* of 1958. Later still, the dummy funnel was eliminated completely and the bridge deck and associated structure extended aft. The twin exhaust flues themselves may well, as a result, have been painted with the company's colours. At the same time, paintings depicting the planned public rooms and exterior facilities were also released, which gave an impression of the superior standard of appointments that were intended for the vessels.

… underwent several metamorphoses on the drawing boards. *Nippon Yusen Kaisha*

Although the Nippon Yusen Kaisha still remained hopeful that the construction of the liners might take place, the issue was more or less resolved against them in the end with the publication of a Japanese Government policy statement in 1963. Entitled '*Two Laws of Maritime Traffic Reconstruction*', this document posed the question whether or not passenger service reorganisation was attainable – or even desirable. It left the construction of new passenger ships as a problem to be resolved in the future, by which time, in the event by the late 1960s, it no longer required deliberation due to the replacement of ocean passenger travel by aircraft.

Oddly, another Japanese company, the Toyo Yusen Kaisha, also featured on the projected liner scene at about this time. This firm's plans involved the construction of a 50,000 gross ton, triple-screw passenger ship with a speed of 35 knots for scheduled service between Japan, Australia and the United States and, depending on the availability of a government subsidy, it hoped to have the vessel in operation by 1967. As might be expected, maintaining its unfavourable fiscal stance, the Japanese Government did not offer any financial inducements and, in consequence, the huge liner did not materalise. Had she been built, she would have been by far the largest liner to have been owned by a Japanese shipping company but, with her abandonment, the Japanese dreams of large post-war liners were

finally dashed, since the ensuing years were not conducive to even contemplation on this subject.

Bucking the trend, however, considering the ever-increasing encroachment of air transportation, the early 1960s was a relatively fruitful period for new passenger liner construction. A total of twenty-one new ships of over 20,000grt were built for service on all the major sea routes, across the Atlantic to New York or Montreal, to South America, Africa and to Australia and New Zealand. They included three giant ships introduced on the New York express service, the *France*, *Michelangelo* and *Raffaello*, and the largest ships ever placed on the Sydney run from Southampton, the *Oriana* and *Canberra*.

Yet this was but a temporary respite, for the general decline in passenger shipping services continued unabated, even accelerated, and soon many of these ships were to be dependent solely on cruising to earn an income. Indeed, it is interesting to speculate whether their several owners would have ordered them at all had the situation prevailing when they were completed been the same as that when they were laid down. Certainly, the conditions at this time caused various other germinating schemes to be nipped in the bud. Many of these amounted to no more than announcements of intent, but one or two of them are worthy of more detailed comment.

One particularly interesting project, of which very little is known, also originated in the Orient, in the Chinese People's Republic. As a result of research into nuclear ship projects in the mid 1960s, naval architects at Vickers Ltd at Barrow-in-Furness discovered that Communist China was planning to build a 20,000 gross ton nuclear passenger liner for service between Tsientsin and Shanghai. This ship was apparently intended primarily for the transportation of migrant workers and would, therefore, have had only dormitory accommodation. Although there is no official or authenticated documentation available, and, incidentally, even this information cannot be substantiated by Lloyds, the experts at Vickers (later VSEL and now part of BAe Systems) remained convinced that such a vessel was already in existence or, if not, its construction was imminent. If she had been completed and had actually become operational, it would surely have been incredible if such a nuclear ship had somehow escaped wider notice. It is of interest to note – it is even perhaps something of an irony – the research then being undertaken at Vickers related to British efforts to commission its own nuclear-powered passenger ship (see page 194). Neither of these ships materialised, however, despite what can only be assumed were resolute intentions in both cases. If either had been produced, it would have become only the second passenger-carrying nuclear vessel after the United States' *Savannah*.

Yet another project which reappeared in the 1960s was Russia's elusive giant. First mentioned in 1958 with a gross tonnage of 85,000 and apparently destined for the New York express service, her construction was supposed to have been started in 1961. However, by 1963 the ship had been scaled down to 50,000 gross tons, although most maritime journalists viewed even these reports with much scepticism. In 1965, two years later, a more detailed and plausible report stated that a geared-turbine vessel of around 25,000 gross tons was under construction at the Admiraltieski Shipyard at Leningrad. The secrecy with which Russian officialdom enshrouds itself makes it impossible to even speculate on the rise or fall of this scheme, but it is certain that nothing emerged from it – at all events in the form of a passenger ship – for the only new liners to

be added to the Sovtorgflot fleet before the fall of the Soviet Union were the five units of the *Aleksandr Pushkin* class, all built in what was then East Germany. The whole Russian system at that time was very different from the conditions that prevailed in the West. It might be thought that a project such as the original 85,000-tonner, once agreed, might have had more hope of survival since there was not the same likelihood of a situation where a private enterprise shipowner became embattled with its government in matters of subsidy – the Soviet Government was, in effect, also the shipowner and the Russian national budget was not dictated by entirely the same considerations. Perhaps there never was the necessary unanimity of opinion amongst those concerned, although the fact that the American stevedores union was threatening to refuse to handle Russian ships at that time, could have been a relevant factor in the decision not to proceed beyond the planning stage to actual construction.

As the 1960s drew to their close, very few passenger liners remained employed full-time on scheduled services. The prevailing economic and political climates, subsequently worsened by the oil crisis of 1973, hastened the departure of many still youthful ships to the breakers' yards. Others turned to full-time cruising, and this, in itself, generated a boom in the construction of vessels purpose-built for this expanding and lucrative market. Even Metro-Goldwyn-Mayer, the Hollywood film conglomerate, was reported to be planning a series of 20,000-ton cruise ships prior to its partial liquidation in October 1973. It perceived a synergy between film production and the cruise industry as dimensions within the same entertainment and leisure spectrum. In fact, this was not such a strange association as it has since been pursued more positively and successfully by the Walt Disney Company whose Disney Cruise Line operates a fleet of several large cruise ships out of ports in Florida and Texas. It is therefore apposite that the remaining chapters of the book should largely focus on this theatre of passenger ship operation. But first we should return to the 1940s to consider a comprehensive programme for new passenger liners, launched in the United States, and which, as it turned out, generated minimal results.

6

SHIPS FOR THE SEAS OF PEACE

THE PLANNED RENAISSANCE OF THE UNITED STATES MERCHANT MARINE

The Second World War had been as much a struggle of science and technology as of military strategy and might. Sustained by a massive war effort, both sides had sought to maintain their offensives with more and more sophisticated and ingenious weaponry. A new and unparalleled importance was placed on scientific ingenuity and technical advancement and, through the perpetuation of this research as well as its commercial 'spin-offs', the immediate post-war period came to symbolise the dawning of a new technological age.

Many of the inventions which resulted from this had a direct influence on the passenger shipping business and, bearing this in mind, the different passenger lines began to reassemble their fleets, as far as possible devising applications for these modern contrivances in the replacements they required. Great Britain had fared best in the war with both her *Queens* coming through it unscathed. This enabled the Cunard Line to resume sailings with little difficulty, and then to see how things developed. In France, the veteran *Île-de-France* had survived, while that country was also awarded the *Europa*, which was renamed *Liberté*. Reconstruction of both these ships also allowed the Compagnie Générale Transatlantique time to consider their future plans, although it was rumoured that, for a while, consideration was given to building three new 40,000 gross ton liners immediately. As stated previously, Germany made no attempt to rebuild her pre-war passenger ships at that time, although Italy made enormous strides in expanding her fleet beyond its previous magnitude and splendour. Only the United States stood conspicuously deficient on the sidelines.

One consequence of her desperation to build a respectable passenger fleet for the first time was that the majority of the giant passenger liner projects over the next fifteen years were of American origin although, in the event, the only success stories were those of the *United States*, *Constitution* and *Independence*. The first major campaign for such new ships emanated from the United States Government's own official body, the Maritime Commission.

Following the Second World War, it was realised in the United States that the country could not become a first-class maritime power without making a significant contribution towards future passenger-carrying seaborne trade. The USA had been particularly adversely affected in this direction by the war, having had its entire fleet of passenger ships utilised for government service as troopships. The facts were plain to see: a five-year break in any planned additions to an ageing fleet, and only one large liner, the *America*, having been added to the mercantile marine since the early 1930s. The United States Maritime Commission (USMC), established prior to the War, set its prime objective as the planning of the rehabilitation of the United States Merchant Marine. Following the end of hostilities, the requirement to establish large passenger liners on the key routes of the world was realised very clearly when the USMC released a directive dated 25 October 1944 in which the then President, Franklin D. Roosevelt (himself a keen ship enthusiast), had requested that the USMC prepare a plan for improving the U.S. Merchant Marine and maintaining its future position. Moreover, he had stressed that no time should be lost in the preparations of designs for the construction of vessels for this purpose, and that the building of any new types should be scheduled to prevent interference with ships and materials required for war, whilst contracts should only be awarded on the basis of competitive tenders. The President had insisted that the plan, '*Ships for the Seas of Peace*', should be implemented as an immediate priority, since both the employment situation and the conversion from a war to a peace-time economy had to be considered.

The *Independence* painted black, the guise in which she first entered service. *Alex Duncan*

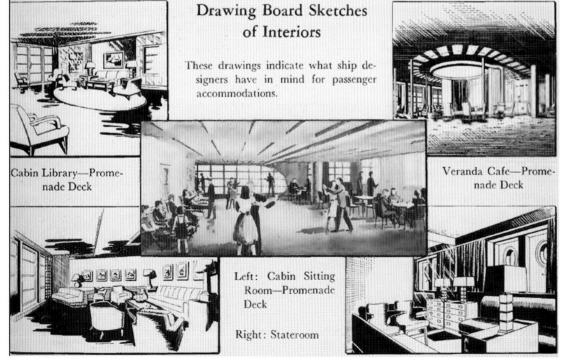

Renderings of the interior accommodations that designers had in mind for the various liners planned under the U.S. Maritime Commission's 'Ships for the Seas of Peace' Programme as depicted in its 'American World Traders' brochure published in 1946. *Authors' collection*

To clarify these proposals, on which the USMC were already actively engaged as a result of President Roosevelt's edict, it is necessary to refer to a paper presented to the Society of Naval Architects and Marine Engineers (SNAME) in 1945. Entitled '*Large Passenger-Carrying Ships for Certain Essential Trade Routes*', it was read by James L. Bates, then Director of the Technical Division of the USMC. In his paper, the author touched on some of the lessons learnt from the war, and on possible future consequences of them that should be taken into consideration and applied to the proposed liners already under review, or to those which had already been accepted.

The Second World War had revealed that the large passenger liner was not generally suited for use as an aircraft carrier. Neither the *Queens* nor the *America* would have been ideal for such a purpose, either with or without elaborate and expensive conversion. It also seemed that neither such vessels nor their smaller sisters were well suited for the auxiliary cruiser role. However, liners such as the *America* and the '*Mariposa*'-class had proved to be extremely valuable for troop transportation, and it would be for this purpose that they – or their future successors – should be viewed when plans were made for future national emergencies.

In considering some of these post-war effects, it was felt that, as a direct result of the enormous destruction of available labour and property abroad, many Western European ports would require the expenditure of much time and money for reconstruction. Even after this was done, it was felt (at that time, in 1945) that they might not attain their pre-war importance as commercial centres. The potential of the United States' interests in the Pacific had been affected favourably, while very attractive possibilities existed for trade with South America. However, one development had emerged from the war which was feared to be about to present itself as a serious competitor, even as far back as 1945, and that was the passenger-carrying aircraft. Mr Bates pointed out how, at that time, the increase in speed and the multiplication of air routes was becoming phenomenal.

As pointed out earlier, with these factors in mind, he considered that, in the immediate post-war years, all types of passenger transport would be utilised to maximum capacity, but he foresaw that air travel would increasingly secure the available First-class passenger traffic,

because of its superior speed. Eventually, the future of passenger ship transportation, he believed, would progressively divert towards the cruise for relaxation and leisure. How very correct his predictions proved to be!

The leading questions to be considered by the US Government, ship operators and by naval architects were: 'Where shall the passenger ships of tomorrow operate and what shall be their outstanding characteristics?' Apart from these, it also had to be asked: 'What future routes should be classed as essential?'

The original intention was to develop high-speed passenger liners which would have had a minimum displacement and a minimum horsepower in order to keep initial costs low, while consuming a minimum amount of fuel. These ships were intended to be passenger carriers only, but it was found that there would be a certain amount of unoccupied space in such vessels which could be exploited profitably for the stowage of high-earning cargoes (i.e. some 1,500–2,500 tons per ship). In these particular designs, speed would have been the major influence. Trends indicated that increases in speed above 20 knots should be accompanied by decreases in the amount of cargo carried, as well as in the time spent in port, in order to exploit this costly characteristic to the maximum. Speed was to be given special consideration because, it was postulated, a smaller number of ships, at greater speed, might do the same work as a larger number at a lower speed. The very real possibilities of encroachment by air travel, with its much reduced journey times, would assuredly make low speeds intolerable anyway.

The radius of operation was to be fixed, with the prime objective of completing the round voyage on one fuelling. However, sufficient fuel capacity was to be provided where possible so that, in the event of being used on military service, a total radius of 12,000–15,000 miles could be achieved at the ship's designed speed. Thus, in spite of the original intentions and in order that the ship's speed should be maintained in rough seas and that passenger comfort should be a prime consideration in these conditions, liners of great length and of large displacement were favoured. In other words, weather experienced on certain routes would exercise a positive influence on the design of the ship to operate on that route.

A number of trade routes were discussed in Mr Bates' paper, not because they were the most important which might have been selected, but because passengers had been carried on them in the past and they looked to be promising for large, fast vessels of the future. Those under consideration were as follows:

(a) The transatlantic service between New York, the British Isles and Western Europe and return – total distance some 8,000 nautical miles,

(b) The eastern seaboard of the United States to the east coast of South America, or New York, Rio de Janeiro, Santos, Montevideo, Buenos Aires and return, calling at Trinidad for bunkering facilities – total distance approximately 12,000 nautical miles,

(c) The service between New York and the Mediterranean and return – total distance about 9,000 nautical miles,

(d) The western seaboard of the United States to the Orient, or San Francisco, Honolulu, Yokohama, Shanghai, Hong Kong, Manila and return – total distance about 14,500 nautical miles,

(e) The western seaboard of the United States to the Pacific Islands, Australia and New Zealand and return – total distance some 16,000 nautical miles.

Each of the above-mentioned routes would have offered both cargo and passenger business but, although the concept related primarily to the carriage of passengers (on which more will be said), this could not be considered independently of the cargo-carrying problem. Route (a), whilst classed as 'essential' and a well-proven 'stamping ground', was, at the time, still highly competitive, and probably could not offer to American interests the same opportunities in future passenger transport development that were offered elsewhere. Route (c) was thought to be of especial importance in developing closer relations between the United States and the Soviet Union, as well as the smaller nations located around the Mediterranean Basin. Routes (b) and (d) offered exceptional opportunities for the development of mutually advantageous commercial and sociological relationships, suggesting a promising future. Finally, route (e), although offering fairly attractive prospects, also presented certain serious difficulties.

In order to meet the necessary requirements on the proposed essential routes, the USMC's studies concentrated on three schemes for its investigations, namely designs for routes (a), (b) and (d) in consultation with prospective operators. The design for route (c), however, resulted from studies sponsored by the American Export Lines, which was the only private company as such to be involved, which came forward with a design of its own for a large passenger ship and was ready to back it with its own money. (Already, prior to the war, the American Export Lines had submitted its own design and money in order to rejuvenate its own dry cargo fleet under the United States Merchant Marine Act of 1936.)

Route (e), apparently, could still be catered for by the Matson Line's passenger ships *Mariposa* and *Monterey* which had initially been built for, and operated under subsidy contract between, Pacific Coast ports and Australia. The *Lurline*, built in 1932 for the domestic trade between California and Hawaii, still operated on that route in 1945. As no further vessels were proposed for the Australian route, which was well served at the time, this route does not come within the scope of this subject.

The proposed liners considered for routes (a), (b) and (d) are dealt with in detail under the succeeding three subheadings. However, the reasons for the demise of some of the projects, or the factors which prevented them from proceeding to the building stage, were not always obvious or made manifest. As a result, the authors can do no more than speculate upon them. Nevertheless, the estimated total cost of establishing passenger fleets on the particular routes was cited at $200–$225 million (£50 to £56 million), which cannot be ruled out as a contributory factor for their failure to materialise. Today, when astronomical budgets, fanned by inflation, have become commonplace, it is easy to forget that such a sum seemed to be immense in the immediate post-war years, yet … it only represented an impost of roughly one dollar per capita of the US population!

DESIGN FOR THE NORTH ATLANTIC ROUTE: THE P4-S2-41

The P4-S2-41 indicated, by the USMC's system of designation nomenclature, a passenger vessel with a waterline length between 700 and 800ft, propelled by twin-screw steam turbines. Design number 41 revealed that it had been commenced between 1941 and 1943. This particular design was determined in collaboration with the United States Lines who had operated a service on the North Atlantic route with the *Manhattan* and *Washington* prior to the war. Their ports of call had been Cobh, Plymouth, Le Havre and Hamburg, before returning via Le Havre, Southampton and Cobh. It was thought that post-war routing might have to be changed when trends were known better.

At that time, the United States Lines had never favoured, as had other operators, departures from New York on a fixed day of the week. But, despite this, the Maritime Commission felt that this was important, and so weekly sailings from New York were accepted as a basic principle. With this in mind, it was assumed that, using three vessels, each would complete a round voyage every three weeks. The success of the service operated by the *Manhattan* and *Washington* lent credence to the belief that this sort of service should be maintained. Furthermore, if there was to be an adherence to this sort of concept, direct competition could be avoided with the super-liners operated at that time by the Cunard White Star Line. Initially, a fleet of four ships with a sustained sea speed of 20–21 knots operating on a 28-day schedule were considered, but their annual capacity for the transport of cargo and passengers could equally be furnished by the three faster ships that were finally considered. At first it was felt that ships of smaller size and lower speed would not have been affected disadvantageously by any future competition, but final economic studies indicated that a fleet based upon three 24-knot ships would be better than one based on four 20-knot vessels.

The proposed statistics of the P4-S2-41 design were as follows:

Waterline length	745ft
Beam	90ft
Depth to strength deck	70ft 6in
Longitudinal co-efficient	0.598
Power plant	steam turbines
Designed displacement	33,500 tons
Fuel oil capacity	4,000 tons
Fresh water	750 tons
Swimming pools	100 tons
Passengers, baggage, crew and provisions	800 tons
Dry cargo	6,220 tons
Reefer (refrigerated) cargo	530 tons
Deadweight	12,400 tons
Designed speed	24 knots
Designed shaft horsepower	55,000
Number of screws	2
Designed steaming radius	8,000 miles
Number of passengers	1,200
Number of crew	669
Bale capacity	450,800 cu ft
Reefer capacity	53,000 cu ft

In order to develop the three-ship schedule, consideration was given to the problem of cargo handling at the various ports of call. The method favoured was arranged so as to have six open holds, which could be served by a system of derricks and king posts. It was proposed that the ships' stores and refrigerated cargo could be handled through side ports by a newly developed type of gear, which would also be considered for the prospective South American liners.

Each ship was planned to accommodate about 1,200 passengers in two classes, and arrangements were to be provided for the alternative use of certain groups of staterooms by either class, so as to ensure flexibility. The exact design speed of the P4-S2-41 proved to be a problem to predict because, under favourable conditions of smooth water during the Atlantic crossing, cargo and passengers would be

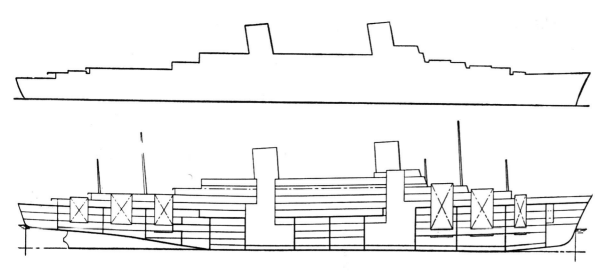

Outboard and inboard profiles of the P4-S2-41 design. *Society of Naval Architects & Marine Engineers*

The *America* had proved to be invaluable for troop transportation during the war as the USS *West Point*. *Kenneth W. Wightman*

handled at the various ports to the desired schedule and, in this case, a sustained sea speed of 24 knots would be sufficient. However, if the crossing was made in rough or foggy conditions, or if any emergencies occurred at the ports of call to disrupt their programme, it would be desirable for the ships to be provided with a liberal margin of power.

Comparison of the P4-S2-41 design with that of the *Manhattan* showed that the length had been increased by some 60ft, and the depth from the promenade deck reduced from 75ft to 70ft, while the beam had been slightly increased. Taking account of existing practice in merchant ships, a novel design feature in the hull form of the P4-S2-41 was put forward – the fitting of twin skegs underneath a relatively broad stern. Each skeg was to carry the propeller shaft and the propeller, abaft of which would be a rudder. The virtues of such a configuration were that a given metacentric height (an important dimension that contributes to the restoring force and transverse stability of a rolling ship) would be obtained on a decreased beam, also that the ships' mobility would be enhanced, because each rudder would operate in a propeller wake. It was feared, however, that, unless proposed model tests predicted a definite reduction in shaft horsepower, a more normal form of after-body would have to be adopted. Apparently the twin skeg form might have introduced certain variations in wake distribution which, if not properly controlled, could have led to objectionable vibration trouble.

The designed displacement of the P4-S2-41 also proved to be difficult to establish. It was thought to be theoretically possible to select a vessel with a smaller displacement than the one proposed. This was a prime example of the weather on a particular route affecting the design of the vessel intended to ply it. The storms and rough weather that would be encountered in the North Atlantic meant that any liner on that run would have to have heavy and carefully disposed scantlings. Quite apart from this, it was also obvious that the greater the size of the vessel relative to the wave size that might be encountered, the more comfortable the passengers would be. The length selected, therefore, was considered to be conducive to passenger comfort, and the approximate displacement of 33,500 tons, whilst smaller in comparison to previous standards, was not decreased radically. In terms of displacement tonnage, the size would

have fallen in the range determined by such pre-war liners as the *Rex* and *Conte di Savoia*, though comparatively less than that of the *Bremen* and of the first *Mauretania*.

With regard to the P4-S2-41's fore-body, two general types had been considered: the first of 'U'-type cross-section as employed in the original design of the *America*, and the second a development of the 'V'-section bow. It seemed that the latter would permit an increase in deck areas for passengers and crew forward, also a positively smaller increase in cargo capacity. For speeds less than 20 knots, it was estimated that the 'V'-section bow would require less horsepower than the 'U'-section, but that at speeds in excess of 24 knots this power requirement would tend to increase. From the greater advantages gained by the 'V'-section, it was decided to settle on this form.

It was considered that the chosen route for the P4-S2-41 would still be competitive, since in the immediate post-war era the flow of high-class freight was considerable. There was also a reasonable volume of passenger traffic to be attracted by the lower fares offered by the intermediate-speed liners. Even as far back as 1945, competition was anticipated from passenger-carrying aircraft, and economic studies, conducted to forecast trends over the next twenty-year period, indicated a falling off in seaborne passenger traffic. The conclusions drawn from this study indicated that the high-class freight business would be beneficial even if passenger volume during the second decade fell to one-eighth of normal ship capacity (which was assumed to be 60 per cent occupancy).

Around this period, when the P4-S2-41 design was being drawn up, the United States Lines (which had been the biggest operator on this route prior to the war) was aspiring to build two 35,000 gross ton consorts for the *America*, in spite of the fact that the P4-S2-41 was available to them and presumably could have fulfilled the same requirements. It was felt that this would be the best way of replacing the *Manhattan* and *Washington*, which remained the property of the USMC but, after some deliberation, a decision was made against the intermediate ships which had been envisaged and in favour of two much larger liners of up to 50,000 tons, one of which emerged eventually as the *United States* in 1952.

The decision to opt for the bigger ships was comparable to that made later by the CGT (French Line) in the mid 1950s. Under pressure from the French Government to construct two 35,000 ton sister-ships to replace the Île-de-France and Liberté, the CGT elected instead to build the single giant France. The French Line justified this on the grounds that one super-liner would not only show the flag much more effectively on an international basis, but would be a bigger and better money-earner than the two less significant, medium-sized vessels. The big ship's prestige value alone should have been sufficient to convince the U.S. Government, as it did subsequently in the mid 1950s, that this philosophy was still important on the North Atlantic route.

Be that as it may, the USMC's P4-S2-41 design never did materialise in any form. The United States Lines re-introduced its Atlantic service in November 1946 when the refurbished America made her first post-war voyage, and she was complemented the same year by the Washington, which was chartered from the USMC.

DESIGN FOR THE NEW YORK TO EAST COAST OF SOUTH AMERICA ROUTE – THE P3-S2-DA1 (DA) DESIGN (AKA THE 'SOUTHERN CROSS SHIPS')

This route had once included calls at Rio de Janeiro, Montevideo and Buenos Aires outward bound, returning via Santos, Rio and bunkering at Trinidad. Based on its pre-war itineraries, Moore McCormack, the principal operator on this trade, considered weekly sailings on the same day of the week from New York to be a major priority.

Before the Second World War they had operated the liners Argentina, Brazil and Uruguay, all with a service speed of 18 knots and dubbed the 'Good Neighbour Fleet'. These were then complemented on this run by a number of C-2 cargo vessels. In this manner, the three liners were able to sail on a six-week round voyage basis, and left New York on alternate weeks. A careful study predicted that a satisfactory programme of sailings could be maintained by five 22-knot cargo-passenger ships, sailing out of New York weekly with a thirty-five-day round voyage schedule. But the same target could

be achieved by four 27-knot cargo-passenger liners sailing from New York on a twenty-eight-day cycle. However, from a profitability aspect, it was assumed that, if the service was operated without competition, it would be more lucrative to operate just two of the faster ships with sailings on alternate weeks.

One of the major requirements taken into consideration when drawing up the operating schedules was that a thorough examination should be made of the time necessary for the vessels to remain in port, both for cargo-handling and for passengers to go ashore for sight-seeing. The proposed speed would have made it possible for the steaming time on the longest leg between New York and Rio to be reduced from about eleven days for the early 18-knot 'Argentina'-class to about seven and a half days. At the time, this was a significant improvement in the face of the emergence of air competition, as well as the fact that many of the prospective passengers would not be able to afford more time at sea and, in any case, might feel that more than a week afloat might become monotonous.

The P3-S2-DA1, otherwise known as the DA, in the USMC classification system indicated a passenger vessel with a waterline length between 600 and 700ft, propelled by twin-screw steam turbines. Design DA, first modification, commenced between circa 1943 and 1945, when the USMC post-war programme was launched. It would be operated on the basis that around 125 passengers per week out of New York could be expected, but she would have to provide for peak loads and expansion in travel. If a weekly sailing schedule was to be implemented, provision would have to be made for a passenger capacity of 250. Alternatively, if sailings were to be every other week, the capacity would have to be for around 550 passengers (470 First-class and 80 Third-class).

The proposed general particulars of the P3-S2-DA1 were as follows:

Overall length	731ft 6in
Waterline length	699 ft
Length between perpendiculars	671 ft
Moulded beam	70ft 6in
Depth to strength deck	56ft 6in
Longitudinal co-efficient	0.57
Designed displacement	22,750–23,500 tons
Fuel oil capacity	5,200 tons
Fresh water	500 tons
Swimming pools	100 tons
Passengers, baggage, crew and provisions	450 tons
Dry cargo	2,100 tons
Reefer cargo	400 tons
Deadweight	8,750 tons
Designed speed	27 knots
Designed shaft horsepower	60,500
Number of screws	2
Designed steaming radius	11,000 miles
Number of passengers	550–560
Number of crew	449
Capacity for cargo	235,000–250,000 cu ft
Refrigerated cargo capacity	42,369 cu ft

It was originally intended that the DA would carry a nominal cargo payload of about 1,000 tons, although Moore-McCormack Lines believed that provision would have to be made eventually for as much high-class freight as would be possible, with due regard to the time required for handling cargo in port, as well as its effect on shaft horsepower and on the fuel consumption brought about by the increased displacement. In the light of this more logical line of thought, provision was ultimately considered for approximately 2,100 tons of high-class package goods in addition to 400 tons of refrigerated cargo.

A significant feature of the DA was that, although she was to have about 235,000 cu ft of cargo space, she would carry no winches, since it was planned that the vessel's entire cargo would be handled through three side-ports. Each of these would be served by a side-port loader comprising hoisting, traversing and boom motions obtained with direct-current motors.

The ships were dubbed 'The Southern Cross Ships' and one of the boasts of USMC literature of 1946 was:

> Passengers will breakfast in their rooms. Luncheon will be served on deck. Dinner will be a formal meal, followed by open-air dancing and fiestas. There will be one standard of service for all passengers, and bigger rooms for those who want them.

Several relevant factors influenced the choice of size and displacement of the DA: the first and most important of these was that the New York to east coast of South America route was considered to be definitely a fair weather run. Hence the ship would be open to the sun and air conditioned below decks. Few severe storms had been encountered and, therefore, the structure of any contemplated ship would not be subjected to the constant buffeting experienced in the North Atlantic. This favoured a more moderate displacement tonnage, even when high speeds were considered.

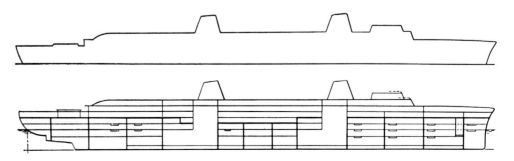

Inboard and outboard profiles of the P3-S2-DA1 design with modified DA design (right) for purposes of comparison. *Society of Naval Architects & Marine Engineers*

Secondly, if the power of the main engines and resulting fuel consumption were to be kept within acceptable and economical limits, a relatively greater length would be required for the high speed desired. The third influential factor was that, due to the shallow waters of the River Plate and the approaches to Buenos Aires, the proposed liner's draught would have to be restricted to 28ft. The last item to have a bearing on the DA's proposed displacement would be the selection of a light but powerful propulsive plant as proven by the United States Navy. The displacement determined after consideration of the foregoing governing factors was moderate, if not actually rather small. The justification for the dimensions and proportions selected were based on those relating to well-known English Channel steamers. It had been demonstrated after years of study and experience that this type of vessel exhibited very high speeds with unusually low displacements. This was in spite of the fact that the English Channel was notorious for its tempestuous and unpredictable waters.

In appearance, the DA's midship design showed a bulge of 2.25ft which would have given an impression that the ship had an external shallow blister. The form of the DA had been selected carefully in every respect in order to provide sea-kindliness, easy manoeuvring and adequate stability throughout her operating range. The same hull form had been well proven in the Hamburg Sud Amerika Company's *Cap Polonio* of 1922, which had been built with a bulged midship section and which represented a prototype for this form of merchant ship. Further model-testing research experiments showed that the underwater cross-section of the DA, as with the P4-S2-41, should have a 'V'-section bow, combined with a bulbous forefoot. With such a form, relatively low water resistance and the requisite stability on minimum dimensions, especially with regard to the beam, were predicted.

The safety requirements for the DA were all to comply with the rules advocated by the International Convention for Promoting Safety

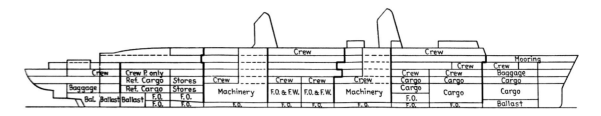

Artist's impression of the P3-S2-DA1 design. *Authors' collection*

of Life at Sea of 1929, and by the United States Senate Report No. 184, covering watertight integrity. Under the recommendations laid down in these documents, the DA would have been a two-compartment-class vessel: that is, the ship would be capable of surviving if any two of her adjacent compartments became flooded. She would have had eleven watertight bulkheads, the minimum watertight compartment length being 44ft long.

The fire detection system of the ship was to be of the zonal type, whereby, if a fire occurred aboard, it could be identified in a certain zone or section of the ship, thus making it unnecessary to search all of the compartments within that zone in order to find its seat. In the DA's cargo spaces, a carbon dioxide (CO_2) extinguishing system would have been employed.

At this stage of the development of the proposed design, the arrangement of passenger spaces was largely a matter of choice and any national influences or preferences would have had to be considered in the internal arrangement of the vessels. The electrical power plant would have been four 1,250 kilowatt, 0.8 power factor, 60Hz, AC generators and the main propulsion system was to be steam turbines. The proposed machinery for the P3-S2-DA1 was tabulated as follows:

Number of shafts	2
Shaft horsepower	60,500
Main boilers	4 × 850 psi and 900°F
Auxiliary boilers	none
Generators	4 − turbo-driven 1,250kW
Emergency generators	1 − diesel-driven 150kW
Circulators per condenser	scoops − 29,000gpm pumps
Fire pumps	4 − motor-driven 400gpm
Flooding pumps	
Bilge	2 − submersible 1,050gpm
Ballast	3 − motor-driven 1,050gpm

Such was the design of the post-war DA that it was believed that it was the only vessel which would have had its machinery so arranged that, in the event of damage being sustained up to the limits of the

safety factors in the subdivision (that is, if two adjacent compartments became flooded), the engines would still be operational. Other unique features of the design were that the use of auxiliary boilers had been considered, but had finally been abandoned, basically on economic grounds, while another significant departure from conventional marine engineering practice lay in the fact that the circulating water for the main condensers was to be supplied from 'scoops'. This method was proposed as an alternative to circulating salt water through the condensers via the pumps. The scoops were protrusions on the shell of the ship which would pick up sea water while the ship was under way, although they would probably have been augmented by sea water circulating pumps while the vessel was stationary or manoeuvering in port. It was claimed that scoops had the advantage of saving space and eliminating the necessity of maintaining two vital and constantly running auxiliaries. The usual practice in European vessels at that time was the use of independent pumps. Condenser scoops were initially fitted in United States Lines' America.

Although some observers felt that the P3-S2-DA1 needed a 'face-lift' with its lack of sheer, pseudo-streamlining and widely spaced trapezoidal funnels, a year later it was still considered to be a viable design and was scheduled for construction in 1949. By this time, consideration was being given to establishing a route between Buenos Aires and New York of ten days' duration, which would be continued on to Europe and, in these circumstances, a service speed of 27 knots would have been required for the same ship.

Moore-McCormack Lines had cooperated with the USMC with regard to research into the operating trends on the South American route and, at the time, Mr Emmet J. McCormack praised the design of the DA both from a speed and competitive aspect, stating that it should prove to be the most satisfactory for the trade. Nevertheless, in spite of this encomium, the DA was never built: perhaps due to its first costs − post-war, the USMC designs as a whole were regarded as no longer viable because, in the intervening years, the cost of shipbuilding materials, especially steel and labour, had risen prohibitively − or perhaps because of the escalating air competition then being established to South America. A prime factor could have been that the original 'Good Neighbour' fleet, consisting of the Brazil, Argentina and Uruguay, was

The *Brazil* ex-*Virginia*, one of the trio of ships that comprised the pre-war 'Good Neighbour' fleet. *Moore McCormack Lines*

reconditioned after the war at a cost of $20 million (£5 million). These ships reached their peak in 1952 when they carried a record-breaking 25,000 passengers. The volume steadily declined thereafter, which may account for the fact that replacements were not ordered until 1956, by which time the original trio had been reduced to two ships, both of them well past the statutory age limit so far as the terms of the US federal loan and mail contract were concerned.

The replacement vessels, the *Brasil* and the *Argentina*, which retained the old names, were designed by the Bethlehem Steel Company, who do not appear to have made any reference to the DA concept. Completed by the Ingalls Shipbuilding Corporation of Pascagoula, Mississippi, these new 15,257 gross ton liners had only two features in common with the DA, namely that they each carried 557 passengers in luxurious style, and they were both specifically designed for the South American service. Apart from this, they could only carry 4,470 tons of cargo.

Sadly, from the date that they were built and throughout the time that they were owned by Moore-McCormack, the new *Brasil* and *Argentina* never operated profitably in any single year. This prompted the chairman of the company, when addressing a United States Congressional hearing shortly before the vessels were laid up, to make the statement: 'Why they were built in the first place remains a mystery of corporate decision-making'.

Why indeed? Many very successful vessels have already been mentioned in the course of this book, in order to provide perspective or comparisons with those which form the burden of its theme – usually grandiose schemes for ships which either never came into existence at all, or which never fulfilled their designed functions. As to the former, the vessels that 'never were', these projects often left their mark on subsequent construction. It might be thought, if viewing these matters rather superficially, that their failure to reach fruition represented something rather negative and, besides, a great waste of money spent on all the origination charges before the projects were finally abandoned. In this context, it must be borne in mind that these charges rare relatively miniscule when compared with the actual cost of constructing and equipping a large vessel but, in any case, they are a constant in the design of a new type of ship, whether she is built in the end or not. Whilst it must be granted that such charges are sheer loss to the promoters whenever a scheme falls by the wayside and, whilst it is only possible to consider the ultimate effects of constructing a ship in retrospect, it is undeniable that it is less unprofitable to scrap origination plans and to proceed no further, than it is to carry on building a ship which proves to run at a loss throughout her career, as in the case of the replacement *Brasil* and *Argentina*.

DESIGN FOR THE TRANSPACIFIC SERVICE FROM SAN FRANCISCO – THE PXE, LATER P5-S2-E1 (AKA 'GREAT CIRCLE LINERS')

Chapter 5 (page 134) has already detailed the story of the pre-1939 War P-4-P (P4-P) design for the Pacific service, for which three vessels were originally contemplated, and of how the two 24-knot ships which were then substituted for them were finally abandoned when the United States entered the war. Certainly, the effects of the attack on Pearl Harbour, and all that followed, scuttled any ideas which the USMC may still have entertained for progressing them, although the indications are that the scheme was already almost moribund – perhaps due to the first cost of any such vessel.

Once the war was over, the USMC considered the Pacific route once again, in consultation with the American President Lines, with the object of operating a service out of San Francisco with calls at Honolulu, Yokohama, Shanghai, Hong Kong, and Manila, with a similar return voyage.

In the years preceding the war, the transpacific route had been worked by the American President Lines' *President Hoover*, *President Coolidge*, *President Cleveland* and *President Taft*. The *President Hoover* was lost in December 1937, the *President Coolidge* was sunk by mine in October 1942 and the *President Cleveland* by torpedo in the

following month off Morocco. The *President Taft*, which also had been taken over as a trooper, survived the war, but she was not returned to her owners. The pre-war schedule operated by these four liners was based on a fifty-six-day round voyage and provided a service for passengers in three classes (First, Tourist and Oriental). They also shipped a large volume of freight.

Three different permutations of the required fleets to serve this route were considered, namely: four 18.5-knot ships operating on a fifty-six-day cycle; three 23-knot vessels working a forty-two-day cycle, and two 29-knot ships on a twenty-eight-day cycle. The number of passengers per vessel and the amount of cargo carried would, of course, have varied with the type of ship and the speed selected as, indeed, would the number of freighters carrying cargo only that would have been necessary to operate in conjunction with the lead ships.

After careful comparisons of these several types, based on economic studies, all the indications were that the two large 29-knot vessels would prove to be more satisfactory than the other two combinations. With this object in view, detailed investigations were then devoted to what was designated the PXE design. This identifier throws up a bit of a conundrum, but if written in the format P-X-E it is possible that this classification indicated a passenger vessel, possibly of the basic E design. At the early stage of development when this classification was allocated, the length and engine arrangement may not have been finally determined, the 'X' representing an unknown quantity at this stage.

The first consideration affecting the design was that of the weather conditions it might encounter. All the evidence showed that the proportion of fair weather would be expected to be much higher than on the transatlantic run, and that such seas as would be experienced would be for a longer period, and more in the nature of a ground swell. For this reason, it was considered that it should be possible to adopt smaller vessels of less displacement tonnage than would be acceptable on the North Atlantic route. This important conclusion had also been borne out by the actual performances of certain types of vessel which had given a good account of themselves during the war in the Pacific theatre, although unable to provide such sea-kindly performances when operating in the Western Ocean.

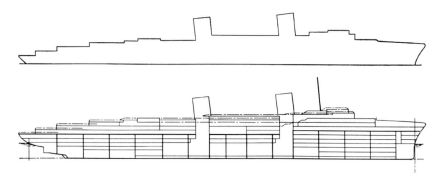

Inboard and outboard profiles of the PXE design of 1945. *Society of Naval Architects & Marine Engineers*

Waterline length	895ft
Beam	85ft
Depth to strength deck	71ft
Longitudinal co-efficient	0.57
Power plant	geared steam turbines
Designed displacement	37,500 tons
Fuel oil capacity	9,500 tons
Fresh water	800 tons
Swimming pools	200 tons
Passengers, baggage, crew and provisions	1,000 tons
Dry cargo	1,350 tons
Reefer cargo	150 tons
Total deadweight	13,000 tons
Designed speed	29 knots
Designed shaft horsepower	100,000
Number of screws	2
Designed steaming radius	12,500 miles
Number of passengers	1,000
Number of crew	496
Bale capacity	150,000 cu ft
Reefer capacity	15,000 cu ft

Once peacetime operations were functioning normally again, it was believed that full advantage would be taken of bunkering at suitable locations in the Philippines but it was also accepted that it would be very imprudent to design a ship which was dependent on a doubtful supply of fuel. Sufficient tanks for bunkers would, therefore, have to be provided for a round trip of some 14,500 miles at the designed service speed of 29 knots. Thus, due to the large amount of fuel which might be carried, the ship's expected deadweight would be relatively large for the high speed anticipated.

During the pre-war design era, the acceptable speed to length ratios (the Froude Number, used in relation to wave-making calculations) for large passenger liners did not usually exceed 0.9 or 1.0. However, ferries in the English Channel (to which reference had already been made when considering the P3-S2-DA1 design for the South American route), reached a value of 1.2, whilst large super-liners, like Cunard's *Queen Mary*, had achieved a value of 0.94 when steaming at around 30 knots. Thus, if the shaft horsepower was to be maintained at a reasonable figure and the vessel able to operate with equally reasonable fuel consumption, it was proposed that the PXE's length should be calculated to be less than 900ft. The proposed principal statistics of the PXE were as follows:

In view of the climatic nature of this semi-tropical route, it was thought to be desirable to avoid the use of inside staterooms wherever possible, and that the installation of outside ones would be made easier by the outstanding proportions of the vessel – a great length and a comparatively narrow beam. On the other hand, from the point of view of the passengers' comfort, it was essential to ensure that the designed beam should be sufficient to ensure a satisfactory period of roll.

For the P4-S2-41 transatlantic design, it had been proposed that the discharge of cargo should be by the use of masts and kingposts, with derricks operated by winches through open hatches. However, in the case of the DA and the PXE, because only small amounts of cargo would be carried and because each ship's beam would also be smaller, it was considered that side-port cargo-handling would be the most practicable in these two types. The PXE would depend on numerous side-ports through which cargo could be discharged by a new type of cargo-handling gear previously suggested for use in the P3-S2-DAI. In this manner, any topside cargo gear would be eliminated, as would any trunked hatchways. Thus the accommodation for the passengers could be extended further forward and aft, although it was felt that they might be uncomfortable if they were berthed too near the ends, where the effects of pitching would be accentuated.

Results from model tests in the Washington ship tank had predicted that the use of twin skegs in the case of the PXE would not be an advantage to the proposed hull configuration, which would have been of full form, but that twin rudders could be a possible alternative which warranted further studies. (A skeg is a protruding metal arm at the after end of a ship to support the rudder and protect the screw. For a single skeg it would be amidships. Twin skegs would be on either side, equidistant from the centre line of the ship.)

The PXE, being a twin-screw vessel, would have been designed to have two boilers per shaft, for pure simplicity and also to save space but, owing to the high horsepower (50,000) required for each shaft, as proposed they would have been the largest marine boilers ever built and would themselves have required special design considerations. The advantages gained by having a small number of boilers were that the associated auxiliaries would also have be in number, thus simplifying the piping, uptakes and boiler mountings, and so on, besides having an influence on all-round convenience in the engine room layout. In the designs that had been put forward for the P4-S2-41 and the DA, the propulsion machinery had been situated amidships and, in each case, there had apparently been ample justification for this location. However, the PXE, which was intended for the Pacific, would have had a much greater length than the other two vessels, so that it was feasible, in theory, to place both machinery compartments in the after third of the vessel. This location would have had the double advantage of reducing the length of propeller shafting, as well as placing the funnels far enough aft to obviate most of the smoke and funnel smut nuisance normally experienced when they were placed in the more conventional position amidships, or almost so. This line of thought seems to have been 'in the pipe-line' before the advent of the *Southern Cross*, *Canberra* and *Northern Star*

which entered service between 1955 and 1961, although its origins actually went back much further, since the early Matson vessels *Lurline* of 1908 and *Wilhelmina* of 1909 might be said to have pioneered this concept. In fairness, though, it must be stated that these two vessels were primarily cargo-passenger ships rather than passenger-cargo liners.

Nevertheless, investigations into stability in a damaged condition revealed that the three-compartment standard required in a vessel of the PXE's length could not be obtained so satisfactorily with the machinery located aft as when it was amidships, and for this reason the engine placement did, after all, follow the pattern set in the P4-S2-41 and DA designs.

Due to the side-port cargo-handling method which was selected, deck obstructions would have been reduced to a minimum. One advantage of this clear profile was that large areas of such unobstructed decks could be used to their fullest advantage for passenger recreation but, equally, the disadvantage was that the apparent wind created by a liner steaming at high speed, especially when added to the effect of a strong head wind, could render such large unprotected areas unsuitable for the purpose of recreation, or even of promenade. In consequence, it would have been necessary to have provided special forms of wind protection on these open decks.

In 1945, aluminium was more readily available and less costly than before the war, and this material was therefore considered for extensive use in the PXE's superstructure, since it would have given the added benefit of reduction in weight. An important consideration in this respect was that, if the vessel was to be entirely or partially 'turtle-backed' with the exception of the forecastle, the use of light metal would have to be applied liberally. Where it would have been undesirable to have provided a turtle-back feature, palisades or similar structures would have been used. These features would have contributed to a marked degree to the radical appearance of the PXE class.

It was thought that the anticipated post-war traffic on the Pacific route had been estimated accurately, as there was no direct competition with the Japanese at that time and there would not be any for some years to come. So long as this situation prevailed, it was clear that, of the various interests which would be capable of carrying the expected freight and passenger traffic across the Pacific, the one with the fleet bearing the lowest capital cost could be expected to earn the highest percentage profit on its capital investment. In other words, when comparing all the possible fleets involved, and assuming on the one hand that they had equal cargo capacities and, on the other, that their operating incomes would be approximately equal, then the capital and fixed charges would be most advantageous for that fleet in which the capital costs had been the lowest. Moreover, it had been gleaned from detailed economic studies that, if expected traffic on the route would support ships of acceptable displacements, cargo would be carried most profitably at up to, but not exceeding, 18 knots; but the optimum passenger-carrying speeds would have to be faster, in the order of 28 to 30 knots. This latter speed was postulated because the overhead charges for victualling passengers were so much higher and because, if they were too long at sea, they would eat up the profits.

For these reasons, the final choice of design for the PXE was for two 29-knot passenger liners with limited space for high-grade cargo to operate across the Pacific on a bi-weekly sailing schedule. These two vessels would be supplemented by C3-class cargo ships. This fleet was not only seen to be the ideal one, but also to represent both the least capital investment and the greatest earning capacity for the future.

The following year, in 1946, the Maritime Commission initiated another proposed design for operation by the American President Lines (APL). Bearing the designation P5-S2-E1, these twin-funnelled liners were presumably intended for APL's round-the-world service

and, as if to bear this out, they were dubbed the 'Great Circle Liners'. The designation letters indicated that they would have been twin-screw vessels driven by steam turbines, with a waterline length between 800 and 900ft – in fact, their estimated overall length was 942ft with a beam of 86ft 4in. They were expected to carry 1,248 passengers in three classes, with a refrigerated cargo capacity of 30,000 cu ft. Detailed plans prepared by the Maritime Commission disclosed extravagant and luxurious public rooms and amenities.

To all intents and purposes, the P5-S2-E1 was a modified and revamped version of the PXE and it is interesting to note that, in her profile, the type of smoke-deflecting cowls intended for her funnel tops were those originally wind-tunnel-tested and considered for use in the United States Lines' *America* in 1939. Tenders for the two P5-S2-E1 liners were invited by 20 September 1946. In the event, they were never forthcoming because, in the interim, the ships had fallen victims to President Truman's austere budget cuts of that year.

Although the USMC's PXE and P5-S2-E1 designs were good and financially viable concepts for the immediate post-war years on the Pacific, and although there is no doubt that the APL endorsed these recommendations whole-heartedly, they were never pursued apart from the requests for tenders on the latter design. As stated, this was partly due to considerations of financial restraint, but it was also influenced by the change of wind in the politics of China which, by that time, was in a state of serious civil war. Instead, the APL purchased two of the last emergency P2-type troopships from the Bethlehem Alabama Shipyard whilst they were still under construction, with appropriate specifications for them to be finished off as luxury liners. In 1947, the company took delivery of the *President Cleveland* and,

Another interpretation of the planned transpacific design, the P5-S2-E1, sporting the American President Lines' funnel motif. *Authors' collection*

The new *President Cleveland* of 1947. Mike Lennon

a year later, of the *President Wilson*. The APL's approach may have been to fill the vacuum on this route as detailed by the Maritime Commission, but not with such an ambitious project as they had had in mind originally. As it was, these two *Presidents* were America's first two post-war passenger liners. The P2 design had already proved itself in all theatres of the war and in all weather conditions so that, in effect, these two vessels were 'de luxe' versions of this troopship design. They each had a gross tonnage of 15,456, and an overall length of 610ft. They could carry 550 passengers in three classes and their turbo-electric power plant could sustain a cruising speed of 19 knots. As originally envisaged, their itinerary was from San Francisco to Honolulu, Yokohama, Hong Kong, Manila and return, and both ships completed twenty-five successful years on this route before being sold in 1972.

This was a model case of how some, but not all, of the recommendations laid down by a government body were followed up with action. Even though the very conceptions of the PXE and P5-S2-E1 designs were dead, a further proposal for a super-liner on the Pacific route was to emerge some 12 years later, as will be seen.

The proposed 'E' type liner was designed for service with Empresa Nacional Elcano on a route from Spain to South America, carrying 600 passengers. Conceived around 1950, she would have measured 20,000 gross tons. Her overall length would have been 640ft. *Navaera Elcano*

7

GRAND PLANS REVIVED DURING THE ERA OF PASSENGER LINER DEMISE

THE 'LIBERTY LINERS'

In 1949 an attempt was made to resuscitate the 'Yankee Clippers' scheme for two massive cabin-liners, which had previously been proposed in the late 1930s, when it had come to naught. A company, called Liberty Liners Incorporated with offices on Broadway, New York, and on K Street, Washington, D.C., was set up to promote the project, and it made a new approach to the United States Government in an attempt to win its support for the construction of these vessels, primarily by stressing their auxiliary potential. Paul Chapman and Theodore Ferris – no less! – were, in fact, urging the government to approve and finance the creation of two high-speed, emergency troop transports and aircraft carriers which, when not commandeered for military purposes, would be operated commercially on the North Atlantic route by Liberty Liners Inc, without any government subsidy once they were in service – essentially a long-term bareboat charter arrangement.

The liners were exactly as they had been devised before the war, except that prices had risen sharply. Unfortunately, estimated construction costs had spiralled to $100 million (£25 million) each, while the one-way passage fare, exclusive of meals, had doubled to $100. Nevertheless, based on this fare and the estimated earnings on weekly sailings with only 50 per cent of the passenger capacity filled, Chapman and Ferris calculated that two such ships would not only manage without the need for an 'operating-differential', but would make a respectable profit besides.

Once again, Chapman and Ferris met with no success but, resolute as ever, they decided to modernise and re-sculpture their design completely to bring it into line with the latest ideas. At the same time, they predicted the forthcoming competition that passenger ships were likely to face from air transport, so contrived further novel features to ensure the viability of their proposed super-cabin liners.

This took them until March 1951. Although the two giant vessels were still basically the same as before – their overall length was still designed to be 1,254ft – their gross tonnage was reduced from the original 100,000, as they now had one deck less. This was the uppermost one, with its 'cathedral' windows, which had been intended for aeroplane storage space but, in spite of its elimination, it was not expected that the auxiliary aircraft-carrying capability would be affected adversely.

In appearance, however, the liners had changed considerably. A revised artist's impression depicted them with a single modern mast above the bridge, replacing the two conventionally placed masts of the earlier design. The two funnels had acquired a streamlined rake, and a distinctive upward trend of the hull colouring forward, starting beneath the fore part of the midship superstructure, gave the vessels a sleek and racy look, while the fifty-eight double-banked lifeboats had been raised from the main to the promenade deck.

The passenger accommodation and troop-carrying potential were naturally rather less since the cabin space had been reduced, but there was the hint of an interesting innovation in the form of cafeteria-style restaurants in addition to the traditional dining saloons. With such an arrangement, the proponents declared: 'The passengers will have a means of controlling their expenses at sea.'

Each vessel was planned to have a dry cargo capacity of 375,000 cu ft and a refrigerated storage capacity of 100,000 cu ft. It was proposed

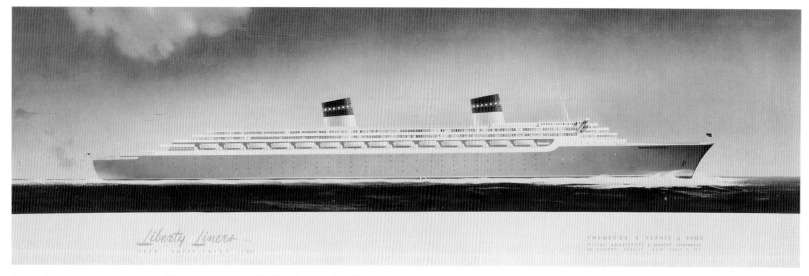

An artist's impression of one of the 'Liberty Liners' in 1952. *Theodore Ferris & Sons*

that cargo and mail stowage would be through the sides of the ships, using 'gear of the extensible-boom type', rather like the gantries used in container ports for the handling of 'box' cargoes.

These new 'Liberty Liners' would have been of entirely fireproof construction, completely enclosed and air-conditioned throughout. The hull was designed to three-compartment safety standard with seventeen main watertight bulkheads.

The propulsion machinery would have been located in two independent, widely separated engine rooms and consisted of four double-reduction-geared turbines designed to develop 280,000 normal shaft horsepower to give a sustained sea speed of 34 knots. Steam would have been furnished by eight boilers at 925psi and 1,000° Fahrenheit.

To promote their scheme still further, Chapman and Ferris engaged a top-ranking public relations firm to 'plug' the super-liners. They had a mock-up of a typical cabin suite built, complete with private bathroom and wall-to-wall carpeting. Further, they explained how the construction of the two monster liners would provide much employment for thousands of industrial and shipyard workers, as well as for 1,700 seamen, whilst additionally providing the United States with two liners which would be the envy of the whole world.

In order to finance the project, however, Liberty Liners Inc. still depended on receiving federal aid. At this time, the government-subsidised *United States* was nearing completion, albeit designed to the United States Navy's specifications, but nevertheless she was America's first giant passenger steamship that was entirely the product of the effort of the United States. The fact that government money had already been spent on this enterprise was one which partly jeopardised the success of the request for similar financial assistance from Liberty Liners Inc., on the one hand, but debate over the proposed size of the ships also caused problems, on the other.

Where the Liberty Liners' proposal was concerned, the sponsors explained that they had designed ships of such unparalleled dimensions so that they could have engines big enough to give the required speed, whilst still able to carry sufficient passengers to make them successful economically even if they were utilised at only half their capacity. As for their tremendous length, this was required to enable them to span three, or to straddle two, 600ft heavy-weather Atlantic waves, thereby reducing the effects of pitching and effectively making them steadier ships, even in extreme conditions.

However, whether because they already had money invested in one project aimed at elevating America's maritime prestige, or

Projected cabin layout for the 'Liberty Liners' ships.

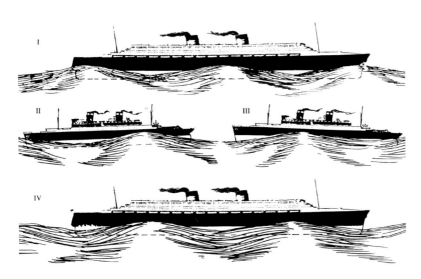

Sketches illustrating the behaviour at sea of a 1,250ft ship (I & IV) compared with that of a 700ft vessel (II & III) under 'heavy weather' conditions of the North Atlantic. The length of seas (horizontally from crest to crest) is 600ft: their height, from crest to trough (vertically), 36ft. *Both Roy Miller from a contemporary brochure*

whether it was because of the unprecedented size of these two liners is not known for certain but, yet again, the Federal Maritime Board was unable to recommend that the Maritime Administration (successor to the Maritime Commission) give its support for the construction of two such vessels.

This ended the final fling of Chapman and Ferris, and both died soon afterwards – Theodore Ernest Ferris' in May 1953 and Paul Wadsworth Chapman the following year. As to the former, his name lives on in maritime history for his many successes and innovations in other forms of ship design, particularly in the two world wars. Although extremely successful before embarking on maritime affairs, Chapman cannot be said to hold the same distinction in this field, since his actual achievements were negligible. Certainly the influence of both men made its impact, even though it may be difficult to demonstrate that it led to any positive results.

Nevertheless, they were both men possessed of enormous resolution, fortified by their unswerving confidence and beliefs in their grandiose conceptions, which were not only intended to be commercial ventures but were equally initiated from a deep-seated sense of patriotism for the greater prestige of the United States. If ever two men might have borne the motto '*Never say die*', these two were they, and, in modern parlance, they were men who could 'think big'. Such vessels as they proposed were never built during the era of the scheduled service passenger liner and, at that time, the likelihood of anything on that scale ever being constructed was very remote. Since then, of course, the emergence of the *Queen Mary 2* at 149,215grt (half as big again) and 1,132ft in length has undermined what was once the conventional wisdom. This has, to some extent vindicated the predictions of not only Ferris and Chapman, but also of Yourkevitch. One may reasonably conclude that their schemes were no mere pipe-dreams and it may be said, with truth, that they were truly 'Damned by Destiny'. Their liner conceptions were indeed 'great passenger ships that never were', yet they might well have come into being.

Had the various schemes set forth in this book finally blossomed onto the passenger routes or cruise circuits of the world, some would probably have had careers attended with financial success and even, in some cases, great fame, whilst others might have found themselves

The partially constructed hull of the Cunarder No. 534 – the *Queen Mary* – on the stocks at John Brown's shipyard at Clydebank. All work on her was stopped on 11 December 1931, while her fate lay in the balance. *Authors' collection*

The *Queen* Mary on trials off the Isle of Arran in early May 1936. Having come close to suffering an ignominious fate – cancellation and demolition incomplete – she became instead the most popular and most successful British ocean liner throughout her illustrious thirty-one-year career. *Glasgow University Archives*

in precisely the opposite case. Who knows? It must be borne in mind that many of those great liners of the past, which became enshrined in the rolls of maritime history, might well have suffered a like fate as could some of the giant cruise ships built subsequently, depending on the circumstances prevailing when each was conceived.

This statement represents no mere flight of fancy, and readers may be familiar with the manner in which the *Queen Mary*, not only one of the biggest, but one of the most successful and charismatic of all the great liners ever built, remained for almost twenty-eight months in a state of uncertain and potentially terminal suspension. Laid down in August 1930 as Yard No. 534 on one of John Brown's slipways in all good faith, the serious economic situation of the time led to all work being suspended when she was in a relatively advanced state of construction, and so she remained, a huge metaphorical question mark dominating the surrounding Clydebank, for nearly two and a half years. Finally, in late 1933, after insistence that the White Star and Cunard Lines be amalgamated (which might not have been accepted), the government of the day agreed to subsidise construction of the vessel to permit her completion. But this, too, was something of a gamble, since all governments are notoriously capricious and the political climate can and does alter the view of the government in power, not to mention that of a successive government through conversion to, or the adoption of widely different opinions and policies.

The gestation period of the *Queen Mary* was both long and difficult but, as it happened, she emerged in the end to become a household name throughout the world. Yet one cannot feel otherwise than that she could equally well have become the subject of another chapter in this book, another great passenger ship scheme 'Damned by Destiny'. Everybody knows that there was nothing wrong with the ship itself, which was not only a record-breaker that captured the Atlantic Blue Riband, but which gave a service, perhaps second to none, in peace and war. Yet had she been abandoned on the stocks, there would always have been a doubt about her achievements had she not gone into commission.

So, too, one must likewise judge the less fortunate vessels documented in these pages. They did not necessarily fail on their potential merits as ships at sea, but often for longshore considerations usually based on finance or the like. But, when one considers the roster of those grandly conceived vessels that 'might have been', and tries to speculate on what they might have achieved, it may be that there are too many imponderables to reach clear-cut conclusions. In many cases, the answer is simply to remember how nearly the *Queen Mary* missed coming into being. Having said that, if there was any question as to the viability of their prospects, it was better to abandon a project in its design stage rather than to proceed regardless only to run a ship that resulted at a loss.

In considering the more immediate problem of the 'Liberty Liners', if, perhaps, the *United States* had not been under construction when they were proposed, one wonders whether they might not have materialised ... who can say? Had they been constructed and gone into service, Chapman and Ferris would have gone down in history as two names with which to conjure, for this alone. Success and failure are inextricably intertwined.

The question of the size of passenger vessels, like those proposed by Liberty Liners Inc., is an interesting one. Certainly, there are valid arguments in favour of such monsters, but the logic of building them is debatable when one considers that their vast size would have prevented their navigation of the Panama Canal and, perhaps of lesser consequence, the Suez Canal. The passage of the former would have been a point of enormous strategic value in their adaptation to military work, as well as having great commercial merit if and when the occasion should arise. The smaller *United States* was able to pass through both canals. Another point which may be remarked, when viewing in retrospect the intervening years – years in which Chapman and Ferris were already dead – and particularly the decades of the 1970s and 1980s when virtually all remaining passenger liners were employed to a greater or lesser extent on cruises, is that these outsize super-liners would have been precluded from using many ports and desirable anchorages due to their excessive draught. Indeed, in this context, it may be noted that a sight not infrequently seen in The Solent back in the years when Southampton, as a major ocean liner terminal, was known as the 'Gateway to the World' was that of the *United States* steaming up Southampton Water while the

Queen Elizabeth or *Queen Mary* lay at anchor down at Cowes Roads, having to wait the deeper water of the full tide.

It is easy to pontificate, and to write with the benefit of hindsight. Entrepreneurs, though, do not have the ability to view the future in crystal balls and, even when the writing is writ clearly on the walls, it often occurs that it is not what they want to read. Certainly Chapman and Ferris could not have foreseen the switch from passenger-carrying on scheduled liner services to cruising, but there was always a school of thought that maintained there was an optimum size for a super-liner which should not be exceeded, if only for the reasons cited above, since any such ship must be expected to be diverted for service in time of war. There was some validity in that contention, even though those who subscribed to it may not have agreed precisely what that optimum size should be. Recent developments in merchant shipping might be said to have completely altered the complexion of the argument for, at the time of writing, there are cruise ships which, in their sheer size, almost overshadow the 'Liberty Liners', while even bigger vessels are forecast, although none of these will ever perform auxiliary duties.

The basis for the existence and promotion of mega-liners and, for that matter, mega-cruise ships lies in the simple economic truth, so well appreciated by the proponents of those 100,000-ton super-liners, that, based on the principle of economies of scale, the larger any unit of transport, the more economically viable it will be, always providing, of course, that it could be kept fully employed and turned round in port with expedition.

There have always been engineers and designers ahead of their times – men like Brunel, for example – but the majority of them have become lost in the mists of time simply because their peers were less far-sighted and too timid to back their ideas. As for Theodore Ferris and Paul Chapman, their great dream may have died unfulfilled with them, but it was not the end of that dream. In 1961, a final ephemeral bid to get their ships, designed ten years previously, into service was made by two close colleagues, William Perott and Walter M. Ballard, who had been associated with Chapman ever since his early days with the United States Lines. Subsequently, Ballard, who had been the design director for the interiors of the liners *Manhattan* and

Washington, had managed the offices of Liberty Liners Inc. on K. Street, Washington, D.C. These gentlemen proposed the construction of the two ships as designed but with the original propulsion system replaced by one combining nuclear reactors with steam turbines. This would have developed a total of 380,000shp, giving a maximum speed of around 40 knots with five propellers.

Nothing came of Perott and Ballard's efforts either, and it seems that the only thing which the Chapman/Ferris projects lacked was the necessary financial support to build the ships. But their lack of success did nothing whatsoever to put off others with similar ambitions, and the American drive for giant passenger liners was soon to have a new champion.

THE CANTOR PROPOSAL – THE *PEACE* AND *GOODWILL*: A CONCEPT 'PAVED WITH GOOD INTENTIONS'

On 5 April 1956, a New York hotelier, Mr Hyman B. Cantor, who was President of the Carter Hotel Group, read an address to the Propeller Club of the United States at the United States Merchant Marine Academy, Kings Point, New York. His subject concerned the construction of two transatlantic super-liners to inaugurate ocean travel to Europe for a one-way fare of $50 (£17) – it seemed that a successor to Paul Chapman and Theodore Ferris had arrived on the scene to perpetuate the American dream of a giant liner and mass tourist transportation by sea.

In his address, Mr Cantor stated that he had been thinking in terms of accomplishing this goal for the past twenty years, but had seen no way of financing such a project until the previous year. At that time, early in 1955, the US Government had made it possible through certain amendments to the Maritime Financing Act. Upon receiving his copy of the amendment, he had seen the possible means of financing two super-liners to make the transatlantic crossing. He foresaw a way of providing ocean travel which the American wage-earning classes could afford by applying mass-handling methods and with the regular American Merchant Marine, yet without an operating subsidy from the government.

The United States, he averred, had a reasonable amount of passenger ship accommodation available for the upper financial strata of its people, but little or no transportation existed for the lower income groups. Cantor's ships were to provide such a feature to a virtually untapped market and, instead of catering to the Waldorf-type clientele in the manner of the existing liners of the day, they would offer ocean passages done in the full American commercial tradition at 'Times Square' prices, permitting fares to Europe within the economic reach of almost everyone.

Originally, his plans called for two ships, each of 100,000 tons, 1,250ft long and with a capacity for 9,200 passengers but, since the U.S. Coast Guard regulations would not permit the carriage of over 6,000 passengers in any one vessel, the plans had to be revised several times in order to conform to this ruling. After these modifications had been incorporated, and following a tremendous amount of work, he eventually evolved a scheme encompassing all of the following features.

His final plans were for the construction of two 90,000 gross ton Atlantic Ocean super-liners, to be named the *Peace* and the *Goodwill*, to carry passengers to Europe for a one-way fare of $50 (£17) minimum. These were to be the largest and fastest ships afloat, each

to have a length of 1,150ft and a 34-knot cruising speed. Their beam would have measured 135ft and their draught 34ft. The two ships were expected to travel between the United States and Belgium in four days, with accommodation for 6,000 passengers and with a crew of 1,350.

The $50 one-way fare would include the transportation and berth only. A single-class catering service was planned, with a large kitchen at the centre of each ship servicing a 1,500-seat cafeteria, as well as a 1,000-seat formal dining room. In addition, there would have been self-service canteens of automat style, with food and beverages at economy prices, located on each guest deck. Four bars and cocktail lounges were also planned for each of the liners.

The passenger cabins would have been prefabricated by the Pullman Company and laid out in two- and four-berth rooms, each with a private bath, television and air-conditioning. Each of the two ships would have had two indoor swimming pools, a skating rink, two theatres, outdoor sports equipment, a concert hall and facilities for religious services. Also planned were shopping centres where goods from both sides of the Atlantic would be sold at reasonable prices.

The vessels were designed to be unsinkable, with twenty watertight compartments in the hulls and, in time of war, they could be converted

Proposed in the mid-1950s, the *Peace* and *Goodwill* were intended to provide cheap transatlantic travel for the masses. The project was killed off, like so many others, by funding difficulties. This model of the planned ships was displayed for many years in the entrance foyer of the Carter Hotel, New York. *Frank O. Braynard*

immediately to aircraft carriers or to division-strength troopships. The top deck would have been a flat, clear space, 450 × 80ft, abaft the funnel, and this would have been used as a sports deck for outdoor activities and also incorporating an outdoor swimming pool. Below this there would have been a glass-enclosed aircraft hangar space two decks deep, which would normally be used as a convention hall with seating capacity for 4,000 people. It would also have featured roll-away doors to enable the space to be divided into meeting rooms for smaller groups.

During off-season periods, the intention was that business groups on both sides of the Atlantic would be contacted to make passenger bookings in order to hold conventions and business 'junkets' aboard the two vessels. Hyman Cantor also planned to exploit his long hotel operating experience to arrange two-week packaged vacations at low cost. Passengers would be offered tours, with all expenses included, for as little as $330 (£110), of which $33 would be paid in cash with the balance in ten monthly instalments, an idea pioneered by the United States Lines in 1940, when it had been compelled to send the newly completed *America* cruising, due to the war in Europe.

Cantor himself headed a group of investors with $25 million (£8 million) in available cash, plus a working capital of $5 million. Since the repayment of a federal loan towards construction costs was guaranteed in twenty years, an operating subsidy from the government would not, therefore, be required. His estimates were that the construction of the two liners would take two years, and he let it be known that reservations for passages would be accepted only after the keels had been laid. Whilst this may seem to have been somewhat optimistic in this age when projects are so prone to fall behind schedule, it was once quite a common practice, and bookings were made on this basis for the maiden voyages of the *Olympic* and the *Titanic*, to cite but two instances.

After numerous reappraisals, the final 6,000 passenger, 90,000-ton ship design seemed to be the most practical, in that it provided ample public space and had complete sports and recreational facilities. There was no question, in Mr Cantor's opinion, but that there was an extremely intense and general need for travel accommodation of this type. Although there were always critics of mammoth ships

per se, there was also the valid concern that they might outgrow the port-handling facilities available to them. But it was felt that these vessels would not be too large on this count, since they would be loaded from their sides, making the length of the piers at which they would berth relatively unimportant.

Hyman Cantor envisaged the operation as a 'Ferry Line' linking New York and Belgium. Initial considerations had covered three ports as the European terminal, namely: Zeebrugge in Belgium, Flushing in the Netherlands and Milford Haven in the United Kingdom. The reasons for the selection of Zeebrugge were that Belgium did not have a major transatlantic passenger line of its own and that the officials there had been very cooperative. The operational base for the company he was setting up would have been at Boston, Massachusetts.

Cantor pointed out that the ships already in service at that time operated with a steward servicing six or eight rooms in the First- and Second-classes. This same steward made the beds, cleaned the cabins, did the valet work such as pressing clothes, shined the shoes, ran errands, acted as room-service waiter and even dispensed pills when a passenger was sick but, as a result of all this activity, he only made up some fourteen to sixteen beds a day. For his part, Cantor was looking for a more efficient productivity approach and had arranged with the unions for a daily target of sixty-five beds per maid. They agreed to this in return for the concession that there would be no overlap of jobs, to whit 'demarcation'. A maid was to be a maid, a waiter a waiter, a doctor a doctor, and so on. Through this more productive method, he was confident that he would be able to reduce the crew requirements considerably.

As an example, he quoted the *United States*, a ship with 1,700 beds and 1,062 crew, and the *Queen Elizabeth* which, with 2,200 beds, employed a crew of 1,600. Compared with these, his super-liners would have had 6,000 beds and, according to the manning scales that he had arranged with the unions, there would be fewer than 1,350 crew. In other words, there would be a ratio of four passengers to one crew member as opposed to about one and a half passengers to one crew in the existing large liners. However, neither caviar, pheasant, nor like delicacies would be offered as part of his service!

The Sea Coach Line's cafeteria ship *Peace*, dramatically illustrated in this rendering by Jochen Sachse. *Arnold Kludas*

The laundry would all be done ashore and, because of the great volume involved, a discount of 40 per cent had been offered by land-based commercial laundries. Most of the food would be pre-cooked, frozen or prepared in advance, and served on individual trays which would be discarded over the ships' sides, thereby eliminating preparation aboard. Had his scheme been fulfilled, there would doubtless have been an outcry from ecological lobbies, especially if the trays were made of plastic and therefore indestructible! Two men in each watch, it was suggested, would be able to keep twenty canteens supplied with food, and each of these canteens, in turn, could supply hundreds of passengers.

Cantor's detailed plans, along with the stress and strain studies, were put on display for the inspection of the Propeller Club audience. He stated that he had been asked by European shipyards to build the ships on that side of the Atlantic, with offers of very favourable financial inducements to do so, but stressed that he himself was an American and that this was a strictly American concept. He continued to say that most of his business would emanate from the United States and, for these reasons, he preferred that Washington should help him to close the deal in his own country. As for the Merchant Marine officers of the future, Cantor saw an opportunity in his enterprise to restore the glory of the American passenger fleet to the nation's advantage. He felt that, in one fell swoop, his project would accomplish passenger ship supremacy for the United States and supply permanent employment for 2,700 merchant seamen, in addition to 4,000 shipyard and construction employees while the ships were being built – all achieved simply by the application of the American concept of mass handling.

In conclusion, he reiterated that no government operating subsidy would be necessary for his ships and that he hoped that the loan guarantee would be favourably received and set in motion very soon, in order that contracts could be signed for the ships' construction.

Apparently, the U.S. Maritime Administration liked Mr Cantor's proposal, and preliminary plans were sent to the United States Navy Department for its approval, since the two vessels would be used as troop transports or aircraft carriers should the need arise and they were, therefore, classified as 'special purpose vessels'. In 1954, the estimated cost of these proposed liners was $200 million (£65 million) if they were to be built in the United States but, owing to large wage increases and rises in the price of steel, by August 1956 this figure had risen to $270 million (£90 million). This posed the question of where the liners should be built, as United States Navy approval would be necessary if Mr Cantor was to benefit from a construction subsidy of between 40 and 50 per cent but, in turn, this would be conditional on them being built in an American yard. On the other hand, if they were built in a foreign shipyard, they would have been much cheaper but, in that case, there would have been no government construction subsidy.

Representatives from a German shipyard visited Cantor to discuss the building of the ships, but nothing concrete resulted. The proposals for the *Peace* and the *Goodwill* remained a subject of much interest in passenger shipping circles for the next three and a half years, by which time another American tycoon, Mr Edgar Detwiler, had arrived on the scene with some proposals of his own to rival Cantor's ideas.

Hyman Cantor's grandiose and bold scheme culminated in September 1959 when, in the midst of rumours that he had negotiated contracts with Deutsche Werft AG at Hamburg for the construction of two 90,000grt liners, it finally transpired that all that he had done was to come to an understanding with the yard that, if and when he had found the money and had made all the other arrangements necessary, they – probably like many other shipyards – would be happy to build the ships. According to one report, Cantor had discussed the matter with Dr Erhard, the West German Finance Minister, in an attempt to conclude an agreement with the West German Federal Government over the cost of the building of the ships. It seems that he was prepared to sign a contract with the Deutsche Werft shipyard involving $168 million (£56 million) if the German Government would guarantee 70 per cent of the building expenses. In this context, and since this supposition may require clarification, the explanation was provided by a letter written by Cantor shortly afterwards, in which he said:

We even signed a contract (for the *Peace* and *Goodwill*) with the Deutsche Werft shipyard at Hamburg, subject to the German

Government providing primary mortgage financing, but negotiations on this never materialised.

By this time, a company named Sea Coach Transatlantic Liners Inc. had been formed to manage the project, and Cantor wanted his 'Hotel Dixie' super-liners, as they had been dubbed, to be in service by 1962 and 1963. Deutsche Werft quoted thirty-six months to build each ship, but against this there was a competitive bid from a Japanese yard of thirty months per ship, with primary financing provided by the Japanese Government. However, the terms of this contract, in respect of amortisation, were considered to be too onerous for the company and, since it was felt to be imprudent to proceed on such terms, this solution to the building of the ships had to be abandoned.

Following that set-back, nothing more was heard of Hyman Cantor's proposals. Just how seriously his scheme should be viewed in retrospect may be uncertain, but he certainly did a great deal of talking and a lot of interested and well-known people listened to him at the time. The fact of the matter was that one practical problem associated with these proposals of 1956 and 1959 was the unfamiliarity of Cantor himself with ships and naval architecture, although he was well versed in hotel management and catering matters. The famous naval architect, Vladimir Yourkevitch, the designer of the *Normandie*, acted as his consultant; in fact the influence of his *Bretagne* concept was quite evident in those proposed *Peace* and *Goodwill*. In this capacity, Yourkevitch must have been much discomfited by day-to-day changes of service speed by as much as 3 knots for such reasons as: 'By getting them in before lunch we can save a meal', or 'This will mean two more round voyages in the year.' The consultants were accused of making difficulties when they explained that such large speed increases might require almost a doubling of power, thereby resulting in a severe reduction in the space available for accommodation!

It is nevertheless interesting to note that, looking back to the 1980s, the largest profit-earning liner in that decade, the *Queen Elizabeth 2*, was owned by Cunard, which was then part of the major holding group, Trafalgar House Investments, which was itself a large hotel and catering organisation. Similarly, it is also ironic to observe that, on 28 September 1977, Sir Freddie Laker, another entrepreneur, inaugurated his 'Skytrain' service between Gatwick and New York, based on cheap one-way fares of £59, thus succeeding in doing by air what Hyman Cantor had failed to accomplish by sea. This was but a brief accomplishment, though, for the spectacular bankruptcy of 'Skytrain' followed in February 1982.

In late 1978, Cantor revealed that he was investigating other liner operation possibilities. These involved the deployment of two large-scale ships with huge public rooms and suitably adapted interiors for conventions and public meetings, along the lines of the *Queen Mary* in her role at Long Beach. He declared that 'this would be very profitable', but nothing ever came of it.

A SECOND *AMERICA* AND THE *PRESIDENT WASHINGTON*

A bid to obtain approval for the construction of the contemplated sister-ship to the *United States* began in 1956, and this scheme was closely linked to another project involving a new transpacific super-liner for the American President Lines. Both vessels, looking very similar indeed to the earlier *United States*, were designed by the Gibbs brothers, although it seems that the APL were not happy with this and were looking for an appearance which reflected the advances made in the years since the previous liner was built. The two projects were linked by the fact that they formed integral parts of a bill presented by Representative Herbert C. Bonner, the North Carolina Democrat and the Chairman of the House of Representatives Merchant Marine Committee, before the 85th session of Congress. The eventual failure to appropriate funds for their construction was yet further evidence of the vacillating attitudes concerning giant liner ownership within the American administration.

The United States Lines' vessel was requested as a replacement for the *America*, which was then nearly twenty years old and due to be superseded at this age under the terms of the federal subsidy agreements. The new liner, which would probably have borne the same name, was virtually a duplicate of the *United States*, although construction costs had increased by 60 per cent since she was built. Plans for her National Defence auxiliary capabilities included the

The *United States* which, in 1952, eclipsed all previous passenger ship records by making the westbound Atlantic crossing at 34.51 knots and the eastbound at 35.59 knots. By no means the largest ship on the run, she was the ultimate in terms of speed. *United States Lines*

An artist's impression of the *President Washington* proposed for transpacific service with American President Lines. Her exterior design showed influences of the earlier *United States* as did the proposed consort of the latter ship. *Gibbs & Cox*

provision for possible installation of a nuclear propulsion unit, as an alternative to the traditional steam generation plant.

The American President Lines' ship – the President Washington – was some 10,000 tons smaller with an estimated gross tonnage of 43,000, an overall length of 956ft and a passenger complement of 1,450 divided between three classes. The President Washington was also considered for the installation of nuclear instead of conventional steam plant and boilers for military reasons and, as a twin-screw ship, would have had the very creditable speed of 29 knots.

Competitive tenders for the two liners were requested, and in each case the lowest bids came from the New York Shipbuilding Corporation at Camden, New Jersey, which quoted around $109 million (£36 million) for the sister to the United States and $97.5 million (£32.5 million) for the President Washington, although construction of the latter vessel was at first considered to be more likely undertaken on the west coast. The progress of the Bill for the two liners was fairly smooth at first, but then a difficulty arose between the United States Lines and the Federal Maritime Board with regard to the subsidisation of the extra speed required for their new vessel. The company argued that experience gained from the operation of the United States showed that a vessel designed with a great emphasis on auxiliary requirements and carrying engines with an excessive margin of reserve speed was an uneconomic proposition. Therefore, the company wanted to have the commercial speed of the new liner set at 28 knots, with the government paying for the cost of increasing the speed above this figure. The Federal Maritime Board, on the other hand, argued – with some good reason, as may be thought – that the average speed at which the United States had been operated was 31.5 knots, and that this should, therefore, be the service speed of the new vessel. This divergence of opinion unfortunately prolonged the negotiations over the two ships and, as a result, the legislation for approving their construction fell as a casualty of budget pruning in the first session of the 85th Congress.

Matters reached a head again by 20 March 1958 when the House of Representatives Merchant Marine Committee once more recommended the construction and sale of two super-liners. The committee proposed that one of them should equal the size and grandeur of the United States with a capacity for 2,000 passengers, while the other would ply a major Pacific route and would accommodate 1,400 passengers. In effect, this was an echo of the new America and the President Washington proposals, and it had a familiar ring about it. By this time, however, the cost of the new running mate for the United States, to replace the old America, had risen to around $128 million (£42.5 million), which would include her defence features, together with luxury facilities and appointments. There was no total cost quoted for the Pacific liner, but estimates were thought to be approximately $200 million (£67 million) as a minimum for both vessels.

The proposal was that the United States Lines should purchase the larger liner for $47 million (£15.5 million) and the American President Lines the smaller one for $34 million (£11.3 million), or 45 per cent of the domestic construction costs in each case, whichever should be the greater. These sale prices to the companies would be fixed but, if shipbuilding and outfitting costs rose above contract specifications, a provision would be made whereby any cost differential between the fixed sale price and that of final construction costs would be borne by the government.

It seems that this provision was in line with congressional legislation that any new passenger liner would have to be ready for troopship duties in times of national emergency. Any construction and sale operations would still be subject to the approval of the Federal Maritime Board. The Bill, which was basically the same as that originally sponsored by Herbert C. Bonner, still required that the repayment terms from the companies should be in accordance with the existing laws but, nevertheless, the terms were felt to be liberal. In this context, the payments made by the respective operating companies would not include U.S. Navy specifications or the costs of features added to the vessels to that end, since these would have to be met at the government's expense.

The contracts for the two ships now depended entirely on congressional action on separate maritime appropriation bills which went before the Senate and the House of Representatives. In the event, the construction of both vessels did finally receive authorisation by Congress and was also fully endorsed by President Eisenhower. These hurdles having been cleared, the schemes now seemed to have no further obstacles before them and merely awaited the actual allocation of federal funds. By 1961, however, there had still been no provision for money in the administration's fiscal budgets. At this point, and despite their contractual obligation to the U.S. Government to build replacement tonnage for the *President Wilson* and *President Cleveland*, the American President Lines shelved the project for its new liner and terminated its arrangements with the lowest bidding shipyard, with which no formal contract had been signed.

The United States Lines, on the other hand, continued to pursue its intention of building a sister-ship to the *United States*, although they appeared to have abandoned the initial design proposal which was, as previously stated, virtually a duplicate of the famous record-breaker. In 1963 it sanctioned the Gibbs brothers to prepare a study for a 'super-*United States*' but nothing developed from this either. Then, in 1965, the Gibbs were approached again to produce designs for 'a new *America*', but this also failed to gain government approval for a federal subsidy, even though the company was still under its obligation to replace the old *America* which, by that time, had become the Greek *Australis*. (Since the 1958 bill before Congress was in respect of both the Atlantic and Pacific vessels, it automatically broke down when the American President Lines reneged on its obligations and, for this reason, the subsequent moves on the United States Lines' projected vessel were subject to separate and unrelated applications for federal approval and aid.)

The reason for the persistent reluctance to aid contract replacement programmes on the part of Congress lay in the ever-increasing shipbuilding costs. So long as these programmes were projected as loss-making operations requiring massive long-term subsidies, the government was not, it seems, prepared to press shipping companies into fulfilling those contractual obligations which had originally been undertaken in a different financial climate.

During the years that the United States Lines lobbied Congress for the financial support to build a consort for the *United States* (probably with a feeling of some frustration in the light of the fact that approval had been given for such a ship in the 1958 bill, and it

was no fault of theirs that the ship had not materialised as a result of it), another quite different bill to appropriate the construction costs of giant passenger liners was laid before Congress, albeit with an equal lack of success. The instigator of this latter bill was Republican Senator John Ray of New York, who called for the approval of the building of two 90,000 gross ton all-Tourist-class liners for the Department of Commerce, which would then sell them to any interested operating concern, including the United States Lines! He advocated two vessels having a length of 1,150ft and a speed of 35 knots, each intending to carry up to 6,000 passengers at low-rate fares, and to be operated like commercial hotels, lacking the splendour, grandeur and elaborate cuisine of the real luxury liners. Senator Ray's proposals, which sounded rather like a revival of Hyman Cantor's plans of a decade earlier, were received with even less enthusiasm than the original ones put forward by the United States Lines and, beyond that, were never sufficiently tangible to warrant further elaboration here.

Around this time, it was rumoured, without much supporting evidence, that the Sovtorgflot – the managing organisation of the Soviet merchant service – was planning the construction of an 85,000 gross ton liner. As usual, Russia was a 'dark horse' about her merchant and naval plans, and little could be ascertained about the ship's design or its intended service. Whether or not there was any fire beneath the smoke of that particular rumour, it seemed to fade into the impenetrable mists and mysteries behind the Iron Curtain, and represented the merest interlude for speculation in a period dominated by projects of American origin.

Ironically, by 1969 the *United States* was experiencing high operational fuel and manning costs along with falling passenger receipts, her balance sheet worsened by the withdrawal by the government of the day of her operational subsidy. In addition to this she was arguably facing more classy competition from French Lines *France* and Cunard's *Queen Elizabeth 2* as well as the incursion of jet airliners. In these circumstances, being too expensive to run on diminishing returns with her high-redundancy engine room configuration, the *United States* was withdrawn from service and laid up. It was barely five years since her owners had been pursuing its last fruitless effort to secure funding for a consort and, reflecting the signs of the times, it rendered the entire matter of a replacement for the *America* as academic. As for the *United States*, she continues to languish in a much deteriorated state at a lay-up berth on the James River near Philadelphia, her abandonment and neglect a reflection of near-total national disinterest in the one-time Atlantic Blue Riband holder and the part she played in the era of the great ocean liners.

THE DETWILER PROJECT – THE *UNITED NATIONS*-CLASS

In the winter of 1958–59, plans were announced for the intended introduction of four 120,000 gross ton passenger liners on the transatlantic route, each of which would carry 8,000 passengers. Mr Edgar Detwiler, President of the American-European Travel Project Inc. of New York, proposed that these vessels, to be called the *United Nations*, *New Yorker*, *Lisbon* and the *Hollander* (the latter alternatively to be named the *Mayflower*), would be built in the Netherlands and would possibly trade under the Portuguese flag. Their projected speed would enable them to cross the Atlantic in about 3.5 to 4 days, and the charge for the all-in fare would be less than $162 (£54) – the lowest ever available!

Mr Detwiler had apparently been planning to carry large numbers of American tourists to Europe in enormous one-class ships ever since 1929, and he hoped that, following the signing of the building contracts, the first of the ships would enter service in 1961. Following these sudden announcements, which displayed Detwiler's initial enthusiasm, the story became more complex and involved as it proceeded. At the time, the estimated cost of each of the ships would have been more than $90 million (£30 million), although he was confident that the money would be raised from 'international sources'. The preliminary design of the liners had been prepared by Mr John Wright, an American naval architect, and this was seen during a visit to the United States by Mr Cornelis Verolme, the Chairman of the Verolme United Shipyards in whose yards it was proposed that the ships should be built.

In order to cater for such a mammoth undertaking, the first step was the formation, in the autumn of 1959, of a Dutch shipping, holding and financing company called American European Lines NV. One of the reasons for its formation was that it was proposed to man the vessels with crews of Dutch nationality as well as other Europeans, thereby incurring lower wage bills and other operating cost benefits than would accrue under the United States flag. No contract had been signed at this stage, and the major problem that lay ahead was the actual financing of the immense project. In the meantime, Mr Detwiler had assured potential backers that arrangements were being made, not only to finance the proposed vessels, but also to cover the cost of the ocean terminals which would have been necessary in both the United States and Europe in order to accommodate liners of such gargantuan proportions. The cost of each fully equipped vessel, including the interest payments involved in financing the construction period and other expenses, the operating capital and a pro-rata proportion of the cost of the ocean terminal facilities was estimated to be some $128 million (£43 million) per vessel. The necessary equity to provide operating capital, amounting to $34.5 million (£11.5 million) per vessel, was said to have been arranged already. The outstanding balance for each of the liners would be paid on an instalment basis at the various stages of construction. The ships would be managed and operated by the Dutch company and, as such, would be registered under Dutch law and be required to fly the Dutch flag, and not the Portuguese, as originally planned.

It will have been noted that Hyman Cantor had been required to amend his original idea of carrying 9,200 passengers to 6,000, so as to conform to the U.S. Coast Guard regulations, and that each of the successive American-flag schemes had settled on the figure of 6,000 passengers for this very reason. Now, of course, by operating his vessels under a flag that was not under the jurisdiction of the U.S. Coast Guard, Detwiler was enabled to set his target for the higher figure of 8,000 berths.

His holding company entered into a contract with Hardy, Tobin and Co., a creditable firm of consultant naval architects, marine engineers and ship surveyors in London, to draught the final designs for the vessels of his proposed fleet – since it was no less! – and, in

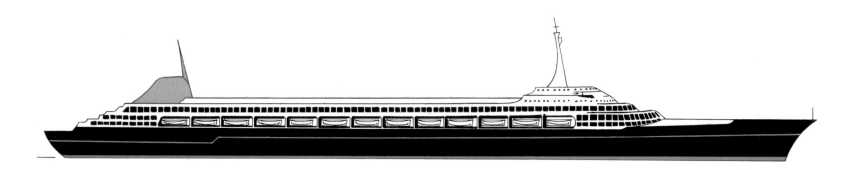

A profile drawing of Edgar Detwiler's *United Nations* class of transatlantic giants, showing the engines aft configuration as envisaged in a press release of 14 May 1960 entitled 'How Europe (and especially Holland) can earn more United States dollars and enjoy greater prosperity' (see also third colour section for alternative conception). *David Hutchings*

this connection, Detwiler had frequent meetings with Mr A.C. Hardy, the director of the consultancy. It was then revealed that much of the design for the ships, besides the broad economic strategy of the scheme, was based on the 'Liner of the Future' concept which had been outlined by A.C. Hardy and Pierre deMalglaive as far back as 1937 (see page 90). Consequently, Hardy, Tobin and Co. were given the responsibility for both the architectural work and interior design of the four passenger liners. In appearance, the two designs are not altogether dissimilar, the principal difference being the substitution of the retractable funnels and unusual exhaust arrangements of the 'Liner of the Future' for a pair of athwartship funnels placed aft in the Detwiler ships. There are even similarities in the dimensions of the two designs and in the type of power plant selected.

The *United Nations*, *New Yorker*, *Lisbon* and the *Hollander* were to be one-class liners with the following main particulars:

Tonnage (gross registered)	108,000–120,000
Length overall	1,275ft
Beam	130ft
Speed	35 knots
Power plant	Turbo-electric
Shaft horsepower	300,000–400,000
Number of passengers	8,000
Number of crew	2,000

The turbo-electric drive selected for the main propulsion of the 'United Nations'-class would have used two land power station-type of turbo alternators which would supply five double-armature motors, each coupled to a propeller. Mr Hardy considered that it was then ten years too early to consider it a viable proposition to install nuclear power plants in such ships.

Special entertainment features planned for each Detwiler vessel included a large theatre to seat 1,200 people, four different kinds of night club, eight different areas in which to dance, a cinema seating 800 persons, where the latest international films would be shown, and eight dining rooms of varying standards accommodating 4,000 people at a time with top-quality food and service. In addition, a number of snack bars, American-type soda fountains and different types of tea, coffee and cocktail lounges would be provided. There would be no cafeteria-type service as originally envisaged in the Cantor project. Detwiler made no apology for the fact that passage aboard his liners would be a relatively basic experience, announcing that there would be 'around 2,000 juke boxes, 3,000 games consoles and as many as 4,000 vending machines of all types'. He explained:

Our ships would require many more coin machines than a normal operation because of our economy-class travel. We will be catering to people with very little money, people who ordinarily would never have the money for a trip to Europe.

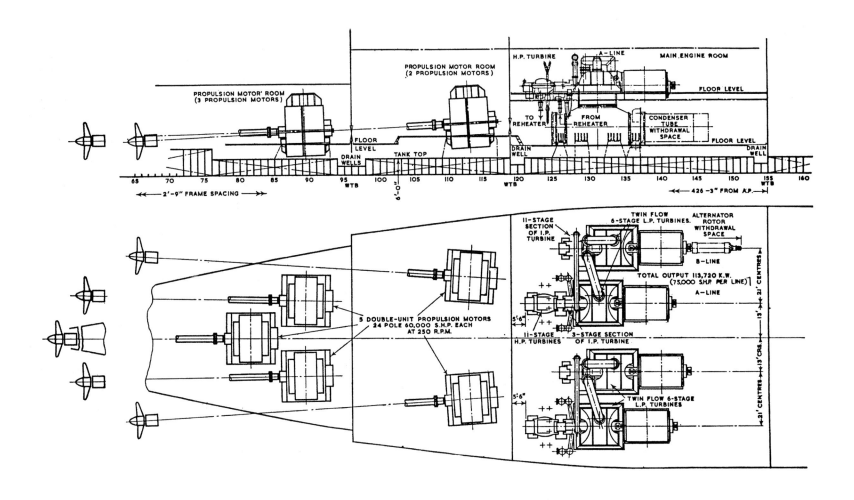

A proposed 300,000shp turbo-electric propulsion arrangement driving five screws devised for the 'United Nations'-class ships by A.E.I. in April 1960. Simultaneously, Pametrada of Newcastle conceived an advanced steam turbine plant as an alternative power option for the four liners. *Authors' collection*

We can't provide them with next-to-nothing transportation and still wine and dine them in the luxury manner. This, we all have to understand. We can give them transportation and a place to sleep – and that is all.

Nonetheless, the ships would have been well-equipped. Facilities would have been provided for many kinds of sports (in the form of swimming pools, etc.) and for recreation, while tax-free goods would have been available in a comprehensive shopping complex of about fifty shops. There would also have been many rooms with the capability of accommodating large conference and convention groups.

These proposed liners would have been completely air-conditioned. Each stateroom was planned to be of the lounge type, with its own bathroom, and would have accommodated from one to four people. Indeed, the accommodation and facilities to be provided by each ship would have somewhat exceeded those of the world's largest hotels of the time.

It was estimated that the building of the first vessel would take about three years and the following sisters about two years each. The intention was that two of the vessels would have operated regularly on the North Atlantic between New York and Amsterdam, with intermediate calls at Cobh (formerly Queenstown) and Plymouth, while the other two would have plied on the more southerly track between New York and Lisbon, with occasional voyages to Italy. Each of the four vessels would have been interchangeable between these routes, depending on the volume of summer or winter traffic available. The estimated round-trip fare for a family, or for a social or student group of three of four people, in a private stateroom with bathroom and including meals was to have been about $175 (£58) per head, but the same facilities for two people would have been $200 (£67) each. Special terms, such as hire-purchase arrangements, were to have been made available to passengers to assist them by spreading the cost of the passage and associated tours, if required.

Detwiler had foreseen the building of special marine ocean terminals, which would have been required in conjunction with these huge liners, in order to expedite the embarkation and disembarkation of their passengers and the handling of their luggage. He also predicted that there would need to be a complex combination of railway, bus, coach and heliport termini with car-parking capacity for 10,000 cars. In addition, he planned that hotels, motels and a complete tourist shopping centre would have to be available and, to provide for layouts of such complexity, he calculated that six piers and over 30 acres of land would be needed. However, Detwiler optimistically promised that all these facilities would be made available at Amsterdam and at Lisbon, not to mention the need to widen the North Sea Canal to Amsterdam to allow the passage of his enormous vessels! During the early part of his various negotiations, he had had talks with the Port of Rotterdam authorities about the use of Europort as the Dutch terminus, since this was one of the few ports able to accommodate such large vessels. It is not entirely clear what the objections to this may have been, although it might be safe to presume that the area of land that was required did not accord with the Europort scheme as already determined. On the other hand, the River Tagus at Lisbon was deep enough to take the vessels and possibly presented less of a problem regarding the size of the ships.

It was predicted that, when the four proposed liners were all in service, they would have been able to carry 900,000 round-trip passengers each year between the United States and Europe, and that the spending potential of this number of tourists might amount to some $500 million (£167 million) while they were in Europe.

We have already considered in previous chapters some very ambitious schemes, upon the viability of which readers may have formed their own opinions. In the full knowledge of the way that events have unfolded after these various proposals were made – and died – they may conclude that some would not have proved to be viable. This would be a perfectly valid conclusion, particularly in the case of the later, post-war schemes, although it must be remembered that the various entrepreneurs and their backers did not possess crystal balls and that, although the threat of air transport as a serious competitor to the passenger liner was certainly looming, no one could then have guessed just how great that threat was to prove to be, or the sudden collapse and withdrawal from regular service of so many splendid passenger ships. In order to take a balanced view of these proposals, it is necessary to project oneself back in time to the years when they were being considered and, without prescience of what the future might hold, having accomplished this rather difficult operation and setting aside the knowledge of those factors which did subsequently occur to sabotage the economics of passenger ship operation, it will be generally found that the various schemes did seem to be perfectly feasible. The reasons for their foundering were usually because the initial costs could not be raised or due to other factors that have been described but which were not immediately concerned with any lack of confidence in them. Indeed, as has been shown, they received the support of influential men of high intelligence and, in some instances, of genius.

So it was in the case of Edgar Detwiler. Monumental projects for immense cruise ships some fifty years later would render his plans as relatively modest but, at the time, his was the most ambitious scheme of all, not only because his ships were to be the largest and because there were to be more of them, but also because the ancillary requirements, in the sense of his vast ocean terminals, were the most grandiose yet conceived. Moreover, he was the last of the proponents of the great American 'dream' – the last to try to place the United States at the forefront of the Atlantic passenger trade – and it might be thought that, by the late 1950s, the writing was on the wall where concepts of this sort were concerned. In fact, this was not the case although, had he come forward ten years later, it is doubtful if anyone would have listened to him. As it was, he received the support of some very influential and respected men in the field of shipping.

Mr Cornelis Verolme of the Verolme United Shipyard at Rotterdam, which later became part of the now defunct Rhine-Schelde Verolme Group, felt that the project was 'extremely serious' and if, in the event, the building contract had been signed, the order would have been worth a total of $340 million (£113 million) and would have achieved a record as the largest shipbuilding order ever placed at that time. Of course, in citing him, it might be argued that he had a vested interest in the project: an interest which would have enhanced the profits and prestige of his firm almost beyond measure, but no businessman of his acumen and experience was likely to undertake such an operation unless he had full confidence in its successful outcome, for the ships were not going to be built overnight, and it is difficult to imagine a more alarming situation than to have such enormous vessels well on the way to completion and then to find that the purchasers could not proceed. These were not vessels which could be 'sold off' elsewhere, and much confidence was required to undertake to build in the first place, regardless of the possible rewards which might accrue from the venture.

A somewhat cynical reader might argue that Mr A.C. Hardy, another party who gave the scheme his backing, had an equally vested interest. A marine engineering and naval architecture consultant of very high standing, he was a sincere man who had already been convinced of the viability of very large Atlantic liners for over twenty years. He did a great deal of work on the project, for which he was presumably paid, but, once again, it must be remarked that it does not help any man's reputation to back a failure, and if Hardy was a naval architect par excellence, he was on a plane which did not ignore the economic considerations involved in the ships he designed. Even the Chairman of the Board of Directors of Mr Detwiler's American-European Travel Project Inc. was no less a

man than the former Prime Minister of the Netherlands, Professor P.S. Gerbrandy, while the Holland America Line, in collaboration with the Fugazy Travel Bureau Inc., was involved as potential ship managers or charter operators. Even KLM, the Dutch airline group, was said to have been negotiating for the helicopter service planned for each terminal, using the recently developed Fairey Rotodyne, because of its capacity, speed and low running costs – three US cents or 2.5d (1.25p) per passenger mile in those days!

Again, it might be argued that all these people and bodies had something to gain, but it was nevertheless considered worth their while expending a good deal of time and money investigating in their several roles. Sadly, like Hyman Cantor's proposal, the one important ingredient that Edgar Detwiler lacked was vast financial backing. However, his case was not the same as Cantor's, nor many of the other endeavours to build and operate the 'might-have-been' liners. In the first place, he was going to operate under a foreign flag, and so, by increasing the number of passengers to be carried, he had, at the same time, abandoned all claims to enhancing the national prestige of his country and, since the ships were obviously not on call to the United States in the event of a national emergency, he had forfeited any hope of federal aid. Nor, by the very nature of his proposed operation, could he hope for aid from any other government, and he was thus left with the remaining option of raising money by the sale of stock in the markets of the world. But this, too, had the disadvantage that the capital so subscribed would not show any return for some considerable time until the ships were actually completed and in service.

Taking the situation as it was at the time, this seems to have been the great weakness in the structure of Detwiler's embryonic empire. Even if some magic wand had been waved and the money had been available to enable the ships to be built, and taking account of the developments in the passenger ship situation in the years which ensued, it is difficult to escape the conclusion that, however statistically impressive they might have been, they would have proved to be the whitest of all white elephants, as they were much too big, as conventional liners, to have been diverted to successful cruising roles.

Sporadic reports about the four giant liners continued right up to the end of 1959, after which there was silence. One of Mr Detwiler's associates was quoted as saying that the trouble with him was that he started things and would put in a lot of his own money, but that when things really got going, he bowed out. Gaston Eyskens, the Belgian premier described Detwiler, perhaps unfairly, as 'the man who launched the passenger liner phantom', while *Time* magazine in its 1 August 1960 business section called him 'the Big Dreamer'. These may or may not be justified comments, for it is too easy to turn on well-intentioned persons when things stall, as Captain Herbert Hartley had experienced through his association with the '*Flying Cloud*' project. It is certain that Detwiler did put in a great deal of time and money in the first instance, but the fact was that the furthest the negotiations ever reached with Verolme United Shipyards was the exchange of 'letters of intent', a fact that seems to substantiate the comments made by Detwiler's colleague and others.

Beyond this, no further substantial progress was made. Other problems which may well have militated against the advancement of the project were, in the first place, the question of the capability of land transportation to handle as many as 16,000 passengers each trip, when they embarked and disembarked at their various European and US terminals. In the second place, the matter of what would have happened to such ships during the winter 'off' season never seems to have been resolved.

There is one aspect of the schemes of both Hyman Cantor and Edgar Detwiler which should be borne in mind, and which must have fortified both of these entrepreneurs in the validity of their proposals. Perhaps rather surprisingly, more people actually crossed the Atlantic by passenger ship in 1958 (which was virtually in the centre of the periods in which these gentlemen were so much to the fore) than in any other year before or since. Despite this interesting statistic, liner shipping was in a state of decline, and the fact of the matter was that the increase in transatlantic aircraft passenger travel was even more remarkable. The figures for the passenger liners may have looked to be superficially encouraging, but those for the airlines were the salient ones, since these represented a clear writing on the wall when predicting the future. Yet … it is easy to make such a comment today

in the light of all that has actually occurred in the ensuing decades, but prescience of the future is quite another matter, and thus judgement on these schemes can only be passed on the basis of the information available at the time when they were initiated.

As already mentioned, the Detwiler project turned out to be the last of the great American liner dreams which never came to fruition.

CUNARD LINE'S Q3 – THE *QUEEN* THAT NEVER WAS

While the smoke of the various American schemes was clouding the sky, there was considerable activity on the building front on the other side of the Atlantic, particularly amongst the Continental lines. In consequence, the Cunard Line was compelled to give consideration to the replacement of the *Queen Mary* and the *Queen Elizabeth*, the former being twenty-five years old at this time. The result was the famous, if unfortunate, Q3 '*Queens* replacement' project.

Cunard had reserved a berth at John Brown's shipyard on Clydebank in 1957 for a vessel to replace the *Britannic*, the last White Star unit in the fleet. It did not, however, proceed with an order at that time and took no further action concerning new vessels for their express service other than to indicate that it was also contemplating two large liners which would cost about £20 million each. As it turned out, the company was to have the two existing *Queens* so extensively overhauled, including the fitting of new cabin suites, lido areas and fin stabilisers, that it was widely believed that they might possibly remain in service for many years to come. Furthermore, there were other suggestions that were designed to prolong their service lives by improving their performance.

One such proposal came from Mr Arthur P. Pedrick, a prolific inventor and register of patents, with a certain knowledge of high speed hull principles and techniques. He claimed that the *Queen Mary* and the *Queen Elizabeth* could be kept in service longer by improving their speed with boundary layer air lubrication, which would reduce both frictional and wave resistance. This would have been effected by feeding compressed air to their underwater hulls through hundreds of small holes, the power required to compress the air coming from a slight up-rating of their engines' power output. This idea was too complicated to detail here in full, but Pedrick's plan included the provision of a false side, or sheet, on either side of the hull and parallel to it, bonded in such a way as to be airtight but attached to the ship's hull along its top edge by a sort of bellows, or diaphragm, in such a way that, when expanded, it would form a reservoir of air. The airholes in this false side, which were necessary to provide the required slipstream for improved efficiency, would be positioned at different levels so that, when the false side was drawn in flush against the hull, it would to some degree act as a valve, sealing the air holes in the hull. The mathematics of this suggestion, documented in Patent Specification 997,737, *Reduction of Hydrodynamic Drag of Water Buoyant Vessels*, published 7 July 1965, were extremely involved, but Pedrick claimed that the power requirements to provide the compressed air would have been so small that there would not have been any need to have turned it off, even in port, when a lower output would have been sufficient to balance the air and water pressures. There is no doubt that Pedrick was both a genius and an eccentric, and that the majority of people found themselves out of their depth when trying to follow all the details of his schemes. While this proposal was mathematically feasible, it was never put to the test at the time, largely because it was overtaken quite swiftly by other developments with surface effect vessels (i.e. hovercraft, hydroskimmers and hydrofoils).

Fast forward to 2015 when Pedrick's concept was finally adopted when Royal Caribbean International's *Quantum of the Seas* and *Anthem of the Seas* were built by Meyer Werft, both fitted with the Air Lubrication System (ALS) designed by Finnish naval architects. According to Royal Caribbean, the system's installation meant that propulsive power could be reduced and that, when the ships were operating at cruising speeds, a net fuel saving equivalent to 7–8 per cent was achieved.

Back in 1965, how much credence Cunard may have attached to this concept or to similar suggestions which were being discussed in the engineering and technical journals of the day is purely academic since the underlying problem was not the speed of the two vessels, but the very age of their hulls. At all events, the Cunard Line took no further action in the matter until 1960, by which time the Compagnie Générale Transatlantique and the Holland America Line had forged ahead with their new *France* and *Rotterdam*, respectively, while the United States Lines, in this period at least, had also achieved reasonable headway in its moves for a second *United States*. All of these vessels were to be subsidised annually by a considerable amount, while the rapidly ageing *Queens* received no similar financial assistance although, rather optimistically, Cunard had stated earlier that they would not need government economic aid for their replacement liners anyway.

By 1960, this rapidly changing situation had become a cause for great concern to the Cunard Line. It would be difficult enough for the company to keep abreast of these foreign competitors, let alone to maintain that degree of supremacy on the North Atlantic which they had enjoyed since 1945, and, to make matters worse, the cost of building the two new ships had risen sharply due to their own prolonged procrastination over the issue. When the company finally approached the British Government with the problem, it had to talk in terms of £40 million worth of aid towards shipbuilding costs, since it was by then estimated that each ship would cost something in the region of £28 million – an increase of 40 per cent on the original figure quoted. The *France*, by contrast, was expected to cost the CGT the equivalent of £25 million.

The government was sympathetic to the Cunard Line's request and set up the independent Chandos Committee to advise on the best way of finding a solution to the company's difficulties. Discussions centered on a proposal for two liners of approximately 75,000 gross tons with an overall length of about 1,000ft and a service speed of around 30 knots. (In 1959, Cunard's Chairman, Colonel Denis Bates, had intimated that the replacement ships for the two *Queens* could be up to 80,000 gross tons and as long as 1,040ft.) At the same time the P&O Line suggested a partial amalgamation with the Cunard Line in the event of no acceptable or adequate monetary help forthcoming from the government. Its idea was that one ship should be built for a joint company for operation on both the North Atlantic and Australian routes at their respective peak periods. This scheme which, in essence, was similar to another proposed merger of interests in 1946, was likewise rejected. In the first place, Colonel Bates had expressed his firm belief in maintaining an all-year-round

North Atlantic service, but Cunard were also worried about the P&O Line's involvement with air transport because, around 1955, Saunders-Roe (later GKN Aerospace) of East Cowes, on the Isle of Wight, had carried out a design investigation, closely linked with this shipping operator, for a massive, 670-ton five-deck flying boat designated the P192.

This enormous aircraft, measuring 318ft in length and having a 313ft wing-span, was so big that a man could have stood upright in the wings to service the engines during flight. Its twenty-four Rolls-Royce 'Conway' by-pass turbo-jet aero engines would have given 18,500 pounds thrust each at take-off and a cruising speed of 389 knots at 35,000ft would have been possible. There would have been accommodation for 1,100 passengers – a normal liner-load – or space for 67,600 cu ft of cargo. Although the P192 was designed specifically for an overland route to Australasia, P&O nevertheless opted to retain their traditional passenger liner service with the new *Canberra*.

Meanwhile the Chandos Committee made its first recommendation to the government to the effect that financial aid for Cunard's new

ship programme should be in the form of a loan rather than a subsidy, which was no less than the decision that had been expected. The subsequent decisions were to be the crucial ones from the company's point of view and were then eagerly awaited.

Rather ironically, however, an unexpected and ill-timed development at this point was Cunard's decision to exercise its rights to operate aeroplanes when it took over Eagle Airways in September 1960, renaming this firm Cunard Eagle Airways. This move prompted the Chandos Committee, in circumspection, to reappraise their recommendations for the amount of government aid that should be made available to the liner replacement programme for what had now become the shipping side of Cunard's widened operations.

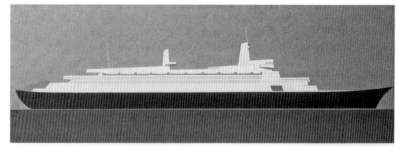

Early drawings of the Q3 lacked a completed funnel but hinted at something along the lines of that of the contemporary *Leonardo da Vinci* of Italia Line whose style exemplified the vogue of the time (see third colour section). *Italia Line*

Under James Gardner's guidance, a variety of more distinctive profile options for the Q3 were considered by the Cunard design team. *Michael Gallagher*

Industrial designer James Gardner was not impressed by the early depiction of the Q3's exterior design as shown in this model created in the Cunard design office. He felt that it did not convey either the bearing or dignity of such an important and high-profile vessel. *Dr Bruce Peter*

Hence its advice was that a Treasury loan of £18 million at 4.5 per cent over twenty-five years should be made to enable the Cunard Line to construct only *one* 75,000 gross ton vessel with a capacity for 2,250 passengers. This seemed to be a fair and reasonable compromise proposal in the circumstances and, with Cunard's acceptance and following the production of a design specification, tenders for the liner's construction were invited during March 1961. It was anticipated that an order for the new ship, which immediately became known as the 'Q3' or the 'Queen 3', would be placed by the autumn of that year at the latest.

James Gardner was appointed as design coordinator and made ultimately responsible for the outside appearance of the ship. He had a background as the Chief Designer of the Festival Gardens at Battersea and the British Pavilion at the Brussels Exhibition. He would later go on to be a joint design coordinator on the *Queen Elizabeth 2*.

As originally envisaged in drawings dating from 3 March 1961, the Q3 would have had a fairly typical hull form and superstructure with partially open promenade decks. The one unusual feature was the twin-funnel arrangement combining a conventional broad-based

The revised appearance of the Q3 in 1961, from a John Brown display model. The parallelogram on the side of the hull below the bridge was an emblematic panel displaying Cunard's lion in gold on a red-painted background. *Dr Bruce Peter*

funnel aft with a funnel-cum-mast, or 'mack', as it is described in the United States, above the bridge. The shape of the conventional funnel had not been finalised, but the authors believe that, taking account of contemporary trends, Cunard had in mind, for one of the options, something resembling the funnel shape of the Italia Line's *Leonardo da Vinci* or even the much later-built *Vistafjord*.

Only a few months later, a completely different profile for the Q3 was unveiled in a display model fabricated by the John Brown shipyard. All the superstructure was now enclosed for complete air-conditioning and the fore-deck had a turtleback configuration for heavy weather wave dispersal. The forward 'mack' was retained, though with a slightly modified shape, and the after funnel was now of similar form. This modified design reflected the thinking of James Gardner who considered the original rendering, conceived by Cunard's own naval architects, as 'clumsy, [with] one vent shaped like an obese streamlined funnel … and the other … disguised as a mast'.

The Q3's dimensions varied from 1,041ft length overall to 920ft in the Vickers-Swan Hunter variant, and 116ft breadth. Her draught was designed as 35ft, while her gross tonnage was expected to work out at nearer 80,000 than 75,000. She would have been a quadruple-screw vessel driven by geared turbines producing 200,000 shaft horsepower. Steam conditions were planned for 850psi and 950° Fahrenheit. It is interesting to note that, with a similar machinery arrangement to the earlier *Queen* liners, the Q3 would only have had eight boilers, compared with twelve in the *Queen Elizabeth* and twenty-seven in the *Queen Mary*. As manning costs represented 85 per cent of the total running costs of ships in the 1960s, any attainable savings in this area would have been carefully evaluated. Serious consideration was given to diesel machinery because experience with Cunard's sole motor-ship *Britannic* showed that, with a need for fewer greasers and engineers, she required an engine room staff of only sixty-three as opposed to 250 on the *Queen Mary* and 220 on the *Queen Elizabeth*, around a quarter the number despite the size difference.

Provision for eventual nuclear propulsion was made in the Q3 design, as it had been in the case of the *France* but Cunard felt that any recommendations for the use of nuclear power would be premature, being an unproven form of propulsion in the case of merchant ships.

Five bids for the construction of the Q3 were submitted to Cunard between 28 and 31 July 1961, the known details of each as shown in the table below:

Shipyard	Passengers	Dimensions	Power shp	Delivery	Cost
Cammell Laird, Birkenhead	2,298	1,041ft loa 942ft lbp		End 1965	£27,980,000
Fairfield SB and E, Govan, Glasgow	2,298	1,040ft loa 942ft lbp	150,000	March/April 1966	£27,177,800
Harland & Wolff, Belfast	2,298	1,037ft loa 942ft lbp	200,000	Dec 1965	£24,650,000
John Brown, Clydebank		990ft loa		End May 1965	£24,051,880
Vickers-Armstrongs and Swan Hunter, Tyneside	2,270	920ft loa	180,000 (140,000)*	April 1965	£21,944,600

Note: * the maximum rating according to Ian Rae, formerly of Swan Hunter; the power output of the John Brown option was said to be comparable to that of the Vickers-Armstrongs and Swan Hunter option.

As can be seen, the lowest tender for the Q3, of approximately £22 million, was from a consortium of Vickers-Armstrongs and Swan, Hunter and Wigham Richardson, and it was intended that the liner would be built on Tyneside. Each tenderer submitted a model mock-up of the future Cunarder, some following the conceptual illustrations of James Gardner, others revealing individual interpretations of the ship's external profile.

The five bids to build the Q3 were, however, overtaken by events within the realms of the Cunard management. With only one such replacement liner, the Cunard Line could no longer expect to dominate the North Atlantic passenger trade but, nevertheless, with a ship of this calibre, it should have been able to compete with other lines on equal terms. Everything seemed to be set fair for proceeding with the Q3 when the Cunard Line, quite unexpectedly, made another move which further endangered the realisation of the newly proposed liner. On 19 October 1961, following a shareholder revolt led by those who felt that a traditional, exclusively line service vessel was an inappropriate and out-of-date solution, the company decided to postpone the order for the Q3 indefinitely. The postponement was partly due to poor trading results for the Cunard Group in 1961 but also, to some extent in the light of the shareholders' concerns, because the company's directors felt that the design of the new ship should be reappraised. Colonel Denis Bates, who had died on 13 September 1959, had been succeeded as chairman by Sir John Brocklebank in

This Swan Hunter model of the Q3 on the crossover berth at Wallsend was displayed in the main entrance hall of the company's offices. Swan Hunter bid for the Q3 construction contract in collaboration with Vickers-Armstrongs. *Ian Rae*

early 1960 and he was fundamentally in favour of a dual-purpose ship, whilst regarding the Q3 design as a recipe for disaster. He felt that a ship of her type – a high-speed luxury liner suited only for the North

Atlantic service – was not the ideal vessel for economic operation in what was then becoming an unprecedentedly competitive business, a reservation subsequently justified by the problems experienced by CGT's *France*.

In Tom Kameen's article 'More than a Century of Machinery Progress in the Cunard Line Passenger Vessels' in a 1972 edition of The Motor Ship, he wrote:

> … consideration was again given to diesel machinery, although the Q3, which was the original replacement concept, was to have had a turbine installation with four screws which would have been similar in many respects to the old *Queens* [albeit with a smaller engine room complement of 146]. However, the Q3 investigations made it evident that marine technology had advanced to a situation whereby the required passenger complement and speed could be achieved in a much smaller ship driven by twin-screws. Thus, the Q4 was born.

Cunard's 'Queens Replacement' plan, originally projected in the form of the Q3, was finally manifested in the *Queen Elizabeth 2*, referred to as the Q4, seen here in her original form in an aerial view. *Cunard Line*

Therefore Cunard's revised requirements called for such a liner of reduced size, suitable for off-peak cruising in both the Atlantic and the Pacific, and thus able to negotiate the Panama Canal, and with construction costs nearer to £22 million. Described as the Q4, this specification ultimately resulted in the *Queen Elizabeth 2*.

The immediate dilemma confronting the Cunard Line late in 1961, however, was that the granting of government aid for a new ship was subject specifically to a vessel of the Q3 type being built. Although this condition was abrogated subsequently, it was Cunard's failure to place such an order in 1961 that finally necessitated the cancellation of the project.

Viewed with retrospection, the failure of the Q3 can hardly be considered to be the Cunard Line's equivalent to the White Star Line's ill-fated *Oceanic* of the 1920s, for a new super-liner for the company did finally appear in the form of the *Queen Elizabeth 2* – clearly a more appropriately designed ship and one which accrued a creditable success record despite some difficult years immediately following her entry into service. After a year's silence following the cancellation of the Q3, Sir John Brocklebank spoke further on the

company's replacement policy when he addressed the shareholders in July 1963. He then promised a decision on the Q4 in 1964, and it was on 30 December of that year that an order was placed, with the *Queen Elizabeth 2* eventually entering service in April 1969.

It is worthwhile comparing this latter ship with other contemporary liners of the day in order to illustrate the advantages in her design, which had been advocated by Sir John Brocklebank. Measuring 66,863 gross tons and 963ft in length overall, her draught, at 32ft 6in, was less than that of the much smaller *Canberra*. The draught of the *France* was 34ft 6in, the same as that of the *Canberra* which was restricted on the cruise circuit as a result of this disadvantage, since the shallow waters of certain Caribbean Island ports denied her essential berthing facilities.

For the purposes of making the transit of the Panama Canal locks, the *Queen Elizabeth 2*'s beam was restricted to 101ft – 15ft less than the Q3 – and, additionally, she had a high-capacity distilling plant which enabled her to make voyages on routes longer than the North Atlantic. The *Queen Mary*'s fresh water tanks limited her time at sea to six days!

An artist's impression of the *Phoenix World City*, showing the three-tower permutation. *Knud E. Hansen*

A model of the planned four-tower 'Phoenix' super-cruise ship was displayed aboard Norwegian Caribbean Cruise Line's *Norway*. *Lars Helge Isdahl*

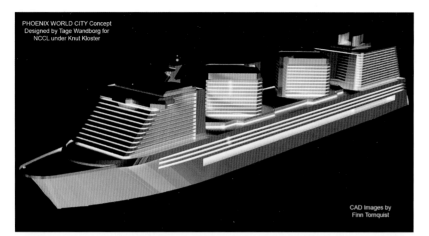

PHOENIX WORLD CITY Concept
Designed by Tage Wandborg for
NCCL under Knut Kloster

CAD Images by
Finn Tornquist

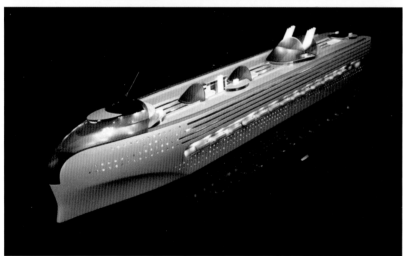

Clockwise from top left: A CAD (computer-aided design) projection of Klosters' *Phoenix World City*. *Finn Tornquist*; A wind tunnel model of Tikkoo's 'Ultimate Dream', a potential rival to the *Phoenix World City. Authors' collection*; Model of the *Pearl of Miami*, a concept cruise ship developed by *Wärtsilä* in 1993 for display at the Seatrade Conference, Miami. The model shows a longitudinally split superstructure, a solution later used in the 'Oasis'-class vessels of Royal Caribbean Cruise Lines. *Dr H.C. Kai Levander and Guy Design Group.*

The incomplete *Regent Sky* laid up at Ambelakia, Salamis, on 31 July 2005. At the bow, her faded new name is also evident. *Frank Heine*

SUPERSTAR SAGITTARIUS II

A postcard image of the *Superstar Sagittarius II* planned for Star Cruises with a sister-ship, *Superstar Capricorn II,* around the turn of the millennium but cancelled before construction had started. Had they been built, they would briefly have been the largest passenger ships in the world. *Star Cruises*

Profile view of the Carnival Pinnacle, developed from the FUN Ship. *Fincantieri*

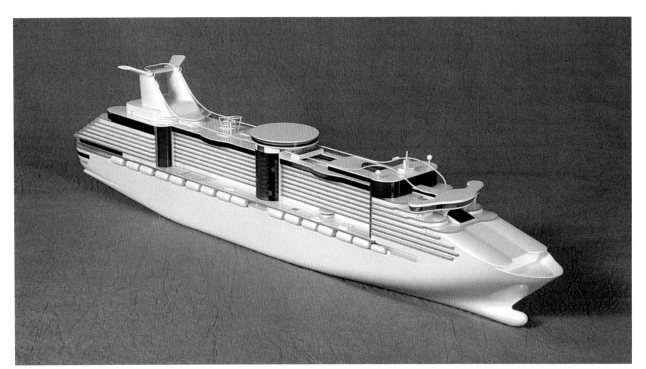

The model of the FUN Ship viewed from bow and stern quarters. The circular structure at the centre of the upper deck is the planned rotating restaurant. *Both Fincantieri*

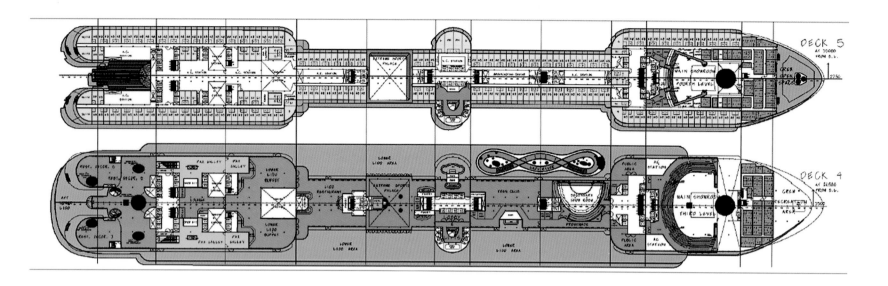

A section of the Carnival Pinnacle's deck plan showing the 'Lazy River' feature on the port side of deck 4. This drawing also reveals how the wider lido deck space was to be achieved by corrugating the sides of the superstructure. *Fincantieri*

A close-up view of the 'people mover' system for passenger transportation around the Carnival Pinnacle. *Fincantieri*

An artistic portrayal of the *Eoseas* pentamaran cruise ship proceeding under full sail. *STX France/Chantiers de l'Atlantique*

A Study of A New Concept for Cruise Ships

KAGUYA

Japan Contents Network Inc.

The *Kaguya* or *Princess Kaguya* was intended as more than just a study of a new concept for ocean cruising. An image of the Princess Kaguya from Japanese folklore is painted on the ship's side near the bows. *Japan Contents Network*

Another impression of the *France II* seen from the starboard stern quarter, showing the cascading aft decks descending to an extremely low freeboard stern structure. *Tillberg Design*

A bow quarter view of the *Titanic II* from the port side. Intended to look as closely as possible like the original *Titanic*, the SOLAS safety requirements mandated for modern passenger ship operation, initiated in the wake of the *Titanic* disaster, enforced vital design deviations on the *Titanic II*. Although not fully evident in this illustration, these related primarily to the navigation and emergency evacuation equipment. Another replica of the *Titanic*, contracted for assembly in China by Wuchang Shipbuilding at a cost of $160 million (£115 million), was reported to be half-complete by September 2017. However, as it is destined to remain on display as a tourist attraction in a land-locked dock near Suining, on the River Qi, it is not intended to put to sea. *Blue Star Line*

POLONIA

In 1961 it was announced that Polish Ocean Lines was considering the construction of a 23,000grt motor-ship as a replacement for the ageing *Batory*. Identified as the *Polonia*, she would have had berths for 100 First-class and 700 Tourist-class passengers. The proposed builder was Stoczni Warskiego, Szczecin (Stettin), in the former shipyard of AG Vulkan and Stettiner Oderwerke. These images reveal how, as in the case of other planned passenger ships at that time, the external design of the *Polonia* gradually evolved. Nothing came of the plans, though. When the *Batory* was retired in 1969, her owners acquired the former Holland–America liner *Maasdam* and instead had her reconstructed as the *Stefan Batory*. *Both Author's collection*

THE BRITISH NUCLEAR PASSENGER LINER

After thermonuclear bomb tests had revealed the devastatingly destructive capability of nuclear weapons, the 1950s witnessed a drive to utilise atomic energy for a ubiquitous range of more peaceful applications. Among them was the propulsion of merchant vessels, substituting reactors for oil as the fuel for the boilers of steam-turbine-driven ships and, specifically, passenger vessels. Under its 'Atoms for Peace' initiative, the United States had commissioned the cargo-passenger ship NS *Savannah* in 1959, the only passenger-carrying nuclear-powered ship ever to put to sea. Germany and Japan focused their attention on pure cargo vessels but Great Britain and France concentrated their efforts on true passenger liners. How far the French progressed with the research and development of a nuclear liner is not known, but the UK reached the point where an order for construction, supported by government money but conditional on an operational agreement with an established shipping line, was on the cards in the early 1960s.

An artist's impression of the proposed British nuclear passenger ship, developed by Vickers Limited under a government contract, was released on 1 February 1963. Vickers had already gained significant experience installing these power plants in nuclear submarines built by them at Barrow-in-Furness. In parallel, an announcement was made the following day in the House of Commons that the decision had been made to proceed with construction of the ship for delivery in 1967 in a joint enterprise with industry and an established operating company. But just how much the government intended to invest in the programme was not disclosed.

The impression showed a sleek and stylish vessel of 30,000 gross tons to carry 1,500 passengers on an unspecified route. It was said that the ship would most probably have twin reactors generating sufficient power for a service speed of 24 knots.

There were, however, misgivings as to the economic viability of running such a liner without it requiring expensive, sustaining operational subsidies despite claims that it would be cheaper to operate than an oil-driven ship. The project was viewed as motivated by nebulous national prestige rather than commercial need. *Shipbuilding and Shipping Record* had this to say on 14 March 1963:

> The recent announcements which appear to indicate that Britain may build an economic or almost economic nuclear-powered merchant ship by about 1967, should be treated with reserve.

It continued:

> Weight and space limitations make the building of an economically attractive nuclear plant [for a merchant ship] far more difficult than for a power station.

The preliminary design for the planned British nuclear passenger ship, dated 2 December 1963. *NS Savannah Association*

Besides that, a profoundly fundamental problem that threatened, amid ratcheting costs, to undermine the development of the nuclear passenger liner, was the government's engagement of numerous committees as part of the procurement process. An industry observer voiced his opinions on this:

> The Danes have a proverb which says 'When God intends that nothing should be done, he appoints a committee'. The history of the possible use of nuclear power for merchant ship propulsion has been plagued by committees … but virtually nothing has been achieved.

Sir Donald Anderson of P&O, one of the companies believed to be under consideration to operate the nuclear liner, was also critical. His observations, expressed with a measure of aplomb, were reported in the *Shipping World and Shipbuilder* of April 1963:

> How much better it would be if only … decisions at each stage were taken on grounds of hard economic and technical facts, instead of on those of national prestige.
> My own ignorant view is that nuclear power will only be of interest to us if it is not only cheaper overall, but also if it is simpler overall.

Less diplomatically, he concluded:

> The main advantages of nuclear power are of enormous assistance to warships but of no use to merchant ships.

No one who was alive in the mid 1960s could forget the 'I'm Backing Britain' campaign to support British industry as the nation's economic fortunes faltered. The fact was that the bleak outlook necessitated some serious national belt-tightening, and among the casualties of clipped government budgets was the nuclear-powered passenger liner which, it seems, in actuality no shipping company really wanted anyway.

CUNARD'S 'CENTURY 21' PROJECT, THE Q5 – ANOTHER ABANDONED *QUEEN*

The question might reasonably be asked by the reader, just how serious were the projects related in these pages, with the exception of those completed or partially completed vessels which mainly fell foul of the circumstances of war? Many, of course, were the visions of 'ships of the future' as perceived at various times by naval architects or designers operating either independently or representing shipyards for which it was hoped that firm orders would eventually be received. Without exception, though, all the endeavours described herein were pursued with a commitment of much effort and a great sense of purpose, the proponents in each case convinced of their worth and viability, especially where comprehensive structural designs and in-depth specifications were developed, and detailed studies and analyses carried out. Thus, a measure of sorts of the genuine intent behind these projects could be the sheer amount of work devoted to their pursuit – none more so than for a sequence of new ship plans that emanated within Cunard throughout a decade commencing from the late 1980s. A great deal of technical application and considerable sums of money were expended in the generation of designs, the evaluation of business potential and the compilation of marketing plans.

Much of the attention of Cunard's project office at that time was given to new cruise ships, the need being to preserve the company's ranking as a prestige operator at a time when competition in the cruise market was hotting up. Company executives considered the style of the recently completed Wärtsilä-built *Song of America*, delivered to Royal Caribbean, to be particularly attractive and explored the commissioning of similar vessels. Ultimately, though, it proved too expensive a proposition to adapt the design to meet Cunard's unique requirements. So the '1300/160' concept, as it was called, was shelved. Cunard was also keen to break into the Hawaiian cruise business out of America's west coast and was prepared to have ships built specially in the USA. In association with the Hyatt hotel chain and Tampa Shipyards, Florida, a 'Tampa Ship' project was hatched in 1988 for a pair of cruise vessels with a capacity for around 1,500 passengers each. There were numerous obstacles to overcome for the venture to proceed – higher US building costs, unionised American crewing, U.S. Coast Guard regulations, berthing issues in Hawaii as well as Hawaiian state regulations – all of which were thoroughly investigated. The result was that the scheme rumbled on for several years, only to re-emerge later as the 'Eagle' project.

For Cunard, it was frustrating for so much effort to be expended for so little return, but for all the concern about reinvigorating its cruise fleet, the maintenance of its seasonal transatlantic operation remained paramount. In 1987, the *Queen Elizabeth 2* had completed an expensive, £100 million life-extending engine change, from steam turbine to diesel-electric. Assessments carried out simultaneously suggested that her hull was fundamentally sound and that the company could reasonably expect her to survive for another twenty years – which she did! But back at the end of the 1980s this remained conjecture, albeit technically substantiated, and it was considered to be prudent to commence planning for her eventual replacement sooner rather than later.

The fact that the company would be celebrating its 150th anniversary in 1990 gave greater impetus to a project for a new *Queen*, the 'Century 21' project or Q5 as it was known. It was intimated that Trafalgar House, Cunard's owners since 1971, were hoping to use this big occasion to announce the construction of the new ship. Of course, it would have been preferable to have the ship actually enter service during that year, just as had been intended with the *Queen Elizabeth* on the 100th anniversary in 1940, but it was already too late for that.

Moreover, development of the Q5 became a protracted affair as concerns about aspects of the concept necessitated rethink after rethink, a matter which also exposed a deep divergence between the operating philosophies of Cunard's British and American marketing teams. The designers, too, were briefed to evaluate a wide range of power and propulsion options, all of which added to the mounting costs.

Several conceptual assessment documents were released through 1990 into 1991 but probably the '*Outline Specification for a Passenger Cruise Vessel/Ocean Liner – Project Q5 for Cunard* (reference: P3197), dated 12 December 1991, was most conspicuously detailed and informative. Covering every aspect of the prospective ship's design to a meticulous level of complexity, it was prepared for Cunard by the Finnish consulting naval architects, Deltamarin Ltd. Essentially, it was a bidding guide for prospective builders.

The opening passage confirms the intention for the Q5 to emulate the *Queen Elizabeth 2* as a dual-role ship: 'a modern luxury dual purpose ocean liner and cruise vessel for transatlantic and worldwide cruise service'. Initially to consort the older liner, it was clear that the Q5, with its designed 50-year longevity, would ultimately replace its predecessor. As a larger ship, measuring approximately 90,000 gross tons, the Q5 would have been only marginally longer with an overall

length of 984ft 4in. Her other dimensions were 940ft length between perpendiculars, 128ft maximum beam, and 204ft air draught to the top of the funnels. The cruising draught was 34ft 7in, slightly less than on the transatlantic, at 35ft 4in.

The internal layout provided for a maximum complement of 3,800, of which the passenger element was distributed through three or, more realistically, four classes: a Super-class was sub-divided into 150 of Penthouse standard and 450 of de luxe standard. A further 570 passengers would have been in First-class staterooms with 1,076 Tourist-class accommodated in generous size cabins. No doubt some flexibility was intended, given that the 2,246 passengers along

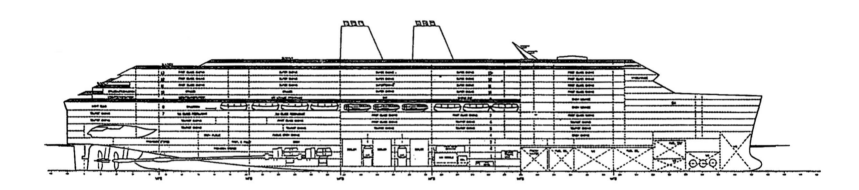

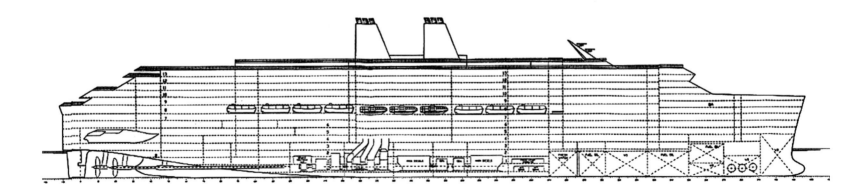

Profile drawings of the original Q5 design showing alternative engine arrangements, steam turbine (top) and gas turbine (bottom). *Deltamarin*

with the officers and crew, numbering 1,203, totalled only 3,449. The crew accommodation was to be in 728 cabins with a fair degree of sole occupancy, and all passenger and crew quarters were to have private bathroom and toilet facilities.

Restrictions occasioned by the ship's dual role dictated that, as on the later Queen Mary 2, the distribution of the accommodation spaces was something of a compromise. Typically, inside cabins are always more difficult to sell, especially on cruises, but the architects were able nevertheless to contrive that 75 per cent of the private passenger spaces would be outside.

The general arrangement drawings 0.3197.150.1/1-4, dated 11 October 1991 and appended to the specification document P3197, show a diesel-electric main engines arrangement with gas hydraulic gearing to three propeller shafts. However, many different power systems were considered for the Q5 and an earlier drawing set, from 26 April 1991, shows a steam turbine configuration comprising six propulsion boilers connected to the triple shafts via all-mechanical gearing. This latter form of prime mover was outlined in considerable detail. It was to comprise three MPU propulsion turbine units of the non-reheat cross-compound type, each consisting of a single-flow HP turbine and a double-flow LP turbine. The turbine units were designed to deliver a maximum of 73MW (97,855hp) at 120rpm to the wing shafts and a maximum of 80MW (107,238hp) at 105rpm to the centre-line shaft, each unit double-reduction-geared to the shafts. There would be fixed-pitch propellers on all three shafts, 24ft (7.3 metres) diameter on the wings and 26ft 4in (8.0 metres) diameter on the centre-line. An auxiliary boiler, four diesel generators and a turbo-alternator would have supplied electrical power.

Among the other power arrangements evaluated were gas turbine and a variety of combination systems. Likewise, various fuel options were appraised including coal, diesel, heavy fuel oil and AV fuel.

Whichever of these power-plants would have been settled on, the intended speed of the Q5 was a matter of some controversy within Cunard. The engine arrangement was to be organised in such a way that she could operate at high speed on Atlantic crossings and at low speed when cruising. The specified requirement was for a year-round

transatlantic service speed of 37.5 knots, a speed which almost certainly would have made the Q5 a serious contender to wrest the Atlantic Blue Riband honours from the United States. Maximum speed at a total shaft power output of 210MW (281,501hp) was to be demonstrated on the acceptance trials at a sustained 39.5 knots over 24 hours with a loaded draught of 35ft 5in (10.75 metres) but without the fin stabilisers deployed.

As a whole, the sea trials, all arranged in accordance with the Society of Naval Architects and Marine Engineers' 'Code for Sea Trials, C2' of 1973 were to be extremely demanding. Besides the high speed run, an endurance test involved the maintenance of 37.5 knots over a period of 72 hours in Beaufort Sea State 5 conditions. The builders were also to be required to demonstrate a range of 4,200 nautical miles continuous sailing at 37.5 knots and 7,000 nautical miles at 28 knots. Furthermore, the Q5 was to be capable of unassisted harbour manoeuvring in a continuous wind speed up to Beaufort Force 8 and a tidal current of 2 knots.

The matter of the Q5's high projected transatlantic speed is an interesting one to reflect on. It appeared to be in conflict with the accepted wisdom of the day and was the cause of much consternation within Cunard. Since the 1970s, when fuel prices had experienced a five-fold increase and operators had been seeking to reduce running costs by slowing down their ships. Part of the reasoning behind the installation of the new engines in the Queen Elizabeth 2 had been to reduce her fuel consumption, her single largest cost element. At an annual cost of £5 million, the engine conversion had cut it in half. So why was such high speed sought for the Q5? In essence, there was a counter-opinion concerning the impact of fuel costs on the bottom line as expressed by Kai Levander of Wärtsilä in his address entitled 'Converting Concepts to Reality' given at the Cruise 85 Conference in London:

Very often we forget to look for improvements on the income side. In passenger shipping we can achieve a greater increase in profitability by persuading each passenger to spend five dollars more a day than by saving 10 per cent in bunker costs.

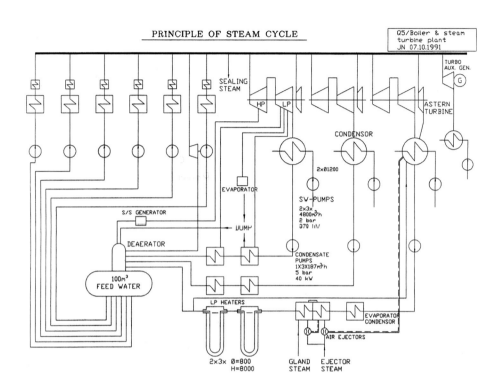

A schematic drawing from the Q5 design specification of 7 October 1991, showing the steam cycle of the boiler and turbine plant of the steam turbine variant. *Michael Gallagher*

Another of the several engine arrangements evaluated for the Q5, in this case diesel-electric. Note the three-screw propulsion arrangement. *Deltamarin*

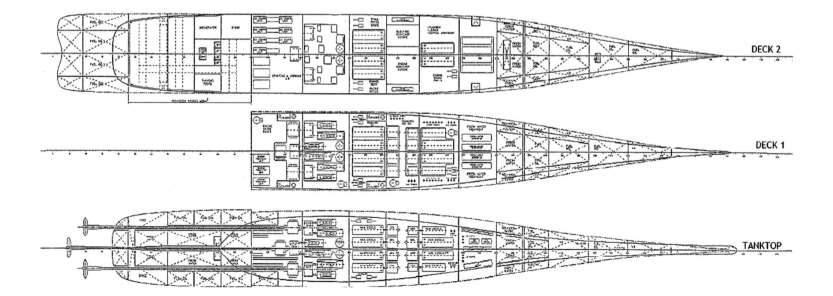

Nonetheless, the question of the Q5's high operating speed was to prove one of the project's Achilles Heels.

An allusion to the later *Queen Mary 2* has already been made where the Q5 was concerned and there were other similarities between them. The Q5's interior appointments comprised many of the features that later would be incorporated in the *Queen Mary 2* which, it could be argued, was a larger reincarnation of the earlier concept. There was to have been a show lounge, a separate ballroom, an observation lounge, casino, theatre and cinema, besides a disco club, a teen's room and a games room. Dining amenities were a 285-seat First-class restaurant and a 900-seat Tourist buffet dining room. Two grill restaurants would have catered for 100 and 200 Super-class passengers, respectively, and there would have been two small speciality restaurants for which a dining supplement would be charged. One difference from the *Queen Mary 2* was a planned outdoor buffet restaurant for 200 diners.

A range of sport and recreational facilities would have included a designated jogging track around the outer decks.

The décor was to be of a very high calibre, the quality and workmanship to be at least equivalent to that aboard the *Queen Elizabeth 2* in her original, delivery condition and the level of refinement to reflect ultra de luxe hotel, retail and catering design attributes as the reference guideline.

The ship's hull was to meet Lloyd's two-compartment classification and the Special Survey of Lloyd's Register of Shipping as +100A1 passenger ship. Damage stability was to be in accordance with the latest International Maritime Organisation (IMO) and Safety of Life at Sea (SOLAS) rules, the subdivision and compartmentation to be arranged such that, as far as possible, unsymmetrical flooding could be avoided. The double bottom was to extend from the engine room aft bulkhead to the bow thruster room aft bulkhead with stiffening of the transverse frames and the longitudinal shell and plates.

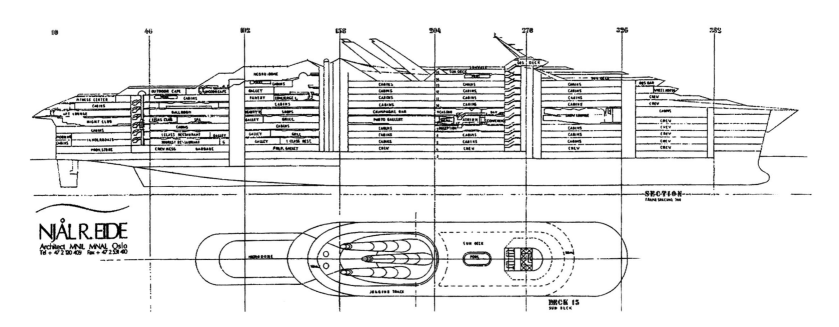

Profile and plan drawings of the Q5 as developed by Njal Eide, showing hull extensions fore and aft which increased the ship's overall length. The plan view shows the grouping of the three pipe-like funnels that were introduced in place of the two more conventional funnels of the original design. *Michael Gallagher*

In the *Queen Mary 2*, the largest and longest passenger liner ever built, Cunard commissioned a ship to deliver what had been intended with the Q5. She was, in fact, a hybrid in that she was designed as much for cruising as for line voyages. *David L. Williams*

As a whole, the ship and all its systems were to conform to a plethora of classification rules, conventions and protocols. The Q5 was destined to operate under the Red Ensign primarily in accordance with all UK national regulations. Other conformity measures were to include Panama Canal Commission and Suez Canal Authority Rules of Navigation and Tonnage Regulation, the consolidated SOLAS 1974 Convention plus the 1978 Protocol and 1981 and 1983 Amendments, the MARPOL 1973 Convention for the Prevention of Pollution from Ships, the International COLREG 1972 regulations for Preventing Collisions at Sea, and the U.S. Coast Guard's CG-515 Rules and Regulations for Foreign Flag Vessels Operating in the Navigable Waters of the United States.

By revealing the breadth of the design and regulatory detail outlined here, extracted from the Q5's design specification, the intention is to convey the extent of the effort that is committed to the consummation of the Q5 project. But the Q5 represented a huge challenge for Cunard and Trafalgar House at an inauspicious time. Neither organisation was happy with the ship's proposed exterior profile and questioned both the class segregation and high operating speed, both of which were preferences of the US office. Unable to agree on the final appearance and style of the ship, the Norwegian naval architect Njal Eide was approached to refine the design.

The result was far more streamlined and modern in comparison with the original two-funnel concept. Instead, the ship was given three clustered, acutely inclined pipe-like funnels and a mast above the bridge similarly leaning steeply aftwards. Projections to the hull at the bow and stern increased overall length to 1,045ft 6in but, as a whole, the new look certainly eradicated the stumpiness of the original profile.

Astonishingly, at the same time and with no apparent justification, the ship's speed was to be increased, to 41 knots maximum service speed and 44 knots maximum trials speed! Passenger numbers were amended to 750 total in Super-class, 700 First-class and 1,050 Tourist-class. The dining arrangements were also modified to a 350-seat single-sitting First-class restaurant and a 525-seat double-sitting Tourist-class restaurant.

All this was to no avail. The design and development costs of the Q5 were spiralling out of control and the truth was that Trafalgar House was reluctant to invest in the new ship having only a few years earlier spent so heavily on the *Queen Elizabeth 2*'s life-extension refit and engine change. The group had raised £400 million through a rights issue, ostensibly for the Q5, but other investments, among them some that were performing poorly, had swallowed up the available funds. By 1992, it seemed that any money set aside for the Q5 had disappeared.

The net result was that the Q5 concept had to be shelved and, in the end, nothing came of it. Meanwhile, the *Queen Elizabeth 2* soldiered on alone, entering a period in which she was so successful that, viewed in retrospect, it became her glory years. It has been stated already that it is a matter of regret that clear corporate decisions such as on this occasion by Trafalgar House were not made earlier in order to avoid much wasteage of time and money.

Within four years, the Cunard Line would briefly have new owners. Then two years later again, there would be another change of ownership when the company was acquired by the Carnival Corporation. Just weeks later, on 8 June 1998, designs for two 84,000grt 2,000-passenger liners for Cunard were completed. These were quickly abandoned, though, when it was recognised just how successful Carnival Cruise Line's 100,000grt *Destiny*-class and Royal Caribbean International's 137,000grt *Voyager*-class schemes were proving to be. Cunard's new ship or ships needed to be bigger. Six months later, in December 1998, the first details of 'Project Queen Mary' were released, for a vessel of even greater size – a truly prodigious ocean liner, the first new ship for the transatlantic service since the 1960s, that would also undertake an annual programme of cruises. The incredible *Queen Mary 2* eventually entered service on 12 January 2004, and the rest, as they say, is history.

8

EXTRAORDINARY SCHEMES FOR THE EMERGING CRUISE INDUSTRY

KLOSTERS REDERI'S SEMI-CATAMARAN CRUISE VESSEL *ELYSIAN*

The cruising boom of the 1970s, precipitated by the need to keep conventional passenger ships employed profitably, distinguished itself from other similar periods of intense activity in this direction in a number of respects. Whenever passenger figures became low or depressed, or when certain ships were past their prime, or during the scheduled service low season, shipowners were prone to resort to cruising as a temporary expedient, which was the primary reason on all such occasions in the past. By the mid 1970s, however, the situation was rather different since, although the reason was the same, the liners which had become diverted from their normal schedules were, in fact, being transferred into cruising roles permanently and, whereas the need for distinctive dual-role ships had been apparent in the 1950s and 1960s, this form of shipping business, by now highly competitive and catering for a more discerning and sophisticated clientele, had begun to create a demand for specially designed cruise vessels.

At the same time, with the involvement of public relations and marketing experts, cruise itineraries were no longer the rather haphazard schedules which had characterised them in the past, when the voyager had been tempted by a few exotic place names, interspersed with monotonous days at sea. Instead, carefully planned cruise circuits had been evolved, in order to provide the cruise passenger with the maximum amount of sight-seeing and the least amount of transition time between the various stopping–off points. Hence, the three most popular areas which emerged were the Mediterranean, the Baltic and the Caribbean. The latter undoubtedly headed the list, primarily catering

for the American market and, quite uncharacteristically, it was the Norwegians who became the most dominant in exploiting it.

Amongst the first major companies to recognise the potential of cruising the Caribbean waters out of Miami, Florida, was Klosters Rederi A/S of Oslo, which operated under the name Norwegian Caribbean Line (NCL). Norwegian Caribbean was responsible for many of the cruise innovations that have become standard throughout the industry and it was for this company that a new and most unusual cruising vessel project was first announced in the late 1960s.

The Norwegian Caribbean Line commenced operations from Miami in 1966 with the small passenger cruise vessel-cum-car ferry *Sunward*. This vessel was first complemented by, and later replaced with, three larger passenger ships, thus indicating the remarkably rapid growth of the Kloster Company's cruise business. By 1972, however, when the third new ship had joined the NCL fleet, other Norwegian companies had begun to appreciate the significance of Miami as an operational centre and were also beginning to establish themselves there. The first of these to arrive was the Royal Caribbean Cruise Line in November 1970, followed closely by Norwegian Cruiseships and the Royal Viking Line in 1972. These contenders for the business were quite apart from such foreign competitors as the Cunard, Home and Holland America Lines.

As a result of this situation, Klosters Rederi decided to embark on a second programme of new construction which would augment its already popular fleet of ships. In the first instance, they ordered a sister-ship to the 16,500grt *Southward*, its latest ship, from the same builders, Cantieri Navali del Tirreno e Riuniti in Italy. Planned to bear the name of the company's inaugural ship, the *Sunward*, which had been disposed of in the interim, the new vessel, like the *Southward*, was

Even though her catamaran stern is not immediately apparent in this artist's rendering of the *Elysian*, it shows her to have been one of the most radical departures from conventional passenger ship design for over a century. *Klosters Rederi*

contracted on a fixed-price basis, but the builders ran into financial difficulties and asked Klosters to pay an additional £10 million. This they refused to do, with the result that the contract was terminated and the new *Sunward* was taken over instead by P&O Lines and launched and completed to their specification as the *Spirit of London*.

Therefore, Klosters' other new building scheme, for a completely unique cruise vessel, now took precedence over everything else. First mentioned in 1969, it had been revived as part of this expansion programme. Designed specifically for the Caribbean cruise circuit, she was probably the most revolutionary ship conceived for many years and would have introduced more new features into a single vessel than had ever been attempted previously.

Described in detail for the first time in May 1972 when Klosters announced its firm intention to build her, the proposed ship would have had a semi-catamaran hull, that is, a conventional bow and fore section but a double-hulled stern. The reduction in her length/beam ratio resulting from this arrangement would have reduced her rolling characteristics radically, especially in beam seas. Apart from the advantages of this additional stabilisation, and even of classification, Klosters also intended to exploit the proposed ship's unusually broad configuration to the maximum in the planned passenger facilities. As to the classification benefits inherent in such a design, Mr Cedric Barclay, a former technical employee of Klosters, offered some explanation in saying:

The *Elysian* had a certain resemblance in her bow and bridge areas to the *Oriana* of 1960, one of the last big passenger liners to be built for a regular trade. *Chris Howell*

The cost of a catamaran would be prohibitive. In a passenger vessel, the only saving likely to arise [in such a ship] would be in the fire-fighting classification of one of the hulls, if not intended for passenger use.

Amongst the facilities proposed were a partial glass bottom through which the marine and coral life below the surface might be viewed; a vast sun deck terraced around a large swimming pool and an extensive inside sports area with numerous tennis courts. The most spectacular of the interior attractions was a huge, all-purpose room on the uppermost deck covered by a clear bubble-dome which would permit, late at night, the observation of the stars in order to gain, so it was said, an appreciation of their role in celestial navigation – a kind of live floating 'Planetarium' in fact – and which could also be used for dancing, cabarets and other activities.

An artist's impression of the proposed cruise ship which was released to the press exhibited all the space-age characteristics as described, while it also revealed a certain resemblance to the P&O liner *Oriana* in the bow and bridge areas. Painted on the bow was the name *Elysian*, conjuring up the Elysian Fields of Greek mythology, whither favoured heroes were borne without passing through death to dwell in a state of sustained happiness and bliss. This may have been only a working name for the project, as Klosters had maintained a consistent naming policy in all their undertakings, even to bestowing the title 'Landward' to the construction programme for their new office block in Miami. If, however, the name *Elysian* had been given to the planned semi-catamaran liner, it would have represented a dramatic break from the Norwegian Caribbean Line's tradition of having names ending in '-ward'. Although displayed on the ship's hull, more likely it was a project name chosen for marketing purposes to conjure up the happy and blissful on board ambience the company aimed to promote.

Around 20,000 to 22,000 gross tons, the futuristic semi-catamaran's passenger capacity would have been nearly 1,000, with the construction costs being estimated at £20 million in 1972. In commenting on the ship, Mr Knut Utstein Kloster, [then] the chairman of the parent company, Klosters Rederi, said: 'The broad beam would allow for the greatest flexibility of facilities and freedom of passenger movement on any cruise vessel afloat.'

The Norwegian Caribbean Line was undoubtedly very enthusiastic about its latest enterprise, but spiralling costs, compounded by the 1973 oil crisis, forced them to defer the project temporarily. Most observers held the view that it had been cancelled completely at that time.

In fact, this was not the case. Almost two years later, in July 1974, press announcements indicated that the scheme had not been abandoned. The Norwegian Caribbean Line's Miami-based Sales Vice-President, Mr Bruce Nierenberg, declared that a suitable shipyard was being sought and that the final decision on whether to proceed with the vessel would be made that September. He added: 'If the go-ahead is given, the ship could be in service by late 1977.' However, the optimism of the summer made a marked contrast with the gloom in the company's Miami offices that autumn when Knut Kloster announced yet again his decision to shelve his ambitious plan to build the world's first semi-catamaran liner.

The reasons were entirely financial, and a common enough problem – inflation and sky-high operating costs. As Knut Kloster put it: 'Even with full ships, today we are not making much money.' Despite this statement there were apparently still firm intentions to keep the project alive, and Knut Kloster confirmed this when he said:

The plans have not been dropped, but it is difficult to see how it could be justified from a prudent business point of view to build a ship which, due to tremendous inflation and price increases in the past two or three years, will probably cost four or five times as much as [each of] our present ships.

In the years that immediately followed, the economic climate did not improve sufficiently to favour the resumption of the project, with construction costs rising higher than ever. Another ominous factor was the return of all the data relating to the *Elysian* to the company's headquarters office at Oslo in 1977.

Klosters Rederi was nevertheless quick to scotch any rumours that the semi-catamaran cruise vessel scheme was finished. That her construction might yet proceed became evident from statements made by Knut Kloster in a communication on the subject of the

The cruise ship *Norway*, converted from the former transatlantic liner *France*, seen in the River Hudson in May 1980 on her inaugural New York call. It was perhaps her purchase by Klosters Rederi for cruise operations that finally doomed the *Elysian* project. *Bill Miller*

ship in 1978, when he remarked, inter alia, '… the project is still very much at the sort of "fluid planning stage" with a highly uncertain prospect for realisation'. More optimistically, he further stated: 'All the particulars [of the ship] are preliminary, and subject to a lot of future changes.' Al Wolfe, the Norwegian Caribbean Lines' Director of Public Affairs, added his own sanguine observations:

I would be very reluctant to say that it [the ship] has been permanently shelved. We continue to hope that, at some future date, conditions will permit us to pursue it.

One pertinent new factor, unforeseen at that time but certain to have had a significant bearing on the prospects for the *Elysian*, was the purchase by the Norwegian Caribbean Line in June 1979 of the former French luxury liner *France* for Caribbean cruise duties. Re-named *Norway*, the former CGT North Atlantic vessel, one of the last great ships built for scheduled passenger services and very much a flag-waver for France, was extensively re-furbished for her new role at the Hapag-Lloyd AG shipyard in Hamburg. As part of this programme, previously enclosed promenade decks were opened up and numerous additional recreational and dining facilities were installed.

In the light of this, it was difficult to endorse the optimism of the Norwegian Caribbean Line's officials regarding the company's project for a semi-catamaran cruise vessel. An investment of the size involved in the purchase of the former *France* would take some considerable time to recoup, apart from the fact that the company expressed a desire to buy another similar-sized vessel should the *Norway* prove to be very successful, perhaps the former United States Lines' flagship *United States* with which the *France* had operated a joint service and which was laid up looking for a buyer.

Two years later, the *Norway* was established in her new cruise service although it may be disputed whether she was a qualified success, although she continued in her new role for many more years than she had as the *France* on the Atlantic run. Either way, her emergence made it extremely unlikely that the *Elysian* would ever be constructed, at all events in the form originally suggested, and so it turned out to be. Despite the absence of her realisation, her conception was a catalyst for more radical thinking in the design of dedicated cruise ships. It merits suggestion that she launched the drive for more specialised cruise ships and it was seen as likely that, sooner or later, either the Norwegian Caribbean Line or one of the other leading cruise operators would introduce an equally revolutionary ship, a ship which would change the trends of cruise vessel design irreversibly, yet be affordable enough to construct, and remain a viable concept in the first place.

The boom in cruising that began in the early 1980s, manifest in the number of large new cruise vessels by then on the order book or under construction, created the climate in which experimental design thinking could flourish. While some of the more imaginative and unorthodox, occasionally bizarre, designs that have emerged in the years since have not been accompanied, as will be seen, by any greater success than the *Elysian*, the new-found freedom of creativity has since had an impact. The modern cruise ship, with its amenity-driven approach to interiors and its ranks of balconied staterooms, bears little resemblance, other than superficial, to the ocean passenger liner of the past, a contention that is borne out in radically different internal layouts and the extensive provision of leisure amenities.

WÄRTSILÄ'S SWATH CRUISER

As a clear indication that ocean cruising was continuing to thrive and expand as the 1980s progressed, certain shipbuilders and operators unveiled plans for what they perceived would make a future generation of ideal cruise vessels. The ships they proposed were not only intended to increase the number of available berths for the growing market but, with futuristic shapes and features previously undreamt of, they were intended to completely revolutionise the whole concept of the cruise holiday. As four of these particular projects, all of which failed to appear, have a closely related ethos, they are dealt with consecutively in this and the next three sections.

For some years, at the time when the available cruising tonnage still largely comprised adapted ships originally constructed for the liner trades, it had been recognised that there was a need for highly specialised vessels for the modern cruise market. Some relatively advanced thinking had been reflected in such new ships as Royal Caribbean Cruise Line's *Song of America* (1982), P&O's *Royal Princess* (1984) and Carnival Cruise Line's trio *Holiday* (1985), *Jubilee* (1986) and *Celebration* (1987) but the belief in many quarters was that designers had not yet gone far enough. While many technical advances had been achieved, especially in fuel economy, it seemed that there remained a persistent adherence to the view that the cruise ship should continue to bear some overall resemblance to the traditional passenger liner that had once operated on the world's ocean ferry routes. The problem with that approach, they contended, was that the ships' designs were dominated by the 'marine' side, with the passenger functions incorporated in the hull wherever space was

An artist's portrayal of the Wärtsilä SWATH Cruiser. Her unusual catamaran configuration with submerged pontoon hulls is clearly visible, as is the broad area of open space on the upper deck. A typical cruise package for the ship would have constituted seven days out of Miami combining calls at three established resorts with two 'sea-holiday' days in the waters of the Bahamas. *Wärtsilä*

available, almost as a secondary consideration. In effect, because the needs of the modern cruise ship, as they perceived them, were so completely different, such a doctrine severely limited the possibilities where fundamental shipboard improvements were required.

Financially, the world recession of the 1980s had brought severe competition into the cruising market, resulting in slender profits. Certain designers were convinced, therefore, that the competitive edge and future prosperity in the cruising business could only be gained through a revolutionary departure from the traditional cruise philosophy and conventional design attitudes. Such radical changes would permit a complete rethink of the on board layout of the accommodation and amenity spaces as well as of the overall focus of a cruise vacation, potentially resulting in cruise ships that would bear little resemblance to those already in service.

Hence, totally new concepts like the SWATH Cruiser (Small Waterplane Area Twin Hull) emerged as just one of a number of unorthodox proposals from the design team at Wärtsilä, in Finland, under the leadership of Chief Designer Dr Kai Levander. At that time, the Wärtsilä Group could be said, with little fear of contradiction, to have been the world's leading builder of passenger ships, having delivered, over a twenty-year period, more than twenty major passenger/vehicle ferries and fifteen assorted cruise vessels. With such a pedigree, Wärtsilä's observations and predictions deserved to be treated with respect. Significant among the methods employed by the Wärtsilä design team for evolving their ideal cruise ship were special computer programmes – then something of a novelty – which analysed the impact of various factors, both economic and technical, on the projected performance of each subject design.

Bow and stern views of the SWATH Cruiser. *Wärtsilä*

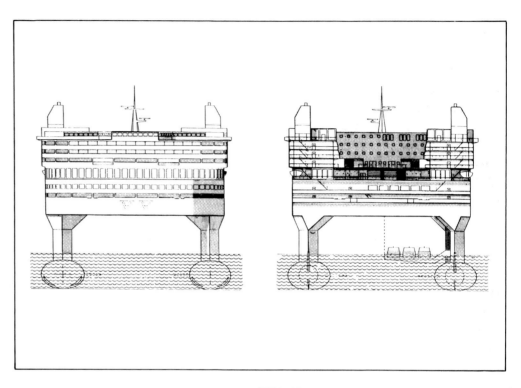

The 'Riviera Terraces', the inner area between the wings of the SWATH Cruiser's superstructure. *Wärtsilä*

To support such a radical diversion from orthodox marine architecture as the SWATH Cruiser, Wärtsilä claimed a number of important advantages in the design. Basically, a SWATH or SSC (Semi-Submerged Catamaran) ship consists of three main components, namely two submarine pontoons attached via struts of streamlined section to a superstructure platform connecting the two demi-hulls. Such an arrangement, it was postulated, offered many benefits.

With the engine rooms and propeller shafts situated in the two submerged pontoons, separated from the accommodation quarters and public spaces so that there was no underwater hull above the propellers, vibration and noise levels would be greatly reduced. Also, the vessel's extremely wide beam relative to its length would give enhanced stability such that exceptional sea-keeping characteristics, both at anchor and underway, were claimed for the design.

Of greatest significance from the point of view of commercial operations was the vast amount of extra deck space made available by the catamaran configuration. In the SWATH Cruiser, this lent itself to architectural and functional innovation on an unprecedented scale for the public rooms while, for open-air recreation and promenade purposes the extensive, unhampered deck space was at least twice as great as that on a conventional mono-hulled cruise vessel of comparable tonnage. The SWATH Cruiser's design offered 6,500 square metres of indoor public passenger space which included, in addition to the usual dining, entertainment, sports and recreation areas, a submersible saloon complete with aquarium.

Though ultra-modern and, to some extent, futuristic in appearance, the SWATH Cruiser was not an altogether novel concept. The general principle had been the subject of some detailed research for over twenty-five years and had been exploited already in the construction of oil rig and offshore support and survey vessels where large areas of free deck space were called for. Nor was it the first application of these design principles to a passenger-carrying vessel. For the record, the Mitsui Shipbuilding and Engineering Company of Tokyo, Japan, had also been progressively involved in the development of SWATH craft types and had built two 690 gross ton SSC passenger ferries, the *Meisa 80* – a demonstration craft completed in 1979 – and, two

years later, the *Seagull* which entered commercial service for Sanzo Kigyo KK, a Tokyo-based ferry company.

However, SWATH Cruiser was by far the most ambitious such project. The first ship of this type specifically designed for a cruising role and a massive step forward in terms of size and general dimensions, having an overall length of 534ft, a maximum beam of 202ft and a depth to the struts of 82ft. Draught to the underside of the submerged pontoons measured as 36ft. Its approximate gross tonnage would have been 44,250, indicating a cruise ship of not inconsiderable size.

The ship's designed capacity was for 1,500 passengers in 704 fully air-conditioned cabins, each with private toilet and bathroom facilities. In excess of 70 per cent of this accommodation would have been outside, either overlooking the sea or a unique inner area imaginatively named the Riviera Terraces. Consisting of a wide boulevard of palm tree-lined walkways around swimming pools and a sports area, this latter feature extended through the centre of much of the length of the superstructure, from the ship's stern to just abaft the bridge. Adjoining it were a shopping precinct, a casino and various bars and lounges, while terraced on either side at the fore end were the balconies and verandahs of inner cabin suites. Crew numbers would have been approximately 420, the majority of whom were to be accommodated in single cabins on the lower decks.

Apart from the largely revolutionary characteristics of the SWATH Cruiser already described, there was one further particularly innovative feature which, more than any other, reflected the predicted change of emphasis conjectured for future cruise holidays. Situated on the starboard side of the lowest deck in the superstructure, there was to be a huge mobile platform some 580 square metres in area which could be lowered to sea level as and when required. Equipped with three motor launches, each of 150 persons capacity, and a range of sports equipment: windsurfers, scuba diving equipment, water-skis, in fact all manner of apparatus for every conceivable aquatic activity, the hydraulically operated platform was also intended to serve as a sheltered boarding stage, protected from the elements within a form of dock between the struts.

For its main propulsion, the SWATH Cruiser would have had four Pielstick 8 PC2 L400 diesel engines of 12,600kW (approximately 17,150bhp) total output coupled to two controllable pitch propellers. Such an installation would have permitted a cruising speed of 16 knots. Additionally, an auxiliary engine of 9,600kW (approximately 13,050bhp) maximum output would have generated power for all on board services.

It can be concluded that a lot of thought and detailed preparation had been expended by the Wärtsilä design team in the development of the SWATH Cruiser concept. Sadly it was all to little avail, for no operator took up the design in a new-build contract with the shipyard. Written on every publicity document published by Wärtsilä was the slogan: 'We believe that the only limit to a man's creativity is his own mind'. The company finally lost its identity in 1989 when it filed for bankruptcy and was reorganised as Masa Yards.

Wärtsilä's slogan was intended as an exhortation towards broader-mindedness in design attitudes and the acceptance of progress. It could also be interpreted as a sober recognition of that ever-present, conservative resistance to change which has threatened the prospects of many new ideas, killing them off in their infancy and which, perhaps, ultimately augured unfavourably for the SWATH Cruiser. On a positive note, though, the radical SWATH cruise ship concept that Wärtsilä had proposed was subsequently realised in a somewhat smaller scale when, just three years later, in 1992, the smaller all-balcony luxury SWATH vessel *Radisson Diamond* was completed by the Rauma Finnyards, another Finnish shipbuilder. Measuring 20,295 gross tons with main dimensions of 430ft length overall and 105ft maximum beam, and having capacity for 354 passengers, the *Radisson Diamond* is to date the only twin-hulled cruise ship ever to have been built. The fact that its active career extended for over

The only example of an ocean-going SWATH cruise ship to be actually built is the *Radisson Diamond*, later renamed *China Star*. At 20,295grt, she was approximately half the size of Wärtsilä's projected SWATH Cruiser.
Frank Heine

25 years, latterly under the name *China Star*, suggests that, despite being the lone ship of its type, it has not been unsuccessful.

Prior to the demise of Wärtsilä as a shipbuilder, its design team continued to develop new concepts, persistently advocating a break from tradition by designing ships around the passengers and their on board vacation experience rather than simply as a means of conveyance, albeit well-appointed, between a string of resorts. Around 1989, its 'Project Rio' design emerged, a vision for a 100,000 gross ton cruise ship intended for the high-volume seven-day Caribbean market. The 722ft-long delta or wedge-shaped vessel would have, at 250ft, had an extremely wide beam for its length, more than double that of other mooted cruise ships of this tonnage. It was said that these dimensions, giving a length to breadth ratio of 2.9:1, would make for good sea-keeping qualities as well as high speed.

A total of 3,500 passengers would have been catered for in two separate hotel towers mounted upon the hull's uppermost deck. The 'Project Rio' certainly broke the boundaries with the astonishing array of passenger amenities incorporated into its vast, broad hull. It was suggested that new spaces and new activities would be discovered on every day of a cruise. Several restaurants would offer a variety of décors, cuisines and views of the sea. There would be various health and fitness suites, many locations for musical and theatrical entertainment and even an amusement park for children. A ship-board marina, complete with cafés and bars, would have a 'pontoon-sheltered outer harbour' for water sports and operating ship-to-shore tenders. Most incredible, the ship was to have an internal rail system serving three decks on a circular track, an idea that was resurrected later in Carnival's 'Pinnacle' project (see page 237). A veritable 'City at Sea', it was no wonder that the estimated cost to build and equip the ship was stated to be $360 million! (£180 million)

NIPPON KOKAN MACS 3000

Like Wärtsilä with its SWATH Cruiser and other concepts, the 1980s and 1990s were a period in which shipbuilder-led design ideas for new cruise ships were prevalent, though not all from yards well established in passenger ship construction. One such was the Japanese

yard Nippon Kokan KK located in the Tsurumi/Shimizu prefecture of Yokohama. Better known for steel production, Nippon Kokan entered the shipbuilding business in 1940, benefitting from the upsurge in demand for naval construction as Japan triggered the Pacific war. Post-war, the yard engaged in a greater variety of commercial work until financial difficulties in the mid 1980s led to a reorganisation of the parent corporation's business activities and, in particular, its Heavy Industry Division. Simultaneously, as part of a process of increased diversification, the shipbuilding business launched its bid to become a builder of cruise ships, presenting its design for what was described as 'the cruise ship of the 1990s', a futuristic conception called the MACS 3000 or Multi Activity Cruise Ship.

In keeping with the philosophy behind the SWATH Cruiser, the MACS 3000 featured an approach to cruising intended to establish the vessel as a destination in itself or at least as the primary focus of a quite different type of cruise holiday. After locating the ship in suitably temperate waters, recreational activities would then take over as a major part of the holiday programme rather than the pursuit of an itinerary of port calls with shore excursions as offered in a traditional cruise. As an added benefit, it would save the operator both fuel costs and docking fees. Clearly it was aimed at a younger, fitter and more active clientele!

The MACS 3000 was a displacement vessel with what appeared to be a basically orthodox hull shape, although the external complexity of the design tended to conceal this. It was quoted as being 858ft long with a beam of 142ft. Depth from the upper deck to the keel was 177ft although the designed draught was only 28ft. The lofty superstructure was to be exploited to the full in the amenities to be offered for passenger entertainment, recreation and dining, while the shallow draught was intended to permit access to offshore waters of restricted depth such as over coral reefs. As projected, the MACS 3000 would have had a gross tonnage of around 85,000 (some reports gave a figure of 152,000grt but this figure does not appear in any of the Nippon Kokan publicity literature).

The design of the MACS 3000 resulted from collaborative effort between Nippon Kokan and Iko Maritime with the Norwegian naval architect Njal Eide, later engaged for the Q5 project, acting as consultant.

The MACS 3000 Multi-Activity Cruise Ship as depicted in an early impression, revealing the twin-skeg stern configuration with floating marina. *Nippon Kokan*

A cross-section of the MACS 3000 accommodation showing the public spaces and cabin areas situated in the superstructure wings. *Nippon Kokan*

Accommodation aboard the MACS 3000 would have been provided for 2,000 one-class passengers in 1,000 cabins, all located in two longitudinal wing structures running along either side of the ship. As a result, all cabins would have been outside, facing either the sea or an atrium, one of two inner areas of gardens, boulevards and fountains similar to the Riviera Terraces of the SWATH Cruiser, and a design feature adopted aboard countless later cruise ships. Areas for sun bathing, sports and other pastimes were situated on the top deck where there would also have been swimming pools.

The most remarkable innovation proposed for the MACS 3000, which distinguished it from other contemporary cruise ship designs, was what was described in publicity documents as a 'stern inside harbour area'. This consisted of a circular marina and floating island secured at the stern from where it could be allowed to drift away from the ship itself, while remaining attached. It was intended that this would have launches and other water craft docked within it and all along its outer rim. It is not clear whether this structure would have remained extended at all times or whether it would have been retracted into the hull when the ship was underway. Emphasising the 'ship as the cruise centre' approach, the marina would have been the focal point for all manner of water sports such as wind surfing, scuba diving, sailing and water skiing while it would also have acted as a unique social centre provided with its own cocktail and snack bars.

The key to the design which permitted this extraordinary feature was the vessel's wide beam that projected aft into a twin-skeg configuration at the stern. Apart from the recreational advantages already highlighted, it was claimed that this also gave the MACS 3000 improved operational efficiency.

Repeating the point made earlier, passenger facilities and amenities in the MACS 3000 design took priority over all other considerations. So extensive were the recreational facilities that would be on offer, it was said that the only thing that the vessel lacked was an 18-hole golf course. In exploiting the ship's scale for those purposes, some 23,000 square metres of deck area would have been dedicated to public spaces of which 13,000 square metres would have been inside. That corresponded to 11.5 square metres per passenger, certainly a high figure.

The engine installation proposed for the MACS 3000 was four NKK-SEMT Pielstick 6PC40K diesels which would have permitted a service speed of 22 knots, though this was, to some extent, irrelevant given the ship's intended role.

Common to the SWATH Cruiser and the MACS 3000 was the philosophy that the ships themselves should be the focus of cruise holiday entertainment in exotic settings with the more familiar visits to a rota of destinations largely abandoned. Thus, almost any sunny and sheltered anchorage, lagoon or coral reef could be a satisfactory locale for a cruise operation independent of the traditional itinerary of resort centres. The result, it was said, would be youthful relaxation and considerably more physical activity.

However, one can only speculate on how much market research was conducted in parallel with the running of computerised design and evaluation tools when assessing these concepts. Novelty is definitely a defining factor in the modern cruise business, both where the provision of on board diversions are concerned, as well as in defining or recasting the operational application of a given vessel. But if the niche the designer is aiming at is too narrow then the justification for investment in construction can become so marginal as to be, for all practical purposes, non-existent.

A more detailed view of the stern 'inside harbour' seen from water level. *Nippon Kokan*

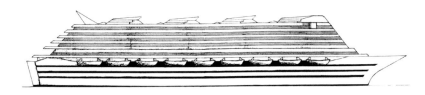

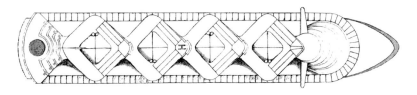

Confronting the perennial challenge, as to how the maximum provision of outside cabins could be achieved – even 100 per cent if possible, Aalborg Vaerft, the Danish shipbuilder which was actively contending for modern passenger ship business in the 1980s, offered its own, unique solution for a forthcoming new generation of cruise ships. The emphasis of its approach was more on the decentralisation of the passenger accommodation than on the recasting of the ship's fundamental role. The resulting design, having cabin sections located on the upper deck arranged diagonally like a series of diamonds or lozenges, was arrived at by what was described as a 'square root' principle: 'By creating a greater outside surface many more real outside cabins can be provided while the cores of each section lend themselves to the creation of all manner of suitably conducive environments'. Looking at the side elevation, the symmetrically arranged cabin sections on the top deck do not appear to have sufficient height to provide much of the vaunted outside accommodation spaces! *Roy Miller from an Aalborg Vaerft sketch*

Experience has demonstrated that certain novel concepts have not captured the level of interest anticipated, and their success, if that is the right term, has been questionable at best. The residential or time-share apartment cruise ships are one example of this. No doubt, such dubious prospects could equally have faced those schemes that projected 'fun in the water' as their primary raison d'être. Today, for the adventurous-minded cruise passenger with a hankering for physical exertion and a desire to go 'off piste', there are the smaller themed 'expedition' and 'discovery' cruise ships which, being of compact size and having smaller complements, take their intrepid explorers for adrenalin-filled thrills in polar regions and up mosquito-infested tropical tributaries, inaccessible to the larger cruise ships.

PHOENIX RISING – THE '*WORLD CITY*' GIANT

Probably the most extraordinary project for a new-generation cruise ship emerged in the late summer of 1984. The 'Project Phoenix', as it was called, was developed for Norwegian Caribbean Line (NCL) – Norwegian Cruise Line since November 1987 – motivated very much by the owner of NCL's parent company, Klosters Rederi. At the time, NCL already owned and operated the *Norway* ex-*France*, then the world's largest cruise ship, employing her in a rather unconventional cruising role which hinted at the changing cruise trends then being advocated. Based at Miami, the *Norway*'s itinerary involved typical cruise visits to a small number of ports on the Caribbean cruise circuit, followed by a period acting as an offshore hotel at one of two private NCL-owned islands, Harvest Caye, Belize, and Great Stirrup Cay, Bahamas.

Based on this experience and having already demonstrated a willingness to innovate, it was not entirely surprising that NCL should next pursue a project as unorthodox and ambitious as the 'Phoenix', especially as it carried a price tag as high (then) as the $350 million (c. £175million) quoted. Indeed, the 'Phoenix' would have dwarfed the *Norway* in terms of both cost and size. Originally envisaged as a 250,000 gross ton vessel measuring 1,250ft overall length (it later grew to 265,000grt on a length overall of 1,268ft) with a 253ft 4in beam but having a draught of just 33ft. With accommodation for up to 5,200 passengers and a crew of 1,850, the 'Phoenix' would then have been the largest passenger ship ever seriously contemplated. Prior to NCL's 'Phoenix', the previous largest were the four Detwiler 'boatel' liners of the late 1950s which would have had a tonnage of 120,000 gross and a length overall of 1,275ft. Of course, in the years since, the size and dimensions of these phenomenally large concepts have been virtually matched by the 'Genesis'-class ships of Royal Caribbean Cruise Lines which weigh in at 225,000 gross tons on a length of 1,187ft, the first of which, the *Oasis of the Seas*, entered service in December 2009.

It wasn't long before the 'Project Phoenix' had adopted the code name *Phoenix World City* – not necessarily the name which would have appeared on the ship's hull had she been completed.

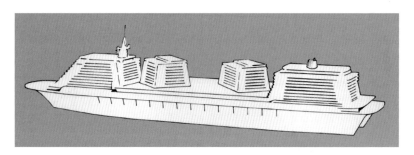

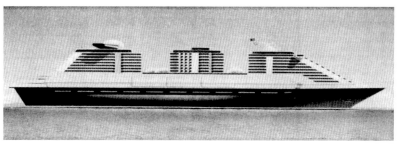

The 'Phoenix' floating holiday resort. The drawing belies the immense size of the ship, four times the gross tonnage and almost quarter as long again as the *Norway*, then the largest passenger ship in the world. *Roy Miller*

The three-tower configuration of the *Phoenix World City* concept. *Travel Trade Gazette*

Her design reflected the principle known as 'decentralisation' whereby all cabin accommodation would have been in three or four high-rise blocks (both configurations were revealed in models and impressions) erected upon the main deck of a dory-like hull, thereby separated from the rest of the ship. This arrangement would allow all cabins, distributed around the sides of the blocks, to have unobscured sea views.

The Danish firm of marine architects, Knud E. Hansen of Helsingor, led by Tage Wandborg, worked on the design of the 'Phoenix' for Norwegian Caribbean Line under project number KEH 83029, contributing extensively to its evolution as a practical ship, but its most ardent enthusiast was Knut Utstein Kloster, the owner of Klosters Rederi. Identifying himself positively as a supporter of the emerging new spirit of cruising, he is quoted as having said of the 'Phoenix':

A lot of people are sceptical about its design but that is because the design of all cruise ships today is rooted in the old concept of a passenger ship as a means of transportation. If you think of a cruise ship as a resort in itself, why would you want to put the bulk of the passengers in cabins below decks, many of them without windows? We think the 'Phoenix' is beautiful because it is functionally perfect and escapes the strictures of traditional concepts.

Indeed, Knut Kloster was so committed to the 'Phoenix' project that he had $34 million (£17 million) invested in its development.

Like the Nippon Kokan MACS design discussed earlier in this chapter, the *Phoenix World City* would also have had a twin-skegged stern under the shelter of which there would have been a marina or harbour. From this, four huge, high-speed 400-capacity day cruisers would shuttle passengers rapidly from ship to shore. Evidently, the *Phoenix World City* was to have followed the arrangement established with the *Norway* but beyond that, the *Phoenix World City* was also to assume the role of a mother ship with the tenders acting as feeder vessels stationed at destinations and embarkation ports within a 50-mile radius. Acting as a vast floating, offshore hotel, it was intended that guests could join and leave the ship at will without the constraints of a fixed or predetermined voyage duration.

With the cabin accommodation arranged in the tower blocks, the main part of the ship's hull space was left free for leisure, recreation, dining and entertainment provision. It was intended that these should include an Olympic-standard swimming pool, a gymnasium and complexes of full-size tennis and squash courts complete with saunas and jacuzzis and an 800-metre jogging track. Conference and education centres, along with a planetarium and a 100,000-book library would have provided for those less interested in energetic pursuits, while for entertainment there would have been cinemas and a 2,000-seat theatre. In keeping with Kloster's concept of a 'floating city or resort', the interior of the hull was to be arranged with 'streets, villages and shopping malls', besides numerous restaurants offering the widest possible choice of dining and culinary options. A comprehensively equipped hospital and a heliport were also among the trend-setting amenities planned for the ship.

An artist's rendering of the entrance into the aft docking bay of the 'Phoenix', located under the stern and between the sides of her dory-type hull. *Knud E. Hansen*

A sketch showing the main deck of the *Phoenix World City* and one of her accommodation towers. *Knud E. Hansen*

The potentially ground-breaking thinking behind these amenities brings to mind Thomas Ismay's decision back in 1871 to shift the saloon passenger spaces in the original *Oceanic* quartet from the aft end to amidships where there was less vibration and movement. Though considered to be most radical at the time, it set a trend that all other liner companies subsequently followed. Another example was the dining arrangement where food would be bought separate from the passage fare, as first proposed for the one-class cafeteria ships of the 1950s, then perceived to be the means of providing rock-bottom fares as the declassification of social strata gathered pace in the tourist era. Now this custom, once thought to be an unacceptable practice, is being adopted aboard an increasing number of cruise ships.

A gas turbine power plant was considered for *Phoenix World City* but it is understood that the design team ultimately settled on a diesel-electric propulsion system comprising two 20MW main motors per shaft each driving a 23ft (7 metre) diameter variable pitch propeller for a service speed of 19 knots. Eight 9,600kW diesel generators would have supplied auxiliary power and there would have been eight 2,500kW side thrusters, four forward and four at the aft end to assist manoeuvring. Test tank trials using large-scale models proved to be very encouraging, presumably based on the sort of performance that could be expected from the power system finally selected.

Speculation was rife in the shipping world, closely following the unfolding project, that the order for the first 'Phoenix' ship would be placed before the end of 1984 with entry into service in 1989. The lucrative order was earnestly pursued by several competing shipbuilders, among them the Kockums yard in Malmö, Sweden, and Wärtsilä in Finland. However, time passed without a contract and in the absence of any sign of imminent construction the project seemed to have 'gone off the boil'.

It seems that finance for such a staggeringly ambitious scheme was the problem. In *Lloyds List* of 29 January 1988 it was stated that

A model of the four-tower version of the 'Phoenix' undergoing trials in a manoeuvring test tank. *Klosters Rederi A/S*

the build cost, which had previously increased to $500 million (£250 million), had escalated to $1 billion (£500 million), although the proponents had already raised $200 million (£100 million) through the US market. The balance was to be sought, it was explained, through 'corporate subscriptions', essentially mammoth high-value share holdings, each of $1 million, obtained from large, international 'blue-chip' corporations. To make these 'shares' more exclusive, they were to be rationed in number by country according to the size of its gross national product, viz: United States of America 70 units, Japan 22, West Germany 14, the United Kingdom 10, and so on. The remaining funding was to be raised through conventional shipyard financing and other credit-generation facilities, which is where the potential shipbuilders came in.

By this point both Kockums and Wärtsilä appear to have been sidelined but it was clear that the project had not been abandoned. It transpired that a Japanese consortium representing Mitsubishi, Ishikawa Harima and Nippon Kokan had become the favourites to secure the order, only for a protocol of agreement to be signed with another consortium led by Howaldtswerke Deutsche Werft in West Germany on 18 July 1988. This included Bremer Vulkan, Blohm and Voss and Thyssen Nordseewerke, each of whom would be responsible for fabricating component sections that would be assembled in the Kieler Forde yard of Howaldtswerke Deutsche Werft. Kloster considered that collectively these yards had the financial clout to execute a project of this enormous scale. In the hope of gaining the building contract, the lead company had in fact been involved with the 'Phoenix' project right from the start, having assisted considerably with the design development. It was estimated that construction of the ship would absorb 80 per cent of West Germany's shipbuilding capacity. A revised delivery date in 1993 was forecast but finance remained the stumbling block after the West German government, like its Japanese counterpart, expressed an unwillingness to underwrite the project costs.

Securing the investment to cover first costs of large passenger vessels of unproven design has consistently been difficult, going right back to the 1920s. The highly speculative character of such projects tends to be off-putting, but it is felt that there are also other, less tangible obstacles to the progress of designs like that of the 'Phoenix'. Ships of extraordinarily novel design require not only operators but also investors of considerable courage in order to proceed. It is likely that the latter, in particular, are better able to perceive the greatest potential hurdle to be faced: the attitudes of the targeted paying customers, the reactions that may be provoked by the ship's unconventional appearance or function. Even in today's push button, silicone chip age, the public in general still has pre-conceived notions as to what a car, an aeroplane or a cruise ship should look like, both inside and outside, despite being wowed by some of the novel features that are now on offer. The criticism that accompanied the inauguration, not so very long ago, of the innovative *Queen Elizabeth 2* or Holland America's *Rotterdam* of 1958 is sure evidence of this. Klosters Rederi and the Norwegian Caribbean Line clearly demonstrated that their place was at the forefront of innovative change but how many other organisations, financial or maritime, were prepared to exhibit such a bold and pioneering spirit?

Ironically, twenty or so years after the 'Phoenix' project was first announced, the emergence of Royal Caribbean's *Oasis of the Seas*-class suggested that the 'Phoenix' design as originally conceived was not as extreme as it had first appeared and was essentially viable. But in the late 1980s, long before such vast ships finally appeared, cruise industry 'pundits' regarded the 'Phoenix' as outlandish, having far from realistic prospects. So much for the 'experts'!

Despite the fact that the endeavours to get the ship built in Germany had been thwarted, it was not the end for the 'Phoenix' for the efforts to turn the dream into reality persisted over the next twenty years. In the mid 1990s and again in the mid 2000s, the seemingly moribund project resurfaced. In fact, it had never gone away but had only been dormant, awaiting resurrection by its advocates. Though originally promoted by cruise visionary Knut Kloster, in 1996, the Westin Hotels and Resorts Group had taken an interest in reviving the project, renaming it *America World City*. And, by the time an application was lodged for federal loan guarantees to permit construction of the ship in the United States, the project was being fronted by the World City Corporation headed by Stephanie Gallagher, who had been a member of Kloster's original team.

A very upbeat marketing campaign was launched under the name 'The America Flagship Project', with the slogan: 'We were ahead of our time, but our time has come'. As part of its approach to the United States Government for support funding, a hard-hitting, patriotically loaded pitch was made to sell the project, highlighting the many benefits it could offer to the American nation.

It would provide, it was said, 15 million hours of work for thousands of workers and hundreds of US supply businesses. There would be long-term, self-sustaining jobs in shipyards and component firms and, later, operational and administrative jobs aboard ship and ashore. The volume of business created by the 'Phoenix' project would generate billions for the U.S. Treasury in corporate and payroll taxes. As there would ultimately be three of these giant vessels, all operating in US territorial waters – one on the west coast, one on the east coast and one around Hawaii – it would provide an estimated $500 million in annual economic benefits to US ports and coastal communities. It would reverse the multi-billion dollar drain on the national trade deficit through countering the foreign dominance of the US-based and US-driven cruise industry and it would not cost American taxpayers anything except 'vision, determination and confidence'.

Reminded, perhaps, of the fact that the 'Phoenix' had been conceived originally by the Norwegian Cruise Line – one of the foreign companies that was conveying American cruise passengers but not paying federal taxes – and concerned not to undermine that company's goodwill, a concession was offered. A strategic cooperation and technology exchange between the USA and Norway was thus proposed as part of the package, allowing the World City Corporation to benefit from Norwegian experience in the operation of cruise ships as well as permitting Norway to supply key marine components during the build phase, to the tune of $100 million. More generally, despite the heavy emphasis on American 'competitiveness, ingenuity, productivity and resourcefulness', it was also said that, while the America World City constituted a solid business opportunity for the American economy, it was in no way intended to undermine the recognised benefits to America of the existing foreign-flag cruise industry!

When the 'US-Flag Cruise Ship Pilot Project' was passed by Congress in 1997, a statute designed to revitalise the malingering ocean-going cruise fleet of the United States, the World City Corporation saw an opportunity to exploit this in order to obtain the Title XI channel construction funding it was seeking.

Commonly referred to as Title XI, the Federal Ship Financing Program, to give it its official title, derives from the Merchant Marine Act of 1936. Its purpose was to promote the growth and modernisation of the U.S. Merchant Marine and American shipyards and, by so doing, to stimulate employment creation. Authorised by 46 US Congress Chapter 537, it achieves its goal through U.S. Government debt guarantees (effectively loans) which have extended repayment terms and interest rates that are lower than those charged by commercial lending sources.

Despite the World City Corporation's optimism, it was pipped to the post when the U.S. Maritime Administration (MARAD), part of the Department of Transportation responsible for implementing the Title XI policy, awarded funding instead to a rival 'Project America' scheme under which American Classic Voyages of Chicago, Illinois, ordered two 72,000grt cruise ships from Ingalls Shipbuilding at Pascagoula, Mississippi, on 9 March 1999. Subsequently, however, exacerbated by the shock waves of the attacks on the World Trade Centre in September 2001, this enterprise collapsed with huge financial debts and the American taxpayer was forced to pick up the tab with little or nothing to show for the outlay of close on $500 million (£250 million).

Arising from this episode and having burnt its fingers once, MARAD explained, in rejecting the World City Corporation's request for a Title XI loan:

> The Department of Transportation has adopted a policy prohibiting MARAD from financing overnight passenger vessels under 46 USC Chapter 537. This policy is based on MARAD's long history with troubled passenger vessel projects.

While it did not impose an objection to the filing of a new application, MARAD also pointed out that any future Title XI financing would guarantee no more than $350 million (£175 million), considerably less than the amount World City required.

With considerable acrimony, the feud over funding rumbled on as efforts to push the American Flagship Project continued, and a bid was made to reinstate the application for more generous federal loan guarantees. During 2012, in the run-up to the US presidential elections of that year, a direct appeal was made to both candidates, Barack Obama and Mitt Romney, requesting the next administration, whoever headed it, to instruct MARAD and the Department of Transportation to reinstate the World City Corporation's full, economically sound Title XI application.

Given that the fundamental requirement for receipt of federal maritime funding was all-American construction and all-American operation and manning, the World City Corporation explained at this juncture how it intended to satisfy some of those conditions:

> The hull modules and machinery sections of *America World City* are well within the technical capability of several US commercial shipyards, but the United States has not built a major passenger ship in over 60 years. Therefore, the complex [modular] hotel construction and highly-detailed outfitting of the city-ship will be undertaken – to marine standards and specifications – by a leading hotel builder who has worked extensively with the U.S. Coast Guard and the American Bureau of Shipping to qualify for this marine-specific contract. Similarly, the complex assembly of hull modules will be taken by a leading offshore contractor, Kiewit Offshore Services, based in Corpus Christi, Texas.

It is probable that the lack of evidence of any real experience in cruise ship construction revealed by this statement did little to enhance the chances of any application for loan provision, whether from federal or commercial sources. All this had a ring of familiarity to it, reviving memories of the attempts over the years, by such persons as Lawrence Wilder, Edgar Detwiler and Hyman Cantor, to obtain monies from the U.S. Government in the pursuance of grand passenger liner schemes that were at the boundaries of practicality. So what, realistically, were the prospects for the construction of the *America World City* aka *Phoenix World City* cruise ship being accomplished?

It is understood that the basic design was financially proven and substantial operating profit was forecast even at fairly low levels of occupancy. Notably, fuel costs were projected to represent a much reduced percentage of total operating costs when compared with a traditional cruise ship. Despite this, what purported to be a sound business case proved not to be strong enough to attract investment in the venture. Despite the upbeat pronouncements, it was rejected when European and Far East governments distanced themselves from the scheme, precluding construction by foreign shipyards and, as in the passenger liner age, it proved to be lacking in appeal to US federal institutions. The US political framework, dominated by representatives and senators from land-locked states, remained fundamentally disinterested in the world of passenger shipping, particularly if it involved the erosion of hard-pressed budgets required in difficult times for other, more worthy domestic projects.

As far as is known, the most recent World City Corporation appeal was not acted upon, the parlous state of American and worldwide finances in the wake of the 2008 crash having had a great bearing on this. Since then, the Corporation's website has vanished and it may be concluded that the project has sadly but finally come to an end, and this is one 'Phoenix' that is doomed never to rise.

THE TIKKOO RIVAL, THE '*ULTIMATE DREAM*'

Four years after the launch of the 'Phoenix' project, a scheme for another mega-sized cruise ship was revealed, not as large as the Norwegian giant but still well beyond the size of any passenger ship actually constructed up to that time. Once again, it brought to mind the monster ocean liners planned for the North Atlantic service from the 1930s to the 1950s in that it exhibited extraordinary features: a design that was radically at variance to contemporary practices and an operational approach that reflected the principles of 'economy of scale' in its thinking although it was intended that the cabins would be 40 per cent bigger than the industry average.

The proponent was an established and respected Indian shipping tycoon, Ravi Tikkoo, known for operating super-tankers, having already owned and placed on long-term charter the world's two largest, the

484,000 deadweight tons, 1,246ft long *Globtik London* and *Globtik Tokyo*. The shipyard earmarked to build his world-beating cruise ship, a concept which had preoccupied Mr Tikkoo for over four years, was Harland & Wolff with whom negotiations were said to be underway, a major fillip for the Belfast yard at a time when orders for new ships were in steep decline.

The intention, as was the case with the 'Phoenix', was to exploit a gap in the world cruise market, or more specifically in the burgeoning demand for cruise vacations from American holiday-makers. In 1988, the year when this new project was announced in industry journals, the US cruise market was estimated to be worth $35–50 billion (£17.5–25 million) a year and growing annually at a rate of 14 per cent. Yet, by that year, some 95 per cent of Americans had never taken a cruise. For eight months of the year, the projected ships – for more than one was planned – would operate seven-day Caribbean cruises out of Miami. For the remaining four months they would be based at New York. Cruise fares were set at £160 per person per day.

Given the project name 'Ultimate Dream', the actual name or names of the ships that would result were then undecided and, apparently, would not be disclosed until 1991 when the first vessel was ready to be launched or, as was more likely, floated out of the giant Harland & Wolff graving dock where they would be constructed. It can only be assumed from his comments that other shipyards had been considered for the task by Mr Tikkoo but Harland & Wolff had been selected because, he intimated, it had been the most enthusiastic. In a BBC interview, he said:

> They [Harland & Wolff] were the first to transfer my concept into plans for a beautiful liner.

The 'Ultimate Dream' ships were to have a gross tonnage of 160,000 with main dimensions of 1,132ft overall length, 208ft beam and a depth of 159ft. The draught was designed to be lower than 29ft to allow access to shallower ports and anchorages. Provision was made for 3,026 passengers in a single class, the accommodation comprising 1,322 standard cabins, 127 suites, 61 de luxe suites and 3 penthouse

A model of the 'Ultimate Dream' envisaged for construction for the Tikkoo Cruise Line by Harland & Wolff. *Press Association*

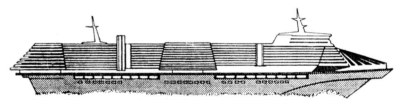

Ultimate Dream - Length: 1,132 feet; Tonnage 160,000 tons

Queen Elizabeth - Length: 1,030 feet; Tonnage: 83,000 tons

QE2 - Length: 963 feet; Tonnage: 67,139 tons

The 'Ultimate Dream' compared with the *Queen Elizabeth* and *Queen Elizabeth 2* at the same scale. While her great size was impressive, she would have been a less attractive ship than Cunard's iconic pair. *Travel Trade Gazette*

suites. Each ship would be manned by 90 British officers and a 1,000-strong mixed Asian and British crew.

Like the 'Phoenix' concept, the 'Ultimate Dream' featured a wide, barge-type hull but where the hull of the 'Phoenix' would have been surmounted by tower blocks, aboard the 'Ultimate Dream' a continuous eight-deck superstructure to be erected above the main deck was to have a zig-zag or 'S' configuration. This would ensure a clear sea view from every cabin, all of which would have been outside with a private balcony.

Lifeboats were to be sited below an overhanging extension to the upper-most deck of the main hull and there would also be two 400-passenger tenders, available for emergency evacuation, housed within the aft section in the inevitable – by then – retractable wharf. The hull would have contained another twelve decks, eight of them dedicated to public rooms, entertainment facilities and recreational spaces. There would be the familiar plethora of passenger amenities: a three-tier 1,500-seat theatre, two cinemas, twelve swimming pools, the largest casino afloat, an exhibition centre, a 500-metre jogging track, and so on. Catering for the eight restaurants, all offering flexible meal times, and all other on board hotel services would be contracted out by a franchise to a large, international hotel group.

The provisional specification called for two 8-cylinder MAN B&W L70MC slow-speed diesels for the main propulsion system, generating 50,000 total horsepower and driving twin screws for a maximum speed of 21.5 knots. On the face of it, industry specialists considered the power rating to be modest in relation to the vessel's main dimensions and gross tonnage. The selection of a slow-speed diesel-mechanical installation (probably direct-diesel drive) was also viewed as unusual for the time when the industry was generally moving to diesel-electric power plants because of the characteristically high totel load of cruise ships. More typically, when a diesel-mechanical system was adopted, the preference was for medium-speed machinery. As for the in-house fabrication of the chosen engines, this was well within Harland & Wolff's capability, as the company already had an existing license agreement with MAN BandW.

On 19 April 1988 it was announced that the order for the first 'Ultimate Dream' ship had been placed with Harland & Wolff at an estimated cost of $500 million (£250 million), to enter service in 1992. In reality, only a 'heads-of-agreement' had been concluded and a final contract would not be signed until that September after financial details had been satisfactorily completed. As released on 18 July 1988, these involved a construction subsidy from the UK Government of £74 million ($140 million) or 28 per cent of the total cost, the maximum permitted under the Common Market's (then the EEC) Sixth Directive on Shipbuilding. With Hambros Bank acting as Mr Tikkoo's financial adviser for the negotiations, the deal under discussion also involved the acquisition of Harland & Wolff by the Indian businessman, a proposal which conveniently was in unanimity with the government's declared intention of shedding all British shipbuilding facilities into private ownership. Essentially, it seems, the deal was for both or nothing: as far as Tikkoo was concerned the 'Ultimate Dream' and the purchase of Harland & Wolff were intrinsically linked. For the government, Tom King, the Northern Ireland Secretary, was non-committal. In discussions with John Parker, the Chief Executive and Chairman of Harland & Wolff, he would only say that the project was 'imaginitive … but major issues have to be looked at'.

As Ravi Tikkoo intended that the ship would fly a flag of convenience, he registered a new company as the owners, the Tikkoo Cruise Line based in the Bahamas. Operated as a foreign venture, this meant that the construction order would qualify as an export contract, a matter of some importance at the time. Also, because the ships would be based overseas, the construction contract would qualify for UK Export Finance or ECGD (Export Credits Guarantee Department) loan guarantees on OECD (Organisation for Economic Co-operation and Development) terms, i.e. 80 per cent of the cost at 7.5 per cent over 8.5 years. Simultaneously, Vikram Tikkoo, Ravi Tikkoo's son, was appointed as the Project Manager to work with Harland & Wolff during the build phase.

The water was rather muddied when, at almost the same time, another project for a giant cruise ship began to attract a lot of media interest, not least because, unusually, it also heralded Harland & Wolff as the potential builder. For its part, the Belfast company declared through a spokesperson that it did not perceive any difficulty in undertaking both projects – a potential bonanza – as it was capable of building the two ships in parallel.

First announced in *Lloyd's List* on 9 January 1988 and dubbed the 'Great British Cruise Ship Project', the second scheme was fronted by representatives of the Midlands-based Institute of Production Control (IPC) on behalf of a group of unidentified professional British businessmen. Though not as comprehensive in the details released, the plan involved the construction of a single cruise ship of 75,000 gross tons, 1,030ft long overall and 120ft in its beam, with a capacity for 2,500 passengers. To be based loosely on Cunard's first generation *Queens* – the *Queen Mary* and *Queen Elizabeth* – it was intended for an unusual, almost unique role, certainly for a ship of that size. The cost was forecast to be £260 million ($468 million).

Its size would have made it 1,000 gross tons bigger than the *Sovereign of the Seas*, then nearing completion for Royal Caribbean Cruise Lines, so that on delivery it would become the world's largest cruise ship. Key to the project, distinguishing it from all other contemporary cruise ship schemes, was the intention to operate the ship essentially as a combined floating exhibition centre and cruise vessel. Its primary function would be to voyage worldwide as a showcase of British products, much like the Japanese-flagged *Sakura Maru* and *Shin Sakura Maru* but on a far grander scale. This helped to explain the selection of Harland & Wolff as the builder, there being no other suitable UK shipyard then remaining, because the engagement of a foreign yard would have severely undermined the central ethos of its 'British-built' message. The 1980s were a difficult time for British industry and the nation would certainly have benefitted from a floating shop window exhibiting British products to foreign customers.

All that said, the media reports expressed the view that there was really insufficient information to go on to permit the industry to determine whether the project was 'firm or viable' even though it was stated that the anonymous business syndicate had already raised sufficient finance and that the IPC was ready to go ahead with a contract on their behalf for 'one of the most luxurious ships afloat' with delivery scheduled for 1991–92.

Negotiations between the IPC, Harland & Wolff and the Northern Ireland Industry Minister, Peter Viggers, concerning funding possibilities were held in Belfast from 4 to 8 January but the parties declined to comment on how they had gone on or what stage, if any, had been reached.

Some six months into the discussions with Harland & Wolff it turned out that the ship's promoters had still not settled on a definitive design, implying that an order, if there was ever to be one, was still a considerable way off. Besides, what had never been explained by IPC was how it was hoped to make enough money with the venture to pay off the construction costs, quite apart from all the operating liabilities: fuel, crew wages and so on. It was not even clear whether the 'passengers' were to be excursionists or exhibition stand personnel or foreign buyers as invited guests or a mix of the three.

After that, irrespective of the proponents' laudable objectives, nothing transpired and no more was heard of the 'Great British Cruise Ship Project'. It was a familiar problem – how to finance such an ambitious scheme – which frustrated efforts to proceed and killed off the project in its infancy.

Another model of 'Ultimate Dream' on display at Ravi Tikkoo's London offices on 19 April 1988, the occasion of the announcement of the impending construction of the mega cruise ship. *Authors' collection*

Meanwhile, the 'Ultimate Dream' continued to draw media attention with much public relations hype, the unveiling of showy display models and TV interviews with leading Northern Ireland political figures like Lord Gerry Fitt, former MP and deputy leader of the power-sharing Northern Ireland Executive. But the euphoria that had been witnessed in Belfast at the announcement of an order gradually waned with the acceptance that it was not so clear cut and, in the absence of funding from Whitehall, it wasn't going to happen.

On the other hand, one optimistic Ulsterman, Ernie Adams, the landlord of the Anchor Inn in the village of Kesh and a former merchant seamen, was so confident that the new ship would be built that he contacted the shipyard and Mr Tikkoo's offices in an attempt to book on the maiden voyage! Gradually, however, the publicity died away and it could have been assumed with good reason that the scheme had been aborted and was now dead. Not so! As late as August 2000, the 'Ultimate Dream' concept resurfaced.

After returning to London from ten years of self-imposed exile in the Bahamas, Ravi Tikkoo declared his ambition to revive the project. One cannot imagine the scepticism with which this announcement was greeted by the once-delighted, 1,500 remaining Belfast tradesmen, the remnants of the 4,000-strong workforce of twelve years earlier, who nonetheless were anxious about the security of their jobs. The official reaction of the ailing shipyard, by then owned by Fred Olsen, as expressed by a spokesman was not exactly enthusiastic. In confirming that a new approach had been made by Mr Tikkoo, he said that all opportunities for work would be considered but 'the Ultimate Dream was a long-term prospect'.

For his part, Tikkoo remained confident that his ship would be built, and in Belfast. Speaking to the Irish News on 31 August 2000, he said:

> Harland & Wolff designed the Ultimate Dream. No other shipyard is going to undertake a ship that has been designed by another yard … and they [Harland & Wolff] have a dock large enough.

Explaining why he had resurrected the 'Ultimate Dream' project, he added;

I think the [cruise] industry from the early 1990s onwards has been very buoyant. It has been growing over 10 per cent compounding in the United States and around 10-11 per cent in Europe. I think the industry is still very backward in Europe, only one per cent of people who go on holiday go on cruise ships.

I can predict that the European demand for cruises will probably grow at 11 per cent compounded per annum from here onwards.

On that score, he was close to foreseeing exactly what in fact happened in the years since, but his accompanying predictions regarding his ability to secure funding proved to be less accurate:

> The funding is there because it is dependent on getting the normal loan under European regulations which amounts to about 80% (£320 million), and the only funding required is 20%. It is not very much.
>
> The £80 million is no problem. I'll personally put in 50% and the rest will come from partners.

The remaining funds, he said, could be provided as a DTI-arranged loan through the Ship Mortgage Finance Corporation. He revealed that he had received encouragement from Stephen Byers, the Trade Secretary, on behalf of the UK Government. In a letter to Sir Teddy Taylor, MP, who was acting as Mr Tikkoo's adviser, Mr Byers declared that 'the Northern Ireland Industrial Development Board will, of course, stand ready to assist Mr Tikkoo in any way it can'. Anyway it can, that was, short of providing public funds. Finance remained the obstacle and, ultimately, the dream was not to be.

One of Mr Tikkoo's final quotes, prophetic as it turned out, served as an epitaph of sorts both for Harland & Wolff and the British shipbuilding industry as a whole:

> If Harland & Wolff undertakes to build this cruise ship, it will save the shipyard and probably save the shipyard [shipbuilding] industry in the United Kingdom too.

The 'Ultimate Dream' was not built and Harland & Wolff as a shipyard was not saved. And realistically, British shipbuilding, as an industry of substance and international credibility, has also ceased to be.

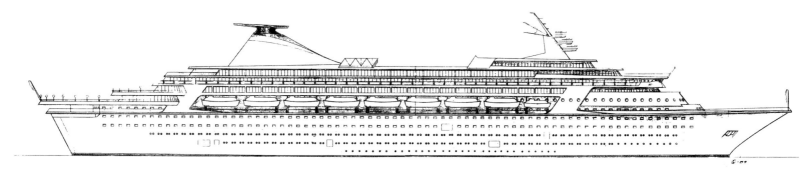

A design for a never-built cruise ship of more traditional appearance, intended for Klosters in 1983. *Dr Bruce Peter*

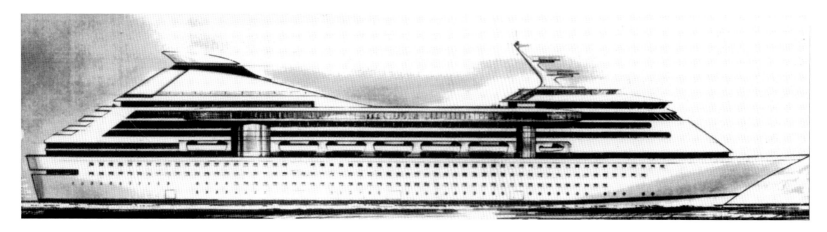

Exhibiting similarities in its broad concept, the Eagle Hawaii cruise ship, or 'Eagle Project', a design prepared for Cunard in the early 1990s. *Michael Gallagher*

BACK TO CUNARD'S ROOTS: A NEW *MAURETANIA* AND THE *AMERICA* AND *BRITANNIA*

Hardly had the Q5 project been laid to rest than another much more ambitious new-building scheme emerged within Cunard. The fact was that, if the 1980s had been dominated by Klosters 'Phoenix' and Tikkoo's 'Ultimate Dream', then the 1990s was certainly the decade of Cunard's many abortive attempts to get new ships into service. The company may well have been able to continue to monopolise the remnants of the transatlantic passenger trade with the dual-role

Queen Elizabeth 2 but it was apparent that it was falling behind in the cruise market.

In 1993, an industry commentator had said that Cunard 'had done absolutely nothing in the cruise industry for the last ten years'; this was not entirely accurate, although there was no physical evidence of progress. Another inferred that Cunard was 'a sleeping giant', possibly an overstatement given the company's size relative to the fast-growing Royal Caribbean and Carnival outfits. It was true that the last major ship built for Cunard, the *Queen Elizabeth 2*, was approaching thirty years of age. It was true, too, that Cunard's fleet at that time was the least balanced and least impressive mix of ships it had ever owned. The problem was certainly not a lack of ingenuity or innovation. It was a situation that had arisen, not from want of trying but rather as the consequences of years of under investment. The fact was that the world of passenger shipping was in accelerating transition and Cunard was being left behind, all of which exacerbated Cunard's predicament.

A variety of prospective cruise ship designs had already been pursued, all of which had metaphorically run onto the rocks, and others were to follow. There was a bid to have two ships like the *Asuka* of Nippon Yusen Kaisha built in Japan by Mitsubishi Heavy Industries, and the earlier 'Tampa Ship' scheme re-emerged as the 'Eagle Project'. This proposed two 40,000grt ships each to carry 1,542 passengers at a speed of 21.5 knots, operating from San Francisco or Los Angeles on short cruises around the Hawaiian archipelago. With entry into service scheduled for 1992 and 1993, it was busy times in Cunard's fleet design office, but, as before, these endeavours were fruitless.

Little more is known of the 'Eagle Project' but barely had its dossier been filed away in Cunard's archives than its place was taken by an undertaking of far greater significance, for a totally revolutionary cruise ship. It was all the more unusual because the proposed mode of operation was completely at variance with the way Cunard had traditionally conducted its affairs up to that point.

Under a joint venture agreement, the ship would have been procured and owned by one company, Swift Line Incorporated of Coral Gables, Florida, but marketed by Cunard and operated under its colours, with the option for Cunard to acquire the vessel outright after an agreed period. The objective was to take advantage of Cunard's long-established international experience, recognising that over 40 per cent of its passengers came from outside the US. But for all its untypical *modus operandi,* it offered Cunard the opportunity to restore its status as an industry leader.

Code-named the 'Swift Project', it was given the working name *Mauretania* by Cunard personnel, to integrate it into the Cunard brand. Whether it was ever intended to bestow this already famous name on the final ship is not known but the prospect had a mixed reception. Certainly, there were critical voices within the company regarding such a choice, given that the ship was to be so radically modern, described as 'new in concept, design and capabilities' and as 'the world's first 21st-century ship'. One Cunard executive had this to say about the possibility that it could become the third *Mauretania*:

I'm not sure of the name – it sounds old fashioned rather than state-of-the-art.

The ship was also dubbed the 'Masa-Swift Project', identifying Kvaerner-Masa Yards of Finland early-on as the intended builders, not least because that shipyard had been intimately involved from the project's inception. Its design had been developed from Masa's concept for 'the ship of the future', a rather hackneyed expression widely used and seemingly reflecting a wide variety of visions.

Norman Bel Geddes' 'whale ship' in model form. It is thought that the design of the planned Cunarder *Mauretania* aka *Swift* may have drawn on aspects of Norman Bel Geddes' radical concept. *Authors' collection*

In October 1993, Cunard released the 'Swift Project Marketing and Sales Plan' which provided a detailed description of the planned vessel and its leading particulars, as well as the 'Marketing Strategy', proposed 'Deployment and Itineraries' and the target 'Source of Business' for the ship, complete with an analysis of the competition.

The 'Executive Summary' contained the following passage:

> The *Mauretania* will be, in design and operation, truly revolutionary. From her striking exterior – which will instantly set her apart from her contemporaries – to her unique three-class General Arrangement and high speed, this vessel will carve a unique niche in the cruise market.

A 'Key Elements' section highlighted the primary ingredients, already alluded to, which were to distinguish this cruise ship from all others currently (then) in service. Anachronistically, as with the Q5, it was to have three grades of accommodation, a particularly unusual arrangement for a cruise ship at a time when the universal direction of the cruise industry was towards the total de-stratification of passenger classes.

A totally separate Concierge-class would occupy apartments at the top of the ship with its own exclusive five-star restaurant. The bulk of the accommodation would be in Premium-class, again with its own dining facilities, and finally there would be a Family-class catering for passengers with children for whom the fare structure would be more than 25 per cent lower than the average berth rate. These passengers would be served by a smorgasbord-style buffet restaurant. Family-class cabins would be modelled on those aboard the Baltic ferries *Silja Serenade* and *Silja Symphony*, two ships built by Kvaerner-Masa for Silja Line, a company owned by Effjohn, another participant in the 'Swift Project'. The *Mauretania* was essentially to be three ships in one, a matter over which some had their concerns.

The *Mauretania* was also to be capable of high speed compared with other cruise vessels, another diversion from contemporary practice. Although the engine type was not specified, the aim was to have a top speed of 26 knots (later increased to 28.5 knots) and a service speed of 24 knots. This it was said was for operational flexibility, to allow for more varied and interesting itineraries within

the envelope of the shorter, 7-day cruise on which the marketing strategy was focused. The plan was for Cunard to operate the *Mauretania* from two centres – from October to April it would be in the Caribbean based at Fort Lauderdale, and from May to September it would operate in the Mediterranean with its home port at Barcelona. Taking the latter phase as an example, the intention was to sail deeper into the Mediterranean within the limitations of the 7-day cruise, effectively to reach places others could not without extending their cruise duration and increasing their fare costs. Affordability was to be a key component of the *Mauretania*'s marketing philosophy. Typical itineraries would be Fort Lauderdale–St Thomas–St Lucia–Barbados–St Maarten–Fort Lauderdale or Barcelona–Nice–Ajaccio (Corsica)–Civitavecchia (Rome)–Valletta (Malta)–Palma (Majorca)–Allicante–Barcelona.

In its external form, the *Mauretania* was to be radically different from conventional cruise ships that were likened to 'floating hotel blocks'. It would be streamlined from bow to stern. In fact, it would not have a bow in the traditional sense of the word. Instead it would have 'a bullet-shaped prow, which will sweep back, instead of forward,

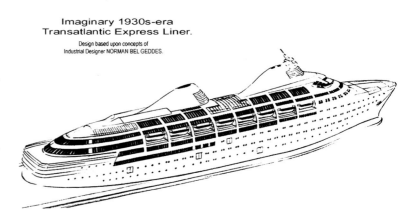

Imaginary 1930s-era Transatlantic Express Liner.

Design based upon concepts of Industrial Designer NORMAN BEL GEDDES.

A speculative vision of a streamlined express passenger liner from the 1930s era based on Norman Bel Geddes' 'whale ship' but with a more conventional hull shape. In fact, Bel Geddes had developed his own ideas along these lines for Henry J. Kaiser whose shipyard may have been 'in the frame' as the potential builders of either the 'whale ship' or a derivative. *Finn Tornquist*

from the waterline over to her bridge'. Hinting of the later inverted X-bow configuration, this feature along with huge glass windows sweeping along her sides and facing forward, would make the *Mauretania* look, so the description claimed, 'not so much like a cruise liner but a water-borne space ship'.

The *Mauretania* was not huge by the standards of the day or even by comparison with the earlier *Queens*. She was expected to have a gross tonnage measurement of 74,000. Her main dimensions were an overall length of 880ft and a beam of 95ft. Her passenger accommodation for a total of 2,000 was distributed 400 Concierge-class, 1,200 Premium-class and 400 Family-class. Her crew would have numbered 800.

She would have ten decks within which there would be a 1,150-seat two-level restaurant, a 947-seat two-tier show lounge, a shopping atrium, a cinema, a casino and a world-class spa besides the other ballrooms, lounges and bars that had become by then established cruise ship amenities. Much was made of the planned implementation of digital and fibre optic technologies in her suite of features and in that regard she was described as an 'electronic showcase'. Interactive access to on board TV from all staterooms was one objective, also the provision of business and computer centres, a space observatory and a virtual reality facility, presumably for amusement purposes. The quest for radically different amenities to provide a passenger experience that contrasted distinctly from that offered by other cruise ships went to unheard of extremes, with even the suggestion that an area of her open deck spaces should be set aside for nude sun-bathing!

On 8 December 1993, on behalf of the Cunard Line, the Executive Vice President, Joseph P. Smyth, despatched a confirmation of the intended joint venture agreement in respect of the *Mauretania* project to Kenneth A.B. Trippe of Swift Line, for his signature. Subject to board approvals, the partnership was in place. Besides the marketing and operational aspects of the deal, the agreement showed that the construction costs at $320 million (£285 million) were to be met by Swift Line, the finance to be derived by a private equity issue for $80–90 million (c. £60–75 million), arranged with the assistance of Lehman Brothers, and a loan of $256 million (£225 million) to be raised through OECD-type debt financing. Kvaerner was confirmed as the ship's designers and builders, which permitted in parallel the conclusion of an offset arrangement between the shipbuilders and Northrop Corporation, as suppliers of F18 fighter jets to the Finnish Air Force, with the approval of the Finnish Government's Offset Committee. Of the various parties involved in these convoluted arrangements, no mention was made of two other important participants who, despite their significant contribution, were in the shadows of the big players. These were the consultant designers, Kai Levander and Guy Lønngren who assisted in the evolution of the ship's radical hull configuration.

The firm order for the *Mauretania* was expected to be placed in early 1994 with entry into service scheduled for April 1996, a very ambitious build programme. But it never happened. In 1994, various contingents within Cunard were still debating the primary elements of the ship's specification and the marketing plan: issues surrounded the class breakdown, the high-speed component, the proposed operational areas, as well as the target market, for none of which was there any measure of consensus.

An impression of the forecast 55,000 gross ton Peace Boat 'Ecoship' scheduled for entry into service in 2020 provides a hint of how the *Mauretania* was perhaps intended to look, with its distinctive bow that extends up and over in an arc to the navigating bridge. Also featuring 'wing sails' for reduced fuel consumption, in this picture they are in the stowed position. *Peace Boat*

It had been on the insistence of Cunard's US people that the *Mauretania* had been laid out as a three-class ship, in complete conflict with the UK office, which preferred adherence to the *Queen Elizabeth 2*'s model – essentially a one-class ship open to all but with exclusive dining and superior accommodation for Grill passengers. As for the intended cruising speed, it was thought that little would be gained in return for the greater fuel consumption at a time when fuel costs remained historically high.

There was also disagreement as to the most suitable regions for the ship's annual cruise programme. Although the marketing and sales plan had predicted healthy revenues from both Mediterranean and Caribbean operations, it was proposed that Alaskan itineraries should be substituted for the cruises out of Barcelona. Another view expressed suggested that concentration on a year-round Caribbean circuit would be better still. These concerns were amplified by misgivings about the assessment of the *Mauretania*'s target market.

An overview of the cruise industry, conducted as part of the marketing and sales plan, had concluded that the predicted growth in cruise holidays which had seen an increase in passenger numbers from half a million per annum in 1980 to 4 million in 1993 could be extrapolated to 8 million by 2000, with the greatest annual growth expected in the UK market. The survey revealed that the momentum for such exponential expansion arose from the high satisfaction level expressed by cruise passengers compared to other vacation types, manifest in an 80 per cent repeat factor ('returners'), that is four out of every five passengers would take more cruise holidays based on their positive experience. Cunard's own figures showed that on average 65 per cent of its customers had sailed with the company on one or more occasions previously. Against those upbeat assessments, the target market for the *Mauretania* was eclectic in the extreme – traditional mass-market cruise passengers from the USA and Europe, affluent North Americans and Europeans seeking exclusivity, the American family market who were seeking distinct features for parents and children, both West European package holiday consumers and East European first-time cruise vacationists, plus business charter groups and clients of major European and American health spas. If, in its accommodation arrangement, the aim was to make the *Mauretania* 'three ships in one', in its target market it was to be 'all things to all men'. Perceiving difficulty in making such a mélange gel together, and questioning whether concierge service was appropriate to passengers heading for 'mass market' destinations, one Cunard executive also doubted whether premier-grade passengers would be prepared to pay over the odds to be on a ship with boisterous and noisy children running around out of control.

There is an expression that says 'timing is everything', a truism that is relevant to countless situations but none more so than to the luckless *Mauretania*. Debate over her specification certainly contributed to her downfall, the prevarication hindering the placement of a firm construction order but, as has been said already, it was clearly better not to proceed at all than to proceed with uncertainty. Besides, it was a fact that, while the *Mauretania* scheme was unfolding, Trafalgar House's fortunes were also in steep decline. Many of the group's investments were delivering poor results and the lacklustre performance was leading to shareholder desertion. Complete collapse seemed inevitable unless things picked up. As it was, rescue came on 18 April 1996 in the form of a takeover by Kvaerner, the Anglo-Norwegian conglomerate whose main activity was in the marine industries. If the *Mauretania* project was not already dead, this amounted to the final nail in its coffin. The new owners were experiencing financial difficulties themselves and did not have the spare capital to invest in a revolutionary cruise ship.

In fact, Kvaerner was completely transparent from the outset about its intentions where Cunard was concerned. It had no desire to retain a company which it considered did not fit its portfolio and it proposed to sell Cunard at the first opportunity. Despite this, just a year later it launched its own bid to build two new large passenger ships, essentially cruise ships but vessels which would also undertake occasional transatlantic voyages. It may be regarded as a cynical deduction, but perhaps this had as much to do with boosting the order book of its shipbuilding division as to the rejuvenation of the Cunard passenger fleet.

The names *America* and *Britannia* were apparently allocated to the vessels under consideration, once again drawing on famous identities from the line's long and prestigious heritage. They were to measure 60,000grt, very large ships considering their low passenger capacity of just 960 berths in each case but, unlike the Q5 and the *Mauretania*, they were to have as few classes of accommodation as possible. Uniquely, they would have all outside cabins, 70 per cent of which would have their own private verandahs. Reflecting this near one-class status – there would still have been a small ultra-luxury component in the form of penthouse suites – they were to have one large restaurant with single-sitting dining for 1,100. Presumably, the allowance in capacity was to provide for an increase in passenger berths should it prove to be desirable. As a concession, two small intimate dining rooms would be provided, and also a lido café.

Similarly, there was to be only a single, 850-seat show lounge but there would have been other more relaxed and informal social and entertainment settings figured in the ships' layout – a night club, a piano bar, a disco and casino. There would also have been a cinema, library and reading room and a shopping arcade. A spa, a gymnasium and two outside pools would have been provided for healthy recreation.

Although the concern about multiple classes of accommodation had been resolved in the specification for the *America* and *Britannia*, they were nevertheless projected to be fast ships with a cruising speed of 26 knots. Certainly there appears to have been a preoccupation with speed by the Cunard people at that time. No decision had been reached regarding engine type at that stage, since the ships' conceptual specification was still provisional.

However, there were revelations regarding the ships' planned operational envelope. It was to be ubiquitous to an extraordinary degree with hardly a cruise region excluded from their annual itineraries. By rotation, they would tour northern Europe from June to August, followed by transatlantic crossings between Dover and Miami, calling en route at Montreal and New York. Next would be a session of short overnight cruises on America's east coast and, after transiting the Panama Canal, another series of coastwise cruises linking San Diego, Los Angeles and San Francisco. The Christmas period would be spent in the Caribbean, followed by a world cruise each winter. Returning to the US west coast, they would then commence an Alaskan season before returning to the Atlantic to repeat the cycle. It was hinted that somewhere in this busy schedule they could squeeze in South America, the Mediterranean and the Far East!

In the absence of any surviving visual record, the external appearance of the *America* and *Britannia* cannot be evaluated, but it is thought that they would have been heavily influenced by the Crystal ships *Crystal Harmony* and the *Crystal Symphony*, the former built by Kvaerner Masa Yards, but both of them rated very highly by Cunard.

The fulfillment programme for the twin ships was to be launched in December 1997, with a minimum of four months allocated for the completion of the detailed design and construction specification. Signing of the contracts to permit physical construction to begin was scheduled for March 1998 followed by an overlapping build period of thirty months per ship, making a total of forty-two months to the completion of the second ship. Thus, delivery was set for June 2000 and June 2001, respectively. This was an intensive schedule by any standard but the view was expressed that the period from laying the first keel sections to completion could be contracted to twenty-six months if an existing hull design, such as that of the Crystal cruise ships, could be adopted for the *America* and *Britannia*.

In the event, these planned Cunard cruise ships suffered a similar fate to the *Mauretania*. Kvaerner achieved the sale of Cunard that it had been pursuing from day one when, on 4 April 1998, the company became part of Carnival Corporation. The *America* and *Britannia* were immediately abandoned but, within two months, Carnival had launched new plans of its own for Cunard, as described earlier.

THE *REGENT SKY* – A UNIQUE CASE?

An unusual and rather different ill-fated project is worthy of mention here, if only because it demonstrates how diverse the reasons are why certain passenger ships never materialised. This is the case of the *Regent Sky*, intended originally as a Baltic ferry and, therefore, not exactly what might be described as significant or a 'great passenger ship', being a fairly run-of-the-mill vessel. Somewhat reminiscent of the experiences of the *Caracciolo*, briefly related in Chapter 3, though without that ship's naval origins, the *Regent Sky*'s story deserves to be related nonetheless.

She was initially ordered in 1979 by Stena Line as one of a quartet of large 39,000grt ferries for the Gothenburg to Kiel overnight route, all to be built in the Polish shipyards of Stocznia Gdansk, in her case at Stocznia im Paryskiej. As such, allocated yard number 494/04, the name bestowed upon her was *Stena Baltika*. Her sisters were the *Stena Germanica*, *Stena Scandinavica* and *Stena Polonica*.

All went well at first and, though delayed, the *Germanica* and *Scandinavica* were completed and entered service in April 1987 and February 1988, respectively. The *Stena Baltika* was laid down in 1985 but problems in the shipyards slowed construction on the third and fourth ships until, during 1988, Stena Line terminated the contract for the remaining incomplete pair and abandoned them to the shipyards for them to find alternative buyers. Being the further advanced of the two, with her Zgoda-Sulzer engines already installed, the *Stena Polonica* attracted interest from other companies operating ferry services. She was acquired that year by Fred Olsen and renamed *Bonanza* but a year later she was sold again, to Anek Lines of Greece, finally making her first commercial voyage as the *El. Venizelos* in 1992.

In 1989, the *Stena Baltika* was also purchased by a Greek concern, A. Lelakis, the owners of Regency Cruises, who planned to complete her as the company's first new ship, having previously owned only second-hand tonnage. Launched on 16 October 1990, she was towed first to the Avlis shipyard at Perama, which was also owned by Lelakis, only to be subsequently moved to the company's Elefsis yard where, in a $200 million (£100 million) modification programme, she was to be turned into a 55,000grt, 1,600 passenger cruise ship named *Regent Sky*.

In part, the work involved the insertion of a 174ft hull extension, increasing her overall length to 748ft. Her beam, at 101ft, and her draught, at 22ft were to remain unaltered. Other modifications reshaped the forward end of her superstructure while huge

The *Stena Germanica*, showing the originally intended appearance of the *Regent Sky* prior to her conversion from an incomplete Baltic ferry. Comparison with the next illustration shows the extent to which the forward end of her superstructure was extensively remodelled. *Frank Heine*

The incomplete *Regent Sky* ex-*Stena Baltika* laid up at Eleusis in 2009, some years after her cruise ship conversion had been aborted. The sections inserted into her hull to increase her size can be clearly seen; also the huge aperture cut in her sides for lifeboat stowage. *Peter Fitzpatrick*

elongated apertures were cut in her sides for lifeboat stowage. At the same time, Wärtsilä diesel engines were also fitted. Completion was forecast for 1997–98, already a protracted interval at around eight years.

In 1995, six years after work commenced, Regency Cruises ceased operations and filed for bankruptcy. Regent Sky, was around 60 per cent complete, and had by then been relocated to a shipyard at Chalkis. All activity abruptly ended and she languished in the shipyard until July 1999 when she was seized jointly by the National Bank of Greece and the Hellenic Industrial Development Bank.

Moved to various lay-up berths at Perama, then between Ampelakia and Kinosoura, attempts were made to sell her at auction but all failed. The incomplete *Regent Sky* was latterly moved to an anchorage in the Gulf of Elefsis around which time it was reported that she was to be completed as the *Zoe* – artist's renderings were released showing her in white livery with a stylish red funnel. However, the name *Regent Sky* remained on her heavily rusted hull and in July 2011, having never been completed, she was sold for breaking up. A year later, to the month, she arrived off Aliaga, Turkey, under tow – her Wärtsilä diesels having been removed in the interim – where demolition commenced. All told, she had existed for some 27 years and considerable amounts of money had been expended on her construction and conversion, yet in that time she had earned not a single penny in return, a singularly wasteful enterprise!

9

BEYOND THE MILLENNIUM: BIG, BIGGER, BIGGEST

CARNIVAL'S 'PINNACLE' AND 'NEXT GENERATION' PROJECTS

Already, by the turn of the millennium, the relentless rise and rise of the cruise industry had thrown up two mega companies which were dominating the trade, Royal Caribbean International (formerly Royal Caribbean Cruise Lines) and Carnival Corporation. The former is a giant stand-alone operating entity founded by a consortium of Norwegian shipping companies (Anders Wilhelmsen, I.M. Skaugen and Gotaas Larsen), the latter a vast conglomerate, reminiscent of the International Mercantile Marine of the early twentieth century, with numerous subsidiaries such as Costa, Cunard, Holland America, P&O, Princess and others.

These two massive businesses vied with each other, not only to corner the market but also to operate the most impressive ships with the most innovative features. The rivalry extended to bids by both concerns to possess the world's largest cruise ship, partly to realise the benefits of economies of scale but just as much for the prestige value that went with it. As with the great ocean liners of the past, the biggest and fastest get noticed, they attract more publicity and by association they tend to elevate the perception of their owners as the market leaders by the people who really matter – the prospective passengers.

In the early years of the twenty-first century, a new cruise ship project was instigated by Fincantieri for Carnival in the most audacious bid up to that time to top the charts and steal the limelight. It was a project which, as Joseph Farcus, long-term Carnival interior designer, put it, 'would blow everything else out of the water' and 'really outdo all their competition'. It was to be the first ship of a design that would be unlike any other, enormous in size at 180,000grt with a raft of exceptionally novel features. Sadly, the 'Pinnacle Project', as it came to be called, turned out to be the largest ship that Carnival never built.

Although both had resurfaced briefly, by the start of the 2000s the projects for the mega cruise ships 'Phoenix' and 'Ultimate Dream' were essentially dead in the water, but they had been the catalyst for the pursuit of cruise ship conceptions of a hitherto unheard of order of magnitude. The growth in cruise ship size had been extraordinary by any measure. In 1990, the *Sovereign of the Seas* (Royal Caribbean Cruise Line) was the largest at 73,192grt. By 1995, she had been superseded by the *Sun Princess* (Princess Cruises) at 77,441grt but only a year later, the *Carnival Destiny*, at 101,353grt, became the first passenger ship to exceed the size of the *Queen Elizabeth* of 1940 and the first to surpass 100,000grt.

The next attempt to take the lead was made not by either Royal Caribbean or Carnival but by Star Cruises, a subsidiary of the Malaysian-based Genting Group which ranked as the world's fifth largest cruise operator. Mentioned off and on throughout 1998, Star Cruises' projected cruise vessels *Superstar Capricorn II* and *Superstar Sagittarius II*, were ordered from Meyer Werft at Papenburg, Germany, on 2 August 1999, as part of a $1 billion (£600 million) new building programme. At 110,000grt and 1,039ft 8in overall length, the duo were expected to enter service in October 2003 and October 2004 but they were cancelled before construction even began. No definite explanation has been discovered for the abandonment of what then would have been the largest cruise ships in the world. After a majority shareholding stake was taken in Norwegian Cruise Line in 2000, most fleet enhancement effort was focused on the new acquisition, which may provide some rationale for the cancellation of the big ships. More than a decade later, in 2016, Genting ordered two even larger 201,000grt, 1,119ft length overall Global-class ships for Star Line, to be purpose-built for the Asian cruise market in a bid, perhaps, to implement the earlier plans in modified form. As before, construction was due to take place in Germany, at the Wismar yard of Lloyd Werft Group, taken over by Genting in January 2016, with delivery scheduled for 2019 and 2020.

The 'Pinnacle Project', more than half as big again, was, though, in an altogether different league to the cancelled Star ships. As conceived initially by Maurizio Cergol, Fincantieri's Senior Chief Designer in its Cruise Ship Division, under the project name 'FUN Ship' (Fincantieri Ultimate New Ship), chosen by him, it was intended to introduce a raft of innovative design and recreational features. It had twin Carnival-style funnels set aft with a roller coaster ride along the length of the upper deck, extending up to the top of one funnel and downwards from the other. Within the superstructure at the ship's centre a large multi-level passenger area would have had glass walls in Carnival's logo colours and at the top of the superstructure, there would have been a disc-shaped revolving restaurant. Other features included large, open lower decks and a navigating bridge of inventive shape.

Presented to Carnival, it immediately captured the imagination of Joseph Farcus who saw the possibility of taking the concept further. Substituting the new project name 'Pinnacle', he envisaged an even larger cruise vessel based on Cergol's concept, measuring 210,000grt. Just as extraordinary were the hull dimensions, a key component to allow the implementation of some of the fantastic amenities that were now forecasted. The hull length was to be 1,245ft overall and the maximum beam dimension of around 200ft, but the breadth of the superstructure above the main deck, apart from two tower-like enclosures amidships to port and starboard, was to be somewhat less at 148ft, in order to leave expanded wide-open areas at Promenade Deck level (deck 4) on each side of the ship.

These spaces were to be utilised for some idiosyncratic components: along the port side an amenity called the 'Lazy River', a double-8 artificial stream which would criss-cross over and under itself while, on the starboard side, full-size basketball courts and other sports areas were planned for an open lower lido area.

Originally envisaged as shown here, the FUN (Fincantieri Ultimate New) Ship was developed into the 'Pinnacle' Project through the influence of Carnival Corporation's preferred interior designer, Joseph Farcus. The lines of the roller coaster, a feature intended for the ship at this stage, can be seen running along the sides of the upper deck leading up to and over the funnels. *Fincantieri*

Modified with a huge single 'whale tail' funnel in place of the two athwartships exhausts planned by Maurizio Cergol, Fincantieri's lead designer, the details of the 'Pinnacle' cruise ship were released to a cruise industry audience at Miami on 11 March 2005. *Fincantieri*

Between these features, accessed from either side of the Promenade Deck and extending the full width of the superstructure, a massive public room (even bigger than Maurizio Cergol had planned), many decks high, was planned in which entertainment extravaganzas and spectacular shows were to be held, including a high-seas version of the 'Cirque du Soleil'.

Pinnacle's thirteen-deck-high superstructure was split at the aft end from decks 4 to 15, creating a cavity that projected inwards for some distance. On either side of the cavity there would have been glass-laminated tower atriums with scenic lifts looking down on the stern deck and leading up to an ornate grill or supper restaurant on deck 17 above. Set within what would now be a large, single funnel structure, this too would have been enclosed by immense glass canopies in blue and red, Carnival's distinctive brand colours.

At the aft end, located within the split superstructure, two giant water chutes, dropping through ten or more decks, would descend to an infinity pool on deck 5. This, in turn, would over-spill into another pool on deck 4. Two more outdoor pools were sited on the Sun Deck, deck 16, one with a mini-mountain edifice with a cave and slides hidden within it and a rock climbing face on one side. For the crew, there would have been a multi-level lounge and a greater number of single occupancy cabins.

More novel still was a monorail 'people mover' system instead of the roller coaster ride. This was to circle the ship, according to one drawing, on tracks fitted around deck 16 and deck 4 while a general-arrangement deck plan shows the lower track on deck 2. The system was to have vertical intersection lines with transfer stations at midships on each side of the superstructure. Although the capacity of the monorail cars appeared to be limited, based on the released images, this method of conveyance was promoted as being more practical than ornamental, intended primarily to assist passenger flow dynamics by helping in the movement of so many people – over 6,000 at full capacity – around a vessel of such immense proportions.

The aim behind all these 'wow factor' features was to bring aboard ship, to the extent that the vessel's scale permitted, the kinds of amenities typically found ashore in holiday hotel complexes, water parks and other comparable vacation centres.

The unique glass-enclosed restaurant sited within the funnel structure as mooted for the 'Pinnacle' was introduced in practice aboard the 'Carnival Spirit'-class ships. Shown here is the funnel restaurant aboard the Carnival Miracle, a shipboard feature that is best appreciated in colour when the red and blue light of the atrium skylight can be seen illuminating the dining area. Jim Zimmerlin (www.jimzim.net)

The layout of the 'Pinnacle's aft decks, showing the two immense water flumes. Fincantieri

In addition to the innovative passenger features, some creative thinking also went into the technical side of the ship's operation. The power plant was to be a combination system of gas turbine and diesel electrical generators operating in tandem. Maximum power output of the single gas turbine generator and the six diesel units was 128,000kW (approximately 174,250hp). It is not clear whether the 'Pinnacle' would have had four shafted propellers or four propulsion pods but the combined power output would have been 60,000kW (approximately 81,650hp). Service speed was calculated at 21.5 knots with a maximum capability of 23 knots.

Despite her size and bulk, the 'Pinnacle' would have drawn only 32ft when fully loaded. It was intended that she would carry no fuel in her double bottom tanks and, with both environmental and fuel efficiency considerations in mind, she would be fitted with plasma incinerators to convert rubbish and other organic matter into a synthetic gas fuel.

While Maurizio Cergol was to develop the design of the evolved concept, Joseph Farcus was to be responsible, as on previous Carnival Cruise Line ships, for the internal décor and the accommodation layout as well as the technical aspects of the new passenger features. This culminated in a series of promotional videos and a presentation to the owners at Miami on 11 March 2005 under the title 'Pinnacle Project: Data and Comparisons' which was expected to kick-start the project for real.

As it turned out, though, it never happened and there was a single, fundamental reason for this – cost! Each 'Pinnacle' ship, assuming there would have been more than one, was expected to cost $1.5 billion (£1 billion), not that this was necessarily prohibitive for the well-resourced Carnival Group. But the deal with Fincantieri called for payment in euros and it just so happened, at the very point when construction orders were about to be placed, that the exchange rate between the currencies changed alarmingly to the disadvantage of Carnival. Introduced in January 1999, initially the euro had a relatively minor status on world financial markets, its exchange value tending to slip downwards. This changed dramatically in 2002 when all the old European national currencies it was replacing were withdrawn, being legal tender no longer. This, along with a sharp increase in the use of the euro as a reserve currency, triggered a sharp appreciation in its value, an upward trend which continued through to 2008 when the financial crisis in the United States caused the dollar to devalue further. Against this background, the cost of the 'Pinnacle' ship had increased by around 40 per cent. Carnival Corporation expected its subsidiaries to work to strict guidelines with regard to profitability and return on investment, calculated on the basis of anticipated revenues from a given level of lower berth occupancy. By this reckoning, as a result of its higher euro capital cost and the tight operating margins, the 'Pinnacle' project was deemed not to be financially viable. It was concluded that there would be no return on the huge investment that each ship represented for more than five years from entry into service and so the scheme was abandoned and cancelled altogether later that same year.

Joseph Farcus' regret at not being able to turn this astounding and challenging project into reality was undeniable. 'We studied all the technical requirements and the ship, the proposal we had on the table, was a real ship. We had talked to the people who supply these things and they calculated a real price', he said. He went on to add, 'In my view, Pinnacle really was outstanding and it was probably my biggest professional disappointment that the project wasn't built'.

In its place, Farcus was assigned by Carnival Corporation to conceive and develop an alternative, less elaborate design – the 'Project Next Generation'. As strikingly unique, it was still of considerable size, believed to have measured in the 150,000grt category. Likewise, it was also a long ship though with a smaller length to beam ratio compared with the 'Pinnacle'. Simpler in concept, too, it lacked such radical features as the 'people mover' and the 'lazy river' although it retained the split in the superstructure at the aft end. In place of the single, immense, glass-surrounded funnel of the 'Pinnacle', the 'Project Next Generation' ship had two widely spaced funnels, one right aft, the other amidships with a pool separating them.

Even less progress was made with the 'Project Next Generation', the concept having advanced little further than rudimentary sketches. Ultimately, Carnival elected instead to persist with its tried and proven ship designs, a format that had been progressively evolved and enhanced over the years.

The 'Project Next Generation' design which was contemplated as an alternative to the 'Pinnacle' in a pen-and-ink rendition derived from sketches by Joseph Farcus. *Redrawn by David L. Williams*

Only a short time after the cancellation of the 'Pinnacle Project', Royal Caribbean International set in motion its 'Project Genesis' for four massive cruise ships comparable in size and dimensions at 225,000grt, 1,186ft 6in overall length and 198ft maximum beam. Laid down in November 2007, the first to enter service was the *Oasis of the Seas* in October 2009, followed by the *Allure of the Seas* in December 2010, the *Harmony of the Seas* in May 2016 and the *Symphony of the Seas* in April 2018. The 'Project Genesis' ships have vindicated the ambitious intentions of Fincantieri and Carnival but, unfortunately for the American concern, they have stolen the 'Pinnacle's' thunder. As this book has already demonstrated, it is generally only the ships that have been actually built that get remembered, just as few people can recall the names of the runners-up to Olympic champions.

The 'Pinnacle Project' did, however, leave a positive legacy, with some of its more distinctive features adopted on other cruise ships: its characteristic broad promenade decks found on the *MSC Seaside* and Norwegian Cruise Line's sisters *Norwegian Breakaway* and *Norwegian Getaway*; the extreme waterslides have a near parallel in the Ultimate Abyss dry slides on the *Harmony of the Seas*; and the glass-encapsulated restaurant within the 'Pinnacle' funnel structure has been duplicated aboard other Carnival cruise vessels.

It is a matter for conjecture whether the exchange rate difficulty was the sole reason for the cancellation of the 'Pinnacle' scheme.

Undoubtedly, there would have been more than one ship produced out of that mould, spreading some of the first costs, but surely the currency exchange impact would also have been felt by all ships purchased in euros at that time, whatever their size, while Carnival's established dollar-trading profitability formula would have also proportionately applied to them. Between 2004 and 2008, Carnival Cruise Line took delivery of the post-Panamax *Carnival Valor*, *Carnival Liberty*, *Carnival Freedom* and *Carnival Splendor*, all built by Fincantieri in Italy. But then, they were less sensationally different.

Will Carnival ever resurrect its 'Pinnacle Project' or a developed derivative? It seems that would require quite a leap of faith and only time will tell.

JULES VERNE'S 'FLOATING CITY' BY ANY OTHER NAME

In 1895, science fiction author, Jules Verne's book *Propeller Island* was published. In it he envisaged an enormous ship called *Standard Island*, 27km square, which was capable of producing its own food and water, and could accommodate some 10,000 people (or passengers). The vessel Verne described could carry millionaires on a permanent voyage in the Pacific Ocean between the latitudes of 35°N and 35°S, thus avoiding winters and other inconveniences (could these include taxes?). Essentially, Verne's concept was not so much a ship but more a floating island.

In September 2002, Cunard's *Queen Mary 2* was under construction at Chantiers de L'Atlantique, Saint Nazaire, but the order book was empty and there were no orders in the pipeline for future building. Parisian architect, Jean-Philippe Zoppini, together with Alstom, the holding company of the Chantiers de L'Atlantique, published plans for an ambitious project not too far removed from Verne's concept with the hope that the idea might have been taken up and materialised. Philippe Kasse, a spokesman for the Chantiers de l'Atlantique at the time stated:

> This time we are doing it the other way around and trying to create a desire.

The project, originally designated *Ile d'AZ* (A for Alstom, Z for Zoppini), was proposed to be an oval craft 400m (1,316ft) long by 300m (990ft) in width, with a lagoon and beaches at its centre. There was to be a yacht and ferry harbour at the stern and blocks of cabins or flats up to fifteen storeys high. In addition, the craft would accommodate shops, theatres, bars, casinos and other entertainment centres. Passengers would be able to travel from one part of the ship to another by monorail, not unlike Carnival's 'Pinnacle' class. Another idea put forward was that it could be marketed as a time-share holiday resort or even as permanent off-shore homes for stateless billionaires.

One of the disadvantages of the *Ile d'AZ* was that by virtue of its dimensions, as big as Club Med village, it would be too large to enter any ports, severely restricting its role as a cruise ship. This meant that any prospective passengers would have to reach her by ferry, helicopter or seaplane. The latter two methods of approach would probably have precluded those passengers who do not like the fly-cruise option!

At the time, Alstom said such a project would present no technical difficulties, but being too large a vessel to be built in their existing facilities, it would have to be constructed off shore, similar to an oil rig. It was to be powered by conventional engines and propellers, mounted in pods around its circumference with a cruising speed of 10 knots. The name that might have been chosen for this vessel, which would have cost £2 billion to build, was speculated as being *Jules Verne*. At the time of writing there has been no uptake for the *Ile d'AZ/Jules Verne* for it would be a leap in the dark for any prospective operator. As a concept, it goes against the purpose of a cruise ship calling at various ports of call offering historical or cultural interest to visitors. If prospective punters wanted a Club Med or theme park, would they choose a floating one that actually couldn't go anywhere, rather than those already available to them ashore? It could possibly find its niche as an offshore gambling vessel, a sort of floating Las Vegas, but it was probably a case of the concept being industry-driven rather than customer-driven. So for the time being, this particular *Jules Verne* remains more a Mysterious Island rather than a Propeller Island.

Not to be discouraged the *Jules Verne* resurfaced, albeit in a more conventional guise, exhibited at the Alstom Marine stand at the Seatrade Cruise Ship Convention held during March 2005 in Miami. Once again the concept design had been developed by Chantiers de l'Atlantique although this time the idea was no longer a floating

Alstom's concept for an eco-friendly trimaran cruise ship for which the name *Jules Verne* was proposed. *Alstom/Chantiers de l'Atlantique*

island but the return to a true 'ship', with some innovative refinements with an emphasis on on board leisure activities. Its design was the concept of two of Chantiers' engineers, Frederic Savarin, General Architect, and Christian Gaudin, a Naval Architect. They had hoped to seize the industry's attention with 2005 being the centenary of Jules Verne's death.

The *Jules Verne* was to have a trimaran hull, which comprised a central monocoq hull with two SWATH lateral outriggers, a configuration which would contribute to its stability and sea-keeping qualities and thus enhance passenger comfort. Further consideration was given to the design of its bow and stern form, such that it would minimise motion in a seaway in an attempt to further improve comfort on board.

The outrigger arms were designed to act as structural reinforcement to the hull, and by this technicality any total glazed surface area of the main superstructure could be increased to approaching that of shore-based large buildings. In this manner it was hoped that a lot more space could be allocated for public spaces, cabins, private decks and the like. It was estimated that the total area for public spaces would be 26,000m² and the 1,700 passenger cabins would occupy some 34,000m², each cabin area being 20m².

Four on-board marinas were planned, which aimed to give the passengers opportunities for sea discovery excursions on submarines or small boats. It was designed such that all these marinas would be covered by large glass domes by which it was intended that light would penetrate all the way down to the waterline. The ship's

The tiered stern of the sail-powered pentamaran cruise ship *Eoseas*, devised by STX France with a strong bias to environmental considerations. In reality, prevented from entering narrow channels and unable to pass under bridges over essential cruise routes, such as the Verazzano Narrows at New York and the *Øresund* in the Baltic, the *Eoseas* would have suffered from a restricted operational envelope. *STX France/ Chantiers de l'Atlantique*

wheelhouse was intended to feature panoramic views that would be partially open to visiting passengers.

The *Jules Verne* was to be propelled by the latest models of pod diesel-electric propulsion system which would guarantee enhanced sea-keeping, manoeuvrability and an absence of vibration. In addition to this, solar panels on the port and starboard sides would provide the necessary energy for on board consumption. With a power output of 60–80MW (approximately 81,650–108,850 hp), her speed would have been 24 knots.

The *Jules Verne*'s principle particulars were: length: 280–320m (920–1,053ft); beam: 60–80m (197–263ft); draught: 8m (26ft 4in). Her displacement would have been 50,000–60,000 tonnes.

Again, the potential of the innovative *Jules Verne* design was not capitalised upon and the project came to nothing.

The Alstom group of Saint Nazaire was taken over in August 2008 by the Korean STX group as their European satellite. A year earlier, the yard came up with another unique design, the 'Eoseas Concept Cruise ship'. This was subsequently developed by STX Europe in collaboration with a firm called Stirling Design International as part of the Ecorizon programme. The 'Eoseas' was essentially aimed at developing innovative marine clean technologies and alternatives to oil fuels. [MARPOL Annex IV]. After two years of research and development work jointly funded by STX Europe and the Regional Council of Pays de la Loire, the project matured in 2009. Ecorizon was made up of five major programmes which included energy management, air emission management, water management, waste management and sustainable design. Ecorizon felt that they could address the entire environmental footprint of the ship throughout its design, construction and operation. The original long-term mission of the concept was to reduce the use of non-sustainable energy to 50 per cent by 2015!

Probably the most ground-breaking aspect of the design was that the ship would have five hulls or a 'pentamaran' configuration or, more specifically, the ship was envisaged to be a trimaran on five hulls of which the two outer hulls were to be fore-and-aft plane. In addition an air cushion under the main hull was designed to optimise the hydrodynamic characteristics of the vessel. The double hull design was to feature long promenade decks on both sides of the ship. The hulls' double skin was designed to be a natural air-conditioning system. Boundary layer lubrication effected by air film injection was built in to reduce frictional resistance and the introduction of a vertical bow was to be incorporated to reduce the ship's Froude Number.

The question of fresh water was to be addressed by having it generated on board by a combination of multistage evaporators and reverse osmosis plants. Advanced waste water plants were to be used to purify and treat 'grey' and 'black' waters. In addition, an absorption chiller would absorb rain water from the upper decks, and any heat used would be from the engines. The big claims by the 'Eoseas' project were that it would reduce power consumption by 50 per cent, emissions of carbon dioxide by 50 per cent, sulphur dioxide by 100 peer cent, nitrous oxide by 90 per cent and ash by 100 per cent.

'Eoseas' was designed to carry 3,311 passengers in 1,403 cabins to be catered for by 1,089 crew occupying 555 cabins. The cabins were designed to use natural lighting and each was to be fitted with light sensors. In this manner, it was claimed that energy consumption could be reduced by 30 per cent.

Turning to the propulsion system for 'Eoseas', she was to be propelled by four dual-fuel LNG diesel generator sets. Each unit was to provide 8MW (10,900hp) power for propulsion and hotel load. She was to be quadruple screw driven, which comprised two pump propeller pods on its central hull and two pump propellers driven through shafts on the outriggers. The LNG was to be stored in a storage system similar to that of LNG carriers prior to being transferred into a pressurised service tank. In addition to this, in order to recover any thermal energy, the ship would have a heat recovery plant. Photoelectric/solar panels of 8,300m² area were to be shipped on the side and upper deck in order to provide a maximum power of 108MW (approximately 147,000hp) and an average each of 270kW (367.5hp). It was estimated that an on board organic waste treatment plant would generate some 300kW (408hp) of synthetic gas (primarily made up of hydrogen, ammonia and methanol), which could be used to drive the generator units.

The structurally obvious form of propulsion was by wind, as the ship had five masts which could carry 12,440m² of sail, a system that had been patented by STX France. To support its claims, STX had conducted thirteen tank tests with different hulls and propulsion configurations during 2008 and 2009 which achieved 17 per cent improvements compared with conventional propulsion/hull systems, and enhanced fuel efficiency, redundancy and manoeuvring.

The main principal dimensions of Eoseas were to be 105,000 gross tons, 305m (1,003ft) long and 60m (197ft) beam. This latter dimension could have precluded her from transiting the Panama and Suez Canals (the Queen Mary 2's beam at the waterline is 41m/135ft). Also, the 100m (329ft) height of the masts to support such a large sail area could prevent a vessel of this type from passing under the Golden Gate and Verrazano Narrows bridges. These factors could have severely limited the ship's cruise itineraries, but then again this may well have been the idea.

PRINCESS KAGUYA – CRUISE SHIP ZENITH?

By 1997, having surpassed the size of the greatest passenger liners ever built by a considerable margin, there seemed to be no limit to the future enlargement of individual cruise ships. Could, realistically, even larger ships than the Carnival Destiny and her sisters be seriously contemplated? The opening years of the new millennium witnessed vessels of around 150,000grt already being built and the first 200,000grt cruise ships were on the drawing board, if not already under construction. They would soon follow.

Aspiring for the biggest is nothing new. It was a feature of the ambitious liner plans of the 1930s and 1950s, and it was fundamental to Kloster's 'Phoenix' project, though there were good reasons in all these cases for their huge scale – they were not giants simply for some nebulous reason of prestige. Yet these grandiose schemes were destined, by comparison, to seem relatively modest.

As Lloyds Cruise International revealed early in 2000, for one proponent it was a case of even bigger is better, in fact much bigger is best! A Bahamas-based casino group Casino Vegas del Mare confounded the pundits by announcing that it had signed a contract with the Yantai CIMC Raffles Shipyard, in Shandong Province, China, for the construction of three 450,000grt cruise ships, to be the first consignment in a deal that included options for seventeen more vessels of these gargantuan proportions. Furthermore, a potential follow-on order for twenty more of these monsters was under consideration! Each of the ships was to be able to accommodate 9,600 passengers in 3,000 suites laid out over 21 decks, with sufficient facilities to provide for 10,000 more day passengers. It was said that the first of the ships would commence cruise service in 2003. It was hardly surprising that this grand plan did not materialise but the very fact that it had been ventured at all raised the question whether it was the practical limit to which passenger ships could be increased in size physically.

Subject to engineering constraints, making passenger ships much bigger, whether in terms of their tonnage and dimensions or in the capacity of their accommodation for a given size of vessel, may generate lucrative profitability benefits through the principle of economy of scale, but such growth also introduces potentially insurmountable obstacles – regulatory, safety, logistical, technical, navigational and environmental.

The United States Coast Guard, wisely it may be thought, issued a directive limiting to 6,000 the maximum number of passengers that US-flag ships were permitted to carry. Presumably this regulation was not in place when Ferris and Chapman proposed to build vast liners with a complement of 10,000 and later, Detwiler, whose United Nations-class ships were designed to accommodate 8,000, was able to ignore it completely since his ships were to be built in Europe and operated under the Dutch flag. Nonetheless, the USCG restriction had not been imposed without good reason. Introduced largely to mitigate safety concerns, it recognised the dangers associated with the evacuation of so many people in an emergency but it also took into account the port handling and infrastructural limitations of processing up to 12,000 persons at a time – their transportation with their luggage to and from the port, along with the immense disembarkation, registration and boarding processes involved, not to mention the logistical management of laundry services, the replenishment of fuel, food and beverages, plus sewage disposal and so on.

These days, the small islands on the cruise circuits suffer the impact of being swamped by huge numbers of passengers as ship after ship enters their small ports, thus overwhelming the local infrastructure. Apart from the saturation of the immediate urban area surrounding each port, this detrimentally undermines the established economic order of these small communities – and this has been occurring with ships discharging only 3–4,000 passengers at a time. It is not difficult to imagine the repercussions that would be felt if ships capable of carrying half as many again were to be placed in service.

The navigational restrictions, in respect of channel depths, which once prevented such large vessels from entering these waters have been largely overcome by minimising draught and increasing beam dimensions to preserve safe stability. For instance, the *Oasis of the Seas* at 225,000grt draws just 31ft when fully loaded compared with the 39ft of Cunard's 83,650grt *Queen Elizabeth*. But there are other technical and engineering questions that increase in complexity as ships grow in size. A particular concern with regard to the proposed giant *United Nations*-class liners was the enormous stresses that would have been encountered in the main strength decks of such long vessels when operating in the high sea conditions of the open ocean. Of course, depending on their region of operation, modern cruise ships tend to keep to relatively sheltered waters, close to the coastline, but from time to time, whether for re-positioning or for shipyard visits for routine maintenance, they need to make transoceanic voyages.

There is also the question of how large cruise ships perform in inclement weather and rough sea conditions from the passengers' perspective. It is known that, even though they are 'weather-routed', by having flat-bottomed hulls, lacking hydrodynamic form, they tend to exhibit inferior sea-kindliness. It is also now recognised in an age of greater environmental awareness that cruise ships are targeted as big polluters, through the emissions from the fuel they burn, from the 'grey' water that is routinely discharged direct into the sea and, no doubt, for other reasons. Although efforts are underway to eliminate these various shortcomings, it is a case of the bigger the ship, the bigger the problem. These and other technical issues continue to exercise the minds of naval architects and classification bodies alike, while organisations representing professional seafarers still have reservations about the efficacy of the emergency evacuation procedures that have been advocated in the wake of recent incidents.

Taking into consideration these several factors, it would not be unreasonable to conclude that cruise ship size may already have exceeded its practicable zenith, if not for the valid reasons of passenger safety and environmental protection, outlined above, then for the fundamental matter of declining on board comfort and ambience which passengers may experience through the sheer pressure of numbers.

Two senior executives expressed opposing views on this. William Burke, the Chief Maritime Officer of Carnival Corporation, contended that larger ships are not only more profitable but also are more efficient: from a crew perspective because the numbers of technical personnel remain constant regardless of ship size and from a power perspective since engine capacity and fuel consumption are also much the same, so that the ship also becomes more efficient from an environmental perspective. On the other hand, despite the obvious irony of representing a company which had just placed orders for the most capacious cruise ships up to 2017 – its 6,000 passenger 'World'-class ships – Rick Sasso, President of MSC Cruises USA, instead expressed a cautionary view:

> There comes a point when size benefits the cruise operator more than the fare-paying customer.

Be that as it may, just as the creation of the first 1,000ft passenger liner was once a prime target that designers and companies sought to attain, so the challenge to be the first to have a ship that exceeds a particular size remains a prized achievement. As if to bear this out, the contemplation of creating an immense passenger cruise ship along the lines proposed by Casino del Mare resurfaced around 2005. Initially quoted at 370,000grt, its tonnage was soon scaled up to 450,000grt with commensurate principal dimensions of 1,661ft length overall, 191ft maximum beam and, extraordinarily, 31ft design draught.

It was the brainchild of Hajime Tanaka, a maverick Japanese tycoon who had previously been involved in the development of championship golf courses and a Formula 1 racing circuit, the T1 Circuit Aida, at Mimasaka, north-east of Okayama.

The *Princess Kaguya* proposition may not have been achievable, at least at the time it was heralded, but as an innovative, alternative approach to cruise ship operation, it was undoubtedly unique and possibly amounted to an indicator of future trends. It is a perfectly conceivable extrapolation that cruise ships will be introduced in the fullness of time having entirely franchised hotel accommodation, restaurants, bars and fast food outlets. Equally, such gigantic vessels may also extend their revenue stream by offering hotel rooms to shore visitors when in or near ports. *Japan Contents Network*

This stern aerial view taken from a promotional video shows the two stadium complexes on the *Princess Kaguya*'s upper deck with a helipad between them. *Japan Contents Network*

Described using well-worn epithets like 'a revolutionary concept' and 'a true floating city', the ship, named *Princess Kaguya* after a character from Japanese folklore, was in fact to be a combination of floating hotel resort, timeshare condominium and day visitor centre. It was to have 3,610 cabins or suites distributed over twenty decks to accommodate 8,400 passengers when at sea, with scope to take up to 10,000 day guests while in port. Crew numbers were 4,000, indicating that the vessel's maximum complement could be as high as 22,400.

The *Princess Kaguya* was designed to have eight diesel-electric main engines producing a total power output of 153.6MW (approximately 209,000hp) with four 17.0MW (23,150hp) propulsion pods for motive power to give a top speed of 22 knots. Four 5.0MW (6,800hp) bow thrusters would aid manoeuvrability at slow speeds.

The usual plethora of dining, entertainment and recreational amenities were announced for the ship. Not only was their quantity of a dramatically different order of magnitude compared to other cruise ships – fifty-five restaurants for instance – but among them there were some exceptional public spaces, made possible by the ship's vast scale: two stadium-type open sports and concert arenas on the upper deck, a complete shopping mall, a 300-metre-long gallery, a 6,000-square-metre reception hall and a massive convention centre.

Developed by the Tanaka-owned company Ocean Silk Road, the intention was to have *Princess Kaguya* built by the Aker Yards in Finland under the supervision of Japan Contents Network, another Tanaka business. To provide ship management, crewing and regulatory compliance support as well as design and build services for the project, Tanaka engaged V. Ships, part of V Group Limited, a global leader in cruise and cargo operating services for the marine industry with its headquarters in London.

As a sort of belt-and-braces contingency, a scaled down version, *Princess Kaguya II*, was also planned. This 'smaller' variant, still as big as Royal Caribbean's 'Genesis'-class ships, was to measure 250,000grt. Overall length and maximum beam were approximately 1,217ft and 160ft. Similarly, passengers and crew numbers were also lower at 5,600 and 2,400, respectively. Despite her reduced dimensions and tonnage, it was intended that *Princess Kaguya II* would, like her bigger variant, also have twenty decks.

On the face of it, Tanaka and his team appeared to be guilty of performing only a perfunctory assessment of the technical and economic issues involved in constructing and operating such a giant ship, having focused instead on the public relations and marketing aspects of the project. The fact that the Akers shipyards did not have a large enough graving dock in which such a long ship as *Princess Kaguya* could be built was one apparent oversight. Equally vague, it was not explained how, assuming it were possible to build the ship in Finland, it would be able to leave the confines of the Baltic given that the maximum clearance under the Øresund Bridge, completed in 2000, is 187.5ft whereas the designed air draught of the *Princess Kaguya* was 214ft.

Turning to the financial aspects, it was perhaps the case that Tanaka had devised an imaginative formula for capitalising his gigantist venture, whose build cost was estimated to be $2.5 billion (£1.8 billion), and for subsequently generating a healthy revenue stream. As already stated, the *Princess Kaguya* was envisaged as more than a conventional cruise ship, more even than a residential cruise ship.

Although the description 'floating city state', as used in the publicity material, does not convey exactly what the purpose of the ship was, it becomes clearer when it is understood that its proposed operational philosophy was meant to embrace a combination of apartment blocks and independent hotels. Reading between the lines, it seems that Tanaka's intention was to sell part of the accommodation as time-share residential and vacation units and, simultaneously, to franchise three separate and distinctive hotel complexes to major hospitality chains. Each of these major concessionees would be expected to invest in the construction of the ship, just as they would have had to for a land-based hotel development. Ocean Silk Road would presumably have then taken a percentage of each hotel's revenue but each would have been able to sub-let to other third-party commercial organisations for the restaurants, cafés, bars and so on. It was stated that of the fifty-five restaurants planned, each of the hotels would have five, another twenty would be reserved for the residential passengers, while the final twenty would be set aside for day visitors. Likewise, the shopping mall would contain franchised outlets and it was even

The *Harmony of the Seas* and her three sister-ships are barely half the gross tonnage of the *Princess Kaguya*, yet their very commissioning has confirmed that giant passenger ships of the size that was advanced in the 1930s, 1950s and 1980s – but mostly refuted as impractical – are both attainable and viable. *David L. Williams*

hinted that it would have a mini-market selling general produce for the benefit of those persons living aboard. From such a scenario, one can imagine the intended presence aboard the *Princess Kaguya* of such hotels as Marriott, Hilton or Best Western, with at one end of the scale five-star à la carte restaurants like Morton's and Flemings, or Hawksmoor and Heston Blumenthal, and a string of fast food outlets and coffee shops such as McDonalds, Subway, Starbucks and Pret à Manger at the other, besides pubs run by Punch Taverns or Wetherspoons – a markedly different cruising concept to anything else that currently exists – in effect a resort at sea.

The intention was for the *Princess Kaguya* to make mainly long voyages in the Pacific and Far East, though how a consensus would have been reached on the ship's itineraries, with so many stake-holders, is beyond contemplation. Similarly, how the marine side would have been able to marshal the involvement of the hospitality personnel in assisting an emergency evacuation, with so many 'land-lubbers' working on board, beggars the imagination. Access to ports for shore excursions and visits would have been by the ship's plentiful tenders, with the *Princess Kaguya* herself laying-off in the deep water approaches.

It has to be recognised, when considering something that seems as outlandish as the *Princess Kaguya* scheme, that in the modern world the orthodox and traditional are fast disappearing and every day new ways of doing things are overtaking established practices. The *Princess Kaguya* project was put on hold following the world financial crash of 2008 and, realistically, the ship is now unlikely to see the light of day. But who can say that one day soon, if the bespoke funding arrangements described here could be agreed, such a cruise ship will not become reality, taking ocean passenger shipping, quite literally, to new dimensions.

FRANCE II AND TITANIC II

One of the ploys to ensure continuity of passenger clientele is for shipping companies to revive old names for new buildings. This in part is to recall the history and the past glory of ships that were particularly popular with the travelling public and cruise-passenger 'returners'. P&O revived the *Oriana* and Cunard the *Queen Mary 2* and the *Queen Elizabeth*. It is therefore no surprise that two iconic ships' names were planned for revival in the early part of the twenty-first century, these being the *France II* and *Titanic II*.

In 2012, the former, the *France II*, was the brainchild, of STX, France and Tillberg International Design of Miami, led by Didier Spade, the founder of Paris Yacht Marina, who dubbed the project 'Le Nouveau France'. The original Swedish company under Tomas Tillberg had previously worked on the design of ships such as the *Queen Mary 2*, *Celebrity Eclipse*, *Regent Seven Seas* and the *Paul Gaugin*.

Mr Spade had been in negotiations with the STX shipyard of Saint Nazaire who had the facilities and capacity to build a vessel of the size envisaged. The design called for 796 passengers with principle particulars of 255m length, (850ft) 32m beam (105ft 4in) and a gross tonnage of 64,000, to be built at a cost of 400 million euros.

The project was put forward and a model produced of what appeared to be a rather conventional hull with a tiered superstructure at the stern, which stepped down to the waterline as a floating 'beach'. Another feature was an almost vertical bow for low cruising speed of around 14–16 knots. Atop the superstructure were two very large, frustum-shaped structures with wings, to give the illusion of funnels, with the name *France* on the after one. Within these 'funnels' would be sited cabins, luxury suites, restaurants, shops and other public rooms; a 1,500-square-metre palm-lined garden was to be positioned between the 'funnels'. As well as these, there would be the bridge, main engine control room and radio/communications centre. These large structures gave the vessel a rather top-heavy appearance although most likely they would be constructed from aluminium alloy. The model had no lifeboats or motor tenders stowed aboard, although they may have been substituted by life rafts. The old chestnut in ship design of functionality versus aesthetics was clearly resurrected in the minds of the travelling public and of travel writers and, as anticipated, the design concept was given a mixed reception.

Stirling Design International was engaged to optimise the plans and it was hoped that the keel of the new *France* would be laid at the STX shipyard in Saint Nazaire in 2012 with entry into service during 2015. It was a very ambitious plan but at the time Mr Spade could not raise the 400 million Euros to finance the project. Another factor which might have postponed the project was that on 27 May 2016, the parent company, STX Offshore and Shipbuilders, filed for receivership, being the first South Korean shipbuilders to face liquidation.

Another, more ambitious project was put forward on 30 April 2012 by Australian billionaire Mr Clive Palmer, owner of Minerology, a company which mined large deposits of Australian magnetite, coal and nickel. On the 100th anniversary of the *Titanic* disaster in 1912, he announced his intention to build and launch the *Titanic II*. In order to manage and finance the project he set up the company Blue Star Line Pty, Ltd, Brisbane as a holding company. Two Australian *Titanic* experts, Steve Hall and Daniel Klistorner, were hired as Technical Consultants and Deltamarin, the Finnish-based marine architects, was engaged as designers.

Clive Palmer's plan was to build the *Titanic II* as a full size, modern day replica of the '*Olympic*'-class RMS *Titanic* with the exception that the new ship was to have a gross tonnage of 56,000 rather than the 46,328 of the original vessel. Other technical details that emerged were that the length was to be 269m (885ft). The power plant selected to propel *Titanic II* consisted of two Wärtsilä 12V46F diesels and two Wärtsilä 8L46F diesel sets capable of delivering a combined power of 48,000kW (65,350 hp). Mounting ten decks, the proposed *Titanic II* was estimated to have a cost of around $500 million (£330 million).

On 17 July 2013 Lloyd's Register was appointed to review the design and safety features of the vessel, to oversee class rules and Safety of Life at Sea (SOLAS) aspects in relation to the structures, stability and safety of *Titanic II*.

The project appeared to be gathering momentum, for two months later, on 19 September 2013, a model had completed testing in the Hamburg Ship Model Basin in Germany. Between 9 and 12 September the 9m (29ft 6in) wooden hull model of *Titanic II* was subjected to

An artist's representation of the *France II*. One might readily reach the conclusion that, while her name alludes to an illustrious predecessor, in this new concept there seems to have been an abandonment of much of the elegance which made the design of the original *France* so noteworthy. *Tillberg Design*

A basic and simplified model of the *France II*, thought to be for wind tunnel testing purposes. *Tillberg Design*

The original *Titanic* never reached New York to be able to sail on a return transatlantic crossing but in this artist's impression, Clive Palmer's replica, the *Titanic II* does. *Blue Star Line*

This model of the planned *Titanic II* reveals some of the many differences between her and the original White Star ship despite the intentional vintage look. The new version was designed to have podded propulsion units aft, side thrusters forward and the lifeboats stowed below the boat deck in modern davits. *Blue Star Line*

power and propulsion tests in Hamburg's 300m (987ft) long test tank. The model was run at speeds equivalent to the actual *Titanic*'s top speed of 23 knots to predict the power required for the full-sized replica. Incidentally, in the Hamburg tank's centenary year, the *Titanic II* model became the 5,000th model to be tested there.

Following these tests, Mr Palmer indicated that the *Titanic II* was originally scheduled to be launched from its builders at CSC Jinling in China during 2016. A large amount of money was spent on consultants, publicity, marketing and model testing. However, a financial issue with the Chinese Government stalled its construction. At the end of October 2018, Mr. Palmer announced that the project had resumed, scheduled for completion in 2020. Whether or not *Titanic II* will or will not materialise remains to be seen; very much a case of watch this space.

Our narrative has spanned more than 165 years, during which time the ocean passenger ship has evolved into many forms, from the small packet ship into the modern passenger liner, the latter exemplified as multi-class, dual role, one-class tourist, and 'cafeteria' one-class. Latterly, the dedicated cruise ship has emerged, only itself to be adapted into different semblances, among others as traditional cruise ship, residential cruise ship and, more recently, vacation centre cruise ship. For all the many vessels completed of these various types there have been those, as described herein which, though less numerous, did not reach the commercial employment intended for them but which, as we have demonstrated, were often the ones that broke new ground by introducing important advances, which were subsequently adopted as standard. By raising them from the mists of obscurity and giving them the exposure they deserve, we hope we have achieved our aim of furnishing this missing link in the chain of ocean passenger ship history.

★ ★ ★

Finished with engines!

APPENDIX I

HOW BIG?

In order for the reader to form an impression of the sizes of some of the most immense of the projected passenger ships described herein, the following tables list the largest passenger liners and cruise ships which have been both built (below) and cancelled (page 254) by their gross tonnage, principal dimensions and engine power output:

PASSENGER LINERS (COMPLETE)	Gross Registered Tonnage	Length Overall (ft)	Beam (ft)	Main engines horsepower/screws
Normandie	83,425	1,029	118	165,000/4
Queen Mary	81,235	1,019	119	212,000/4
Queen Elizabeth	83,675	1,031	119	212,000/4
United States	53,330	990	102	240,000/4
France/Norway	66,350	1,035	111	160,000/4
	76,050			40,800/2
Queen Mary 2	148,530	1,132	148	172,480/4

PASSENGER LINERS (INCOMPLETE)				
Boston and Baltimore	55,000	1,001	106	185,000/4
Oceanic	60,000	1,010	120	275,000/4
Yankee Clippers	100,000	1,254	144	380,000/4
Amerika/Viktoria	90,000	1,070	112	300,000/5
Bretagne(Yourkevitch)	100,000	1,148	138	280,000/4
'United Nations'-class	120,000	1,275	130	3–400,000/4
Peace and Goodwill	90,000	1,150	135	Unknown

CRUISE SHIPS (COMPLETE)	Gross Registered Tonnage	Length Overall	Beam	Main engines horsepower/shafted or podded screws
Carnival Destiny	101,510	893	116	84,965/2
RCCL 'Genesis'-class*	225,280	1,187	154	80,400/3

CRUISE SHIPS (INCOMPLETE)				
Phoenix World City	250,000	1,236	300	108,000/2
Ultimate Dream	160,000	1,132	200	50,000/?
Superstar Capricorn II and Sagittarius II	110,000	1,037	Unknown	Unknown
Carnival Pinnacle class	200,000+	1,246	200	172,800/4
Princess Kaguya	450,000	1,662	192	206,000/2

* Oasis of the Seas, Allure of the Seas, Harmony of the Seas and Symphony of the Seas

APPENDIX 2

COMPLETE LIST OF ALL PASSENGER SHIPS
LAUNCHED OR COMPLETED
BUT WHICH NEVER ENTERED COMMERCIAL SERVICE

Vessels marked with an asterisk (*) are below 20,000 gross tons, and do not therefore figure in the main text.

NAME Owners/Builders (Yard No.)	Date Launched	Date Finished	GRT	LOA ft	Notes
PRINCIPESA JOLANDA* Lloyd Italiano/Soc. Esercizio Bacini	21/9/1907	–	9,200	486	Capsized when being launched. Scrapped incomplete. Intended for Genoa-Buenos Aires service.
BRITANNIC White Star Line/Harland & Wolff (433)	26/2/1914	12/1915	48,158	903	Completed as hospital ship. See Ch. 2.
STATENDAM Holland America Line/Harland & Wolff (436)	9/7/1914	4/1917	32,234	776	Completed as troopship *Justicia*. See Ch. 2
AUSONIA* Soc. Italiano di Servizi Marrittimi/ Blohm and Voss (236)	15/4/1915	–	11,300	518	Planned for first German aircraft carrier in First World War. Sold for scrapping incomplete in 1922 when builders and owners could not agree price due to high German inflation. Negotiations between owners and builders 1919–20. Intended for Genoa–Alexandria–Venice service.
AOTEOROA* Union Steamship Co. of New Zealand/Fairfield (499)	30/6/1915	1916	14,744	550	Completed as auxiliary cruiser HMS *Avenger*. Torpedoed and sunk 14/6/1917 by *U69*. Intended for Sydney–Vancouver service via New Zealand.
AURANIA* Cunard Line/Swan Hunter and Wigham Richardson (965)	16/7/1916	3/1917	13,936	540	Completed as troopship. Torpedoed and sunk 4/2/1918 by *UB67*. Intended for London/Liverpool–Boston/Montreal service.

KAISERIN ELISABETH* Unione Austriaca di Navigazione/ Cantiere Navale Triestino	1917?	–	14,000		Bombed incomplete by opposing Italian and Austrian forces during First World War and broken up. Intended for Trieste–New York service.
CONTE ROSSO* Lloyd Sabaudo/Beardmore (519)	2/12/1917	9/1918	15,000	565	Completed as aircraft carrier HMS *Argus*. Scrapped by T.W. Ward, Inverkeithing 1946/47. Intended for Genoa–Buenos Aires service.
CARACCIOLO Navigazione Generale Italiana/ Cantieri di Castellare di Stabia	12/5/1920	–	25,000		Commenced as battleship; planned conversion to battlecruiser, then aircraft carrier; sold for conversion to passenger/cargo liner. Broken up, incomplete. See Ch. 3.
STOCKHOLM Swedish America Line/Cantieri Riuniti dell'Adriatico	29/5/38	–	28,000	675	Burnt out 19–20/12/1938. See Ch. 4.
STOCKHOLM Swedish America Line/Cantieri Riuniti dell'Adriatico (1203)	10/3/40	10/1/1941	29,307	675	Ran trials but delivery blockaded. Sold to Italian Government 11/1/1941 and converted to troopship *Sabaudia*. See Ch. 4.
VATERLAND Hamburg America Line/Blohm and Voss (523)	24/8/40	–	41,000	824	Destroyed by fire in air raid while incomplete 25/7/1943. See Ch. 4.
KASUGA MARU* Nippon Yusen Kaisha/Mitsubishi (752)	19/9/40	9/1941	17,127	590	Completed as aircraft carrier *Taiyo*. Torpedoed and sunk 18/8/1944 by USS *Rasher*. (Sister ships *Nitta Maru* and *Yawata Maru* converted to aircraft carriers *Chuyo* and *Unyo*, respectively, but both saw limited commercial service). Intended for Yokohama–Hamburg service.
ZUIDERDAM* Holland America Line/ Wilton-Fijenoord (672)	Spring 1941	–	12,150	518	Sunk incomplete in air raid 28/8/1941. Scuttled 22/9/1944. After second salvage considered as not worth repairing. Scrapped 1948. Intended for Rotterdam–New York service.
MIIKE MARU* Nippon Yusen Kaisha/Mitsubishi (760)	12/4/41	9/1941	11,739	535	Completed as troop transport. Torpedoed and sunk 21/4/1944 by USS *Trigger*. Intended for the Kobe–Vancouver–Seattle service.
IZUMO MARU Nippon Yusen Kaisha/Kawasaki	24/6/41	7/1942	27,500	722	Completed as aircraft carrier *Hiyo*. See Ch. 5.
KASHIWARA MARU Nippon Yusen Kaisha/ Mitsubishi (900)	26/6/41	5/1942	27,700	722	Completed as aircraft carrier *Junyo*. See Ch. 5.
GOKOKU MARU* Osaka Shosen Kaisha/Tama and Mitsui	2/4/1942	9/1942	10,348	537	Completed as auxiliary cruiser. Later converted to troop transport. Torpedoed and sunk 10/10/1944 by USS *Barb*. Intended for Japan–Europe service.

AKI MARU* Nippon Yusen Kaisha/ Mitsubishi (761)	15/5/42	10/1942	11,409	535	Ex-*Mishima Maru*. Completed as troop transport. Torpedoed and sunk 26/7/1944 by USS *Crevalle*. Intended for the Japan–Australia service.
AWA MARU* Nippon Yusen Kaisha/ Mitsubishi (770)	24/8/42	3/1943	11,249	535	Completed as troop transport. Torpedoed and sunk, despite diplomatic immunity (flag of International Red Cross) 1/4/1945 by USS *Queenfish*. Intended for the Japan–Australia service.
AMERICAN MERCHANT* United States Lines/Ingalls (268)	23/1/42	9/1942	12,093	489	Launched as *Pascagoula*. Completed as troop transport *George W. Goethals* (T-AP182) due to the Second World War. Scrapped 1970/71. Intended for New York–London service.
AMERICAN BANKER* United States Lines/Ingalls (297)	11/11/42	2/1943	12,090	489	Launched as *Biloxi*. Completed as troop transport *Henry Gibbins* (T-AP183) due to the Second World War. Transferred to New York State Maritime College in 1960 as a training ship and renamed *Empire State IV*. Intended for New York–London service.
AMERICAN FARMER* United States Lines/Ingalls (298)	22/8/42	4/1943	12,097	489	Launched as *Gulfport*. Completed as troop transport *David C Shanks* (T-AP180) due to the Second World War. Scrapped 1973/74. Intended for New York–London service.
AMERICAN SHIPPER* United States Lines/Ingalls (299)	12/9/42	6/1943	12,093	489	Launched as *Pass Christian*. Completed as troop transport *Fred C Ainsworth* (T-AP181) due to the Second World War. Scrapped 1973/74. Intended for New York–London service.
PRESIDENT JACKSON* American President Lines/New York S.B. (485)	27/6/50	12/1951	12,660	533	Completed as troop transport *Barrett* (T-AP196) due to the Korean War. Transferred to New York State Maritime College in 9/1973 as training ship *Empire State V*.
PRESIDENT ADAMS* American President Lines/New York S.B. (486)	9/10/50	9/1952	12,660	533	Completed as troop transport *Geiger* (T-AP197) due to the Korean War. Laid up in April 1971. Transferred to Massachusetts Maritime Academy in 1979 as training ship *Bay State IV*. Destroyed by fire December 1981.
PRESIDENT HAYES* American President Lines/New York S.B. (487)	19/1/51	12/1952	12,660	533	Completed as troop transport *Upshur* (T-AP198) due to the Korean War. Transferred to the Maine Maritime Academy in 1973 as training ship *State of Maine*. Later to U.S. Coast Guard.
NOAH'S ARK* Chariot International Holdings/ Kamitsis	2/6/1979	–	12,000	436	Intended as Mediterranean ferry *Taygetos*. Sold 1987 when part-built for conversion to cruise ship *Sea Venture*. Renamed 1996. Laid up 2001. Broken up incomplete 2004 at Aliaga, Turkey.
REGENT SKY Regency Cruises/Stocznia im Komuny Paryskiej (494/04) and Avlis Perama	16/10/90	–	55,000	748	Ordered as Baltic ferry *Stena Baltica*. Purchased for conversion into a cruise ship. Broken up incomplete. See page 235.

BIBLIOGRAPHY

BOOKS AND ARTICLES

Anderson, Roy, *White Star Line* (T. Stephenson, 1964).

Armstrong, Warren, *Atlantic Highway* (Harrap, 1961).

Ardman, Harvey *The Normandie, Her Life and Times* (Franklin Watts, 1985).

Barnaby, Kenneth C., *Basic Naval Architecture* (6th edn., Hutchinson and Co., 1969).

Bonsor, N.R.P., *North Atlantic Seaway* (T. Stephenson, 1955).

Braynard, Frank O., *Lives of the Liners* (New York, Cornell Maritime Press, 1947).

Braynard, Frank O., *By Their Works Ye Shall Know Them* (New York, Gibbs and Cox, 1968).

Braynard, Frank O., *Leviathan, The World's Greatest Ship* (South Street Seaport Museum, Vols. 1–5, 1973–9).

Braynard, Frank O., *Dreams of Half a Century – Those Great Super-Liners That Were Planned but Never Built* (article in Tow Line, date unknown).

Brown, J. J., *Ideas in Exile* (Toronto, McLelland and Stewart, 1967).

Brown, Dr T.W.F. *Machinery Proposals for a Mammoth Liner* (The Marine Engineer and Naval Architect, April 1960).

Brown, Dr T.W.F. *Geared Steam Turbine Machinery for a Mammoth Liner* (The Marine Engineer and Naval Architect, June 1960).

de Kerbrech, Richard P., *Ships of the White Star Line* (Ian Allan, 2009).

Dunn, Laurence, *Famous Liners, Belfast Built* (Adlard Coles, 1963).

Eliseo, Maurizio and Piccione, Paolo, *Transatlantici: The History of the Great Italian Liners on the Atlantic* (Tormena Editore, 2001).

Flounders, Eric and Gallagher, Michael, *The Triumph of a Great Tradition: The Story of Cunard's 175 Years* (Ferry Publications, 2015).

Gallagher, Michael, *The Building of the Queen Elizabeth 2* (Ferry Publications, 2017).

Hogg, R.S., *Naval Architecture and Ship Construction* (Institute of Marine Engineers, 1956).

Isherwood, J.H., *Steamers of the Past* (Journal of Commerce, 1966).

Kludas, Arnold, *Great Passenger Ships of the World* (Patrick Stephens, Vols. 1–5, 1975–1977).

Kludas, Arnold, *Record Breakers of the North Atlantic: Blue Riband Liners 1838–1952* (Chatham Publishing, 2000).

Maber, Lt Cdr John M., *North Star to Southern Cross* (T. Stephenson, 1967).

Munro-Smith, R., *Elements of Ship Design* (Marine Media Management, 1975).

Munro-Smith, R., *Ships and Naval Architecture* (Institute of Marine Engineers, 1973).

Oldham, Wilton J., *The Ismay Line* (Charles Birchall, 1961).

Parker, H., and Bowen, F.C., *Mail and Passenger Steamships of the 19th Century* (1928).

Polmar, Norman, *Aircraft Carriers* (Macdonald, 1969).

Pounder, C.C. *Diesel Engine Principles and Practice* (George Newnes Ltd, 1955).

Potter, Neil, and Frost, Jack, *The Mary* (Harrap and Co., 1961).

Rohbrecht, Gerhard, *Schiffe die niemals fuhren* (article in Schiffahrte Seekiste/International, date unknown).

von Münching, L.L., *Ships That Never Sailed* (article in Sea Breezes, April 1963).

Watts, Anthony J., *Japanese Warships of World War II* (Ian Allan, 1966).

Wilder, Laurence R. *Four-Day Liners for the North Atlantic* (Marine Engineering and Shipping Age, February 1928).

Wilder, Laurence R. *The United States and the North Atlantic* (The Marine News, November 1928).

Williams, David L., *Cunard's Legendary Queens* (Ian Allan, 2004).

Williams, David L., *Dictionary of Passenger Ship Disasters* (Ian Allan, 2009).

Williams, David L. and de Kerbrech, Richard P., *Cabin Class Rivals* (The History Press, 2015).

Wilson, R.M., *The Big Ships* (Cassell and Co., 1956).

PRIMARY RESEARCH TECHNICAL PAPERS, OFFICIAL RECORDS AND PATENTS

Bates, James L., *Large Passenger-Carrying Ships for Certain Essential Trade Routes* (Society of Naval Architects and Marine Engineers, New York, 1945).

de Malglaive, Pierre and Hardy, A.C., *The Transatlantic Liner of the Future* (Institute of Marine Engineers, London, 14 December 1937).

Ferris, Theodore E., *Design of American Super-Liners* (Society of Naval Architects and Marine Engineers, New York, 20 November 1931).

Hansen, Bent (Aalborg Vaerft), *Ship Design for the Further Development of the Cruise Market* (paper presented at the Cruise 85 International Conference, London, June 1985).

Jacob, F.J.C., *Shipbuilding and Marine Engineering in Germany during the period 1939–1945* (British Shipbuilding Research Association and British Intelligence Objectives Sub-Committee, 1948).

Levander, Kai (Wärtsilä), *New Approaches in Passenger Vessel Design* (paper presented at the International Marine Transit Association Conference, Copenhagen, 1981).

Levander, Kai (Wärtsilä) *Wärtsilä SWATH Cruiser* (Helsinki Shipyard Research and Development, 1981).

Levander, Kai (Wärtsilä), *Converting Concepts Into Reality* (paper presented at the Cruise 85 International Conference, London, June 1985).

Pounder, C.C., *Human Problems in Marine Engineering* (Institute of Marine Engineers, London, March 1960).

Pratt, H.R. and Spofford, W.P., *Investigations of the Latest Ship Designs and Operating Experiences with the Technical Personnel of the Hamburg-American Steamship Line, Hamburg* (Combined Intelligence Objectives Sub-Committee, July 1945).

Schmeltzer, J.E., *Engineering Features of the Maritime Commission's Program* (Society of Naval Architects and Marine Engineers, New York, 15 November 1940).

Schmeltzer, J.E., *Confidential Movements of Vessels on Government Service* (Guildhall Library, London).

Log of SS *Justicia,* Official Number 137544, 13 April 1917–20 July 1918 (National Archives, Kew; reference BT165/1874).

Outline Specification for a Passenger Cruise Vessel/Ocean Liner – Project Q5 for Cunard (Deltamarin reference P3197, 12 December 1991).

Payment of Compensation to N.A.S.M. [Holland America Line] for the loss of the SS *Justicia*, requisitioned when building by HM Government (National Archives, Kew; reference T1/12517/13342).

Canadian Patent No 55620 Marine Vessel (13 April 1897).

UK Patent No 2343, Silver and Moore's Improvements in Steamships, etc (19 September 1861).

US Patents Nos D0091579 and D0049617, Design for a Boat (25 October and 1 November 1933).

World Ship Society Shipyard List compiled by Captain John Landels et al.

INDEX

Names of ships are in italics; ships never built or commissioned are in bold italics